REDUCING PREJUDICE
AND DISCRIMINATION

The Claremont Symposium on
Applied Social Psychology

This series of volumes highlights important new developments on the leading edge of applied social psychology. Each volume focuses on one area in which social psychological knowledge is being applied to the resolution of social problems. Within that area, a distinguished group of authorities present chapters summarizing recent theoretical views and empirical findings, including the results of their own research and applied activities. An introductory chapter integrates this material, pointing out common themes and varied areas of practical applications. Thus each volume brings together trenchant new social psychological ideas, research results, and fruitful applications bearing on an area of current social interest. The volumes will be of value not only to practitioners and researchers, but also to students and lay people interested in this vital and expanding area of psychology.

REDUCING PREJUDICE AND DISCRIMINATION

Edited by

Stuart Oskamp
Claremont Graduate University

The Claremont Symposium on
Applied Social Psychology

LEA LAWRENCE ERLBAUM ASSOCIATES, PUBLISHERS

2000   Mahwah, New Jersey   London

Lawrence Erlbaum Associates, Inc., Publishers
10 Industrial Avenue
Mahwah, New Jersey 07430

Library of Congress Cataloging-in-Publication Data

Reducing prejudice and discrimination / edited by Stuart Oskamp.
    p.   cm.
"The Claremont Symposium on Applied Social Psychology."
Includes bibliographical references and index.
ISBN 0-8058-3481-8 (cloth : alk. paper) – ISBN 0-8058-3482-6 (pbk. : alk. paper)
    1. Prejudices. 2. Discrimination. I Oskamp, Stuart. II. Claremont Symposium on
Applied Social Psychology (1999)
HM1091 .R43 2000
303.3'85–dc21

                                                      00-035388

Printed in the United States of America

10 9 8 7 6 5 4 3 2 1

Contents

Preface

Stop and think for a moment about examples of prejudice in our current world: "Ethnic cleansing" in the former Yugoslavia. Tribal genocide between Tutsis and Hutus in Rwanda. Cold-blooded killings of Blacks in the rural United States. Murders of gays or foreigners in U.S. cities. Hostility toward immigrants and systematic campaigns to deny them housing, education, or medical care--let alone equal treatment. Religious persecution. Gender and ethnic bias in employment, education, and the legal system. The prevalence and severity of these evils shows how dramatically and destructively they affect people's lives and corrupt our society.

Finding ways to *reduce* prejudice and discrimination is *the* central issue in attacking racism in our society. Yet this book is almost unique among scientific volumes in being focused on that goal.

As far back as the 1920s, prejudice has been a major topic of study in the social sciences. In fact, it is one of the most-studied areas in all of psychology and sociology. However, most of the research has been aimed at describing the nature of prejudice and understanding its causes, and also, to some extent, at documenting its consequences in people's lives. Probably almost all the researchers wanted to attack prejudice and destroy its pernicious effects, but few of them have concentrated their research energies on the key question of how to reduce prejudice and create a society where equality and social justice are the norm instead of the exception.

This book is different. It combines careful analysis of theories about how to reduce prejudice and discrimination with cutting-edge empirical research on that applied topic, conducted both in controlled laboratory situations and in real-world social settings. The authors of its chapters are some of the best known and most highly regarded researchers in the world on topics related to prejudice, and here they have focused their attention specifically on the question of how to combat and reduce it. Thus, this book is an important companion to other scientific volumes that have focused almost entirely on analyzing the nature and causes of prejudice, discrimination, and racism.

Another benefit of this volume is that its chapters are written in clear, understandable, reader-friendly prose. The authors discuss a wide variety of approaches to prejudice reduction, covering both how-to-do-it and principles behind the methods.

The book should be of great interest to teachers, social workers, administrators, organizational managers and other social practitioners who have to deal with prejudice and discrimination in their jobs. It will be a valuable foundation of knowledge for college courses or individual reading by undergraduate and graduate students and researchers in many fields, including psychology, sociology, communication, political science, and public policy. It can also be read with profit by concerned citizens and community leaders who are trying to improve intergroup relations in their neighborhoods and cities.

A Preview of the Contents

The initial chapter by Stuart Oskamp introduces the many ways that prejudice can be successfully attacked. Next, Walter and Cookie Stephan present a theoretically based summary of many of the important causes of prejudice. Jim Sidanius and Rosemary Veniegas challenge some past theorizing by describing ways that racial and gender discrimination combine in societies throughout the world. The real-world social context is emphasized by Marylee Taylor, both as a determinant of discrimination and as a factor that can help to reduce it.

Part II of the volume presents recent findings by many eminent researchers on varied ways of combating prejudice. Thomas Pettigrew and Linda Tropp report a massive meta-analysis that shows how strongly intergroup contact can affect prejudice, and some of the key factors that moderate its effect. Susan Fiske summarizes research demonstrating that being dependent on an outgroup member, either for positive or negative outcomes, increases attention to that person's individual characteristics rather than stereotypic thinking about them. However, she finds that dependence on a *group* of others does not have this desirable effect. John Dovidio and his colleagues describe a successful technique for attacking implicit (unconscious) prejudice, and another method that reduces explicit prejudice. They also demonstrate how recategorizing one's social identity (e.g., "we're different groups, but all on the same team") can diminish intergroup bias and discrimination. Marilynn Brewer extends this dual-identity notion, pointing out that people have multiple social identities; she then shows how these cross-cutting identities can be used to reduce discrimination against outgroups. Patricia Devine and her colleagues demonstrate ways to "break the prejudice habit" and learn to treat others more fairly, but they also document the risk that some more-prejudiced individuals will exhibit a backlash against such influence attempts.

Part III of the volume discusses applications of research findings in real-world social settings. First, Brenda Major and her colleagues analyze ways that a target of prejudice can use in attempting to reduce unfair treatment by another person. David and Roger Johnson describe systematic approaches within school settings to create cooperative groups, reduce intergroup conflict, and build desirable civic values. Frances Aboud and Sheri Levy summarize research on five other major types of prejudice-reduction interventions that have been used with children and adolescents. Michele Wittig and Ludwin Molina present an evaluation of a multi-cultural education program, which shows that students' orientation toward out-groups can have a strong anti-prejudice effect. Finally, Stuart Oskamp and James Jones report on "promising practices for racial reconciliation" that have been developed by highly regarded community organizations and collected by the President's Initiative on Race.

Readers, enjoy this abundance of riches! And take away examples of its wisdom that can be used to attack prejudice in your own life's setting.

Stuart Oskamp

1 Multiple Paths to Reducing Prejudice and Discrimination

Stuart Oskamp[1]
Claremont Graduate University

Prejudice is one of the most-studied areas in all of social science. However, most of this study has been directed at understanding the *nature, causes, and consequences* of prejudice. Though reducing prejudice has been the implicit goal of many researchers, relatively little research has been directed specifically at the crucial topic of *how to reduce* prejudice and discrimination in our societies. That is "where the rubber hits the road"—where psychological theory and re-search findings must combine to create effective programs for improving social conditions. The vital importance of this topic is emphasized in this quotation:

> [Though they may have had] a possible evolutionary advantage, prejudiced inter-group attitudes—with their potential for periodic eruption in overt intergroup con-flict—have now become an extremely serious threat to the continued survival of human society and civilization. (Duckitt, 1992, p. 250)

We are all aware of horrendous examples of nations that have erupted in open warfare between rival ethnic or religious groups, such as the former Yugo-slavia, Rwanda, and Northern Ireland. On a smaller scale, the United States also still suffers every year from hundreds of vicious hate crimes, including killings of African Americans, gays, and other minorities. Despite these appalling cases, we should keep in mind that remarkable positive changes have occurred in our society and others, in the direction of greater harmony and reduced prejudice. Examples of this kind of progress include the marked change in cultural values and norms affecting intergroup relations in the United States since World War II and the more recent transformation to a more equalitarian political system that has replaced apartheid in the Union of South Africa.

Empirical demonstrations of these favorable intergroup changes can be seen in the dramatic upward trend of responses to all the standard survey questions concerning tolerant racial attitudes and beliefs, as measured in national samples of the U.S. White population since the 1940s (cf. Schuman, Steeh, & Bobo, 1985; Schuman, Steeh, Bobo, & Krysan, 1997). As one example, note the sharp rise over 40 years in approval of even the most controversial interracial topic—opposition to laws against racial intermarriage, and approval of intermarriage (see Figure 1).[2]

To counterbalance this apparently rosy picture, research has also pointed out that attitudes and actions aimed at *implementing* these tolerant and equalitarian attitudes have not gained nearly the same degree of acceptance in the U.S., and that we clearly have a long way to go to reach a society where all groups experience equal opportunity and full social justice (Schuman et al., 1997). Terms for the new, more subtle forms of prejudice and discrimination include *modern racism, aversive racism,* and *symbolic racism.* Recent research on *implicit prejudice* has demonstrated that consciously expressed attitudes do not capture the full extent of prejudice in modern societies (Banaji & Greenwald, 1994; Dovidio, Kawakami, Johnson, Johnson, & Howard, 1997). However, despite the indications of continuing prejudice and of backsliding or backlash against racial tolerance, the dramatic changes toward fuller social acceptance of all groups in our society are encouraging marks of progress.

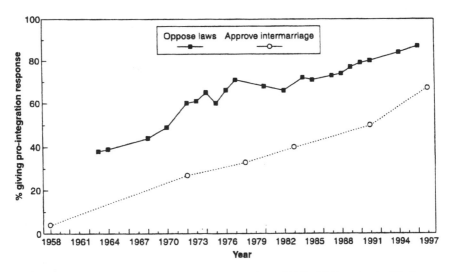

FIG. 1.1. Trends since 1958 in national samples of U.S. Whites about attitudes opposing laws against racial intermarriage (NORC) and approving intermarriage (Gallup). Source: Reprinted by permission of the publishers from Schuman, Steeh, Bobo, and Krysan, *Racial Attitudes in America: Trends and Interpretations* (p. 118), Cambridge, MA: Harvard University Press. Copyright 1997 by the President and Fellows of Harvard College.

CAUSES OF PREJUDICE AND DISCRIMINATION

Efforts to reduce prejudice necessarily have to be built on an understanding of the causes of prejudice. Many authors have noted that the causes of prejudice and discrimination are multiple and elaborately intertwined. For instance, Hamilton and Trolier (1986) wrote:

> Any particular form of stereotyping or prejudice, such as racism, is in all likelihood multiply determined by cognitive, motivational, and social learning processes. . . . Therefore, any attempt to understand such phenomena as a product of one process alone is probably misguided. (p. 153)

The same should be said about attempts to reduce prejudice—they need to consider and combat the multiple causes of prejudice. In analyzing the causes of prejudice and discrimination, Duckitt (1992) proposed a four-level model of possible factors. He listed:

1. genetic and evolutionary predispositions.
2. societal, organizational, and intergroup patterns of contact and norms for intergroup relations—e.g., laws, regulations, and norms of segregation or unequal access, which maintain the power of dominant groups over subordinate ones.
3. mechanisms of social influence that operate in group and interpersonal interactions—e.g., influences from the mass media, the educational system, and the structure and functioning of work organizations.
4. personal differences in susceptibility to prejudiced attitudes and behaviors, and in acceptance of specific intergroup attitudes.

Duckitt further suggested that efforts to reduce prejudice and discrimination need to work at all of these levels, but that "*the higher the level of intervention [i.e., lower numbers], the greater will be its potential impact*" (p. 251).

Prejudice Reduction Interventions. Different approaches are needed in order to counteract these different causes of prejudice. At level 1—genetic and evolutionary predispositions—we may conclude that relatively little can be done on a short-term or intermediate-term basis to change patterns of human interaction that have this kind of built-in biological foundation. However, interventions at the later levels may gradually change humans' evolutionary inheritance of prejudice in the direction of greater acceptance of outgroups.

Thus level 2—laws and widespread norms—becomes the most powerful arena for changing patterns of human interaction. As psychologists, we tend to operate mostly at levels 3 and 4—group influence and interpersonal interactions—but we should keep strongly in mind the importance of efforts toward interventions at level 2. A classic example of level-2 actions is the 1954 and 1964 decisions of the U.S. Supreme Court that outlawed desegregation in public schools. Other examples are equal-opportunity and affirmative-action laws and regulations, which have had nationwide effects on norms, attitudes, and behavior. In the opposite direction, recent reversals of affirmative-action regulations in some states may have the unfortunate effect of increasing prejudice and discrimination.

Moving to level 3—influence processes—we need to distinguish between two rather different sublevels. Duckitt emphasizes *mass* influence processes such as the mass media, the education system, and work roles in organizations, and he pays less attention to smaller-scale group and interpersonal influence processes, which are the type that psychologists most often study in research and try to modify in practical applications. His emphasis is heuristic because, again, the broader the level of change efforts, the more impact they are likely to have.

Thus, in the mass media, programs like *Cosby* or *ER*, which show different ethnic groups interacting in generally friendly, equalitarian, and nonstereotypic ways, are important influences. Within the educational system, programs such as the widely disseminated series on *Teaching Tolerance* from the Southern Poverty Law Center are valuable, and another excellent informational resource is the recent pamphlet *Racism....and Psychology* published by the American Psychological Association (Feinberg, no date). Within work organizations, it is vital to move toward explicit standards for selecting and promoting individuals that guarantee equal opportunity and that value diversity of backgrounds and experiences relevant to the job at hand. At the other extreme, media programs, educational procedures, and work structures that present nonequalitarian or stereotypic models obstruct efforts toward the reduction of prejudice.

Additional Variables in Interventions. Still at level 3, the distinction between *normative* and *informational* social influence (e.g., Deutsch & Gerard, 1955) should be useful in helping to classify and structure influence attempts. The above examples of media portrayals and work-organization standards illustrate normative social influence, whereas informational programs aim to instill cognitive knowledge. Educational programs are mostly informational, though teacher influence processes can certainly also set normative standards. At the small-group and interpersonal sublevel of influence, psychologists' efforts to reduce prejudice often use both normative and informational pressures.

Another useful distinction is between influence attempts where the recipients are *passive*, as in listening to a speech or movie, and ones where they are *active*. Research has found that active participation generally produces stronger and longer-lasting attitude and behavior change than does passive participation (Oskamp, 1991). The active interventions in prejudice reduction programs very often involve interactions with outgroup members.

Examples of actual programs may help to clarify the above categories. Examples of informational approaches include programs of multicultural education in school settings (e.g., Aboud, in press; Banks, 1997; NCSS Task Force, 1992) and training programs about diversity, usually in industrial settings (e.g., Ellis & Sonnenfield, 1994; Tan, Morris, & Romero, 1996). Both informational and normative approaches may be passive (as in exposure to TV or other normative presentations) or active experiences (as in interacting with outgroup members). Examples of interactive interventions include programs of cooperative learning in the schools (e.g., Johnson, Johnson, & Holubec, 1994) and intergroup dialogue programs, usually in college or community settings (e.g., Gurin, Peng, Lopez, & Nagda, 1999).

Finally, at level 4—personal differences—Duckitt places personality factors that make individuals susceptible to prejudiced or nonprejudiced messages and attitudes. He suggests that these factors usually can only be modified through fairly intensive group or individual psychotherapeutic approaches—the province of clinical and counseling psychologists. (He also places at this level attempts to change individuals' specific intergroup attitudes, which seem to me to fit better under the level-3 subcategory of group and individual influence attempts.)

We can conclude, from the above analysis of the varied causal factors in prejudice, that psychologists might try to develop interventions to reduce prejudice using the following different approaches:

- laws, regulations, and widespread norms—the most powerful method
- mass influence processes—either normative or informational, either passive or interactive
- group and interpersonal influence processes—either normative or informational, either passive or interactive
- psychotherapeutic approaches to modify personality characteristics

Another Theoretical Approach

A more fine-grain theoretical view about the causes of prejudice that pertains mainly to Duckitt's levels 3 and 4 (and somewhat to level 2) has been proposed by Stephan and Stephan (Chap. 2 in this volume). They consider intergroup *fears and threats* as major causes of prejudice, and they list four main bases of prejudice:

- realistic threats from an outgroup
- symbolic threats from an outgroup
- intergroup anxiety in interactions with outgroup members
- negative stereotypes of the outgroup

It should be possible to focus on these factors in efforts to reduce prejudice. Stephan and Stephan indicate that the four bases of prejudice are typically interlinked and operate in conjunction with each other rather than separately, and therefore prejudice reduction efforts need to focus on reducing several or all of them together. They further suggest that *cognitive or knowledge-based interventions* can reduce feelings of threat (both realistic and symbolic), and that *group-interactive interventions* can reduce negative stereotyping and intergroup anxiety.

PROGRAMS TO REDUCE PREJUDICE AND DISCRIMINATION

Though most methods of reducing prejudice share some common features, they can be roughly categorized into behavioral, cognitive, and motivational approaches, according to their most prominent elements. Each of these categories of approaches operates primarily at Duckitt's level 3, although in some instances they may also operate at level 2 (through laws or regulations) or level 4 (through psychotherapeutic interventions).

Behavioral approaches include intergroup contact under specified conditions, cooperative learning techniques, and structured experiences as a target of prejudice. Cognitive approaches include attempts to change stereotypes and attitudes through various mechanisms—e.g., recategorization of group memberships into a common ingroup having superordinate goals, or decategorization of group memberships through crosscutting roles and activities that help outgroup members to be seen as personalized individuals. Motivational approaches include reduction of feelings of threat from an outgroup, demonstrating that the outcomes of ingroups and outgroups are interdependent, and emphasizing that each individual has some personal accountability for intergroup events. Two techniques that combine cognitive inputs with motivational pressures are spotlighting of a person's values that are relevant to treatment of outgroups, and the related procedure of inducing guilt feelings about one's individual failure to enact values of equality.

Examples of most of these techniques are given in the following paragraphs, which describe six specific techniques that have been used systematically to reduce prejudice and its expression and which have had some research attention.

1. Reducing Realistic Conflict. Based on Stephan and Stephan's list of the causes of prejudice, a good way to reduce prejudice due to realistic threats from an outgroup is to reduce the bases of realistic conflict. This might be done by sharing power with the outgroup more equally, or ceding the outgroup specific areas of responsibility or authority, or "enlarging the pie" of resources available to the contending groups. These kinds of solutions are often proposed and sometimes accomplished in research on intergroup negotiations (e.g., Fisher & Ury, 1981; Thompson, 1990). Suggested methods have been called "integrative bargaining" or "interactive problem solving." However, a major obstacle to this approach is that it conflicts with the dominant group's usual strong motivation to maintain power over subordinate groups (cf. Sidanius & Veniegas, Chap. 3 in this volume).

2. Publicity About Role Models. Fears based on symbolic threats from an outgroup can often be countered by publicity about or exposure to role models who contradict the symbolic area of threat. For instance, Michael Jordan is admired by Black and White youngsters alike, and the widely publicized achievements of Andrew Young and Ralph Bunche have contradicted many of the stereotypes and symbolic fears that Whites have about Blacks in our society. Similarly, John Kennedy's performance as President contradicted many widespread fears about Catholics in high office, and the clear accomplishments of Sandra Day O'Conner and Madeleine Albright have overturned many of the false perceptions and fears that U.S. citizens have about women in leadership roles. Recent research has shown that exposure to positive role models from minority ethnic groups can reduce (nonconscious) implicit prejudice as well as explicit negative attitudes (Dasgupta, 1999).

This approach to combating prejudice can be one of the strengths of *affirmative action* programs, if they successfully present exemplary individuals who demonstrate the falsity of prevalent fears and stereotypes about a particular outgroup (Pratkanis & Turner, 1994). Making this more difficult, however, is the fact that considerable research has shown that presenting one or two exceptional members of a minority group may allow them to be subtyped as nonprototypic of their group and thus largely discounted as prejudice-reduction influences (e.g., Johnston & Hewstone, 1992).

3. Intergroup Contact. The most prominent interactive approach for reducing prejudice is the *contact hypothesis*, which specifies conditions under which intergroup contact should result in improved relations. This approach has had a long history of theory and research in social psychology, and in several variations, it has become a principal preoccupation of social psychologists in this area. The next major section summarizes some of the voluminous research on the optimal conditions for operation of the contact hypothesis.

4. Cooperative Learning. Going beyond the contact hypothesis, probably the most widespread approach to improving intergroup relations in school settings is cooperative learning programs. Another chief goal of these programs is to improve learning outcomes, using carefully developed procedures in which small groups of mixed ethnic composition work together cooperatively on assigned lessons. They have generally been found to be successful in reducing prejudice and negative intergroup stereotypes (e.g., Aronson & Thibodeau, 1992), and they are described in more detail by Johnson and Johnson (Chap. 11 in this volume).

5. Planned, Personal Experience of Discrimination. This is an interactive, experiential method, in which majority-group members are exposed to prejudice and discrimination, such as minority-group individuals undergo every day. The expectation is that this experience should make them more empathetic and understanding of the problems of minorities. Though this method has seldom been carefully evaluated, there are numerous anecdotal reports of its success in elementary school classes. An example is the teacher-initiated "blue eyes vs. brown eyes" exercise, which is depicted in the film *The Eye of the Storm* (1970). Similar exercises have been used in sensitivity training for public officials such as police officers (e.g., Pfister, 1975; Sata, 1975; Weiner & Wright, 1973). A variety of other techniques that are appropriate for use with school children are described in detail by Ponterotto and Pedersen (1993).

6. Spotlighting Value Conflicts. This is a technique that combines cognitive and motivational bases for reducing prejudice. By demonstrating inconsistencies among people's values, it engages their self-concept, and it often develops guilt motivation (cf. Devine, Plant, & Buswell, Chap. 9 in this volume). This technique usually aims to motivate people to change their beliefs and behavior in the direction of consistency with key underlying values, such as fairness and equality. Rokeach and his colleagues demonstrated that long-lasting attitude and behavioral changes could be produced with this relatively simple technique, which they termed *value self-confrontation* (e.g., Ball-Rokeach, Rokeach, & Grube, 1984; Rokeach, 1971).

Grube, Mayton, and Ball-Rokeach (1994) have summarized the results of 27 such studies, reporting that 96% of them demonstrated changes in the values that were targeted, and that large but lower percentages also showed changes in relevant attitudes (73%) and behaviors (56%). For instance, Rokeach (1971) found behavioral changes that lasted as long as 21 months—specifically, increased enrollment in ethnic relations courses, and membership in civil rights organizations such as the NAACP. Thus, this method of value-confrontation seems a promising intervention to use in attempts to reduce prejudice and discrimination. However, a recent series of studies by Altemeyer (1994), using a similar procedure to increase sympathy for Indian-rights activism in Canada, reported mixed findings about its success. Monteith and Walters' (1998) research results also suggest that Rokeach's method may only work well with a subset of high-prejudice individuals.

RESEARCH FINDINGS ON THE CONTACT HYPOTHESIS

As mentioned above, it is important to consider the optimal conditions for operation of the contact hypothesis. Recall that Allport (1954) predicted that intergroup contact would lead to decreased prejudice, but only under the following four conditions:

- equal status between the groups in the situation
- cooperative activity toward common goals
- personalized acquaintance ("that leads to the perception of common interests and common humanity"—Allport, 1954, p. 281)
- support for the contact by authorities or local norms.

Later researchers have suggested a number of additional conditions, and some have particularly stressed the importance of an intimate situation that allows personalized understanding of members of the other group, or a situation that provides participants with the chance to make friends among outgroup members (e.g., Brewer & Miller, 1984; Pettigrew, 1998).

The contact hypothesis, in its several variations, has received support in many studies, conducted in various situations and with stigmatized social groups ranging from foreign students to the elderly (e.g., Ellison & Powers, 1994; Gaertner et al., 1994; Sigelman & Welch, 1993). Fiske and her colleagues have conducted a series of studies demonstrating that the social interdependence that is inherent in cooperative interactions toward common goals is what gives contact situations their power to reduce prejudice (Fiske, Chap. 6 in this volume).

Pettigrew and Tropp (Chap. 5 in this volume) have recently conducted a massive meta-analysis of 203 studies on intergroup contact as an influence on varied measures of prejudice. Overall, 94% of these studies found an inverse relationship between contact and prejudice, and the meta-analysis showed that contact has a mean effect size (d) of -.42 in reducing prejudice—a moderate effect—and a larger effect size (-.72) in programs where the participants had no chance to avoid being in the contact situation. An important goal of this research was to investigate the importance of many variables that might moderate the size of the contact effect, and the findings are reported at length later in this volume.

Another crucial theoretical question in Pettigrew and Tropp's research was whether beneficial effects of contact with specific outgroup individuals would generalize to new social situations, to the whole outgroup, or to other outgroups. Their findings showed that intergroup contact's prejudice-reducing effects can generalize across situations and even generalize to different outgroups than the one in the contact program. A hopeful conclusion from this research is that successful contact with members of one outgroup can extend to greater tolerance of and willingness to interact with other outgroups.

Different Models of Contact

Much of the research interest in the contact hypothesis has been generated by conflicting predictions about the best way to structure the intergroup contact, and the ensuing question about which way leads to the greatest chance of generalizing prejudice reduction effects to other outgroups. These debates use concepts of social categorization and social identity theory to understand the processes by which cooperative intergroup contact influences prejudiced attitudes and behavior. Brewer (Chap. 8 in this volume) has described three related but different views as to the most effective way to conduct intergroup contact interventions:

1. **Decategorization**, in which the initial ingroup-outgroup categorizations are weakened and superseded by other cross-cutting similarities between ingroup and outgroup members (Brewer & Miller, 1984). These similarities are learned about through a personalized interaction process (e.g., "that outgroup member is like me in doing, thinking, or feeling ____").
2. **Recategorization**, in which the initial ingroup-outgroup categorization is weakened by uniting both groups in a common superordinate identity (e.g., "we're all Americans"—Gaertner et al., 1994).
3. **Mutual differentiation** is a pertinent term for the third model, because it recommends maintaining the initial social category distinctions but explicitly emphasizing that the groups are mutually interdependent (e.g., "our groups are different, but we need to work together to accomplish ____"—Brown, 1995).

The first two of these models are more compatible with an assimilationist view of majority-minority relationships, whereas the third model is closer to a pluralistic view. However, the three models are not completely in opposition, and Brewer suggests that their elements can be combined in interventions that aim to maintain minority groups' social identity while still achieving the goal of social integration for the broader society (Brewer, Chap. 8 in this volume). Dovidio, Kawakami, and Gaertner (Chap. 7 in this volume) have termed this approach a "dual identity" model—like "different groups on the same team"—an image which avoids th- group-identity-loss liabilities of the "melting pot" image. There is evidence that this model is beneficial to intergroup relations in societal contexts (Huo, Smith, Tyler, & Lind, 1996; Smith & Tyler, 1996), not just in laboratory experiments.

Dovidio and his colleagues (this volume) have gone farther in suggesting ways that prejudice can be combated on implicit, nonconscious levels, as well as explicitly. Similarly, Monteith, Sherman, and Devine (1998) have proposed that self-regulatory processes of suppression can help to control the activation of stereotypes—eventually modifying implicit, nonconscious attitudes—and thus reduce overt expressions of prejudiced behavior.

An important further question concerning prejudice-reduction programs is whether their results can generalize beyond the immediate outgroup members to other outgroup individuals and groups. Brown (1995) has suggested that only his model—which aims to maintain the salience of the ingroup-outgroup distinction while at the same time maximizing Allport's favorable conditions of contact—has a good chance of generalizing decreases in prejudice to other members of the outgroup beyond those in the current interaction. This is the case, he held, because then the interacting outgroup members are seen as representatives of their group rather than as isolated individuals. Brown admitted the practical difficulties in maintaining the group distinction while simultaneously trying to efface its negative associations, but he cited unpublished experimental evidence that doing so is possible and that it does have effects that generalize to the outgroup as a whole (Vivian, Brown, & Hewstone, 1994).

Note that Dovidio et al.'s dual-identity model in this volume is aimed at accomplishing this same goal, so there seems to be increasing convergence on the idea that the intergroup contact situation should not completely obscure the fact that participants are members of a social outgroup. Other evidence has shown that dissonance-reduction processes can generalize beyond the focal topic being considered, and thus reduce prejudice toward an outgroup more generally (Leippe & Eisenstadt, 1994). Going still further, it is encouraging that Pettigrew's (1997) findings suggest that successful contact with members of one outgroup can even generalize to greater tolerance of and willingness to interact with *other* outgroups.

However, beyond laboratory studies and carefully structured, intergroup-contact interventions, a practical obstacle is present in most real-life intergroup-contact situations in most modern societies. That is the fact of *segregation*, which dictates that contacts across ethnic or class lines will rarely be of a self-involving or personalized sort, let alone featuring equal-status relationships or cooperative activity toward common goals. Thus, most intergroup contacts do not come close to meeting Allport's (1954) specifications for situations that might reduce prejudice. Returning to Duckitt's (1992) classification of factors producing or opposing prejudice, the reality of societal segregation underlines the importance of actions at level 2—laws, regulations, and widespread norms—which will reduce segregation and encourage equalitarian interactions across ethnic and class lines.

CONTENTS OF THIS VOLUME

Background Factors Affecting Prejudice

The first section of this volume discusses background factors that need to be understood in attempting to reduce prejudice. Following the present introductory chapter, Walter and Cookie Stephan offer a theory that aims to describe the main intergroup bases of prejudice. As mentioned above, their theory stresses intergroup threats and fears as major causes of prejudice and discrimination, and classifies these threats as realistic threats, symbolic threats, intergroup anxiety in interactions with the outgroup, or negative stereotypes of the outgroup. The authors present research findings showing the impact of all of these dimensions on prejudiced attitudes toward several different outgroups. This classification scheme is helpful in suggesting which kinds of techniques for improving intergroup relations will be most effective in reducing particular types of threats, and the authors briefly review findings on several frequently used types of prejudice reduction programs.

Next, Jim Sidanius and Rosemary Veniegas present a challenge to all attempts to reduce prejudice, by emphasizing the evolutionary basis of intergroup conflict. Their approach stresses that a social dominance orientation is typical of all human societies, and that one of its chief features is to cause hostility and discrimination to be directed especially at outgroup males as targets, much more than at outgroup females. They present research data supporting this prediction, and their evolutionary perspective leads them to question whether prejudice, discrimination, and other forms of oppression will ever be able to be completely eliminated from human society, though they may be gradually ameliorated if their origins are properly understood.

The final chapter on background factors, by Marylee Taylor, stresses the importance of the social context, both in allowing and encouraging prejudice and discrimination, and alternatively in contributing to their reduction. Taylor describes housing segregation and employment discrimination as two forms of racial equality that are amenable to policy remedies, and she outlines four social contextual factors that can foster public support for effective remedies: institutional leadership, media framing, political discourse, and economic security among Whites.

Psychological Research on Reducing Prejudice

The second section of this volume contains five chapters that present recent research on various related but different psychological mechanisms for reducing intergroup prejudice and discrimination. First, Thomas Pettigrew and Linda Tropp summarize extensive new meta-analytic findings on the effectiveness of intergroup contact in reducing prejudice. As mentioned above, they show that intergroup contact under the proper conditions does indeed have a substantial, highly significant effect in reducing a wide variety of measures of prejudice toward outgroups. Even more important, their findings demonstrate many of the key conditions that moderate the size of the contact effect, such as the quality of the research, contact in work settings versus less intense and long-lasting settings, the type of outgroup studied, the formation of intergroup friendships, and the use of structured contact programs with optimal contact conditions. These authors also present evidence that contact effects generalize beyond the immediate participants in the contact, reducing prejudice toward other members of the outgroup as well.

Susan Fiske's chapter investigates the variable of outcome interdependence, based on the principle that interdependent types of social relationships influence people's social cognitions and affect toward other people. Her research shows that individual-level interdependence (both cooperative relationships and even competitive ones) create attention to the other person's individual attributes and reduce stereotypic thoughts and evaluations about them. However, group-level interdependence, in which another group is competitive with one's own group (as in team sports) does not have these individuating and prejudice-reducing effects. Fiske concludes that, when people need other people, they pay attention to them as individuals, but that dependence on others-as-a-group produces stereotypic views and evaluations of the group. In addition, individuals in high-power positions are more likely to stereotype people who are dependent on them, but making them aware of their interdependence with others can reduce their stereotypic thinking.

The next chapter, by John Dovidio, Kerry Kawakami, and Samuel Gaertner, builds on the authors' concept of aversive racism as being typical of many people. Aversive racists are people who sincerely believe themselves to be unprejudiced, but who still harbor some negative feelings (often unconscious ones) toward ethnic minority groups. The authors report on a series of studies aimed at reducing people's automatic negative stereotypes about outgroups. In individual-level experiments using extensive cognitive retraining, and others creating awareness of discrepancies between one's actions and values, they demonstrated methods by which both explicit and implicit stereotypes could be reduced. They also investigated conditions for optimal intergroup contact in which two groups were encouraged to *recategorize* their boundaries in the direction of sharing a common ingroup identity (e.g., "we're different groups, but all on the same team"). As predicted, they found this intervention led to reduced intergroup bias and prejudice. The authors emphasize that a strong advantage of this kind of dual-identity procedure is that it does not require minority groups to forsake their own unique group identity when they adopt a broader, superordinate identity.

Marilyn Brewer's chapter continues the focus on cognitive restructuring of intergroup situations. Her past work on *decategorization* has emphasized that ingroup boundaries can be broadened by cross-categorization on more than one dimension—e.g., thinking of one's ingroup as including both Hispanics and women. Here she reviews experimental evidence that cross-cutting characteristics and roles can reduce ingroup bias, which can exist even in equal-status, cooperative-interaction situations. She then extends this dual-identity concept, pointing out that most people have *multiple* social identities that include many cross-cutting social dimensions, such as ethnicity, gender, religion, and occupation. In this chapter she states theoretical principles describing the conditions under which multiple, cross-cutting social identities should reduce discrimination against outgroups based on any single dimension. Carrying this line of thought into real-world situations, she presents data indicating that individuals whose cognitive pictures of their ingroup are more complex or inclusive are more tolerant and accepting of outgroup members.

The final chapter on prejudice-reduction research perspectives, by Patricia Devine, Ashby Plant, and Brenda Buswell, is aimed at understanding and reducing both intentional and unintentional (conscious and nonconscious) forms of prejudice. The authors point out that low-prejudice individuals, in contrast to high-prejudice ones, have relatively low discrepancies between their questionnaire responses as to how they would versus should behave in various intergroup situations. Past research shows that, when low-prejudice individuals find themselves violating their personal standards, they feel guilt, and they try to improve their future responses—that is, to "break the prejudice habit." However, this chapter suggests that high-prejudice individuals may resent social pressures toward tolerance of outgroups, and reactance motivation may cause them to lash out behaviorally against nonprejudiced norms. In testing these notions, the authors developed scales of internal motivation (IMS) and of external motivation (EMS) to respond without prejudice, and they studied the personal consequences for individuals who responded with or without prejudice. In experimental studies they found that individuals who were low in IMS but high in EMS responded to pro-minority influence attempts with anger and with behavioral backlash against the advocated policy. An important implication of this finding is that attempts to reduce the prejudice of such individuals need to avoid the conditions that lead to anger and behavioral backlash, and the authors suggest that Rokeach's (1973) value self-confrontation technique may be useful with such individuals because of its subtlety and lack of external pressure.

Applications in Social Settings

The third section of this volume contains five chapters that examine issues of prejudice reduction in various real-world social settings. First, Brenda Major, Wendy Quinton, Shannon McCoy, and Tony Schmader change the focus of attention from the prejudice holder to the target of prejudice, and analyze strategies that members of socially stigmatized groups might be able to use to reduce prejudice toward themselves or their group. They classify such strategies as prejudice deflection, deterrence, or destruction, and their analysis draws on theory and research findings regarding people's appraisal of and coping with stressful life events. The various possible origins of prejudice (e.g., group differences, stereotypes, threats, etc.) suggest quite different relevant strategies for opposing it. Furthermore, characteristics of the target of prejudice, the prejudice-holder, and the situation all can moderate the appraisal of events as indicating prejudice and the nature of the resulting coping strategies. The authors discuss the potential costs and benefits of a variety of strategies, and they point out that the ultimate risks and rewards of any strategy are borne by the target much more than by the prejudice-holder.

Next, David and Roger Johnson discuss the practical aspects of reducing prejudice and discrimination in school settings, based on over 30 years of research and experience. Starting from the principle of social interdependence, they emphasize three main requirements: establishing a cooperative community, resolving conflicts constructively, and internalizing civic values. A great deal of research on cooperative learning approaches has demonstrated that they not only produce more positive relationships among diverse groups of students, but also greater learning, more frequent and accurate communication, better social perspective-taking, greater mutual influence, and higher self-esteem. Nevertheless, individual and intergroup conflicts still occur, and they need to be handled constructively. The authors briefly outline principles of constructive controversy, problem-solving negotiation and peer-mediation training, and peacemaking in school settings. Finally, they emphasize that in a cooperative community, members must share common goals and values, aimed at increasing the overall quality of life. Their research and theorizing go far beyond the contact hypothesis to show how cooperation must be structured at all levels in a school or in other types of cooperative communities.

Another chapter dealing specifically with children's prejudice is presented by Frances Aboud and Sheri Levy. They review the research literature on five broad types of interventions that aim at reducing prejudice in school-age children (not including cooperative learning, which was covered in the preceding chapter). Two interventions—ethnically integrated schooling and bilingual education—are based on intergroup contact theory. The third—multicultural and anti-racist education—is based on socialization theory and can be conducted with or without intergroup contact. The final interventions—training in social-cognitive skills, and in role-playing and empathy—are aimed respectively at students' cognitive and emotional capabilities. The authors present selected examples of each type of intervention and evaluate their success. They also summarize the strengths and weaknesses of each type, and analyze each one's target of change, its theoretical rationale, and the methodological adequacy of the pertinent research.

The chapter by Michele Wittig and Ludwin Molina describes evaluation research conducted on a multicultural education program that included contact between numerous ethnic groups. The research investigated several psychological processes that have been proposed as explanations of how intergroup contact reduces prejudice toward outgroups. Specifically, it contrasted the effectiveness in reducing prejudice of Gaertner et al.'s (1994) common ingroup identity model with that of two variables suggested by Phinney (1992): exclusive maintenance of ethnic identity, and openness to interaction with outgroups. With this multicultural education program and this sample of nearly 800 Los Angeles area middle- and high-school students, the findings showed a strong positive anti-prejudice effect of outgroup orientation and a weaker negative effect of ethnic identity, compared to a nonsignificant effect for the common ingroup identity model. A second study yielded supportive results, and these findings suggest new theoretical variables to consider in accounting for the effects of intergroup contact. They indicate that valuing and maintaining one's own ethnic identity need not be a barrier to reducing intergroup prejudice, if openness to interactions with members of other ethnic groups is also encouraged.

The final chapter, by Stuart Oskamp and James Jones, reports on a prestigious nationwide survey of programs directed at racial reconciliation. This survey was part of President Clinton's Initiative on Race, and it collected information about "promising practices for racial reconciliation"—outstanding examples of both local community-based groups and national programs directed at improving racial and ethnic relations in the U.S. The report of the President's Initiative is not a scientific document, but it deserves attention and dissemination as a broad survey of the current status of practical, operating programs to improve race relations. Accordingly, this chapter summarizes facts about the programs described in the report, classifies them in various ways, and discusses their goals, the methods by which they aim to reach those goals, the psychological mechanisms apparently implied by their methods, and the degree to which their efforts have been professionally evaluated. Such community programs should profit from using the research findings and theoretical principles for reducing prejudice summarized in the present volume, and in turn their activities will provide new challenges to researchers to explain their effects and improve their procedures.

CONCLUSION

The theories and research findings summarized in this volume give ample evidence that there are many possible paths to reducing prejudice and discrimination between social groups—and also that each path has potential pitfalls that must be avoided if prejudice-reduction efforts are to be successful. Though much meticulous research has been done in experimental laboratories, the full test of the efficacy of their findings is to apply them through careful intervention research in real-world intergroup situations and in community-wide programs. We need many more such applied studies in order to determine the value and the limits of our current theories of prejudice-reduction approaches. Toward this goal, the contributors to this volume hope that their efforts will lead to better methods and more far-reaching success in helping diverse social groups live together peacefully, productively, and pleasurably.

NOTES

1. I want to thank the many people who facilitated this volume and the conference which provided its starting point, the annual Claremont Symposium on Applied Social Psychology. Most of the Claremont Colleges helped with financial support, Pomona College provided physical facilities, and President Steadman Upham of Claremont Graduate University hosted a dinner for the speakers. The chapter authors worked diligently to perfect their manuscripts, my colleagues Bill Crano, Ximena Arriaga, Cherlyn Granrose, and Catherine Cameron gave advice and encouragement, Jessica Johnson and Trina

Moreno ably carried the burden of secretarial support, Amber Garcia performed faithfully as an editorial assistant for the volume, Art Lizza and Debra Riegert provided helpful editorial advice, and many graduate students in social psychology aided in tasks during the conference. My heartfelt gratitude goes to all of them.

2. Of course, it is important to realize that perceptions of the national social climate by minority-group individuals, who have felt themselves the targets of prejudice and discrimination, may differ sharply from these more upbeat viewpoints of the White population (cf. Major, Quinton, McCoy, & Schmader, Chap. 10 in this volume).

REFERENCES

Aboud, F. E. (in press). Evaluation of a fifth grade program to reduce prejudice. *Journal of Social Issues.*

Allport, G. W. (1954). *The nature of prejudice.* Reading, MA: Addison-Wesley.

Altemeyer, B. (1994). Reducing prejudice in right-wing authoritarians. In M. P. Zanna & J. M. Olson (Eds.), *The psychology of prejudice: The Ontario Symposium* (Vol. 7, pp. 131-148). Hillsdale, NJ: Erlbaum.

Aronson, E., & Thibodeau, R. (1992). The jigsaw classroom: A cooperative strategy for reducing prejudice. In J. Lynch, C. Modgil, & S. Modgil (Eds.), *Cultural diversity in the schools* (Vol. 2, pp. 231-256). London: Falmer.

Ball-Rokeach, S. J., Rokeach, M., & Grube, J. W. (1984). *The great American values test: Influencing behavior and belief through television.* New York: Free Press.

Banaji, M., & Greenwald, A. G. (1994). Implicit stereotyping and prejudice. In M. P. Zanna & J. M. Olson (Eds.), *The psychology of prejudice: The Ontario Symposium* (Vol. 7, pp. 55-76). Hillsdale, NJ: Erlbaum.

Banks, J. A. (1997). *Educating citizens in a multicultural society.* New York: Teachers College Press.

Brewer, M. B., & Miller, N. (1984). Beyond the contact hypothesis: Theoretical perspectives on desegregation. In N. Miller & M. B. Brewer (Eds.), *Groups in contact: The psychology of desegregation* (pp. 281-302). Orlando, FL: Academic Press.

Brown, R. (1995). *Prejudice: Its social psychology.* Oxford, England: Blackwell.

Dasgupta, N. (1999, June 4). *Exposure to admired group members reduces implicit prejudice.* Paper presented at American Psychological Society meeting, Denver.

Deutsch, M., & Gerard, H. (1955). A study of normative and informational social influences on individual judgment. *Journal of Abnormal and Social Psychology, 51,* 629-636.

Dovidio, J. F., Kawakami, K., Johnson, C., Johnson, B., & Howard, A. (1997). On the nature of prejudice: Automatic and controlled processes. *Journal of Experimental Social Psychology, 33,* 510-540.

Duckitt, J. (1992). *The social psychology of prejudice.* New York: Praeger.

Ellis, C., & Sonnenfield, J. A. (1994). Diverse approaches to managing diversity. *Human Resource Management, 33,* 79-109.

Ellison, C. G., & Powers, D. A. (1994). The contact hypothesis and racial attitudes among Black Americans. *Social Science Quarterly, 75,* 385-400.

The Eye of the Storm. (1970). ABC News documentary film. Available from Guidance Associates, The Center for Humanities, Communications Park, Box 3000, Mount Kisco, NY 10549.

Feinberg, M. (no date). *Racism...and psychology.* Washington, DC: American Psychological Association.

Fisher, R., & Ury, W. (1981). *Getting to yes.* New York: Penguin.

Gaertner, S. L., Rust, M. C., Dovidio, J. F., Bachman, B. A., & Anastasio, P. A. (1994). The contact hypothesis: The role of a common ingroup identity on reducing intergroup bias. *Small Group Research, 25,* 224-249.

Grube, J. W., Mayton, D. M., II, & Ball-Rokeach, S. J. (1994). Inducing change in values, attitudes, and behaviors: Belief system theory and the method of value self-confrontation. *Journal of Social Issues, 50*(4), 153-173.

Gurin, P., Peng, T., Lopez, G., & Nagda, B. R. (1999). Context, identity, and intergroup relations. In D. A. Prentice & D. T. Miller (Eds.), *Cultural divides: Understanding and overcoming group conflict.* New York: Russell Sage Foundation.

Hamilton, D. L., & Trolier, T. K. (1986). Stereotypes and stereotyping: An overview of the cognitive approach. In J. F. Dovidio & S. L. Gaertner (Eds.), *Prejudice, discrimination, and racism* (pp. 127-158). Orlando, FL: Academic Press.

Huo, Y. J., Smith, H. H., Tyler, T. R., & Lind, A. E. (1996). Superordinate identification, subgroup identification, and justice concerns: Is separatism the problem? Is assimilation the answer? *Psychological Science, 7,* 40-45.

Johnson, D. W., Johnson, R. W., & Holubec, E. J. (1994). *Cooperative learning in the classroom.* Alexandria, VA: Association for Supervision and Curriculum Development.

Johnston, L., & Hewstone, M. (1992). Cognitive models of stereotype change: (3) Subtyping and the perceived typicality of disconfirming group members. *Journal of Experimental Social Psychology, 28,* 360-386.

Leippe, M. R., & Eisenstadt, D. (1994). Generalization of dissonance reduction: Decreasing prejudice through induced compliance. *Journal of Personality and Social Psychology, 67,* 395-413.

Monteith, M., Sherman, J., & Devine, P. (1998). Suppression as a stereotype control strategy. *Personality and Social Psychology Review, 1,* 63-82.

Monteith, M. J., & Walters, G. L. (1998). Egalitarianism, moral obligation, and prejudice-related personal standards. *Personlaity and Social Psychology Bulletin, 24,*186-199.

NCSS Task Force. (1992). Curriculum guidelines for multicultural education. *Social Education,* September, 274-294.

Oskamp, S. (1991). *Attitudes and opinions* (2nd ed.). Englewood Cliffs, NJ: Prentice Hall.

Pettigrew, T. F. (1997). Generalized intergroup contact effects on prejudice. *Persponality and Social Psychology Bulletin, 23,* 173-185.

Pettigrew, T. F. (1998). Intergroup contact theory. *Annual Review of Psychology, 49,* 65-85.

Pfister, G. (1975). Outcomes of laboratory training for police officers. *Journal of Social Issues, 31*(1), 115-121.

Phinney, J. A. (1992). The multigroup ethnic identity measure: A new scale for use with diverse groups. *Journal of Adolescent Research, 7,* 156-176.

Ponterotto, J. G., & Pedersen, P. B. (1993). *Preventing prejudice: A guide for counselors and educators.* Newbury Park, CA: Sage.

Pratkanis, A. R., & Turner, M. E. (1994). Nine principles of successful affirmative action: Mr. Branch Rickey, Mr. Jackie Robinson, and the integration of baseball. *Nine: A Journal of Baseball History and Social Policy Perspectives, 3,* 36-65.

Rokeach, M. (1971). Long-range experimental modification of values, attitudes, and behavior. *American Psychologist, 26,* 453-459.

Rokeach, M. (1973). *The nature of human values.* New York: Free Press.

Sata, L. S. (1975). Laboratory training for police officers. *Journal of Social Issues, 31*(1), 107-114.

Schuman, H., Steeh, C., & Bobo, L. (1985). *Racial attitudes in America.* Cambridge, MA: Harvard University Press.

Schuman, H., Steeh, C., Bobo, L., & Krysan, M. (1997). *Racial attitudes in America: Trends and interpretations.* Cambridge, MA: Harvard University Press.

Sigelman, L., & Welch, S. (1993). The contact hypothesis revisited: Black-White interaction and positive racial attitudes. *Social Forces, 71*, 781-795.

Smith, H. H., & Tyler, T. R. (1996). Justice and power: When will justice concerns encourage the advantaged to support policies which redistribute economic resources and the disadvantaged to willingly obey the law? *European Journal of Social Psychology, 26*, 171-200.

Tan, D. L., Morris, L., & Romero, J. (1996). Changes in attitudes after diversity training. *Training and Development*, September, 54-55.

Thompson, L. (1990). Negotiation behavior and outcomes: Empirical evidence and theoretical issues. *Psychological Bulletin, 108*, 515-532.

Vivian, J., Brown, R. J., & Hewstone, M. (1994). *Changing attitudes through intergroup contact: The effects of membership salience*. Unpublished manuscript, University of Kent.

Weiner, J. J., & Wright, F. E. (1973). Effects of undergoing arbitrary discrimination upon subsequent attitudes toward a minority group. *Journal of Applied Social Psychology, 3*, 94-102.

I

Background Factors
Affecting Prejudice

2   An Integrated Threat Theory of Prejudice

Walter G. Stephan
Cookie White Stephan
New Mexico State University

"It was the best of times, it was the worst of times." (Dickens, 1950/1989, p. 1).

It seems to us that the same could be said of the state of race relations in our country at the present time.

On the "worst of times" side of the ledger is the fact that the great legislative initiatives that were designed to improve intergroup relations are becoming relics of the past. Certainly this has happened to school desegregation and the war on poverty, and it appears to be happening with affirmative action. Of the major legislative initiatives of the 1960's, only one stands unchallenged today. Americans are still strongly in favor of civil rights. White Americans generally agree with the premises underlying the other programs, but they increasingly object to the policies that are used to implement them. In a recent book, Kinder and Sanders (1996) present data indicating that attitudes toward government policies related to race are sharply divided by race. National opinion polls indicate that 90% of African-Americans favor racial preferences in hiring, but only 46% of Whites favor such policies. Similarly, 80% of African-Americans approve of the use of quotas in college admissions, but only 30% of Whites approve of quotas. On race-related public policies such as these, the divide between African-Americans and Whites is often as high as 50%. Furthermore, Kinder and Sanders believe the opinion gap between African-Americans and Whites is growing.

It seems that members of all racial and ethnic groups in America feel that their group is under siege. Whites now believe they are in the minority in the U.S. (*New York Times* Poll, 1995). They are opposed to affirmative action and the use of quotas in higher education; their fear of crime has not abated even though crime itself has; and they are increasingly opposed to immigration and programs to help immigrants, such as bilingual education (Kinder & Sanders, 1996). They feel that their way of life is under assault.

Minority groups have *always* been under siege in America. Prejudice, stereotyping, and discrimination are part of the fabric of their lives. Minority group members must live with a system of power and privilege that favors Whites and disadvantages all others. They are exploited in the workplace, are the target of hate crimes, and are segregated in housing (Jones, 1997). A disproportionate percentage of minority group members live in poverty and suffer the consequences—illness, inadequate healthcare, and poor housing and education (Cose, 1999; Jones, 1997). The White militias are still with us, hate-mongers are still among us, and race is still used to divide us in elections.

On the other hand, there are reasons to feel optimistic about the future of intergroup relations in our country. There are more elected officials from minority groups than ever before. African-Americans and members of other minority groups are represented in a broader array of professions than at any time in the history of our country and the middle class is expanding in most minority groups (Hacker, 1992). There have also been great strides in educational attainment for most minority groups in the last several decades, although most minority groups still lag behind Whites (Cose, 1999; Jones, 1997). The very fact that this volume can be devoted to techniques of improving intergroup relations is a reason for optimism.

Encouragingly, more research is being done on techniques of improving intergroup relations than ever before. More importantly, such techniques are being put into practice at a higher rate than ever before. New techniques are appearing every year. Racial dialogue is being promoted at the highest levels of government (see Oskamp & Jones, Chap. 14 in this volume). Businesses have come to recognize that promoting intergroup relations is good for their bottom line. More and more schools and universities are taking multicultural education seriously. There is a movement toward intergroup dialogues in communities around the country. The number of books on intergroup relations has exploded, as has the number of journal articles in our field and in related fields. We are far from winning the battle against racism, discrimination, prejudice, and stereotypes, but we have developed better weapons with which to fight these enemies.

In this chapter, we will discuss the role that fear plays in causing prejudice, and how we might go about overcoming fear as a means of reducing prejudice. Our interest in these issues stems from our earlier work on the role of ignorance and anxiety as causes of prejudice (Stephan & Stephan, 1984, 1985). Over time we became increasingly dissatisfied with the prevailing theories of prejudice because they did not seem to be useful in understanding some of the worst consequences of prejudice. It seemed obvious that fear and threats to people's ways of life were at the heart of the ethnic barbarity in the former Yugoslavia, the slaughter in Rwanda and Burundi, the terrorism in Northern Ireland, the conflict between Palestinians and Israelis, and the discrimination that is still woven so deeply into the fabric of so many societies.

There was also a growing interest in ideas of threat appearing in the literature on intergroup relations. Bobo (1988) and others were studying realistic threats. Sears, Esses, Sidanius, and others were studying symbolic beliefs and symbolic threats (Esses, Haddock, & Zanna, 1993; Sears, 1988; Sidanius, Devereux, & Pratto, 1992), while Eagly, Stangor, and others were showing that negative stereotypes played an unappreciated role in prejudice (Eagly & Mladinic, 1989; Stangor, Sullivan, & Ford, 1991). But most of this research was occurring in isolation and it seemed to us that each investigator was only examining a part of the picture. In recent years we have tried to integrate their efforts and our own into a model that is more broadly applicable than most other approaches using threats or fear as antecedents of prejudice. In the pages that follow we will present an overview of the theory, a series of tests of the theory, and some of the implications of the theory for improving intergroup relations.

AN OVERVIEW OF THE COMPONENTS OF THE INTEGRATED THREAT THEORY

The basic threat model currently includes four types of threat that we believe play a role in causing prejudice. These four threats are: realistic threats, symbolic threats, intergroup anxiety, and negative stereotypes.

Realistic Threats

The first type of threats included in our model consists of realistic threats posed by the outgroup. Realistic threats are threats to the very existence of the ingroup (e.g., through warfare), threats to the political and economic power of the ingroup, and threats to the physical or material well-being of the ingroup or its members (e.g., their health).

This concept of realistic threats has its origins in realistic group conflict theory. This theory, as developed by LeVine and Campbell and by Sherif, was primarily concerned with competition for scarce resources, such as territory, wealth, or natural resources (Bobo, 1988; LeVine & Campbell, 1972; Sherif, 1966). Our concept of realistic threat differs from the idea of threat emphasized in realistic group conflict theory in two ways. First, our focus is broader, encompassing any threat to the welfare of the group or its members. Second, we focus on subjectively perceived conflict between groups. We emphasize *perceived* realistic threats because the perception of threat can lead to prejudice, regardless of whether or not the threat is "real."

Symbolic Threats

The second type of threat is symbolic threats. Symbolic threats primarily involve perceived group differences in morals, values, standards, beliefs, and attitudes. Symbolic threats are threats to the worldview of the ingroup. These threats arise, in part, because the ingroup believes in the moral rightness of its system of values.

Some of the most prominent theories of prejudice in social psychology deal with symbolic threats of one kind or another. However, these theories take a different approach to symbolic threats than we do. They argue that feeling that your values are threatened by an outgroup is a form of prejudice (e.g., Kinder & Sears, 1981; McConahay, 1986; Sears, 1988), whereas we believe that feeling that your values are threatened is a cause of prejudice.

The theories of symbolic racism and modern racism argue that the hostility of Whites in the U.S. toward African Americans is a response to the belief that African Americans violate traditional values shared by most Whites (Kinder & Sears, 1981; McConahay, 1986; Sears, 1988). For instance, symbolic racism is defined as "a form of resistance to change in the racial status quo based on moral feelings that Blacks violate such traditional American values as self-reliance, the work ethic, obedience, and discipline" (Kinder & Sears, 1981, p. 416). Sidanius has reformulated symbolic racism theory as a theory of social hegemony, which he terms social dominance theory (Sidanius, Devereux, & Pratto, 1992). This theory explains prejudice toward subordinate groups as a function of dominant groups' attempts to maintain social control, and it holds that symbolic attitudes serve to justify the desire for group dominance. It seems to us that the legitimizing myths, which Sidanius says that dominant groups use to justify their positions, include realistic threats and negative stereotypes as well as more purely symbolic attitudes.

Ambivalence-amplification theory (Katz, Wackenhut, & Glass, 1988) posits that many stigmatized groups, including African Americans, are thought to violate the values of the dominant group, particularly those associated with the Protestant ethic. Yet, the dominant group also holds egalitarian attitudes, and the combination results in ambivalent feelings toward members of stigmatized groups (e.g., sympathy and aversion).

Most of the above symbolic-threat theories have focused mainly on threats associated with the values incorporated in the Protestant ethic (Sidanius' social dominance theory is an exception). Our concept of symbolic threats includes threats posed by the outgroup to any of the central values held by the ingroup. In measuring symbolic threats, we have attempted to distinguish clearly between realistic and symbolic threats. All previous measures of symbolic racism have included aspects of both of these types of threats.

The approach to symbolic attitudes that is closest to ours has been formulated by Esses, Haddock, and Zanna (1993), who argued that the more the ingroup's values, customs, or traditions are blocked by an outgroup, the more negative the ingroup's attitudes toward the outgroup will be. One difference between their approach and ours is that their measure of symbolic attitudes assesses the degree of frustration caused by blocking the ingroup's value system, whereas in our integrated threat theory, feelings of threat that are generated by challenges posed to the ingroup's value system are measured.

Intergroup Anxiety

The third threat is intergroup anxiety—the original concept that led to the current model. In our earlier work on intergroup anxiety, we argued that people feel personally threatened in intergroup interactions because they are concerned about negative outcomes for the self, such as being embarrassed, rejected, or ridiculed (Stephan & Stephan, 1985).

The idea that anxiety has negative effects on intergroup relations appears in several theories (Gaertner & Dovidio, 1986; Gudykunst, 1995). For instance, aversive racism theory suggests that unacknowledged negative affect toward African Americans is one of the essential components of racism (the other component being egalitarian values). According to this theory, the negative affect involves, "discomfort, uneasiness, disgust, and sometimes fear" (Gaertner & Dovidio, 1986, p. 63). These theorists argue that aversive racism motivates avoidance of outgroup members, rather than direct expressions of prejudice.

The concept of anxiety that we use in the integrated threat theory differs from the idea of anxiety in other theories in several ways. The most important difference is that we explicitly measure anxiety levels and relate them directly to prejudice.

Negative Stereotypes

The fourth type of threat is negative stereotypes. Almost all outgroup stereotypes embody threats to the ingroup because one of the functions of stereotypes is to serve as a basis for expectations concerning the behavior of members of the stereotyped group (Hamilton, Sherman, & Ruvolo, 1990). To the extent that the expectations are negative, conflictual or unpleasant interactions are likely to be anticipated. The essence of threat is the fear of negative consequences, and that is exactly what negative stereotypes create.

It has long been argued that stereotypes are associated with prejudice (Allport, 1954; Brigham, 1971; Ehrlich, 1971), but until recently studies of stereotyping and prejudice have failed to reveal a substantial relationship between the two. A major reason was that most studies of the relationship between stereotypes and prejudice have ignored the valence of the traits in the stereotypes. Since stereotypes frequently consist of both negative and positive traits, failing to consider valence may have rendered summary trait indices meaningless. Studies employing multiplicative indices, in which the stereotype percentages are multiplied by the evaluations of the stereotyped traits and the products are added to form a summary index of stereotyping, have found such indices to be consistent predictors of prejudice (Eagly & Mladinic, 1989; Esses et al. 1993; Stephan & Stephan, 1993).

Attitudes Toward Outgroups

In the integrated threat theory, these four threats are used to predict attitudes toward outgroups. We have defined prejudice as negative affect associated with outgroups (Stephan & Stephan, 1993). Our definition of affect includes both emotions and evaluations. This definition of affect has allowed us to include emotional reactions like hatred and disdain, as well as evaluative reactions like disliking and disapproval, in our measures of prejudicial attitudes toward other groups.

TESTS OF THE MODEL

Attitudes Toward Immigrants to the U.S.

In this section we will briefly summarize a number of studies that have tested our integrated threat theory of prejudice.

The first study we will describe concerned prejudice toward immigrants from Mexico, Asia, and Cuba to the U.S. (Stephan, Ybarra, & Bachman, in press). Anti-immigrant attitudes were quite intense in the U.S. at the time of the study, as evidenced by anti-immigrant bills that were being considered in Congress. The conflict over immigration makes attitudes toward immigrant groups a good test of the model. We expected that all four types of threat would predict prejudice toward immigrant groups because these groups are perceived to pose real threats to Americans, their values are perceived to differ from those of mainstream Americans, many Americans are anxious when interacting with people from other cultures, and Americans often have very negative stereotypes of immigrant groups. The following measures were employed in this study:

Realistic Threats. The measure that was created to assess realistic threat consisted of 12 items including such threats as crime, drugs, disease, job loss, and economic costs for health, education, and welfare. An illustrative item about Mexicans stated, "Mexican immigrants are contributing to the increase in crime in the U.S."

The items in this scale, and in all of the other scales, were evaluatively balanced, and favorable items were reverse-scored. Then they were combined into summary indices. The format for all of the items in all of the scales included 10 response options.

Symbolic Threats. To capture the threats posed by perceived differences in values and beliefs, a measure consisting of 12 items was developed. These items tapped perceived differences in work, family, religious, and moral values, among others. For example, "Mexican immigration is undermining American culture."

Intergroup Anxiety. The measure of intergroup anxiety was a modified version of the intergroup anxiety scale developed by Stephan and Stephan (1985). It consisted of 12 items that asked participants how they would feel when interacting with members of the respective immigrant groups. Examples of the anxiety-related feelings that were used are: apprehensive, confident, worried, at ease, and anxious.

Stereotype Index. To assess stereotypes, participants were asked to indicate the percentage of immigrants (Cuban, Mexican, or Asian) who possessed each of 12 traits that pretesting had shown to be associated with immigrant groups. Examples of the traits are: dishonest, unintelligent, clannish, hard-working, and friendly. The participants also rated the favorability of each trait. For each trait, the percentage estimate and the favorability rating were multiplied, and then the resulting products were added across traits to create a summary stereotype/evaluation index reflecting the negativity of the stereotype.

Prejudice. For the measure of attitudes, participants were asked to indicate the degree to which they felt 12 different evaluative or emotional reactions toward immigrants. The items included: hostility, admiration, disliking, acceptance, superiority, affection, disdain, and approval.

The sample for this study consisted of students at universities in Florida, Hawaii, and New Mexico (over 100 in each state). The participants were asked only about the immigrant group that predominated in their area. Simultaneous regressions were run on each sample separately. Attitudes toward each of the three immigrant groups were regressed on the four threat variables. Only the data for Mexican immigrants are presented here because the results of all three samples were almost identical. For attitudes toward Mexican immigrants among New Mexico college students, three of the four predictors were significant at conventional levels (beta coefficients were .27 for realistic threats, .34 for symbolic threats, and .28 for negative stereotypes, all with $p < .01$), while intergroup anxiety was a marginally significant predictor (beta = .13, $p < .10$). The four predictors accounted for 72% of the variance in attitudes toward Mexican immigrants.

Thus, the model received very solid support in this study. Prejudice toward immigrants was predicted by all four threats in all three samples ($p < .05$). These results suggest that opposition to immigration is probably not solely due to considerations of realistic threat, although that is generally the only kind of threat that enters into the public debate concerning these issues. The data suggest that value differences, discomfort about interacting with foreigners, and negative stereotypes are probably equally important, but unacknowledged, reasons why opposition to immigration is so strong in the U.S.

Attitudes Toward Immigrants to Spain and Israel

The second study concerned immigration to Spain and Israel. It was conducted to determine whether or not results obtained in the U.S. would generalize to other countries experiencing high levels of immigration under different political and economic circumstances. In this study the integrated threat theory was used to examine the attitudes of Spanish citizens toward Moroccan immigrants and of Israelis toward Russian and Ethiopian immigrants (Stephan, Ybarra, Martinez, Schwarzwald, & Tur-Kaspa, 1998). Only the Moroccan data are presented here. The immigration of Moroccans to Spain involves the movement of people from a developing country to an industrialized country, and it occurs primarily to fill the labor market needs of Spain.

For this study, the scales measuring realistic and symbolic threats and stereotypes were modified to be locally relevant, but the scales for intergroup anxiety and attitudes remained the same. Again, attitudes toward Moroccans were regressed on the four threat variables. The sample consisted of students at a university in Southern Spain. For attitudes toward Moroccan immigrants to Spain, intergroup anxiety ($p < .01$), stereotyping ($p < .01$), and realistic threats ($p < .10$) were significant or marginally significant predictors. The regression model accounted for 60% of the variance in attitudes toward Moroccan immigrants.

Although the predictors accounted for a substantial amount of variance in attitudes toward Moroccans and the findings provided considerable support for the threat theory, there was one failure to replicate the U.S. data. Symbolic threats were not a significant predictor in the Spanish sample, as they were in the U.S. The reason is most likely that symbolic threats are not very salient in Spain. The number of immigrants is relatively small, but more importantly, the Spanish students did not expect them to alter Spanish culture. In fact, Moroccan immigrants cannot become citizens. Thus, respondents who did perceive major value differences between the two cultures might not fear that these value differences would have any impact on Spanish culture, and therefore their evaluations of Moroccan immigrants would not be tied to their views on these differences in culture.

In these first two studies, some relevant psychometric issues were also addressed. In one study, the items in the four predictors were factor analyzed to determine if they loaded as expected on different factors, and they did (Stephan et al., in press). A separate sample of students was also asked to rate each item on the degree to which it assessed the four threats, to see if the four threats were conceptually discriminable, and they were (Stephan et al., in press). In addition, structural equation modeling was used to examine the latent structure of the four threats, and the best model was one suggesting that they all tap into one underlying dimension—feelings of threat (Stephan, et al., 1998). Also, the Cronbach alphas for these measures were consistently above .80, with most of them hovering about .90. In addition, the multicollinearity diagnostics for the regressions indicated that, despite intercorrelations among the threat variables, multicollinearity was not a problem in these analyses.

Women's Attitudes Toward Men

The next study examined threats as antecedents of women's attitudes toward men (Stephan, Stephan, Demitrakis, Yamada, & Clason, in press). Recently, considerable attention has been focused on the measurement of attitudes toward women (e.g., Frieze & McHugh, 1997). As a result, a number of new measures of sexism have been developed, including measures of neosexism (Tougas, Brown, Beaton, & Joly, 1995), modern sexism (Swim, Aikin, Hall, & Hunter, 1995), and ambivalent (hostile and benevolent) sexism (Glick & Fiske, 1996). The new sexism scales were developed to measure men's attitudes toward women. By comparison, little work has examined the parallel phenomenon, women's attitudes toward men. In this study we sought to redress this imbalance by examining women as subjects and not just as objects.

In this study a new variable was added because we were interested in the predictors of feelings of threat. The added variable was the extent of negative contact women had with men. There is considerable evidence linking contact to prejudice (Pettigrew, 1998; Stephan, 1987), but most of this research is concerned with positive, not negative, contact. It was expected that negative contact would be directly associated with negative attitudes, as well as having an indirect effect on attitudes through its effects on feelings of threat.

The amount of negative contact the participants had with men was measured with 17 items (e.g., being treated as inferior, manipulated, rejected, sexually harassed, sexually assaulted, threatened, physically harmed, and discriminated against). The participants were students at two different universities, although only the data from New Mexico State University are presented here.

Structural equation analyses were performed on the data (see Figure 2.1). The model accounted for 27% of the variance in attitudes toward men. In this analysis, symbolic threat and intergroup anxiety had significant direct effects on women's attitudes towards men. The findings also indicated that negative contact with men was related to disliking them and to high levels of symbolic threat and intergroup anxiety. Contrary to prediction, realistic threat and negative stereotyping were not significant antecedents of attitudes toward men.

Why did these two types of threat fail to predict attitudes? The experience of women within a patriarchal society may provide an explanation for both of these

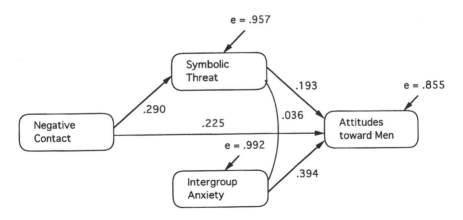

FIG. 2.1. Structural equation model of the role of threats in women's attitudes toward men. Source: Stephan, Stephan, Demitrakis, Yamada, & Clason, (in press). Reprinted by permission of Cambridge University Press.

nonsignificant effects. American women have always had less power and status than men, and most women believe that this condition has pertained in all societies at all times. College women may well perceive patriarchy as an inevitable condition that will never change, and therefore not use it as a basis for their attitudes toward men as a group. Stereotypic male traits, too, may be viewed as direct conse-quences of greater power and status. As such, stereotypes may not be seen as characteristics which should engender liking or disliking, but rather as natural by-products of history and men's social position.

Intergroup Attitudes of Mexicans and Americans

The next study focused on the attitudes of Mexicans and Americans toward one another (Stephan, Diaz-Loving, & Duran, in press). One of the greatest sources of difficulties in intercultural relations is the belief that other cultures pose a threat to one's own culture. Wars have been fought because of such fears and, at a lesser level, such feelings of threat commonly interfere with diplomatic, business, and interpersonal relations between members of different cultures. Mexico and the U.S. have a long and troubled history of interrelationships, as do many countries that exist side-by-side (Miller, 1985). Relations between the two countries have often been strained due to problems of immigration, trade, and drugs. The countries differ in terms of language, culture, and to some degree in racial composition and relig-ious preferences. Mexicans perceive the U.S. as attempting to dominate Mexico economically, politically, and culturally. The U.S. economy is dependent to some extent on immigrant labor from Mexico and thus has benefited from Mexico's prox-imity, but at various times in the history of the two countries, Americans have dis-criminated against, deported, and rejected Mexican immigrants.

In this study, prior contact between the groups was again included as an ante-cedent of feelings of threat. The sheer amount of intergroup contact may affect perceived threats because contact provides information about the other group. Even when some of the information is not positive, it can at least reduce uncertainty about the characteristics and behavior of the other group. The types of positive contact that improve intergroup relations—cooperative, individualized, voluntary, and equal status (Allport, 1954)—should also reduce perceived threats. In this study measures of both quantity and quality of contact were included.

Separate but identical path analyses were run on each sample, but here we will present only the data from the Mexican sample, which was comprised of students from the national university in Mexico City. Amount and quality of contact were en-tered as predictors of the threat variables and attitudes, while the threat variables were used only as predictors of attitudes. The path model accounted for 36% of the variance in attitudes toward Americans (see Figure 2.2). The Mexicans' attitudes toward Americans were strongly influenced by intergroup anxiety and negative stereotypes, and less strongly influenced by symbolic threats, while realistic threats were unrelated to these attitudes. The finding regarding realistic threats parallels

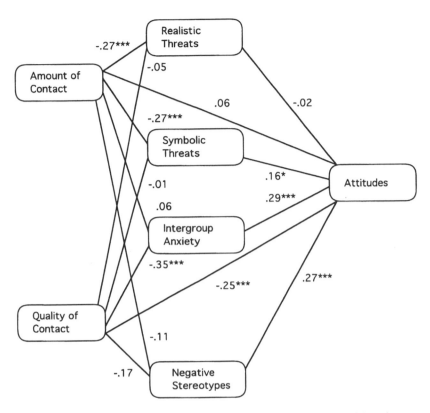

FIG. 2.2. Path analysis of factors related to Mexicans' attitudes toward Americans. Source: Stephan, Diaz-Loving, & Duran (in press). *Journal of Cross-Cultural Psychology*. Reprinted by permission of Sage Publications, Inc. *p < .10. **p < .05. ***p < .01.

that for women's attitudes toward men, and it may be that the explanation is similar as well—i.e., based on the assumed inevitability of the situation. Perhaps the Mexicans who perceive that the U.S. poses real threats to Mexico believe that there is nothing that can be done about the situation, given the relative power of the U.S. in this relationship, and therefore they do not use perceived realistic threats as a basis for their attitudes.

The Mexicans' attitudes toward Americans were also influenced by having favorable contacts with Americans, but not by the amount of contact they had with Americans. These findings suggest that it is the quality of contact, not the quantity of contact that affects attitudes most. The number of *favorable* contacts Mexicans had with Americans strongly affected intergroup anxiety, but did not have a significant impact on the other threat variables. The sheer amount of contact the Mexicans had with Americans affected the perception of both symbolic and realistic threats from Americans. This seems to represent an instance in which extensive contact does dispel threat, perhaps because the threats were overblown. Much of the information that Mexicans have about Americans comes from the mass media, which may present a distorted picture that can be countered by extensive personal contact.

Attitudes Toward the Beneficiaries of Affirmative Action

The next study extended the theory by using threats to predict attitudes toward the beneficiaries of affirmative action (Duran & Stephan, 1999). One of the main strengths of studies of modern racism and symbolic racism is their ability to predict attitudes toward social policies such as busing and bilingual education (Sears & Huddy, 1990). This study was conducted to determine whether or not the threat theory could predict attitudes toward a group described as "the people who benefit from affirmative action." Two new variables were added as predictors of threat: identification with the ingroup, and the personal relevance of affirmative action to the participants' lives. In general, it seems that the people who identify most strongly with their group would be the most likely to feel that their group was threatened by other groups. Similarly, when a social policy is thought to involve personal costs, it seems likely that people would feel threatened by it, although some previous studies have failed to obtain such an effect (Sears, 1988).

In the measure of personal relevance, participants were asked about the degree to which they felt that affirmative action would hurt their own chances of getting jobs for which they were qualified, and hurt the chances of other people close to them. The measure of ingroup identification was taken from Luhtanen and Crocker (1992) and included questions such as, "In general, being a White male is an important part of my self-image." The participants were 98 White males from New Mexico State University.

Again we used path analysis to analyze the data. The whole model accounted for 68% of the variance in attitudes toward the beneficiaries of affirmative action (see Figure 2.3). All four threat variables had significant or marginally significant direct effects on these attitudes. In addition, strength of group identification as a White male had a direct effect on attitudes. Personal relevance directly affected all four threat variables, while group identification only affected intergroup anxiety.

Previous studies have found that realistic and symbolic threats are powerful predictors of attitudes toward social policy (Kinder & Sanders, 1996; Huddy & Sears, 1990). This study indicates that these two threats, plus intergroup anxiety, negative stereotypes, and group identification, play an important role in attitudes toward individuals who benefit from these social policies. In addition, the results show that the personal relevance of this social policy is related to perceptions of all four types of threat.

It should be noted that the data from all of the above studies are correlational. There is probably some reciprocal causation involved in these relationships between threat and prejudice, but we are comfortable arguing that the predominant

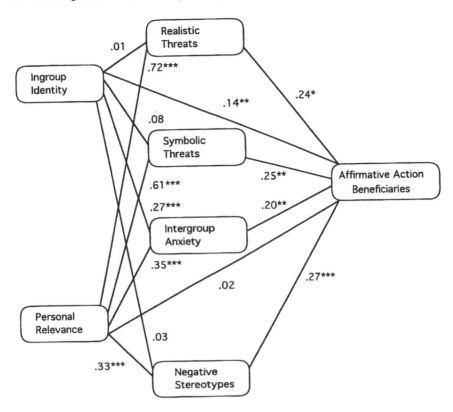

FIG. 2.3. Path analysis of factors related to attitudes toward the beneficiaries of affirmative action.   *p < .10.   **p < .05.   ***p < .01.

direction of causality is from threat to prejudice, rather than vice versa. We base this argument on the accumulating evidence showing that when threats to the in-group are manipulated in experimental studies, they consistently lead to prejudice toward outgroups (Maio, Esses, & Bell, 1994; Esses, Jackson, Nolan, & Armstrong, in press).

Attitudes Toward Rwandan Refugees—An Experimental Study

The final study we will summarize was designed to test causal predictions from the threat model (Martin, Stephan, Esses, & Stephan, 1999). This study examined atti-tudes toward a real national group that could plausibly be expected to immigrate to the U.S.—Rwandan refugees. The participants were 88 students at New Mexico State University. The design was a 2 X 2 X 2 factorial, in which we manipulated the presence or absence of realistic and symbolic threats and examined high vs. low identification with the ingroup. We asked students to read information about Rwandan refugees that was presented in a newsmagazine type of format. In all conditions, the article started with a description of Rwanda and the background of the civil war there. Then, in the high realistic threat conditions, the article described the costs of bringing the refugees to the U.S. and providing social services to them, and further said that they would need jobs when they arrived, that they might bring contagious diseases with them, and that they might be prone to violence. In the high symbolic threat conditions, the article said that Rwandans have very different values than Americans with respect to work, that they have no real experience with democratic ideals, that they prefer tradition over change, believe in folk medicine, and are not Christians. The low threat conditions merely omitted the threatening information on the given dimension.

In this study, the Luhtanen and Crocker (1992) measure was again used to assess identification with the ingroup, in order to test the idea that only people who identify strongly with their ingroup will be concerned about threats to it. Thus, it was expected that people who identified themselves strongly as Americans would express more negative attitudes toward Rwandans in the high threat conditions than in the control condition. The participants were divided at the median on the index of strength of ingroup identification.

Table 2.1 displays a three-way interaction indicating that the threat variables had the predicted effects in the high-ingroup-identification conditions. For the participants who strongly identified themselves as Americans, the condition in which the Rwandans posed both realistic and symbolic threats produced the most negative attitudes, while the high realistic threat and the high symbolic threat conditions produced less negativity, and respondents in the control condition displayed the least negative attitudes toward Rwandans. In the low-identification conditions, the Rwandans were again rated most negatively when they were presented as posing both types of threats, but the pattern of means in the other conditions suggests that neither realistic nor symbolic threats by themselves led to disliking Rwandans. Thus, the results provide evidence that realistic and symbolic threats can *cause* prejudice, at least among people who identify strongly with their ingroups.

TABLE 2.1
Attitudes Toward Rwandan Immigrants

Realistic Threat	Strength of Ingroup Identification			
	Low		High	
	Symbolic Threat		Symbolic Threat	
	Low	High	Low	High
Low	3.60	2.91	3.70	4.13
High	2.61	4.81	3.88	4.45

Note: High numbers indicate more negative attitudes.

THE CURRENT STATE OF THE MODEL

The core of the model is still the idea that threat causes prejudice. For attitudes toward outgroups, we have added two important antecedents—the idea that strong identification with the ingroup predisposes people to react to threat with prejudice, and the idea that negative contact predicts feelings of threat. Correspondingly, positive contact diminishes perceived threat, and this may be one reason why, under certain conditions, contact reduces prejudice.

In the future we intend to explore further the antecedents of threat and see if we can come to a better understanding of the circumstances under which the different types of threats predict prejudice. It currently seems to us that perceptions of threat depend on the strength of identification with the ingroup, the personal relevance of social policies favoring the outgroup, the nature of the contact between the groups, knowledge of the outgroup, the level of prior conflict between the groups, and the relative statuses of the groups (see Figure 2.4).

Ingroup Identification. Strong identification with the ingroup should increase the salience of all four types of threat. People who do not identify with their ingroup should not be concerned with threats to it and should not interact with outgroup members in terms of their group memberships. People who strongly identify with their ingroups are likely to experience greater feelings of threat from outgroups than people whose identity is less closely tied to ingroup membership.

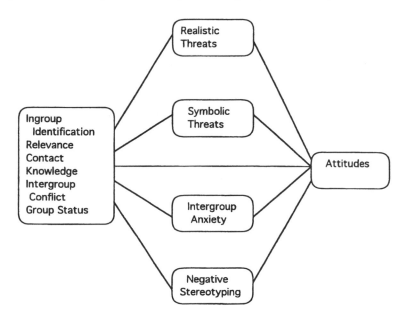

FIG. 2.4. A model of the integrated threat theory.

Relevance. For social policies involving preferential treatment of outgroup members, the more negative the personal impact of the policy, the greater should be the perceived threats.

Contact. The amount and especially the quality (positive or negative) of contact with the other group also affects feelings of threat. The greater the frequency of positive contacts (e.g., cooperative endeavors, successful team efforts, pleasurable intergroup activities) relative to negative contacts (e.g., disagreements, fights, losing team efforts, unpleasant intergroup activities), the lower the threat. By the same token, the greater the frequency of negative to positive contact, the greater the threat. Thus, people whose prior contacts with outgroup members have been predominantly negative are likely to feel threatened by the prospect of future contacts with members of this group.

Knowledge of the Outgroup. When ingroup members know very little about the outgroup, they are likely to perceive the outgroup as threatening. They will think that the other group is dissimilar to them and that its members dislike them. There is a fear of the unknown, a fear of the unfamiliar. If fear is the father of prejudice, ignorance is its grandfather.

Prior Intergroup Conflict. Intergroup conflict is probably the single most important seedbed of prejudice. The important role that conflict and other types of controversy between groups play in causing prejudice is acknowledged in many theories, including realistic group conflict theories, relative deprivation theory, game theory, the theory of graduated reciprocal initiatives in tension reduction (GRIT), and theories stressing the failure of one group to meet the needs of the other (e.g., for recognition) (Burton, 1986; Osgood, 1962; Stephan & Stephan, 1996). The type of conflict that is concerned here is not the current conflicts that may exist between the groups, but conflicts that have occurred in the past, which serve as a backdrop to current intergroup relations. Prior intergroup conflicts can be thought of as occupying a continuum from openly acknowledged, high levels of conflict to low levels of conflict that do not involve direct confrontation and may not even be acknowledged. High conflict may involve direct physical confrontations, but it may also entail competition or controversy concerning scarce resources (e.g., elective positions, jobs, power, money, territory, etc.), or open disagreements over values and rights (e.g., religious values, cultural values, moral values). When prior conflict has been high, perceptions of all four threats are likely to be heightened.

Status of the Groups. Perceived threats may also depend on the relative status or power of the two groups. Both high and low status groups can experience the other group as threatening, but usually in different ways. Members of the high status group may be worried that the low status group would like to reverse the power relationships between the groups, or that their group will be changed in unwanted ways by a group whose customs and values they regard as inferior. They may also experience intergroup anxiety when interacting with members of the low status group because they fear hostility or resentment, or because they feel guilty. In addition, members of high status groups are very likely to have negative stereotypes of groups they consider to be inferior to their own.

Although it would seem that members of low status groups would have reason to be concerned about realistic threats from the higher status group we have not found evidence for this proposition in the studies we have done. Thus, it is possible that realistic threats do not predict prejudice for low status groups. However, because the value differences between groups are often used by the dominant group as an excuse to discriminate against the subordinate group, symbolic threats should predict prejudice in low status groups. Subordinate groups may also have reason to be anxious about having negative interactions with members of the dominant group. In addition, in many cases they are likely to hold negative stereotypes about the dominant group, even if they do not feel free to express them.

It appears that, as the degree of status inequality increases, so too does the salience of threats posed by the other group. Whenever the ingroup has very high status or very low status relative to the outgroup, threats should be more salient.

Despite its breadth, the integrated threat theory of prejudice is not a comprehensive theory of all the causes of prejudice. For instance, it ignores social structural causes of prejudice and personality approaches to prejudice. The theory simply highlights a category of causes that we regard as particularly important. Our research clearly indicates that not all of the threats are always operative. In fact, one important practical goal is to determine which threats are operative in any given situation. On the basis of the results of the studies we have conducted so far, we can formulate two tentative hypotheses that merit further investigation. First, based on the studies of Mexicans' attitudes toward Americans and women's attitudes toward men, it appears that realistic threats may not be a predictor of prejudice toward dominant groups. Second, based on the studies of Americans' attitudes toward Mexicans, Spaniards' attitudes toward Moroccan immigrants, and Israelis' attitudes toward Russian immigrants, it appears that symbolic threats may not be a predictor of prejudice toward certain types of subordinate groups—those seemingly without power to influence the majority group. We hope that future research will allow us to learn more about the circumstances under which particular types of threat predict prejudice.

IMPROVING INTERGROUP RELATIONS

The threat model has some practical implications for understanding and improving relations between groups. Since our results suggest that different types of threats are related to prejudice toward different groups, policy makers, intergroup relations trainers, teachers, and members of groups disadvantaged by prejudice could profit from considering the specific threats outlined in the model. The model should prove to be particularly valuable in selecting the specific techniques to be used in improving relations between the groups, as discussed below.

If we wish to change prejudice based on fear, we must modify feelings of threat. One approach to overcoming feelings of threat is cognitive and relies on the premise that ignorance causes prejudice (Stephan & Stephan, 1984). In particular, it may be possible to undermine perceived realistic and symbolic threats with information that counteracts them. Although it is true that outgroups often do pose realistic and symbolic threats to the ingroup, in most cases such fears are overblown, and it may be possible to undermine them with accurate information about the other group.

There are several techniques of improving intergroup relations that seem ideally suited to reducing prejudice by counteracting realistic and symbolic threats, including multicultural education and diversity training. *Multicultural education* curricula usually consist of materials on the history and cultural practices of a wide array of racial and ethnic groups (Banks, 1988, 1997; NCSS Task Force, 1992). Often an attempt is made to present history from the perspective of minority groups, rather than from the more traditional perspective of the dominant majority. An explicit goal of most multicultural programs is to reduce prejudice. In one of the few systematic longitudinal studies of the effects of multicultural education, Aboud (in press) examined the effects of an 11-week curriculum designed to teach students about peers from different racial and ethnic groups using a variety of didactic presentations and interactive exercises. The students received instruction for one or two classes per week. The program reduced the prejudices of high-prejudiced White children, but had little effect on the attitudes of Black students. There are quite a few studies of more limited curricula that cover relatively short time spans, and this literature indicates that while the majority of these programs do reduce prejudice, some of them have no effects (Banks & McGee-Banks, 1995; McGregor, 1993; Stephan & Stephan, 1984).

Cultural diversity training programs also seem to be well suited to reducing realistic and symbolic threats. These training programs are used primarily in industrial settings to teach managers and employees to value group differences, increase understanding between groups, and help individuals recognize that their own behavior is affected by their backgrounds (Ellis & Sonnefield, 1994; Hollister, Day, & Jesaitis, 1993). Unfortunately, relatively little is currently known about which of these programs are most effective and why. One study (Tan, Morris, & Romero, 1996) found that a diversity training workshop increased knowledge of (a) diversity issues, (b) barriers to change, and (c) the effects of stereotyping and prejudice, and also created a willingness to identify and prevent stereotyping and prejudice in the workplace. A methodologically superior study found that diversity workshops reduced stereotyping (Kamfer & Venter, 1994).

When these programs are successful, it is most likely because of the information they provide about outgroups. While this information may reduce realistic and symbolic threats , it generally concerns the groups as entities (e.g., their history and values), and thus is unlikely to create the differentiated views of outgroup members that can counteract stereotypes (Rothbart & John, 1985). Nor do such programs typically provide the types of experiences or social skills that are likely to offset intergroup anxiety. To accomplish these goals, programs that are more interactive in nature may be needed. *Interactive techniques* of improving intergroup relations that are based on intergroup contact, such as cooperative learning and intergroup dialogues, may be ideally suited to overcoming negative stereotypes and intergroup anxiety.

In *cooperative learning* techniques, small groups consisting of members of different racial or ethnic categories work together on assigned tasks (Aronson, Blaney, Stephan, Sikes, & Snapp, 1978; Aronson & Patnoe, 1997; Cohen, 1992; Johnson, Johnson, & Holubec, 1994). Cooperative learning groups have been found to increase cross-ethnic liking and helping, as well as empathy (Bridgeman, 1981; Johnson & Johnson, 1992; Slavin, 1992; Weigel, Wiser, & Cook, 1975). They seem to be most effective when students are not explicitly assigned to groups on the basis of racial and ethnic categories (Miller & Harrington, 1990), when the interactions are positive in nature and interpersonally focused (Desforges et al., 1991; Rogers, 1982, cited in Brewer & Miller, 1988), and when superordinate groups or cross-cutting categories are highlighted (Brewer & Miller, 1988; Gaertner, Mann, Dovidio, Murrell, & Pomare, 1990; Gaertner, Mann, Murrell, & Dovidio, 1989).

Intergroup dialogue programs are currently being used extensively in university and community settings (Gurin, Lopez, & Nagda, 1998; Schoem, Frankel, Zuniga, & Lewis, 1993). They involve bringing people of different racial and ethnic backgrounds together under highly favorable contact conditions (i.e., equal status, individualized, cooperative, supported by authority figures). The group size typically varies from 15 to 25, but the technique can also be used with smaller groups. The groups engage in semi-structured interactions under the supervision of trained facilitators. They discuss topics related to intergroup relations, such as stereotyping, prejudice, and discrimination, and they read and discuss assigned materials about current events and issues. Experiential exercises are employed to stimulate discussion. Stress is placed on dialogue between groups, and many opportunities are provided for people to voice their own experiences. Research indicates that dialogue programs lead to a better understanding of issues concerning racial identity, reduced perceptions of racial polarization, and increased perceptions of commonalities across groups (Gurin, Peng, Lopez, & Nagda, 1998; Lopez, Gurin, & Nagda, 1998).

It is likely that when interaction-based programs are successful, they have a greater impact on reducing intergroup anxiety and negative stereotypes than on realistic or symbolic threats. Both cooperative groups and intergroup dialogues provide ingroup members with social skills that facilitate intergroup interaction and should therefore reduce intergroup anxiety. In addition, individualized interaction with outgroup members provides the participants with an opportunity to acquire information that is inconsistent with their stereotypes. Participants also learn that outgroup members vary considerably, which should lead to more differentiated perceptions of the outgroup.

In summary, we suggest that the integrated threat theory of prejudice is useful because it provides knowledge about the causes of prejudice, makes it possible to understand which types of threat are operative in a given situation involving specific groups of people, and provides insight into the specific techniques of improving intergroup relations that may be most effective in reducing particular types of threats.

REFERENCES

Aboud, F. E., (in press). Evaluation of a fifth grade program to reduce prejudice. *Journal of Social Issues.*

Allport, G. W. (1954). *The nature of prejudice.* Cambridge, MA: Addison-Wesley.

Aronson, E., Blaney, N., Stephan, C., Sikes, J., & Snapp, M. (1978). *The jigsaw classroom.* Beverly Hills, CA: Sage.

Aronson, E., & Patnoe, S. (1997). *The jigsaw classroom.* New York: Longman.

Banks, J. A. (1988). *Multicultural education* (2nd ed.). Boston: Allyn & Bacon.

Banks, J. A. (1997). *Educating citizens in a multicultural society.* New York: Teachers College Press.

Banks, J. A., & McGee-Banks, C. A. (1995). *Multicultural education: Issues and perspectives* (2nd ed.). Boston: Allyn & Bacon.

Brewer, M. B., & Miller, N. (1988). Contact and cooperation: When do they work? In P. A. Katz & D. A. Taylor (Eds.), *Eliminating racism: Profiles in controversy* (pp. 315-326). New York: Plenum.

Bobo, L. (1988). Group conflict, prejudice, and the paradox of contemporary racial attitudes. In P. A. Katz & D. A. Taylor (Eds.), *Eliminating racism: Profiles in controversy* (pp. 85-116). New York: Plenum.

Bridgeman, D. (1981). Enhanced role taking through cooperative interdependence: A field study. *Child Development, 52,* 1231-1238.

Brigham, J. C. (1971). Ethnic stereotypes. *Psychological Bulletin, 76,* 15-38.

Burton, J. W. (1987). *Resolving deep-rooted conflict.* Lantham, MD: University Press of America.

Cohen, E. G. (1992). *Restructuring the classroom: conditions for productive small groups.* Madison, WI: Wisconsin Center for Education research.

Cose, E. (1999, June 7). The good news about Black America. *Newsweek,* pp. 29-40.

Desforges, D. M., Lord, C. G., Ramsey, S. L., Mason, J. A., Van Leeuven, M. D., West. S. C., & Lepper, M. R. (1991). Effects of structured cooperative contact on changing negative attitudes toward stigmatized social groups. *Journal of Personality and Social Psychology, 60,* 531-544.

Dickens, C. (1850/1989). *A tale of two cities.* New York: Bantam.

Duran, A., & Stephan, W. G. (1999). *The role of threats in attitudes toward affirmative action and its beneficiaries.* Unpublished manuscript. New Mexico State University, Las Cruces.

Eagly, A. H., & Mladinic, A. (1989). Gender stereotypes and attitudes toward women and men. *Personality and Social Psychology Bulletin, 15,* 543-558.

Ehrlich, H. J. (1973). *The social psychology of prejudice.* New York: Wiley.

Ellis, C., & Sonnenfield, J. A. (1994). Diverse approaches to managing diversity. *Human Resource Management, 33,* 79-109.

Esses, V. M., Haddock, G., & Zanna, M. P. (1993). Values, stereotypes, and emotions as determinants of intergroup attitudes. In D. M. Mackie & D. L. Hamilton (Eds.), *Affect, cognition and stereotyping: Interactive processes in group perception* (pp. 137-166). Orlando, FL: Academic Press.

Esses, V. M., Jackson, L. M., Nolan, J. M., & Armstrong, T. L. (in press). Emotional threat and attitudes toward immigrants. In L. Halli & L. Drieger (Eds.), *Immigrant Canada: Demographic, economic, and social challeges*. Toronto: University of Toronto Press.

Frieze, I. H., & McHugh, M. C. (Eds.). (1997). Measuring beliefs about appropriate roles for women and men. *Psychology of Women, 21*(1), 1-16.

Gaertner, S. L., & Dovidio, J. F. (1986). The aversive form of racism. In J. F. Dovidio & S. L. Gaertner (Eds.), *Prejudice, discrimination, and racism*. Orlando, FL: Academic Press.

Gaertner, S. L., Mann, J. A., Dovidio, J. F., Murrell, A. J., & Pomare, M. (1990). How does cooperation reduce intergroup bias? *Journal of Personality and Social Psychology, 59*, 692-704.

Gaertner, S. L., Mann, J., Murrell, A., & Dovidio, J. F. (1989). Reducing intergroup bias: The benefits of recategorization. *Journal of Personality and Social Psychology, 57*, 239-249.

Glick, P., & Fiske, S. T. (1996). The ambivalent sexism inventory: Differentiating hostile and benevolent sexism. *Journal of Personality and Social Psychology, 70*, 491-512.

Gudykunst, W. B. (1995). Anxiety/uncertainty management (AUM) theory: Development and current status. In R. L. Wiseman (Ed.), *Intercultural communication theory*. Thousand Oaks, CA: Sage.

Gurin, P., Lopez, G., & Nagda, B. R. (1998). *Context, identity, and intergroup relations.* Unpublished manuscript, University of Michigan.

Gurin, P., Peng, T., Lopez, G., & Nagda, B. R. (in press). Context, identity, and intergroup relations. In D. Prentice & D. Miller (Eds.), *Cultural divides: The social psychology of intergroup contact*.

Hacker, A. (1992). *Two nations: Black and White, separate, hostile, unequal*. New York: Scribner's.

Hamilton, D. L., Sherman, S. J., & Ruvolo, C. M. (1990). Stereotype-based expectancies: Effects on information processing and social behavior. *Journal of Social Issues, 46*(2) 35-60.

Hollister, L., Day, N. E., & Jesaitis, P. T. (1993). Diversity programs: Key to competitiveness or just another fad? *Organization Development Journal, 11*, 49-59.

Johnson, D. W., & Johnson, R. T. (1992). Social interdependence and crossethnic relationships. In J. Lynch, C. Modgil, & S. Modgil (Eds.), *Cultural diversity in the schools* (Vol. 2, pp. 179-190). London, England: Falmer.

Johnson, D. W., Johnson, R. W., & Holubec, E. J. (1994). *Cooperative learning in the classroom*. Alexandria, VA: Association for Supervision and Curriculum Development.

Jones, J. M. (1997). *Prejudice and racism* (2nd ed.). New York: McGraw-Hill.

Kamfer, L. & Venter, J. L. (1994). First evaluation of a stereotype reduction workshop. *South African Journal of Psychology, 24*, 13-20.

Katz, I., Wackenhut, J., & Glass, D. C. (1988). An ambivalence-amplification theory of behavior toward the stigmatized. In S. Worchel & W. G. Austin (Eds.), *Psychology of intergroup relations* (2nd ed.). Chicago: Nelson-Hall.

Kinder, D. R., & Sanders, L. M. (1996). *Divided by color: Racial politics and democratic ideals*. Chicago: University of Chicago Press.

Kinder, D. R., & Sears, D. O. (1981). Prejudice and politics: Symbolic racism versus racial threats to the good life. *Journal of Personality and Social Psychology, 40*, 414-431.

LeVine, R. A., & Campbell, D. T. (1972). *Ethnocentrism: Theories of conflict, ethnic attitudes, and group behavior*. New York: Wiley.

Lopez, G. E., Gurin, P., & Nagda, B. A. (1998). Education and understanding structural causes for group inequalities. *Political Psychology, 19*, 305-329.

Luhtanen, R., & Crocker, J. (1992). A collective self-esteem scale: Self-evaluation of one's own identity. *Personality and Social Psychology Bulletin, 18,* 302-318.

Maio, G. R., Esses, V. M., & Bell, D. W. (1994). The formation of attitudes toward new immigrant groups. *Journal of Applied Social Psychology, 24,* 1762-1776.

Martin, T., Stephan, W. G., Esses, V., & Stephan, C. (1999). *The effects of realistic and symbolic threats on attitudes toward immigrants.* Unpublished manuscript, New Mexico State University, Las Cruces.

McConahay, J. G. (1986). Modern racism, ambivalence, and the modern racism scale. In Dovidio, J. F., & Gaertner, S. L. (Eds.), *Prejudice, discrimination, and racism* (pp. 91-125). Orlando, FL: Academic Press.

McGregor, J. (1993). Effectiveness of role-playing and antiracist teaching in reducing student prejudice. *Journal of Educational Research, 86,* 215-226.

Miller, N., & Harrington, H. J. (1990). A model of category salience for intergroup relations: Empirical tests of the relevant variables. In P. J. D. Drenth, J. A Sargeant, & R. J. Takens (Eds.), *European perspectives in psychology* (Vol. 3, pp. 205-220). New York: Wiley.

Miller, R. R. (1985). *Mexico: A history.* Norman: University of Oklahoma Press.

Myrdal, G. (1944). *An American dilemma.* New York: Harper.

NCSS Task Force. (1992, September). Curriculum guidelines for multicultural education. *Social Education,* pp. 274-294.

Osgood, C. E. (1962). *An alternative to war or surrender.* Urbana: University of Illinois Press.

Pettigrew, T. F. (1998). Intergroup contact theory. *Annual Review of Psychology, 49,* 65-85.

Rothbart, M., & John, O. P. (1985). Social categorization and behavioral episodes: A cognitive analysis and the effects of intergroup contact. *Journal of Social Issues, 41*(3), 81-104.

Schoem, D., Frankel, L., Zuniga, X., & Lewis, E. (1993). *Multicultural teaching in the University.* Westport, CT: Praeger.

Sears, D. O. (1988). Symbolic racism. In P. A. Katz & D. A. Taylor (Eds.), *Eliminating racism: Profiles in controversy* (pp. 53-84). New York: Plenum.

Sears, D. O., & Huddy, (1990). On the origins of political disunity among women. In L. A. Tilly & P. Gurin (Eds.), *Women, politics, and change* (pp. 249-277). New York: Russell Sage.

Sherif, M. (1966). *Group conflict and cooperation.* London, England: Routledge & Kegan Paul.

Sidanius, J., Devereux, E., & Pratto, F. (1992). A comparison of symbolic racism theory and social dominance theory as explanations for racial policy attitudes. *Journal of Social Psychology, 132,* 377-395.

Slavin, R. E. (1992). Cooperative learning: Applying contact theory in the schools. In J. Lynch, C. Modgil, & S. Modgil (Eds.), *Cultural diversity in the schools* (Vol. 2, pp. 333-348). London, England: Falmer.

Stangor, C., Sullivan, L. A., & Ford, T. E. (1991). Affective and cognitive determinants of prejudice. *Social Cognition, 9,* 359-380.

Stephan, C. W. (1992). Intergroup anxiety and intergroup interaction. In J. Lynch, C. Modgil, & S. Modgil (Eds.), *Cultural diversity in the schools* (Vol. 2, pp. 145-158). London, England: Falmer.

Stephan, W. G. (1987). The contact hypothesis in intergroup relations. In C. Hendrick (Ed.), *Review of personality and social psychology* (Vol. 9, pp. 13-40). Beverly Hills, CA: Sage.

Stephan, W. G., Diaz-Loving, R., & Duran, A. (in press). Integrated threat theory and intercultural attitudes: Mexico and the United States. *Journal of Cross-Cultural Psychology.*

Stephan, W. G., & Stephan, C. W. (1984). The role of ignorance in intergroup relations. In N. Miller & M. B. Brewer (Eds.), *Groups in contact: The psychology of desegregation* (pp. 229-257). New York: Academic Press.

Stephan, W. G., & Stephan, C. W. (1985). Intergroup anxiety. *Journal of Social Issues, 41*(3), 157-175.

Stephan, W. G., & Stephan, C. W. (1993). Cognition and affect in stereotyping: Parallel interactive networks. In D. M. Mackie & D. L. Hamilton (Eds.), *Affect, cognition, and stereotyping: Interactive processes in group perception* (pp. 111-136). Orlando, FL: Academic Press.

Stephan, W. G., & Stephan, C. W. (1996). *Intergroup relations*. Boulder, CO: Westview.

Stephan, C. W., Stephan, W. G., Demitrakis, K., Yamada, A. M., & Clason, D. (in press). Women's attitudes toward men: An integrated threat theory analysis. *Psychology of Women Quarterly*.

Stephan, W. G., Ybarra, O., & Bachman, G. (in press). Prejudice toward immigrants: An integrated threat theory. *Journal of Applied Social Psychology*.

Stephan, W. G., Ybarra, O., Martinez, C., Schwarzwald, J., & Tur-Kaspa. (1998). Prejudice toward immigrants to Spain and Israel: An integrated threat theory analysis. *Journal of Cross-Cultural Psychology, 29*, 559-576.

Swim, J. K., Aiken, K. J., Hall, W. S., & Hunter, B. A. (1995). Sexism and racism: Old-fashioned and modern prejudices. *Journal of Personality and Social Psychology, 68*, 199-214.

Tan, D. L., Morris, L., & Romero, J. (1996, September). Changes in attitudes after diversity training. *Training and Development*, pp. 54-55.

Tougas, F., Brown, R., Beaton, A. M., & Joly, S. (1995). Neosexism: Plus ca change, plus c'est pareil. *Journal of Personality and Social Psychology, 68*, 842-849.

Weigel, R. H., Wiser, P. L., & Cook, S. W. (1975). The impact of cooperative learning experiences on cross-ethnic relations and helping. *Journal of Social Issues, 31*(1), 219-244.

3 Gender and Race Discrimination: The Interactive Nature of Disadvantage

Jim Sidanius
University of California, Los Angeles

Rosemary C. Veniegas
University of California, Berkeley

While many parts of the world made great strides in reducing racial, ethnic, and gender discrimination during the 1960s and 1970s, a casual glance across the globe quickly reveals that the scourges of ethnic and gender intolerance are far from having been eliminated. Despite intense and almost desperate efforts to eliminate ethnic intolerance and discrimination, they appear to be every bit as bad at the close of the 20th century as at the beginning of the century. The questions addressed by this chapter are: Why are ethnic, racial, and gender discrimination so difficult to eliminate, and what can we do to hasten their demise?

Traditional approaches to the study of prejudice and discrimination within social psychology and sociology have viewed sexism and racism largely within the same broad conceptual framework and essentially as different manifestations of the same underlying phenomenon. In contrast, we will argue that, while these two forms of discrimination are clearly related, they are also qualitatively and dynamically distinct. Using social dominance theory as our conceptual frame of reference, we suggest that we cannot hope to eradicate ethnic or gender prejudice until we have a better understanding of exactly how these two social phenomena are both similar to and different from one another.

Social dominance theory begins with the observation that human societies are structured as group-based social hierarchies, with dominant groups enjoying a disproportionate amount of positive social value (e.g., wealth, power, and status) while subordinate groups suffer from a disproportionate amount of negative social value (e.g., poverty, stigmatization, and imprisonment—see Pratto, in press; Sidanius, 1993; Sidanius & Pratto, 1993, 1999). Social dominance theorists argue that group-based social hierarchies can be classified into three distinct categories: (a) an *age system*, in which adults and middle-age people have disproportionate social power over children and younger adults,[1] (b) a *patriarchal system,* in which males have disproportionate social and political power compared to females, and (c) an *arbitrary-set* system. The arbitrary-set system is composed of socially constructed and salient group categories on dimensions such as "race," ethnicity, caste, clan, social class, "estate," nation, religious sect, region, or any other socially relevant characteristic which the human imagination is capable of constructing. While there are a number of similarities in the structural and functional characteristics of the patriarchal and arbitrary-set systems of social stratification, each system is functionally unique and plays a different role in the overall construction and maintenance of group-based social hierarchy.

DISTINCTIONS BETWEEN PATRIARCHAL AND ARBITRARY-SET HIERARCHIES

There are at least five important differences between patriarchal and arbitrary-set hierarchies. First, most obviously and perhaps most importantly, unlike different categories of the arbitrary-set system, males and females are completely codependent. For example, while it is possible for European Americans to continue in the complete absence of African Americans, and vice versa, it is obviously not possible for one sex to exist more than one generation without the other—at least not yet. This complete codependence of males and females, and the inherent unity of their long-term interest, set limits on the depth and severity of intersexual conflict.

Second, and related to the first point, patriarchy and arbitrary-set hierarchies differ in the nature and depth of the emotional/sexual attachment between dominant and subordinate categories. The emotional/sexual contact between men and women is substantially more positive than the emotional/sexual attachment between dominant and subordinate arbitrary-sets. Many feminists characterize patriarchy as primarily a misogynist structure driven by male hatred of and contempt for women (e.g., Dworkin, 1974; Mies, Bennholdt-Thomsen, & von Werlhof, 1988). However, empirical research shows that patriarchy is primarily associated with *paternalism* (i.e., the intersection of discriminatory intent and positive affect) rather than with misogyny (e.g., Jackman, 1994; see also Reese & Curtis, 1991). While arbitrary-set hierarchies often contain paternalistic elements (see van den Berghe, 1967), paternalism is consistently and substantially more characteristic of patriarchy than of arbitrary-set hierarchies.

The third major distinction between these two forms of social hierarchy follows from the second. It is that, compared to patriarchy, arbitrary-set hierarchy is associated with far greater levels of violence, brutality, and oppression. While patriarchy contains elements of violence, even of a lethal nature, the brutality and terror associated with arbitrary-set hierarchy generally far exceeds that associated with patriarchy in both intensity and scope. For example, the 20th century has witnessed at least eight major episodes of genocidal, arbitrary-set violence. These include: (1) the massacre of the Kurds by Turkey in 1924, (2) Stalin's slaughter of the Kulaks in 1929, (3) the European Holocaust of the 1930s - 1940s, which not only witnessed the execution of some 6 million Jews, but also between 200,000 - 500,000 Roma[2] and approximately 16 million Slavs,[3] (4) the Khmer Rouge terror in Cambodia in the late 1970s, (5) widespread massacre of the East Timorese by Indonesia in the late 1990s, (6) "ethnic cleansing" of Serbs from Croatia, Muslims from Bosnia, and Albanians from Kosovo in the late 1990s, (7) the widespread killings of Kasaians in Zaire (French, 1996), and (8) the massacres of Tutsis and Hutus in Rwanda and Burundi in the late 1990s. This level of slaughter is rarely, if ever, used to maintain patriarchy.[4]

A fourth distinction between patriarchy and arbitrary-set hierarchies concerns the transhistorical and transsituational invariance of these two social constructions. Though there is some degree of flexibility and situational contingency in the manner in which categories of "male" and "female" are defined and constructed across different cultures, this categorical fluidity pales in comparison to the high degree of arbitrariness, plasticity, flexibility, situational and contextual sensitivity used to construct and define salient group distinctions within the arbitrary-set system. Depending on the specific historical and socio-political circumstances, salient arbitrary-group distinctions may be defined in a very wide variety of ways. These include membership in "races" (e.g., "White" vs. "Black"), street gangs (e.g., "Bloods" vs. "Crips"), nationalities (e.g., American vs. Serbian), or social classes (e.g., "working-class" vs. "upper-class").

Furthermore, even with respect to a given salient arbitrary-set dimension, the manner in which categorical membership is defined is highly dependent upon the specific cultural and situational context. The clearest example of this definitional arbitrariness can be found with respect to the construct of "race." While most people in the modern world reify the concept of "race," treating it as if it were a "natural category," the fact of the matter is that there is no consistent set of genetic markers setting off one human "race" from another (Yee, Fairchild, Weizmann, & Wyatt, 1993). Furthermore, the manner in which certain individuals would be classified into "racial categories" shows a very high degree of situational and historical flexibility. For example, a given person who had 1/8 African heritage would be classified as "Black" in early 19th century America, as "mulatto" during the same period in Brazil, and as "White" in late 20th century Denmark.

Finally, patriarchy and arbitrary-set hierarchies differ with respect to transcultural and transspecies generalizability. Patriarchy appears to be a cross-cultural and transhistorical universal. While the *degree* of patriarchy varies substantially across culture and across time, the *fact* of patriarchy appears to be universal across time and place. Despite the claims of some (e.g., Bachofen, 1861/1969; Gimbutas, 1989), there are no societies in recorded human history which can unambiguously be described as "matriarchal." That is to say, there are no societies in which women, as a group, have had control over the political life of the community, the community's interaction with outgroups, or the technology and practice of warfare (arguably the ultimate arbiter of political power). Although there are several known examples of matrilineal societies (i.e., where descent is traced through the family of the mother), matrilocal or uxorilocal societies (i.e., where newly married couples reside with the wife's kin), and societies in which women have near economic parity with men (see Murdock, 1949)—and even though some societies are occasionally ruled by very powerful individual queens—in the aggregate there are no known examples of matriarchal societies (e.g., Collier & Yanagisako, 1987; Lenski, 1984).

While patriarchy is the rule among all known human groups, arbitrary-set hierarchies are generally not found among small hunter-gatherer societies (Lenski, 1984). It has been argued that one major reason for the lack of arbitrary-set hierarchies among hunter-gatherer societies is because such societies do not produce stable economic surpluses (Lenski, 1984). Similarly, because hunter-gatherer societies tend to be nomadic, people within these societies are not able to accumulate large amounts of food-stuffs, and they are also not able to produce, accumulate, and transport large amounts of other forms of wealth. Since all adults are largely engaged in the procurement of life's daily necessities, this leaves little room for the development of highly specialized social roles and social institutions, such as professional armies, police, or other expropriative bureaucracies. Because hunter-gatherers are free from these "coercive specialists," in the aggregate all adult males are essentially the military equals of all other adult males. Therefore, to the extent to which political authority among adult males exists, this authority tends to be based upon mutual agreement, persuasion, and consultation rather than coercion. However, in the aggregate, this military equality appears never to have existed between males and females. Their military inequality is not only a function of physical dimorphism (i.e., the larger size and strength of males) and the greater physical aggressivity of males, but also of the fact that males are more predisposed to establish and maintain systems of group-based social dominance (Eisler & Lowe, 1983; Maccoby & Jacklin, 1974; Sidanius, Levin, Liu, & Pratto, in press; Sidanius & Pratto, 1999; Sidanius, Pratto, & Bobo, 1994; Sidanius, Pratto, & Brief, 1995).

On the other hand, while arbitrary-set hierarchies tend to be relatively rare in hunter-gatherer societies, arbitrary-set hierarchies are completely universal within societies producing sustainable economic surpluses (e.g., horticultural, agrarian, industrial, and post-industrial societies—see Lenski, 1984). An economic surplus allows certain males the luxury of being able to specialize in the arts of coercion (e.g., war-lordism, policing) and religious and/or political sophistry. These role specialists are then used by political elites to develop expropriative economic and social relationships with other members of the society, resulting in the establishment and maintenance of group-based, arbitrary-set hierarchies. The relationship between the production of a sustainable economic surplus and the emergence of arbitrary-set hierarchy is so strong that it is virtually impossible to identify a single society producing a sustainable economic surplus that at the same time does *not* have an arbitrary-set hierarchy.

FEMINIST PERSPECTIVES ON PATRIARCHY AND
ARBITRARY-SET HIERARCHY

According to various feminist and sociocultural theories, the desire for power best accounts for institutionalized social domination (Jaggar, 1993; Lorber, 1998; Reid, 1988). For example, Jackman (1994, p. 101) argued that "The question of power is important here, not as a means to an end, but primarily as the central goal in itself." Men and members of dominant ethnic groups seek to control economic, educational, judicial, and political systems. In establishing such control, dominants gain power and access to desired material and interpersonal resources. Jackman's (1994) analysis of the characteristics of gender, class, and race inequality reflected these themes of power and social control. She argued that race inequality is created and maintained by Whites in order to have access to laborers. The history of immigration and labor practices in the U. S. offers ample illustration of how ethnic hierarchy provided Whites with inexpensive and controllable sources of labor (Takaki, 1993, 1994). Regarding gender inequality, Jackman (1994) argued that men sought power over women in order to have access to emotional and sexual rewards.

A rather parallel sociocultural interpretation can be found in the work of Eagly (1987). According to her, systems of gender hierarchy are maintained by the socialization of women and men into distinct roles, which assign more power to men than to women. Such roles are accompanied by culturally shared expectations regarding the appropriate traits and behaviors of higher status versus lower status group members. Forms of hierarchy are perpetuated by shared beliefs about the roles played by high and low status individuals. Both the feminist and sociocultural accounts of patriarchy and arbitrary-set hierarchy define power as the ultimate resource that men and dominants seek to monopolize. From a feminist and sociocultural perspective, ethnic minority women might be viewed as controllable sources of both labor and emotional/sexual benefits.

THE DOUBLE JEOPARDY HYPOTHESIS

The reasoning outlined above can generate two opposing hypotheses concerning the combined effects of gender and ethnic discrimination. First, some feminist theorists have suggested that gender and subordinate ethnic group membership are two highly salient social identities among ethnic minority women, who consequently suffer from a double dose of discrimination—one based on gender and the other on ethnicity. This thesis is known as the "double jeopardy" hypothesis (Beale, 1970; Bond & Perry, 1970; Epstein, 1973; Jackson, 1973; King, 1975; Lorber, 1998; Reid, 1984).

The notion of "double jeopardy" was originally developed to describe the experiences of African American women. Black women were thought to suffer not only from racism at the hands of Whites, but also from sexism at the hands of both White and Black men (Beale, 1970; Bond & Perry, 1970; Reid, 1984). Over time, the concept of double jeopardy was expanded to describe the situations of Asian American women and Chicanas (Chow, 1987; Garcia, 1989; Gonzalez, 1988; Greene, 1994).

Protagonists of the double jeopardy hypothesis can be divided roughly into two camps. Some argue that the negative effects of one's ethnic and gender status are purely additive. This implies that whatever handicaps one suffers as a result of being an ethnic subordinate are simply added to the handicaps suffered by virtue of being a woman. However, others have argued that the negative effects of these multiple stigmas are interactive rather than additive—i.e., a greater than additive effect due to some multiplicative function (e.g., Almquist, 1975; Greene, 1994; Lykes, 1983; Ransford, 1980; Reid & Comas-Diaz, 1990; Smith & Stewart, 1983).[5]

While some form of the double jeopardy hypothesis (either additive or interactive) is intuitively compelling—almost self-evidently true and consistent with many narrative accounts of the daily lives of many American women of color—there has been remarkably little empirical research actually confirming this effect. In contrast, we will suggest, in a later section, an alternative hypothesis regarding the combination of gender and ethnic inequality that better describes the nature of disadvantage across a wide range of domains.

EVOLUTIONARY PSYCHOLOGY PERSPECTIVES

A second perspective for understanding the dynamics of gender and arbitrary-set hierarchies has been offered by evolutionary theorists. This perspective suggests that the common roots of patriarchy and arbitrary-set hierarchy lie much deeper than suggested by most feminist and sociological theorists. The evolutionary psychology approach suggests that, whenever one finds behavioral similarities within a given set of organisms across a wide range of situational and historical contexts, one should ask what function these behaviors may be serving for the organisms' continued existence. One set of transhistorical and transsituational behaviors that needs to be explained is the consistent tendency for men to establish systems of patriarchal control over women. Second, although the empirical evidence is more limited on this question, a consistent body of research suggests that males are also more hostile toward arbitrary-set outgroups than are females, even when these arbitrary-set outgroups are defined in the most arbitrary manner (Ekehammar, 1985; Ekehammar & Sidanius, 1982; Furnham, 1985; Marjoribanks, 1981; Sidanius, Cling, & Pratto, 1991; Sidanius & Ekehammar, 1983; Sidanius, Levin, Liu, & Pratto, in press; Sidanius, Pratto, & Bobo, 1994; Sidanius, Pratto, & Brief, 1995).

The tendency for males to display higher levels of arbitrary-set outgroup aggression is most unambiguously and cleanly observed in the most extreme form of arbitrary-set outgroup aggression, namely warfare. Both anthropologists and war historians have noted that war-making appears to be an exclusively male enterprise

(Keegan, 1993; Rodseth, Wrangham, Harrigen, & Smuts, 1991; Wrangham, 1982). While this does not imply that women are incapable of being warriors or have never functioned as warriors, the historical and anthropological evidence does show that women do not form military coalitions among themselves for the purpose of making war either on their own sex or on men (Keegan, 1993).

How should we go about trying to understand these consistent male–female differences? Evolutionary psychology suggests that we should expect behavioral and psychological differences between males and females whenever reproductive success for each sex is optimized by different behavioral strategies (Buss, 1996; Malamuth, 1996). One possible avenue for understanding the way in which these male–female differences may be related to differential reproductive strategies for men and women is suggested by "parental investment theory" (Trivers, 1972). Trivers argued that, because the act of reproduction is considerably more costly for females than for males of many species, males are able to produce considerably more offspring than females. This relatively low level of female fecundity is expected to induce females to be much more selective in their choice of a mate and also to invest a great deal more energy in raising the young. Consequently, females are expected to prefer males with social and economic resources, and to prefer males who appear willing to invest these resources in them and their offspring. Thus, everything else being equal, those males who are able to accumulate and control the types of resources that females find most desirable will also be the most reproductively successful males.

Reproductive advantage will not only belong to those males who are able to accumulate resources as a result of their own individual efforts (e.g., skill at hunting), but also to those males who are able to form *successful aggressive coalitions* with other males for the purposes of expropriation of the labor and resources of other males (Betzig, 1993). In addition, across evolutionary time, these males will have a reproductive advantage over other males not only as a result of their ability to form expropriative aggressive coalitions, but also as a result of their willingness and ability to limit the econo-political prerogatives and reproductive freedom of women. These two male predispositions are thought to contribute to the tendencies for human societies to develop both arbitrary-set hierarchies and patriarchy.

However, even though both arbitrary-set hierarchies and patriarchy are hypothesized to be the long-range results of relatively high sexual selectivity among females, and of the resultant male desire for resource control and the accumulation of wealth, this thesis also suggests certain differences in the fundamental natures of patriarchy and arbitrary-set hierarchies. Specifically, we can regard patriarchy as one outgrowth of a limited form of *intersexual competition*—a male attempt to make women more dependent upon them by limiting the women's economic, political, and sexual choices. However, for the most part, patriarchy should not be directed at actually harming, debilitating, or destroying women. Since the ultimate fates of men and women are so intimately interwoven, any system that seriously debilitated women would also damage the reproductive success of men.

In contrast to patriarchy, arbitrary-set hierarchies should be regarded as primarily a form of *intrasexual competition*. They are the result of aggressive male coalitions for the establishment and maintenance of exploitative and expropriative relations against other male coalitions. Because the precise make-up of these aggressive male coalitions is likely to be extremely flexible and contingent upon the exact situational and contextual conditions, these male coalitions are likely to be abstracted into the simple cognitive heuristic of "ingroups versus outgroups," or "us versus them." Furthermore, if arbitrary-set hierarchies are primarily male-versus-male projects, then various forms of arbitrary-set discrimination (e.g., racism, ethnocentrism) should be primarily directed against outgroup males rather than outgroup females.

Rather than being a "just-so" thesis, the evolutionary logic sketched above lends itself to a number of empirically testable hypotheses. One such hypothesis is known as the *invariance hypothesis*. The invariance hypothesis asserts that males will have higher average levels of social dominance orientation (SDO) than females, everything else being equal. SDO is defined as the degree to which one endorses group-based social inequality and group-based dominance. The most well-documented finding generated by social dominance theory is research supporting the invariance hypothesis—i.e., showing that men display significantly higher average levels of SDO than women. Moreover, this higher average SDO level among males does not seem to be moderated by situational or structural factors, such as education, age, social class, political ideology, gender-role norms, ethnicity, religiosity, or degree of patriarchy in the culture. Furthermore, this gender difference also appears to be invariant across a number of Western, quasi-Western, and non-Western cultures, such as the United States, Sweden, Australia, New Zealand, Israel, "Palestine," (i.e., the West Bank and the Gaza Strip), and the People's Republic of China (Pratto, Sidanius, Stallworth, & Malle, 1994; Sidanius & Pratto, 1999; Sidanius, Pratto & Brief, 1995; Sidanius, Pratto, & Bobo, 1994; Sidanius, Levin, Liu, & Pratto, in press).[6] However, rather than concentrate on the invariance hypothesis, in this chapter we will instead focus on another hypothesis derivable from the evolutionary reasoning sketched above.

THE SUBORDINATE MALE TARGET HYPOTHESIS (SMTH)

The reasoning outlined above suggests an intersection of gender and arbitrary-set discrimination (e.g., race discrimination) that is quite different than any version of the double jeopardy hypothesis. In essence, we suggest that women from both arbitrary-set ingroups and outgroups will be subject to gender discrimination and the dynamics of patriarchy. However, outgroup males rather than outgroup females will be the *primary targets* of arbitrary-set discrimination. Although arbitrary-set outgroup females will certainly suffer from the effects of arbitrary-set discrimination—largely as a result of their close associations with arbitrary-set outgroup males as husbands, sons, fathers, brothers, and lovers—we expect that arbitrary-set out-group females will not be the primary targets of arbitrary-set discrimination. The reasoning behind this expectation is that arbitrary-set discrimination is primarily a form of intrasexual competition perpetrated by males and directed against males. As such, arbitrary-set discrimination can also be viewed as a form of low-level warfare directed against outgroup males. Social dominance theorists label this the *subordinate male target hypothesis* (SMTH—see Sidanius & Pratto, 1999).

Evidence supporting the SMTH can be found across several different domains, including the criminal justice system, the labor market, and the educational and retail sales sectors of society.

The Criminal Justice System

Consistent with the expectations of social dominance theory, there is good empirical evidence showing that members of subordinate arbitrary-sets (e.g., "races," ethnic minorities, the poor) are discriminated against within the criminal justice system. Compared to members of the dominant group, subordinate-group members are more likely to be stopped, questioned, and searched by the police than are members of dominant arbitrary-sets, everything else being equal. Once arrested, subordinates are more likely to be beaten by the police while in custody and more likely to be held in custody awaiting trial rather than released on bail. Once tried, they are more likely to be found guilty, less likely to be sentenced to alternatives to prison (e.g., community service), more likely to be sentenced to longer prison terms, less likely to be granted parole, and when convicted of capital offenses, they are more likely to be executed—especially for capital offenses against dominants (for a thorough review of this evidence, see Sidanius & Pratto, 1999). Furthermore, these discriminatory effects are not restricted to any particular nation or political system (e.g., the United States or apartheid in South Africa); rather, they have been found in every nation examined.

While relatively little research has attempted to tease apart the effects of ethnicity and gender within the criminal justice system, the research that does exist is generally more consistent with the SMTH than with the double jeopardy hypothesis. For example, in one of the few studies of its kind, Hood and Cordovil (1992) examined the effects of race and gender discrimination within the English criminal justice system, in a report prepared for the Commission for Racial Equality. After examining 2,884 criminal cases adjudicated by the Crown Court Centres in 1989, the researchers found that male and female ethnic subordinates (e.g., Blacks and Asians) tended to be imprisoned at significantly higher rates than Whites—e.g., Black males were imprisoned at over eight times their proportion in the British population. However, the degree to which subordinate women were imprisoned at higher rates than dominant women could be completely accounted for by the legally relevant variables associated with each case (e.g., seriousness of the crime, previous criminal record, intention to contest the case at trial, etc.).

This was not the case for males. Regardless of which legally relevant control variables were used, subordinate males were still imprisoned at significantly higher rates than dominant males. In other words, there was no evidence of racial discrimination in the criminal justice system against subordinate females, but there was evidence of racial discrimination against subordinate males. Moreover, this evidence was found at all stages of the criminal justice process. Everything else being equal, Black males were more likely to be questioned and searched by the police; once stopped, they were more likely to be arrested; once arrested, they were more likely to held for trial rather than being released on bail; once tried, they were more likely to be found guilty; and once found guilty, they were more likely to serve relatively long prison sentences and to serve these sentences under relatively severe conditions. These British conclusions are similar to findings in the United States, Canada, and Israel (e.g., Cole & Gittens, 1995; Sherer, 1990; Unnerver & Hembroff, 1988).

The Labor Market

While proponents of the double jeopardy hypothesis claim that "women of color" will be particularly disadvantaged in the labor market, careful examination of archival evidence controlling for human capital differences (e.g., differences in education and work experience) throws serious doubt upon this claim. For example, a 1974 English discrimination study found that White women earned a weekly wage about 3% higher than subordinate women (e.g., West Indian, Indian, and Pakistani women), whereas White men earned a weekly wage 10% higher than subordinate men (Smith, 1976, p. 87). Likewise, using 1994 U.S. census data, Sidanius and Pratto (1999) found that Euro-American women earned a 7% higher annual wage than Afro-American women, whereas Euro-American men earned a 44% higher wage than Afro-American men.

Furthermore, after controls for critical human capital differences (e.g., education level) were introduced, the wage difference between dominant and subordinate women essentially disappeared, while the wage difference between dominant and subordinate men remained quite substantial. For example, Figure 3.1 shows the 1994 median income for U.S. Whites, Latinos, and Blacks (men and women separately) at each of five different levels of educational achievement. Not surprisingly, at each level of educational achievement, men earned substantially greater average incomes than women. More to the point, after controlling for educational achievement, there was no significant difference in the incomes of dominant versus subordinate women (i.e., Whites vs. Blacks and Latinos). In contrast, after these controls, among high school graduates and beyond, Euro-American males had substantially higher salaries than either Latino or Black males.

Similar results are found even for individuals educated at the most prestigious colleges and universities. For example, Bowen and Bok (1998) compared the mean 1995 earnings of Black and White men and women who entered America's most

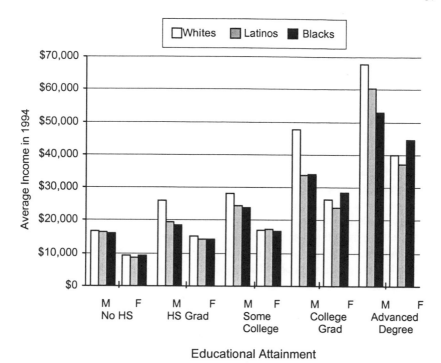

FIG. 3.1. Median earnings in 1994 for Americans 18 years and older as a function of educational attainment, gender, and race. (Source: U.S. Bureau of the Census, 1998.)

selective public and private universities in 1976 (the so-called College and Beyond dataset). Not surprisingly, men had substantially higher annual incomes than women (approximately $98,000 vs. $64,000). More to the point, the White–Black initial and unadjusted earnings gap among women was only about $3,200. However, even at these very prestigious colleges and universities, there were still a number of demographic, personal, and institutional differences between these groups of White and Black women, such as SAT scores, grade point averages, fields of study, socio-economic status, advanced degrees attained, sector of employment, and selectivity of the college or university attended. After controls for these other factors were introduced, the earnings difference between White and Black women disappeared, and Black women earned essentially the same annual incomes as White women ($63,700 vs. $64,000 respectively).

In contrast, a very different picture emerged for men. Overall, White male graduates of these selective colleges earned substantially higher salaries than Black male graduates ($98,200 vs. $76,100). Although these differences were reduced somewhat after controlling for demographic, employment sector, human capital, and institutional differences, they still remained large. Everything else being equal, White males still earned substantially higher salaries than Black males

($98,000 vs. $89,500). In a further effort to account for this residual advantage enjoyed by White males, Bowen and Bok (1998) also entered a number of variables
that might be able to explain these racial differences among men. These included:
detailed differences in their job descriptions and responsibilities, Black–White differences in precollege goals, ambitions, and motivations (e.g., "to be financially
well-off"), and a set of personal and personality differences such as self-confidence
ratings, leadership skills, stubbiness, and physical attractiveness. Consistent with
the SMTH, regardless of what other factors were considered, the economic advantage enjoyed by White males relative to Black males simply refused to go away.

Results congruent with the SMTH were also found using U.S. Census data from
1960 and 1980, when Farley and Allen (1987) examined the amount of increase in
average hourly salary for every additional year invested in higher education (i.e.,
college). While women still received a smaller rate of return than men for every unit
of education, everything else being equal, there was no evidence that White females received a higher rate of return from educational investment than Black females. To the contrary, in both 1960 and 1980, Black females enjoyed a slightly
higher rate of return than White females (i.e., $.62 vs. $.59 in 1960, and $.79 vs.
$.64 in 1980—see Figure 3.2). In contrast, compared to Black males, White males
received a substantially higher rate of return for every additional year spent in
higher education (i.e., $.78 vs. $.56 in 1960, $.96 vs. $.69 in 1980). In addition, this
SMTH pattern in salary differences tended to remain even after controls were introduced for the job description as well as human capital differences (see Sidanius &
Pratto, 1999).

Discrimination against subordinate-group members in the labor market is not
only shown in lower salaries and lower rates of return on human capital investment,
but also in a more restricted sphere of authority in the workplace. That is, subordinate-group members are substantially less likely to hold positions of authority and
power within the workplace. When subordinate-group workers are given more
authority, they are usually only promoted to positions of authority over other subordinate-group members and very rarely to positions of authority over dominant-group
members (de Beijl, 1990).

Consistent with the SMTH, this lack of power is particularly evident with respect
to subordinate males—for example, with Afro-American males, who are less likely
to occupy positions of authority compared to Euro-American males. When Afro-
American males do achieve authority positions, they tend to have a smaller "span
of control" (i.e., number of workers under them), and a smaller "span of responsibility" (e.g., power over promotions and salary) than do White men with comparable
human capital investments (Fernandez, 1975; Kluegel, 1978; Mueller, Parcel, &
Kazuko, 1989). Also consistent with the SMTH, this authority gap appears to be
greater between Euro-American and Afro-American men than between Euro-
American and Afro-American women. Furthermore, while the net authority gap be
tween White and Black American women has tended to become smaller over time,
the net authority gap between White and Black American men has not shown the
same rate of decrease over time (Smith, 1997).

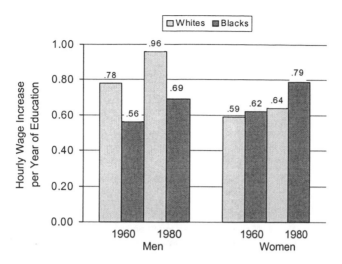

FIG 3.2. Increase in hourly salary for each additional year of college education for White and Black men and women, in 1960 and 1980. (Source: U.S. Bureau of the Census, 1960, 1980.)

In addition to survey and archival evidence supporting SMTH, there is experimental evidence as well. In experimental studies termed *employment audits* (sometimes also known as the situation test), equally qualified male and female, dominant- and subordinate-group members all apply for the same jobs. There are three basic kinds of employment audits: (a) *correspondence audits*, in which two job applicants (e.g., one White and one Black) apply for the same job by mail, (b) *telephone audits*, and (c) *in-person audits,* in which competing applicants actually apply in person. As summarized by Sidanius and Pratto (1999), more than 19 major employment audits have been conducted in at least five different nations and using a variety of dominant and subordinate groups.

As can be seen in Table 3.1, regardless of (a) the nation in which the studies were conducted (i.e., the U.S.A., Germany, Britain, Canada, or Holland), (b) the specific dominant and subordinate groups compared (e.g., Native Dutch vs. Moroccans), and (c) the specific type of audit study conducted (e.g., telephone vs. in-person audit), the studies always showed a significant level of employment discrimination in favor of dominants. Furthermore, this discrimination was found to occur at all stages of the employment seeking process. Thus, dominants: (a) were more likely to be granted a job interview, (b) once interviewed, were more likely to be hired, (c) once hired, were more likely to be given a higher starting salary, and (d) were more likely to be steered into jobs with a greater chance for career advancement (Sidanius & Pratto, 1999).

Importantly, even after controlling for all observed differences between the studies (e.g., the skill level required in the job, the audit methodology used), a meta-analysis revealed that the level of employment discrimination against subordinate

TABLE 3.1
Results of Employment Audits from Five Different Nations

Country	Group Contrasts	Net Discrimination (%)
Correspondence audits		
Britain	Native Whites vs. West-Indians & East-Asians	30
Britain	Native Whites vs. Italian immigrants	10
Netherlands	Dutch vs. Surinamese men	19
Netherlands	Dutch vs. Surinamese women	13
Germany	Germans vs. Turks	10
Telephone audits		
U.S.A.	White vs. Latino men & women	25
Britain	Native Whites vs. West-Indians & Asians	20
Britain	Native Whites vs. West-Indians & Asians	46
Britain	Native Whites vs. Greek immigrants	9
Britain	Native Whites vs. Greek immigrants	10
In-person audits		
U.S.A.	White vs. Black men & women	14
U.S.A.	White vs. Latino men	40
U.S.A.	White vs. Black men	22
Canada	Whites vs. Blacks	9
Netherlands	Dutch vs. Moroccan men	37
Netherlands	Dutch vs. Moroccan women	35
Netherlands	Dutch vs. Surinamese men	40
Netherlands	Dutch vs. Surinamese women	36
Germany	Germans vs. Turks	19

Source: Reprinted, by permission, from Sidanius and Pratto, *Social Dominance*, pp. 165-166. Copyright 1999, Cambridge University Press.

males was substantially larger than the employment discrimination against subordinate females (29.5% vs. 22.5%).

Educational Achievement

Evidence for the SMTH can be found in the domain of education as well. In general, dominants have significantly greater access to quality education and enjoy greater academic success than subordinates (Fischer et al., 1996; Sidanius & Pratto, 1999). However, contrary to the double jeopardy hypothesis, and quite consistent with the SMTH, subordinate females are not usually at greater risk for academic failure than subordinate males, but quite the contrary.

For example, while Euro-Americans tend to have greater high school completion and college admission rates than Blacks or Latino Americans, the high school completion and college enrollment rates for male and female Whites (i.e., dominants) are essentially the same. Among Blacks and Latinos, on the other hand, there is a slight tendency for females to display higher rates of academic success than males (e.g., Simmons, Black, & Zhou, 1991). If one controls for social class and age, there tend to be relatively few differences in academic success between Black and White students. However, where there are significant differences between these ethnic groups, it is African American males, not females, who experience greater academic failure. Moreover, the relatively higher rates of academic failure among African American boys are not restricted to the United States, but have also been found, for instance, on the Caribbean island of St. Croix (see Gibson, 1991).

The relative educational advantage enjoyed by subordinate females in relation to subordinate males can also be seen in attainment of advanced university degrees. The female proportion of Euro-Americans and Afro-Americans attaining the Ph.D. degree showed a steady increase between 1979 and 1989—e.g., for Whites it rose from 30% in 1979 to a little more than 40% in 1989. However, Black females always had higher rates of Ph.D.s relative to Black males than White females had relative to White males. In fact, by 1986, about 60% of the Ph.D.s awarded to Blacks were earned by Black women, while the figure for White women never rose much beyond 40%. Therefore, although Blacks continue to enjoy less academic success than Whites, those Blacks who do achieve high academic success are disproportionately female rather than male (Sidanius & Pratto, 1999).

Retail Sales

A fairly consistent body of research indicates that subordinates are also disadvantaged in retail markets. This disadvantage is not simply due to the fact that subordinate-group members have less disposable income than dominants. In addition, ethnic minorities and the poor are often required to pay higher prices for the same goods and services, and are also often required to pay higher interest rates on consumer loans (e.g., Caplovitz, 1963; Governor's Commission, 1965; Sturdivant, 1971; Sturdivant & Wilhelm, 1968). Part of the explanation for these disparities is the fact that businesses servicing poor and minority clients often have higher overhead (e.g., higher insurance rates), but a substantial part of this difference is directly explicable in terms of discrimination.

The clearest and most unambiguous evidence of this discrimination was found by Ayres (1995; Ayres & Siegelman, 1995) in a series of audit studies of the automobile market. In one set of such studies, teams of male and female, White and Black, auditors were sent to the same Chicago car dealerships to negotiate the best deals they could for new cars. Since audit methodology was used and the auditors were equivalent in all respects except for the characteristics of sex and race, any differences in the amount of money that various groups of auditors were required to pay for these cars could only be attributed either to race and/or gender discrimination. The data showed that, everything else being equal (such as credit history and annual income), Whites were required to pay less money than Blacks for exactly the same cars.

In addition, importantly, and consistent with the SMTH, there was clear evidence of an interaction between race and gender (see Figure 3.3). For example, looking at final offers and auditors who were identical in all ways except for race and sex, White women were required to pay approximately $216 more than White men for

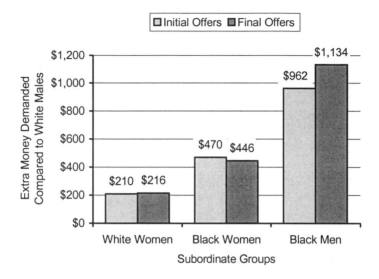

FIG. 3.3. Car sales negotiations: Net amount of additional money demanded of subordinate-group members in comparison to White males. (Data from Ayres, 1995, p. 12.)

the same automobile, while Black women had to pay $446 more than White men. However, Black men were required to pay $1134 more than White men for exactly the same cars. While the differences between White men and women were not found to be statistically significant, the differences between White men and both Black men and Black women were statistically significant.

Furthermore, using a series of game-theoretic models, Ayres concluded that the car salespersons were discriminating against different groups of customers for different reasons. It appeared that the higher prices demanded of White and Black women were primarily motivated by profit-maximization incentives and the salespersons' perceptions that women would be less adept at price haggling. However, because the salespersons continued to push the Black male customers way beyond the point where these customers could be expected to pay, Ayres (1995) concluded that the salespersons' motives were more punitive than strictly economic. In other words, the interaction between the salespersons and Black males went beyond a mere economic exchange and also became an act of aggression.

SUMMARY AND CONCLUSIONS

We suggest that one of the major reasons why humans have made so little progress in eliminating ethnic and gender discrimination is that we do not yet sufficiently understand the dynamics of these phenomena. One example of this lack of understanding is the popularity of the double jeopardy hypothesis, which holds that Black women, for instance, will be more discriminated against than Black males. In contrast, social dominance theorists suggest that, while gender and arbitrary-set (e.g., racial and ethnic) discrimination share many features in common, these two phenomena are qualitatively different types of social discrimination and are driven by qualitatively different motives. We argue that, although patriarchy is ubiquitous and comprehensive, it also has a distinctly paternalistic flavor and is primarily directed at limiting the economic and political prerogatives of women, rather than actually harming or debilitating them. In other words, contrary to popular opinion, *sexism is not primarily an act of aggression, but rather an act of control.*

Arbitrary-set discrimination, in contrast, is largely a male-on-male project. Males are not only the primary and most enthusiastic participants in arbitrary-set intergroup aggression (for instance, "ethnic cleansing"), but males are also the primary targets of arbitrary-set aggression. In support of the SMTH, we have shown much support for the claim that subordinate-group males experience substantially and consistently greater levels of arbitrary-set discrimination than do females. Whereas discrimination against both dominant- and subordinate-group women is not primarily driven by the desire to harm, destroy, or debilitate, arbitrary-set (male-on-male) discrimination has a distinctly more ferocious edge.

For example, while "ethnic cleansing" in Bosnia and Kosovo often ended in the expulsion and rape of women and girls, this "cleansing" often ended in the extermination of men and boys. This difference suggests that dominant males often regard subordinate females as reproductive resources (e.g., rape victims), but they generally regard subordinate males as potentially dangerous rivals and threats. We suggest that not only very extreme forms of intergroup aggression, such as "ethnic cleansing," but even more "normal" forms of intergroup discrimination, which are observable within societies at peace (e.g., employment and housing discrimination), can be regarded as mild and low-level forms of intergroup conflict or warfare primarily directed against outgroup males.

Although we are arguing that subordinate-group males are the primary targets of arbitrary-set discrimination, this does *not* imply that subordinate-group women are unharmed by this form of discrimination. Rather, we argue that subordinate-group women are not the primary and deliberate *targets* of arbitrary-set discrimination. Most of the damage that subordinate women suffer as a result of arbitrary-set discrimination is indirect and "collateral," primarily being the result of their association with and dependence upon subordinate males in their roles of daughters, wives, sisters, lovers, mothers, and friends.

While social dominance theorists have used evolutionary arguments in arriving at the SMTH, some authorities might also suggest that evolutionary arguments are not necessary to reach the SMTH. An alternative explanation of why subordinate-group males are more strongly the targets of ethnic discrimination than are women, is that they are more likely to be found in contexts composed primarily of men. For example, in many work settings, women are excluded from organizations at multiple levels (Benschop & Doorewaard, 1998; Glass Ceiling Commission, 1996). Data on gender and ethnic spatial segregation in various public settings indirectly support this possibility. Jackman (1994, p. 143) reported that, "Almost one-quarter of men describe their work environments as comprised entirely of men, while only 6% of women say they work exclusively with women. In all, about two-thirds of men say their work environments are entirely or mostly male." Complementing these data, Jackman observed that 29% of Blacks work in environments which are "mostly white" or "all white," and she described the situation of Blacks to be one of repeated contact with Whites, often as tokens.

The most comprehensive report on gender and ethnic segregation in the workplace was completed in 1996 by the Federal Glass Ceiling Commission. To identify barriers to women and ethnic minorities in employment, the Commission employed both qualitative and quantitative data, including focus groups, surveys, and "special data runs" of census data compiled for the Commission. In the Commission's report, only 5% of women who held senior-level positions in business and communications organizations were ethnic minority women (Hispanic, African American, or Asian/Pacific Islander), whereas 10% of men in these positions were ethnic minority men. Furthermore, the gender composition of these work settings was predominantly male (62%-67%). In other organizations, including insurance, retail, transportation, utilities, and wholesale trade, ethnic minority women comprised between 2% and 9% of the workforce, while ethnic minority men comprised between 6% and 10% of the workforce. Within the U.S. workplace, the SMTH phenomenon might be at least partially explained by the simple fact that dominant-group males have greater opportunity to discriminate against subordinate males than against subordinate females because women are largely excluded from some of the settings in which discrimination would be most likely to occur.

Related to this point, it could also be argued that dominant-group males might extract more material gain from other males than from females. Some evidence in support of this argument can be found from data that we have already reviewed. Recall that women earned consistently less than men as shown by data from Farley and Allen (1987) and the U.S. Bureau of the Census (1998). White males have less to gain from discrimination against ethnic minority women, who earn less than ethnic minority men and who are less likely to be in positions that would be desired by dominant-group members.

However, although these alternative explanations might be able to account for occurrence of the SMTH effect within the labor and employment sectors, it is difficult to see how they could easily account for the SMTH effect across all of the domains in which it has been observed. For example, how could perception of greater gain from subordinate males possibly account for the fact that arbitrary-set discrimination in the criminal justice system is found against subordinate males, but not against subordinate females? Similarly, it is difficult to see how this "greater gain" argument could be used to explain the consistent tendency for marauding armies to kill subordinate boys and men, while sparing young girls and women. In any case, it is clear that much more research is needed in order to determine definitively which set of processes is primarily responsible for the SMTH effect. We regard this chapter and the work summarized by Sidanius and Pratto (1999) as merely preliminary efforts at such an explanation.

Despite the lack of complete clarity as to the ultimate sources of the SMTH, it is nonetheless quite clear that gender and arbitrary-set dominance systems are not reducible one to the other, nor purely additive. Further, this suggests that a complete understanding of the psychology of gender cannot be reached until we appreciate the distinct gender differences in the predisposition to generate and maintain arbitrary-set hierarchies by means of economic exploitation and physical violence. Most importantly, understanding of discrimination and outgroup aggression will not be complete without appreciation of the fact that males are both the primary perpetrators of intergroup oppression, and also the primary and deliberate targets of this oppression as well.

Finally, what does this perspective imply about our ability to attenuate and possibly eliminate both gender and arbitrary-set discrimination? Of course, the answer to this question is directly dependent upon a theoretical understanding of the forces and factors driving these various forms of discrimination. In general, social dominance theorists have argued that a primary reason for our seeming inability to eliminate the plagues of gender, ethnic, and class discrimination is the fact that we have not properly understood the etiology and functions of these phenomena. Social dominance theorists suggest that these forms of social oppression, rather than being merely products of "improper socialization," simple ignorance, or the exigencies of capitalism, are primarily the result of inherent features of human and primate social organization.

Thus, while social dominance theorists doubt that we will ever be able completely to eliminate these forms of social oppression, a more thorough and valid understanding of their underlying dynamics should at least put us in a better position to try to attenuate and control some of the most ferocious manifestations of these forces. On the other hand, it seems clear that the elimination of discrimination will not be possible until most dominant-group members are at least willing to admit that discrimination continues to exist in modern society. Unfortunately, current empirical evidence indicates that a large majority of American Whites are still in denial about this ugly reality (Kearney, 1997).

NOTES

1. However, it should be noted that this age system is not completely linear. *Very* old people (i.e., 80 years and above) do not always dominate over somewhat younger people (e.g., 60 year-olds).

2. Available: http://www.geocities.com/paris/5121/forgotten.htm

3. These were primarily Poles and Russians. See
   http://www.optonline.com/comptons/ceo/02246_A.html

4. One of the few exceptions to this generalization occurred in the European witch trials of the 16th and 17th centuries. It is estimated that, between 1560 and 1680, approximately 3,000 European women were tortured and put to death for witchcraft (Monter, 1996).

5. For an intermediate position, see Landrine, Klonoff, Alcaraz, Scott, and Wilkins (1995).

6. For a more in-depth discussion of the empirical implications of this evolutionary reasoning, see Sidanius and Pratto (1999).

REFERENCES

Almquist, E. M. (1975). Untangling the effects of race and sex: The disadvantaged status of Black women. *Social Science Quarterly, 56,* 129-142.

Ayres, I. (1995). Further evidence of discrimination in new car negotiations and estimates of its cause. *Michigan Law Review, 94,* 109-147.

Ayres, I., & Siegelman, P. (1995). Race and gender discrimination in bargaining for a new car. *American Economic Review, 85,* 304-322.

Bachofen, J. J. (1969). *Das Mutterrecht: eine Untersuchung uber die Gynaikokratie der altern Welt nach ihrer religiosen und rechlichen Natur.* Bruxelles: Culture et Civilisation. (Original work published 1861)

Beale, F. (1970). Double jeopardy: To be Black and female. In T. Cade (Ed.), *The Black woman* (pp. 90-100). New York: New American Library.

Benschop, Y., & Doorewaard, H. (1998). Covered by equality: The gender subtext of organizations. *Organization Studies, 19,* 787-805.

Betzig, L. (1993). Sex, succession, and stratification in the first six civilizations: How powerful men reproduced, passed power on to their sons, and used power to defend their wealth, women and children. In L. Ellis (Ed.), *Social stratification and socioeconomic inequality: A comparative biosocial analysis* (pp. 37-74). New York: Praeger.

Bond, J. C., & Perry, P. (1970). Is the Black male castrated? In T. Cade (Ed.), *The Black woman* (pp. 115-118). New York: New American Library.

Bowen, W. G., & Bok, D. (1998). *The shape of the river: Long-term consequences of considering race in college and university admissions.* Princeton, NJ: Princeton University Press.

Buss, D. M. (1996). Sexual conflict: Evolutionary insights into feminism and the "battle of the sexes." In D. M. Buss & N. M. Malamuth (Eds.), *Sex, power and conflict: Evolutionary and feminist perspectives* (pp. 296-318). New York: Oxford University Press.

Caplovitz, D. (1963). *The poor pay more.* New York: Free Press.

Chow, E. N. (1987). The development of feminist consciousness among Asian American women. *Gender and Society, 3,* 284-299.

Cole, D. P., & Gittens, M. (1995). *Report of the commission on systemic racism in the Ontario criminal justice system.* Toronto: Queen's Printer of Ontario.

Collier, J. F., & Yanagisako, S. J. (Eds.). (1987). *Gender and kinship: Essays toward a unified analysis.* Stanford, CA: Stanford University Press.

de Beijl, R. Z. (1990). *Discrimination of migrant workers in Western Europe.* Geneva, Switzerland: International Labour Office.

Dworkin, A. (1974). *Woman hating.* New York: Dutton.

Eagly, A. H. (1987). *Sex differences in social behavior: A social-role explanation.* Hillsdale, NJ: Erlbaum.

Eisler, R., & Loye, D. (1983). The "failure" of liberalism: A reassessment of ideology from a new feminine-masculine perspective. *Political Psychology, 4,* 469-475.

Ekehammar, B. (1985). Sex differences in socio-political attitudes revisited. *Educational Studies, 11,* 3-9.

Ekehammar, B., & Sidanius, J. (1982). Sex differences in socio-political ideology: A replication and extension. *British Journal of Social Psychology, 21,* 249-257;

Epstein, C. F. (1973, August). Black and female: The double whammy. *Psychology Today, 3,* 57-61, 89.

Farley, R., & Allen, W. R. (1987). *The color line and the quality of life in America.* New York: Russell Sage Foundation.

Federal Glass Ceiling Commission. (1996). *Good for business: Making full use of the nation's human capital.* Washington, DC: Author, U.S. Department of Labor.

Fernandez, J. P. (1975). *Black managers in White corporations.* New York: Wiley.

Fischer, C. S., Hout, M., Jankowski, M. S., Lucas, S. R., Swidler, A., & Voss, K. (1996). *Inequality by design: Cracking the bell curve myth.* Princeton, NJ: Princeton University Press.

French, H.W. (1996, September 18). A neglected region loosens ties to Zaire. *New York Times,* pp. A1, A4.

Furnham, A. (1985). Adolescents' sociopolitical attitudes: A study of sex and national differences. *Political Psychology, 6,* 621-636.

Garcia, A. M. (1989) The development of Chicana feminist discourse, 1970-1980. *Gender and Society, 3,* 217-238.

Gibson, M. A. (1991). Ethnicity, gender and social class: The school adaptation patterns of West Indian Youths. In M. Gibson & J. Ogbu (Eds.), *Minority status and schooling: A comparative study of immigrant and involuntary minorities* (pp. 169-203). New York: Garland.

Gimbutas, M. A. (1989). *The language of the goddess: Unearthing the hidden symbols of western civilization.* New York: Harper & Row.

Gonzalez, J. T. (1988). Dilemmas of the high-achieving Chicana: The double-bind factor in male/female relationships. *Sex Roles, 18,* 367-380.

Governor's Commission on the Los Angeles Riots. (1965). *Violence in the city: An end or a beginning?* Los Angeles: Author.

Greene, B. (1994). Lesbian women of color: Triple jeopardy. In L. Comas-Diaz & B. Greene (Eds.), *Women of color: Integrating ethnic and gender identities* (pp. 389-427). New York: Guilford.

Hood, R., & Cordovil, G. (1992). *Race and sentencing: A study in the Crown Court. A report for the Commission for Racial Equality.* Oxford, U.K.: Clarendon.

Jackman, M. R. (1994). *The velvet glove: Paternalism and conflict in gender, class, and race relations.* Los Angeles: University of California Press.

Jackson, J. (1973). Black women in a racist society. In C. Willie, B. Kramer, & B. Brown (Eds.), *Racism and mental health* (pp. 185-268). Pittsburgh: University of Pittsburgh Press.

Jaggar, A. M. (1993). *Feminist frameworks: Alternative theoretical accounts of the relations between women and men.* New York: McGraw-Hill.

Kearney, S. M. (1997, June 10). *Black/White relations in the United States: A Gallup Poll social audit.* Princeton, NJ: Gallup Organization.

Keegan, J. (1993). *The history of warfare.* New York: Knopf.

King, M. (1975). Oppression and power: The unique status of the Black woman in the American political system. *Social Science Quarterly, 56,* 123-133.

Kluegel, J. R. (1978). The causes and cost of racism exclusion from job authority. *American Sociological Review, 43,* 285-301.

Landrine, H., Klonoff, E. A., Alcaraz, R., Scott, J., & Wilkins, P. (1995). Multiple variables in discrimination. In B. Lott & D. Maluso (Eds.), *The social psychology of interpersonal discrimination* (pp. 183-224). New York: Guilford.

Lenski, G. E. (1984). *Power and privilege: A theory of social stratification.* Chapel Hill : University of North Carolina Press.

Lorber, J. (1998). *Gender inequality: Feminist theories and politics.* Los Angeles: Roxbury.

Lykes, M. B. (1983). Discrimination and coping in the lives of Black women: Analyses of oral history data. *Journal of Social Issues, 39*(3), 79-100.

Maccoby, E. E., & Jacklin, C. (1974). *Psychology of sex differences.* Stanford: Stanford University Press.

Malamuth, N. M. (1996). The confluence model of sexual aggression: Feminism and evolutionary perspectives. In D. M. Buss & N. M. Malamuth (Eds.), *Sex, power and conflict: Evolutionary and feminist perspectives* (pp. 269-295). New York: Oxford University Press.

Marjoribanks, K. (1981). Sex-related differences in socio-political attitudes: A replication. *Educational Studies,7,* 1-6.

Mies, M., Bennholdt-Thomsen, C., & von Werlhof, V. (1988). *Women: The last colony.* London: Zed.

Monter, W.W. (1996). Witchcraft. In *Grolier Multimedia Encyclopedia.* Danbury, CT: Grolier.

Mueller, C. W., Parcel, T. L., & Kazuko, T. (1989). Particularism in authority outcomes of Black and White supervisors. *Social Science Research, 18,* 1-20.

Murdock, G. P. (1949). *Social structure.* New York: Macmillan.

Pratto, F. (in press). The puzzle of continuing group inequality: Piecing together psychological, social, and cultural forces in social dominance theory. In M. P. Zanna (Ed.), *Advances in experimental social psychology* (Vol. 31, pp. 191-263). San Diego: Academic Press.

Pratto, F., Sidanius, J., Stallworth, L. M., & Malle, B. F. (1994). Social dominance orientation: A personality variable predicting social and political attitudes. *Journal of Personality and Social Psychology, 67,* 741-763.

Ransford, H. E. (1980). The prediction of social behavior and attitudes. In V. Jeffries & H. E. Ransford (Eds.), *Social stratification: A multiple hierarchy approach* (pp. 265-295). Boston: Allyn & Bacon.

Reese, W. A., & Curtis, R. L. (1991). Paternalism and the female status offender: Remanding the juvenile justice double standard for desexualization. *Social Science Journal, 28 ,* 63-83.

Reid, P. T. (1984). Feminism versus minority group identity: Not for Black women only. *Sex Roles, 10,* 247-255.

Reid, P. T. (1988). Racism and sexism: Comparisons and conflicts. In P. A. Katz & D. A. Taylor (Eds.), *Eliminating racism: Profiles in controversy* (pp. 203-221). New York: Plenum.

Reid, P. T., & Comas-Diaz, L. (1990). Gender and ethnicity: Perspectives on dual status. *Sex Roles, 22,* 397-408.

Rodseth, L., Wrangham, R. W., Harrigen, A. M., & Smuts, B. B. (1991). The human community as a primate society. *Current Anthropology, 32,* 221-254.

Sherer, M. (1990). Criminal activity among Jewish and Arab youth in Israel. *International Journal of Intercultural Relations, 14,* 529-548.

Sidanius, J. (1993). The psychology of group conflict and the dynamics of oppression: A social dominance perspective. In W. J. McGuire & S. Iyengar (Eds.), *Current approaches to political psychology* (pp. 183-219). Durham, NC: Duke University Press.

Sidanius, J., Cling, B. J., & Pratto, F. (1991). Ranking and linking as a function of sex and gender role attitudes. *Journal of Social Issues, 47*(3), 131-149.

Sidanius, J., & Ekehammar, B. (1983). Sex, political party preference and higher-order dimensions of socio-political ideology. *Journal of Psychology, 115,* 233-239.

Sidanius, J., Levin, S., Liu, J. H., & Pratto, F. (in press). Social dominance orientation and the political psychology of gender: An extension and cross-cultural replication. *European Journal of Social Psychology.*

Sidanius, J., Pratto, F., & Bobo, L. (1994). Social dominance orientation and the political psychology of gender: A case of invariance? *Journal of Personality and Social Psychology, 67,* 998-1011.

Sidanius, J., & Pratto, F. (1993). The inevitability of oppression and the dynamics of dominance. In P. M. Sniderman, P. E. Tetlock, & E. G. Carmines (Eds.), *Prejudice, politics, and the American dilemma* (pp. 173-211). Stanford, CA: Stanford University Press.

Sidanius, J., & Pratto, F. (1999). *Social dominance: An intergroup theory of hierarchy and oppression.* New York: Cambridge University Press.

Sidanius, J., Pratto, F., & Brief, D. (1995). Group dominance and the political psychology of gender: A cross-cultural comparison. *Political Psychology,16,* 381-396.

Simmons, R. G., Black, A., & Zhou, Y. (1991). African-American versus White children and the transition into junior high school. *American Journal of Education, 99,* 481-520.

Smith, R. A. (1997). *Race and job authority: An analysis of men and women, 1972-1994.* New Brunswick, NJ: Rutgers University, School of Management and Labor Relations.

Smith, A., & Stewart, A. J. (1983). Approaches to studying racism and sexism in Black women's lives. *Journal of Social Issues, 39*(3), 1-15.

Sturdivant, F. D. (1971). Discrimination in the marketplace: Another dimension. *Social Science Quarterly, 52,* 625-630.

Sturdivant, F. D., & Wilhelm, W. T. (1968). Poverty, minorities, and consumer exploitation. *Social Science Quarterly, 49,* 643-650.

Takaki, R. T. (1993). *A different mirror: A history of multicultural America.* Boston: Little, Brown.

Takaki, R. T. (Ed.). (1994). *From different shores: Perspectives on race and ethnicity in America.* New York: Oxford University Press.

Trivers, R. (1972). Parental investment and sexual selection. In B. Campbell (Ed.), *Sexual selection and the descent of man* (pp. 136-179). New York: Aldine de Gruyter.

U.S. Bureau of the Census. (1960). *Census of population and housing, 1960* (Public use microdata samples). Washington, DC: Author.

U.S. Bureau of the Census. (1980). *Census of population and housing, 1980* (Public use microdata samples). Washington, DC: Author.

U.S. Bureau of the Census. (1998, October 10). Table 19. Mean earnings of workers 18 years old and over, by educational attainment, race, Hispanic origin, and sex: 1975 to 1994. Available: http://www.census.gov/population/socdemo/education/table18.txt

Unnerver, J. D., & Hembroff, L. A. (1988). The prediction of racial/ethnic sentencing disparities: An expectation states approach. *Journal of Research in Crime and Delinquency, 25,* 53-82.

van den Berghe, P. L. (1967). *Race and racism.* New York: Wiley.

Yee, A. H., Fairchild, H. H., Weizmann, F., & Wyatt, G. E. (1993). Addressing psychology's problem with race. *American Psychologist, 48,* 1132-1140.

4 Social Contextual Strategies for Reducing Racial Discrimination

Marylee C. Taylor
The Pennsylvania State University

Just as the social context can encourage interracial hostility and inequality, so contextual patterns and events can contribute to reducing racial prejudice and discrimination. This chapter considers two forms of racial inequality amenable to policy remedies—residential segregation and employment discrimination. It then outlines four factors that can foster public support for effective remedies: institutional leadership, media framing, political discourse, and economic security among Whites.

RACIAL INEQUALITY IN NEED OF REMEDY

Residential Segregation

Intergroup contact is no panacea for individuals' negative attitudes and discriminatory behaviors. Pettigrew and Tropp's chapter in this volume describes conditions under which contact yields positive outcomes. As a complement to that analysis, this chapter identifies institutional mechanisms that have the potential to decrease residential segregation. With decreases in residential segregation may come increases in forms of interpersonal contact that enhance positive attitudes. But whether or not residential desegregation improves neighbors' racial feelings and attitudes, it predictably brings other forms of improvement—it weakens many structurally-linked forms of discrimination. Discrimination, in the sociological sense, is:

> a complex system of social relations that produces intergroup inequities in social outcomes...(D)isadvantage accruing from intentional discrimination typically cumu-

lates, extends far beyond the original injury, and long outlives the deliberate perpe-
tration....Direct discrimination occurs at points where inequality is generated, often
intentionally....Indirect discrimination is the perpetuation or magnification of the
original injury. It occurs when the inequitable results of direct discrimination are
used as a basis for later decisions...in linked institutions. (Pettigrew & Taylor, in
press)

Residential segregation has been called the linchpin of racial inequality
(Massey & Denton, 1993; Pettigrew, 1979). Segregated Black neighborhoods,
themselves the products of discrimination, are likely to produce other forms of
discrimination: underfunded, segregated schools (Kozol, 1991); inferior public
services, businesses, and recreational facilities; limited access to a full range of
churches and voluntary associations. In addition, because of the economic hardships disproportionately faced by Blacks, residential segregation brings concen-
trations of poverty in predominantly Black neighborhoods (Massey & Denton,
1993).

With concentrated poverty and joblessness come a panoply of social ills, including teen childbearing, delinquency and crime, demoralization—all of which
perpetuate the hardships faced by Black residents (Wilson, 1987, 1996). Joblessness among Black residents of segregated inner-city neighborhoods is ag-
gravated by "spatial mismatch," the fact that jobs are increasingly located in sub-
urban areas difficult for inner-city residents to reach (Kasarda, 1990). Furthermore, the aggregate circumstances of inner-city residents fuel stereotypes on the
part of employers, making it especially difficult for Black men residing in segregated inner-city neighborhoods to be hired (Neckerman & Kirchenman, 1991).

In sum, the ripple effects of residential segregation by race are extensive and
potent. By the same token, measures that successfully reduce residential segregation can create ripple effects of their own, bringing decreases in many forms of
discrimination.

Identifying successful strategies for reducing racial residential segregation requires some understanding of the forces responsible for producing this segregation. Contrary to conservative analysts' claims that residential segregation re-
flects economics and symmetrical ethnocentric preferences of Blacks and Whites
(e.g., Clark, 1986), federal policy was crucial in producing the "chocolate cities"
and "vanilla suburbs" (Farley, Schuman, Bianchi, Colasanto, & Hatchett, 1978)
that characterize the modern American landscape.

The creation and maintenance of residential segregation in the 20th century
has been a collective enterprise of White America. From the early decades of this
century to 1948, when the U.S. Supreme Court declared them illegal, restrictive
covenants were widely employed. Local real estate boards were often pivotal in
instituting these covenants. Importantly, from 1924 to 1950 the code of ethics of
the National Association of Real Estate Brokers forbade realtors from introducing
into neighborhoods members of any race or nationality whose presence would
bring a decline in property values.

But private organizations were not alone in creating racially divided residential areas. In the 1930s, the federal Home Owners' Loan Corporation institutionalized "redlining," designating predominantly Black areas as too risky for home mortgages. The tradition of channeling federal backing for home ownership into "stable" neighborhoods not threatened by racial mixing was continued in the post-World War II Veteran's Administration and Federal Housing Administration loan programs that propelled the development of the American suburbs. (For a concise account of this aspect of U.S. history, see Massey & Denton, 1993.)

The federal guidelines effectively mandating segregated and unequal residential areas for Black and Whites were abandoned in 1950. Obviously, U.S. history before that time cannot be rewritten. But the federal government's complicity in creating modern patterns of residential segregation and discrimination justifies current calls for the government to intervene in ways that can help undo the damage.

In recent decades, the most overt and egregious forms of discrimination in housing have been declared illegal, but subtle discrimination persists. Realtors, rental agents, home mortgage officers, and the organizations they represent, are important players. Advertising for homes or rental units may deliberately or unwittingly be placed in media that target the racial groups already predominating in the advertised areas. "Steering" by realtors involves selecting and showing prospective rental or purchase properties to clients whose own race matches the racial composition of the neighborhood. Also, rental agents and loan officers may simply give inferior treatment to racial minorities. Over the last several decades, audit studies, using matched White and minority testers, have been used to assess the extent of housing discrimination. Based on 1988 national audit data collected by the U.S. Department of Housing and Urban Development (HUD), Yinger (1991) estimated that about 53% of prospective Black renters and home buyers face racial discrimination as they seek housing availability information and mortgages.

Another contributor to racial residential segregation has been urban renewal and the public housing built to accommodate displaced urban residents. Resistance from prospective White neighbors has affected siting decisions and kept predominantly Black public housing populations in ghetto areas.

The 1968 federal Fair Housing Act was a step in the right direction, but implementation of this legislation became much more effective with the 1988 Fair Housing Amendments Act. The 1988 legislation facilitated the filing and pursuit of discrimination complaints and increased the penalties for violators. Analysts agree, however, that much remains to be done. Massey and Denton (1993) recommended that: HUD increase its support of local fair housing organizations; HUD establish a permanent program of realtor testing; federal oversight of home loan data be institutionalized; federal housing subsidies increasingly be in the form of vouchers for the private housing market; further amendment of the Fair

Housing Act provide for less expensive and more timely adjudication of complaints; hate crimes directed to minority entrants in previously-White neighborhoods be severely penalized; Black realtors be given increased access to multiple listing services; and HUD establish programs to train realtors in fair housing practices. Yinger's (1995) thoughtful recommendations added to this list of needed remedies.

For recipients of federal housing subsidies, Chicago's experience showed provision of vouchers for housing in the private market to be a promising strategy. After years of court battles, tenants of the Chicago Housing Authority (CHA) in 1976 won U.S. Supreme Court acknowledgment that the CHA had discriminated in siting public housing projects in minority neighborhoods and in assigning tenants so as to maintain segregated projects. Ordered to address segregation in Chicago Public Housing, HUD and CHA agreed to the "Gautreaux Program," named after the court case. The federally-sponsored Moving To Opportunity (MTO) program, implemented in five cities in 1994, geographically expanded the Gautreaux approach. In fact, MTO went beyond Gautreaux in format, requiring voucher recipients to locate in low-poverty areas, as well as assisting them with housing counseling. Desegregation by class and race are explicit MTO goals. Unfortunately, Congressional opposition has limited expansion of this promising program (Yinger, 1995).

Some analysts have warned against undue reliance on federal efforts, emphasizing the demonstrated effectiveness of *local* fair housing initiatives and insisting on the continued mobilization of local energy to further fair housing goals (e.g., Saltman, Tisdale, Farmer, & Noel, 1994). Primary among the aims of local efforts have been elevated public awareness, stringent local ordinances, and effective enforcement.

Employment Discrimination

Racial minorities continue to be excluded from desirable jobs. Among the many sources of recent information on inequality in employment, Reskin's (1998) book is particularly accessible. Reskin reports, for example, that in 1996 about 30% of White workers held professional and managerial jobs, while the comparable percentage was about 20% for Black workers and 14% for Latinos. At the other end of the job spectrum, in 1990 about 6% of White men held service jobs, compared to about 14% of African American men and 25% of African American women.

The data indicate that much of this inequality represents inequity—that is, the racial inequality is not explained by such factors as minorities' lower attainment of education and other relevant credentials. Evidence of discrimination comes from a number of sources: discrimination complaints and litigation; audit studies, where matched minority and nonminority job applicants are sent out to test the equity of employer responses; statistical studies showing residual differences between Whites and minorities after "legitimate" background differences are taken into account; employers' reports of how race affects their hiring decisions;

and the prevalence of standard operating procedures that have been demonstrated to perpetuate racial exclusion in the labor market (Reskin, 1998).

Illustrating these problems, "audits conducted between 1989 and 1992 indicate that employers who advertised jobs or recruited through employment agencies discriminated against minorities between one-fourth and one-fifth of the time" (Reskin, 1998, p. 27). Moss and Tilly (1996) found that about half the Detroit and Los Angeles employers they surveyed believed Black men to be inadequate as employees because of poor motivation and social skills.

Aspects of "business as usual" that have been shown to limit access of underrepresented groups include failure to advertise in media accessible to minorities; reliance on word-of-mouth recruiting by current employees; requiring credentials not needed for the job in question; and use of vague and subjective criteria in hiring and promotion. More subtle processes include exclusion of minority employees from informal social networks and mentoring relationships (Reskin, 1998).

Reskin's (1998) suggested focal remedy is affirmative action that involves the formalization of fair procedures, accompanied by goals and sanctions. She marshaled an impressive array of social science findings to discredit three "myths": that discrimination is a thing of the past; that affirmative action is synonymous with quotas and preferences; and that meritocratic employment practices are undermined by affirmative action. Contrary to critics' claims, Reskin found that: "reverse discrimination" is rare; that affirmative action enhances business productivity and enlivens communities; and that Whites' opposition to affirmative action is not invariant, but contingent on the specifics of question wording and context.

Reskin concluded that customary business practices perpetuate discrimination. Dependence on anti-discrimination suits is unfair—because it puts the enforcement burden on the victims—and costly as well as inefficient for businesses and underrepresented groups. The clearly preferable solution, in her accounting, is affirmative action, which "can prevent discrimination by encouraging employers to pursue objective and open personnel practices" (1998, p. 92).

A catalog of specific measures to increase employment equity was provided by Braddock and McPartland (1987, pp. 24-25). In the recruitment stage, employers should: avoid reliance on mouth-to-mouth advertising or walk-in applications; target advertising to minority communities; publicize their equal opportunity policies; list jobs with public employment agencies and with private agencies to which the employer's nondiscrimination policy has been made explicit; use community agencies that specialize in minority referral; work with high school and community college officials to recruit as part-time workers students who may later become full-time employees.

At the applicant-selection stage, measures that promote equal opportunity include relying on objective rather than subjective screening methods and limiting criteria to skills actually relevant to the jobs. Schools should employ creatively devised strategies for sending their students into the labor market with fuller and more positive self-descriptions and credentials. Also, employers should be alert to ways in which initial job placement and the training it brings can affect chances for future advancement within the firm. Promotion-stage measures advocated by Braddock and McPartland (1987) include internal posting and publicizing of advanced jobs and emphasizing objective performance evaluations.

Another employment issue for minorities is the special problems faced by employees who are "tokens"—i.e., rare representatives of their group. Pettigrew and Martin (1987, pp. 66-72) suggested a set of promising remedial measures. These include: circulating information within the firm about the credentials and competence of new minority hires; training managers to recognize organizational practices and aspects of their own behavior that may limit the success of minority employees; structuring cross-race work teams that must cooperate to reach common goals; encouraging generalization of positive attitudes elicited by Black coworkers to the larger minority group; encouraging effective mentorship by rewarding supervisors for successful performance on the part of their Black supervisees. Along with such "microremedies," Pettigrew and Martin suggested that organizations might profitably "cluster" their minority employees so as to prevent the negative dynamics that have been shown to limit the success of tokens. Finally, organizations could "tithe" by voluntarily setting ambitious internal goals for minority inclusion.

FOSTERING PUBLIC SUPPORT FOR REMEDIAL ACTION

Interventions to create the broad changes that would decrease residential segregation and employment discrimination require vision and sophisticated understanding of social institutions. But such interventions also require broad public support. The remainder of this chapter describes four factors that may encourage such public support. The first of these is institutional leadership.

Institutional Leadership

Evidence from research on school, employment, and housing desegregation suggests that people's racial attitudes often shift toward congruence with institutional policy (Allport, 1954; Jaynes & Williams, 1989; Pettigrew, 1971). Such "fait accompli" effects may be mediated by the changed circumstances that policy enactment brings, as when mandated desegregation brings positive intergroup contact (Pettigrew, 1971). However, actual enactment is apparently not a necessary mediator of the "fait accompli" dynamic. Summarizing earlier evidence as well as his own research, Jacobson (1978) insisted that attitude change is sometimes manifested after a legal order or policy shift is announced, but before it is enacted. Probably, the active ingredient in such circumstances is often leadership.

My own research (Taylor, 1995) provides an illustration of a "fait accompli" effect plausibly driven by institutional leadership. Responses to a 1990 national probability sample survey were used to compare the racial attitudes of White workers whose employers did and did not practice affirmative action. Contrary to conventional wisdom, I found no indication that proximity to this form of race targeting created White resentment. Instead, Whites working in affirmative action firms were more supportive of certain race-targeted remedies and were more likely to hold beliefs that served as rationales for intervention on behalf of minorities.

The pattern of findings and the fact that about half of the White employees worked in affirmative action firms make it implausible that Whites whose employers practiced affirmative action were simply an attitudinally select group who had sought out racially progressive firms to work in. Instead, it is most reasonable to conclude that employer policies brought a positive shift in workers' attitudes.

Readers may assume that interracial contact was at work here. That is, affirmative action should increase the representation of Blacks in predominantly White firms, and the positive shift in attitudes of White workers might derive from the cross-race shoulder-rubbing that ensued. But no. The data indicated that interracial contact on the job was not the mediator of the affirmative action effect; in fact, White employees in firms with higher proportions of Black coworkers had, if anything, more negative racial attitudes.

I hypothesize that visible institutional leadership is the key. Management-led promotional campaigns often accompany the institution of affirmative action in modern American firms. Edelman (1992) noted that such campaigns may represent symbolic substitutes for institutional change rather than attempts to propel actual change. But the persuasive impact on the White work force may be the same in either case. In addition, where management enlists the participation of White workers in minority recruitment efforts, still another mediational process is potentially set in motion—attitude adjustment in justification of effort (Abelson et al., 1968; Bem, 1972).

Allport (1954) recognized the importance of educational and public relations efforts. Above all, he believed that leadership has a crucial role in propelling attitude shifts among constituencies. Insisting that stateways *can* change folkways, Allport (1954) wrote: "Administrators, more than they realize, have the power to establish desirable changes by executive order in industry, government, and schools."

This claim is congruent with Reskin's (1998) conclusion that leadership ranks high among the factors making for effective affirmative action in employment. As Reskin noted, indications that commitment among top executives is a prerequisite to effective affirmative action programs for women have been reported by several analysts of workforce opportunities (e.g., Bielby & Baron, 1984; O'Farrell & Harlan, 1984; Shaeffer & Lynton, 1979). Similarly, Hitt and Keats (1984) reported testimony by personnel and affirmative action officers that managerial support is crucial. In the area of minority employment, Xerox Corporation's attempts to broaden its workforce were spurred by institutional leadership. As reported by Reskin (1998, pp. 62-63):

In 1968...the president of Xerox told his managers that the company's failure to hire enough minorities had contributed to urban unrest, and that henceforth company policy would require taking affirmative action to end discrimination. This public commitment paved the way for a very effective affirmative action program. (DiTomaso, 1993; Rand, 1996, p. 67)

Leadership has been demonstrably pivotal in efforts to implement school desegregation as well—both for ill and for good. In the 1970s, Louise Day Hicks and the Boston School Committee put that city on the school desegregation map. The Boston leaders' public intransigence and defiance of the federal court order mandating busing contributed greatly to making war zones of the Boston schools and streets. Fortunately, officials in other communities have taken the opposite stance, and Crain, Mahard, and Narot's (1982) analysis of factors promoting successful school desegregation spotlighted local leadership.

Media Framing and Attributions

Attributions for poverty and racial inequality have been of great interest to sociological social psychologists. Kluegel and Smith (1986), reporting their national survey of "beliefs about inequality," discussed the prevalence and potency of the "dominant ideology" (Huber & Form, 1973), which holds that opportunity is abundant and evenly distributed in America. By implication, since opportunity is there for those who seize it, individuals with inferior outcomes have brought their fate on themselves, especially by neglecting to exert the proper effort. Widespread belief in the dominant ideology limits public support for liberal social programs and other policies representing structural remedies for poverty and disadvantage.

Kluegel (1990) insistently called attention to the impact of these beliefs. He concluded:

As long as White Americans blame Blacks for their economic condition, they have reason to oppose such policies, or to withhold support for them in their private action. While public opinion is only one of several factors shaping government social policy, public support does play a role in the passage of anti-discrimination legislation (Burstein, 1979). More important, public opposition has political consequences as seen in the recent difficulties faced by busing for school integration and by affirmative action. (1990, p. 524)

Several years later, Bobo and Kluegel (1993) reported patterns in Whites' responses to the 1990 General Social Survey that underline the potential importance of assessments of discrimination and beliefs about Blacks' motivation. Both of these factors, particularly assessments of discrimination, predict support for race-targeted policies in the expected direction. That is, Whites who deny discrimination and point to deficient Black motivation are most opposed to "equal opportunity" policies such as enterprise zones and college financing for Black scholars; and these Whites disproportionately oppose "equal outcomes" policies such as federal spending to assist Blacks.

So, if attributions of responsibility for Black disadvantage are important, what can be said about the roots of these attributions and how they might be altered?

Focusing specifically on beliefs about racial inequality, Kluegel (1985) suggested that denial of discrimination, and beliefs that individual failings rather than societal barriers are the cause of racial inequality, have multiple causes. These beliefs may be partly affectively driven—by race prejudice. They also may be "cognitively" driven by group self-interest—Whites' resolve to hold onto their position of social privilege. This latter suggestion is congruent with my own finding (discussed below) that Whites living in localities with relatively large (and presumably threatening) Black populations are particularly likely to assign individual-blame and to avoid system-blame for racial inequality (Taylor, 1998).

Tracing time trends in Whites' beliefs about the causes of racial inequality, Kluegel (1990) focused on causes of individualist attributions and avoidance of structural attributions. Such attributions, particularly the claim that deficient Black motivation is responsible for racial inequality, can be a response to the threat represented by progressive social programs. This pattern of beliefs allows respondents to resist racial change for reasons apparently other than out-and-out prejudice.

Provocative research by Kinder and Sanders (1996) and by Iyengar (1991) suggested another subtle and potentially alterable factor: Media framing of relevant stories. Iyengar drew a crucial distinction between *episodic* and *thematic* television news coverage of policy-relevant topics. Episodic stories focus on individuals and particular incidents, whereas thematic stories are general, abstract, and contextual. Because episodic stories lend themselves to visual portrayal, television news is notoriously episodic. Iyengar hypothesized that episodic coverage promotes attributions of individual rather than social-system causality for social problems, and also encourages assignment of responsibility for remedies to individuals rather than to governments. Along with such attributions of responsibility to individuals come predictable attitudes and policy preferences—particularly opposition to systemic remedial efforts.

Racial inequality and five other topic areas were the focus of Iyengar's (1991) research. Content analysis of 1981-1986 network newscasts showed that racial inequality had received heavier thematic then episodic coverage, largely because discrimination was a major theme; however, a substantial minority of the racial inequality stories were episodic—about 40%. The impact of episodic stories was studied in the innovative experimental facet of Iyengar's research. In it, White middle-class adult subjects were shown randomly assigned episodic or thematic news clips. News coverage of discrimination was found to encourage societal attributions, but stories about Black poverty, especially when episodically framed, encouraged attributions of individual responsibility.

Iyengar explained the impact of episodic framing in terms of the *accessibility bias*. The need for cognitive selectivity and simplification underlies the accessibility bias. As people consider a topic, they do not compile every bit of relevant information stored in their memories. Rather they retrieve a short list of most accessible cognitions. Wyer and Srull (1984) suggested that, within each category of information, the elements that have been most frequently or recently used lie at the top. Thus, when circumstances direct attention to a given category, these most-accessible cognitions will be retrieved first and will dominate opinions.

Iyengar noted that, in thinking about public affairs, people are particularly dependent on the media for their information. Thus the frequency and recency of media messages carries especially heavy weight.

> Episodic reporting tends to make particular acts or characteristics of particular individuals more accessible, while thematic reporting helps viewers to think about political issues in terms of societal or political outcomes. (Iyengar, 1991, p. 134)

Iyengar's experimental data were supplemented with survey data to assess the correlation of causal attributions and assignment of responsibility for remedies with people's racial attitudes and policy preferences. These attitude and policy measures included support for government intervention to help minorities, support for federal spending on civil rights, affect toward Black people, affect toward civil rights leaders, affect toward Jesse Jackson, and appraisal of President Reagan's performance on civil rights. Individualist assignment of causal responsibility significantly or nearly significantly predicted less progressive views on five of the six outcome measures: support for government intervention to help minorities ($p<.01$), support for federal spending on civil rights ($p<.01$), affect toward Black people ($p<.15$), affect toward civil rights leaders ($p<.15$), and appraisal of President Reagan's performance on civil rights ($p<.05$). Individualist assignment of responsibility for remedies predicted less progressive views on support for government intervention to help minorities ($p<.10$), support for federal spending on civil rights ($p<.05$), affect toward Black people ($p<.01$), affect toward civil rights leaders ($p<.05$), and affect toward Jesse Jackson ($p<.05$).

In concluding his report, Iyengar (1991) returned to the point with which this section on Media Framing and Attributions began. Belief in the dominant ideology of abundant and equal opportunity, and the individualist attributions that such belief engenders, both discourage progressive racial views. In contrast, structural and systemic thinking promotes progressive attitudes and support for interventions to remedy discrimination. More extensive thematic news coverage of racial inequality would seem to be one means of encouraging the understanding of structural and systemic dynamics.

When social scientists across a wide range of disciplines serve as consultants and expert discussants on public broadcasting and network news programs, they may have the opportunity to encourage thematic treatment of public policy issues. Also, through college and university programs in communications and journalism, the current generation of scholars has the potential to influence the next generation of those who will shape the media. In addition, the increase in audience participation enabled by the internet has dramatically broadened the opportunities for any viewer to influence the media messages broadcast to others.

Political Discourse

Race-related topics have long been a key element in political discourse, used by one side or another in attempts to attract voters. Recent evidence suggests that such political rhetoric may have effects beyond shifting votes: It may also change the impact of White prejudice in driving racial policy opinion.

Much has been said about the use of the "race card" in political campaigns of recent decades. A concise analysis of the relevance of racial prejudice to electoral politics has been presented by Kinder and Sanders (1996). The gist of their analysis is this: With the 1964 Goldwater campaign against incumbent Lyndon Johnson, racial sentiment among White Americans took on new importance in national elections. By that time, federal civil rights efforts had undermined the hold of the Democratic party on White Southerners. The "Dixiecrat revolt" that almost defeated Truman in 1948 had taught the Democrats they could no longer count on a solid South. From that point on, Democratic politicians faced pressures to keep quiet on race (although Lyndon Johnson defied those pressures). Since Goldwater's use of the issue of "states' rights," Republicans have found various "codewords"—subtle means of using negative racial imagery—to attract White votes. In fact, the Republican party has come to depend heavily on the White South and White social conservatives in other parts of the county.

"Law and order" were codewords used by Richard Nixon, reminding audiences of urban riots. "Law and order" became an issue as well in the Bush–Dukakis campaign of 1988, with the famed Willie Horton advertisement used against Dukakis. Horton was a Black man convicted of murder, who committed another sensational crime, involving rape of a middle-class White woman, while on furlough from a Massachusetts prison. The political ad ostensibly blamed Dukakis for being soft on crime, but the prominence of Willie Horton's picture in the anti-Dukakis ad led to widespread claims that the ad was, above all, an attempt to activate negative racial sentiment among Whites.

Some earlier analysts have claimed that presidential statements—e.g., opposing busing or affirmative action—have led to congruent shifts in public opinion. A more intricate dynamic has been explored by Kinder and his associates (Kinder et al., 1989; Kinder & Mendelberg, 1995). These researchers have focused not simply on main effects that public events may have on racial views, but especially on the interaction of such events with prejudice in affecting policy opinions.

Two different research strategies have been used to assess the purported interactive effect of the Willie Horton ad with prejudice—i.e., to ask whether the ad magnified the negative effect of prejudice on racial policy opinions. First, in a correlational approach, Kinder et al. (1989) used National Election Study interview dates to measure the duration of exposure that survey respondents had to the Willie Horton ad. As predicted, respondents' measured race prejudice was more strongly correlated with their racial policy opinions among those whose late interview date allowed the greatest exposure to the ad before their interview.

Such correlational results are, of course, open to alternate interpretations. To buttress these conclusions, Mendelberg (1997) conducted an experiment in which university students were randomly shown the Horton ad or a racially neutral "control" story, and then were asked their views on a number of racial questions. The predicted interaction was observed, and this effect can be described in two (largely equivalent) ways. Mendelberg emphasized that viewing the Willie Horton ad increased the link between prejudice and negative racial policy opinions—i.e., prejudice was primed, and its impact was accentuated. Equivalently, the data can be described as showing that the Horton ad had a negative impact on racial policy opinions, but primarily among prejudiced individuals. From either perspective, the ad interacted with prejudice to have a negative effect on racial policy opinions, beyond its effect of encouraging White voters to favor candidate Bush.

What does this analysis say about strategies to decrease prejudice and discrimination? It suggests that White public support for efforts to reduce racial discrimination will be encouraged insofar as White politicians, responding to conscience or external pressures, resist negative use of the "race card." And it is reasonable to presume that symmetrical positive effects can be generated when politicians use racial imagery to evoke progressive rather than racist public reactions.

There are some recent examples of such positive effects. The early campaign efforts over a year before the 2000 presidential election brought some potentially positive political messages. Despite the levels of Anglo public support for efforts to limit immigrants' rights and reduce bilingual education programs in the Western United States, the leading candidates of both major parties—George W. Bush and Al Gore—made it a point to court the Latino vote by speaking Spanish on the campaign trail and crafting messages of inclusion. Whatever the motives of these politicians, affirmations of the legitimacy of the Spanish language and of Hispanic Americans thus were reaching the general public.

Although President Clinton's record on policy questions has been mixed, and his credibility has been tarnished by scandal, he has nevertheless sent a number of positive racial messages. For instance, he has supported many race-targeted programs including affirmative action, appointed many racial-minority individuals to visible positions of authority, and maintained prominent cross-racial friendships.

The sociological social psychologist Herbert Blumer would applaud these positive examples. As he wrote:

> race prejudice has...[a] variable and intermittent career...When events touching on [race] relations are not treated as "big events" and hence do not set crucial issues in the area of public discussion; or when the elite leaders or spokesmen do not define such big events vehemently or adversely; or where they define them in the direction of racial harmony...—under such conditions the sense of group position recedes and race prejudice declines. (Blumer, 1958, p. 7)

Economic Security Among Whites

A claim long voiced in the intergroup relations literature is that self-interest drives racial prejudice and discrimination. Levine and Campbell (1972) dubbed this idea "realistic group conflict theory."

Research on Self-Interest. Despite the plausibility of self-interest theories, attempts to demonstrate that self-interest propels racial prejudice have often been unsuccessful (e.g., Taylor, 1995). Sears and his colleagues have repeatedly argued that self-interest effects on racial policy attitudes are weak in comparison to effects of "subtle racism" (e.g., Sears, Hensler, & Speer, 1979). Congruent with this argument, Kluegel and Smith (1983) found that self-interest has only a modest impact on Whites' support for affirmative action. Based on their review of relevant literature, Sears and Funk (1991) concluded that pronounced self-interest effects on social and political attitudes are the exception rather than the rule.

However, these skeptical conclusions rely primarily on individual-level analyses. Typically the test involves correlating survey respondents' individual circumstances with their attitudes. Some analysts, for example Bobo and Kluegel (1993), have insisted that such analyses miss a major point—that *group* self-interest is the relevant predictor of racial prejudice.

Blumer's (1958) classic essay on prejudice as a sense of group position provides a theoretical foundation for the notion that prejudice grows from Whites' collectively defined and maintained sense of their ownership of social privileges. In this view, prejudice is fully activated when this sense of group position is threatened. Aggregate-level analysis of data has the unique potential to document this dynamic.

Research on the Black Population Share. I recently performed such an aggregate-level analysis, and results provided some support for the Blumerian claim (Taylor, 1998). The outcome measures were attitude scales constructed from answers of White respondents to the 1990 General Social Survey (GSS). The respondents were a probability sample of noninstitutionalized, English-speaking adults living in the continental United States. The research related Whites' attitudes to 1990 Census-based indices of the Black population share in the 83 metropolitan areas or nonmetro counties in which these respondents lived. The Black population share across these localities ranged from 42% to essentially 0%, averaging 10% higher in the South than in the other regions of the country.

Controlling for respondent characteristics such as education, and for locality characteristics such as region and population size, the proportion of Blacks in the locality powerfully predicted average scores on three attitude scales: (a) White residents' traditional prejudice, especially stereotyping and aversion to interracial contact; (b) Whites' opposition to race-targeted programs, especially enterprise zones and educational assistance to Blacks; and (c) their policy-related beliefs, especially victim-blaming and avoidance of system-blaming for racial inequality. The pattern was consistent across all these categories of racial views: A larger Black population share brought more negative White attitudes. Thus, much of the observed gap in the racial attitudes of White Southerners and non-Southerners can be attributed to regional differences in Black population concentration (Taylor, 1998).

Unstandardized regression coefficients can be used to translate the impact of Black population share into equivalents of years-of-schooling effects:

- Opposition to race targeting. A 10-point rise in the local percentage of Blacks brought an increase in opposition to race-targeting that was about the same amount as the decrease produced by 3.3 more years of average education level.

- Policy-related beliefs. A 10-point rise in the local percentage of Blacks would produce a negative shift in White residents' policy-related beliefs about Blacks equivalent in size but opposite in direction to the progressive effect that would be produced by about 1.6 additional years of education.

- Traditional prejudice. For traditional prejudice, population proportions interacted with region: The impact of Black population share on Whites' traditional prejudice was negligible in the South; outside the South, however, a 10-point rise in the local percentage of Blacks increased traditional prejudice by an amount greater than the decrease that would be produced by three additional years of schooling (Taylor, 1998).

These results demonstrate the importance of collective circumstances in conditioning racial views. However, they are not directly relevant to discussions of prejudice-reduction and discrimination-reduction strategies because, in the U.S., the local racial population composition is not open to manipulation.

Whites' Economic Security. An aggregate-level variable that is more amenable to manipulation through public policy—Whites' economic security—may also be linked to Whites' racial attitudes. Quillian (1996) created a "threat" scale including White economic status as well as Black population share, and found that, at the level of Census region, Whites' traditional prejudice and opposition to race-targeting both rise with this type of threat.

My micro/macro data file, the 1990 GSS/Census data used in Taylor (1998), allows separation of White economic status from Black population share and also definition of a more detailed geographical unit than Quillian's. Accordingly, in analyses performed for this chapter, I have examined the link between the economic status of Whites in their respective localities and their racial attitudes on the 1990 GSS.

The three attitude scales used in Taylor (1998) were employed here as well. These indices of traditional prejudice, opposition to race-targeting, and policy-related beliefs were constructed from responses to the 1990 GSS (Davis &

Smith, 1990), with the guidance of EQS confirmatory factor analysis (Bentler, 1989). See Taylor (1998) for fuller details. A fourth attitude scale, tapping racial resentment, was constructed for the present analysis. It was the mean of two standardized quantities: (1) estimates of the prevalence of reverse discrimination in employment, and (2) expressed sentiment that, relative to Blacks, Whites have too little influence in American life and politics. (The GSS items that constitute the racial resentment measure are DISCAFF, INFLUWHT, and INFLUBLK in Davis & Smith, 1990.)

As in Taylor (1998), "localities" were the metropolitan areas or nonmetro counties (or pairs of counties) which served as geographical primary sampling units for the 1990 GSS (Davis & Smith, 1990). From 1990 U.S. Census data, I devised a locality-level measure of White economic status. It was the mean of standardized scores representing the proportion of White men who were working and the proportion of White families whose annual income reached or exceeded $25,000.

Each attitude scale was regressed on a set of individual respondent charac- teristics (age, gender, education, occupational prestige, and full-time work status), together with locality characteristics including region (South versus non- South), population size, Black population share, and White economic status. Or- dinary least squares (OLS) regression was used for the analyses reported here.[1]

In these multivariate analyses, the aggregate economic status of local Whites was related to all four attitude measures in the predicted direction—i.e., higher economic status brought more positive racial attitudes. Though the impact of White economic status was not significant for policy-related beliefs ($p < .226$), it was significant for the other three attitudes: traditional prejudice ($p < .002$), sup- port for race-targeted remedies ($p < .022$), and conviction that Blacks are receiv- ing undeserved advantages ($p < .027$). In each case, the standardized regression coefficient (beta) for White economic status was among the largest effects esti- mated for the individual-level and locality-level predictors. Results for the scale of traditional prejudice, which showed the strongest impact of White economic status, are displayed in Table 4.1.

The findings reported in Table 4.1 show that the observed effects of locality- level White economic status were independent from the effects of Black popula- tion share, which I previously found to evoke prejudiced reactions (Taylor, 1998). They were also independent from the effects of region and population size, and of individual respondent characteristics including age, gender, education, occu- pational prestige, and full-time work status.

These results are highly pertinent to discussions of reducing prejudice and discrimination. They tell us that, whatever their individual circumstances, Whites living in economically depressed communities are more prejudiced and resistant to efforts aimed at decreasing racial inequality. Economic policies that improve the status of those communities should predictably increase positive attitudes and support for remedies to discrimination. In addition to (or in lieu of) such eco- nomic improvement, economically depressed White communities can be targeted

TABLE 4.1
Individual-Level and Contextual Effects
on Traditional Prejudice (N = 900)

Variable	Coefficient[a]
Individual characteristics[b]	
Age: pre-Truman	.22***
Age: pre-Kennedy	.12***
Age: post-Reagan	-.04
Male	.00
Full-time employed	.01
Education (years completed)	-.20***
Occupational prestige	-.09*
Locality characteristics[c]	
City population	.00
South	.06
% Black	.17***
White economic status	.15**

[a] Values are OLS regression standardized partial slope coefficients.

[b] Age is represented by three dummy variables designating cohorts exposed to distinct racial climates: Pre-Truman identifies respondents who entered adulthood (age 18) before the presidency of Harry S. Truman, who ordered the desegregation of the U.S. Armed Forces; pre-Kennedy identifies respondents who entered adulthood after Truman assumed office but before John F. Kennedy became president; and post-Reagan identifies respondents who entered adulthood after Ronald Reagan's 1980 winning presidential campaign. Respondents who entered adulthood between the Kennedy and Reagan periods form the reference category. Gender is represented with male coded high. Full-time work status is a dichotomy, employed full-time (coded high) versus all other. Education is indexed as years of schooling completed. Prestige is the Hodge, Siegel, and Rossi occupational prestige index (see Siegel, 1971).

[c] City population and % Black for the locality are based on 1990 Census information. The population measure is the natural log of city size. Region is a dichotomy, with South coded high, non-South low. The measure of White economic status is described in the text.

*$p < .05$. **$p < .01$. ***$p < .001$.

for special attention by social scientists attempting to promote racial change. Presumably, the observed locality-level effects are mediated by the statements and actions of local opinion leaders—political figures and media spokespersons. Interventions might usefully be aimed at modifying their messages to the community.

SUMMARY

Residential segregation and employment discrimination are complex, institutionally structured phenomena. Substantially reducing discrimination in housing and the labor market will require an extensive set of efforts, for which public support must be developed. This chapter has described four factors having the potential to encourage such public support. First, visible leadership on the part of those who head our social institutions is a crucial, insufficiently-used resource. Second, media coverage of topics related to race must offer systematic analysis that encourages the American public to recognize the operation of structural, systematic dynamics in producing racial inequality. Third, political contenders should avoid "the temptations of race" (Kinder & Sanders, 1996)—i.e., politicians must be encouraged to use their platforms to promote racial unity and equality, rather than competing for the votes of White bigots. Finally, policies that bolster the economic status of White communities should also increase White support for racial change.

NOTES

1. A multi-level modeling program such as HLM, which acknowledges the uniformity of locality scores for respondents within a given locality, would produce highly similar effect-size estimates, but the probabilities associated with significance tests for the locality-level contextual predictors would be larger. In other words, readers should realize that the OLS significance test results reported here are somewhat too liberal.

REFERENCES

Abelson, R. P., Aronson, E., McGuire, W. J., Newcomb, T. M., Rosenberg, M. J., & Tannenbaum, P. H. (1968). *Theories of cognitive consistency: A sourcebook*. Chicago: Rand McNally.

Allport, G. W. (1954). *The nature of prejudice*. Reading, MA: Addison-Wesley.

Bem, D. J. (1972). Self-perception theory. In L. Berkowitz (Ed.), *Advances in experimental social psychology* (Vol. 6, pp. 1-62). New York: Academic Press.

Bentler, P. M. (1989). *EQS Structural equations program manual*. Los Angeles: BMDP Statistical Software.

Bielby, W. T., & Baron, J. N. (1984). A woman's place is with other women: Sex segregation within organizations. In B. F. Reskin (Ed.), *Sex segregation in the workplace* (pp. 27-55). Washington, DC: National Academy Press.

Blumer, H. (1958). Race prejudice as a sense of group position. *Pacific Sociological Review, 1*, 3-7.

Bobo, L., & Kluegel, J. R. (1993). Opposition to race-targeting: Self-interest, stratification ideology, or racial attitudes? *American Sociological Review, 58*, 443-464.

Braddock, J. H., & McPartland, J. M. (1987). How minorities continue to be excluded from equal employment opportunities: Research on labor market and institutional barriers. *Journal of Social Issues, 43*(1), 5-39.

Burstein, P. (1979). Public opinion, demonstrations, and the passage of anti-discrimination legislation. *Public Opinion Quarterly, 79*, 157-172.

Clark, W. A. V. (1986). Residential segregation in American cities: A review and interpretation. *Population Research and Policy Review, 5*, 95-127.

Crain, R. L., Mahard, R. E., & Narot, R. E. (1982). *Making desegregation work: How schools create social climates*. Cambridge, MA: Ballinger.

Davis, J. A., & Smith, T. W. (1990). *The General Social Survey: Cumulative codebook and data file*. Chicago: National Opinion Research Center, University of Chicago.

DiTomaso, N. (1993). *Notes on the Xerox case: Balanced work force at Xerox.* Unpublished manuscript. New Brunswick, NJ: School of Management, Rutgers University.

Edelman, L. B. (1992). Legal ambiguity and symbolic structures: Organizational mediation of civil rights law. *American Journal of Sociology, 97,* 1531-1576.

Farley, R., Schuman, H., Bianchi, S., Colasanto, D., & Hatchett, S. (1978). Chocolate city, vanilla suburbs: Will the trend toward racially separate communities continue? *Social Science Research, 7,* 319-344.

Hitt, M. A., & Keats, B. W. (1984). Empirical identification of the criteria for effective affirmative action programs. *The Journal of Applied Behavioral Science, 20,* 203-222.

Huber, J., & Form, W. H. (1973). *Income and ideology.* New York: Free Press.

Iyengar, S. (1991). *Is anyone responsible? How television frames political issues.* Chicago: University of Chicago Press.

Jacobson, C. K. (1978). Desegregation rulings and public attitude changes: White resistance or resignation? *American Journal of Sociology, 84,* 698-705.

Jaynes, D. G., & Williams, R. M., Jr. (1989). *A common destiny: Blacks and American society.* Washington, DC: National Academy Press.

Kasarda, J. D. (1990). Urban industrial transition and the underclass. *Annals of the American Academy of Political and Social Science, 501,* 26-47.

Kinder, D. R., & Mendelberg, T. (1995). Cracks in apartheid: The political impact of prejudice among desegregated Whites. *Journal of Politics, 57,* 402-424.

Kinder, D. R., Mendelberg, T., Dawson, M., Sanders, L., Rosenstone, S., Sargent, J., &. Cohen, C. (1989). *Benign neglect and racial codewords in the 1988 presidential campaign.* Paper presented at American Political Science Association meeting, Atlanta.

Kinder, D. R., & Sanders, L. M. (1996). *Divided by color: Racial politics and democratic ideals.* Chicago: University of Chicago Press.

Kluegel, J. R. (1985). If there isn't a problem, you don't need a solution. *American Behavioral Scientist, 28,* 761-784.

Kluegel, J. R. (1990). Trends in Whites' explanations of the Black-White gap in socioeconomic status, 1977-1989. *American Sociological Review, 55,* 512-525.

Kluegel, J. R., & Smith, E. R. (1983). Affirmative action attitudes: Effects of self-interest, racial affect, and stratification beliefs on Whites' views. *Social Forces, 61,* 797-824.

Kluegel, J. R., & Smith, E. R. (1986). *Beliefs about inequality: Americans' views of what is and what ought to be.* Hawthorne, NY: Aldine de Gruyter.

Kozol, J. (1991). *Savage inequalities: Children in America's schools.* New York: Harper-Collins.

Levine, R. A., & Campbell, D. T. (1972). *Ethnocentrism: Theories of conflict, ethnic attitudes, and group behavior.* New York: Wiley.

Massey, D. S., & Denton, N. A. (1993). *American apartheid: Segregation and the making of the underclass.* Cambridge, MA: Harvard University Press.

Mendelberg, T. (1997). Executing Hortons: Racial crime in the 1988 presidential campaign. *Public Opinion Quarterly, 61,* 134-167.

Moss, P., & Tilly, C. (1996). "Soft" skills and race. *Work and Occupations, 23,* 252-276.

Neckerman, K. M., & Kirchenman, J. (1991). Hiring strategies, racial bias, and inner-city workers. *Social Problems, 38,* 433-447.

O'Farrell, B., & Harlan, S. (1984). Job integration strategies. In B. F. Reskin (Ed.), *Sex segregation in the workplace: Trends, explanations, and remedies* (pp. 267-291). Washington, DC: National Academy Press.

Pettigrew, T. F. (1971). *Racially separate or together?* New York: McGraw-Hill.

Pettigrew, T. F. (1979). Racial change and social policy. *Annals of the American Academy of Political and Social Science, 441,* 114-131.

Pettigrew, T. F., & Martin, J. (1987). Shaping the organizational context for Black American inclusion. *Journal of Social Issues, 43*(1), 41-78.

Pettigrew, T. F., & Taylor, M. C. (in press). Discrimination. In E. G. Borgatta (Ed.), *Encyclopedia of sociology* (2nd ed.). New York: Macmillan.

Quillian, L. (1996). Group threat and regional change in attitudes toward African-Americans. *American Journal of Sociology, 3*, 816-860.

Rand, A. B. (1996). Diversity in corporate America. In G. Curry (Ed.), *The affirmative action debate* (pp. 65-76). Reading, MA: Addison-Wesley.

Reskin, B. F. (1998). *The realities of affirmative action in employment*. Washington, DC: American Sociological Association.

Saltman, J., Tisdale, W., Farmer, J., & Noel, D. (1994, December). *Statement on Massey & Denton's "American Apartheid."* Unpublished manuscript, Kent State University, Department of Sociology.

Sears, D. O., & Funk, C. L. (1991). The role of self-interest in social and political attitudes. In M. P. Zanna (Ed.), *Advances in experimental social psychology* (Vol. 24, pp. 1-91). New York: Academic Press.

Sears, D. O., Hensler, C. P., & Speer, L. K. (1979). Whites' opposition to busing: Self-interest or symbolic politics? *American Political Science Review, 73*, 369-384.

Shaeffer, R. G., & Lynton, E. F. (1979). *Corporate experience in improving women's job opportunities* (Report No. 755). New York: Conference Board.

Siegel, P. (1971). *Prestige in the American occupational structure*. Unpublished Ph.D. dissertation, Department of Sociology, University of Chicago.

Taylor, M. C. (1995). White backlash to workplace affirmative action: Peril or myth? *Social Forces, 73*, 1385-1414.

Taylor, M. C. (1998). How White attitudes vary with the racial composition of local populations: Numbers count. *American Sociological Review, 63*, 512-535.

Wilson, W. J. (1987). *The truly disadvantaged: The inner city, the underclass, and public policy*. Chicago: University of Chicago Press.

Wilson, W. J. (1996). *When work disappears: The world of the new urban poor*. Chicago: University of Chicago Press.

Wyer, R. S., Jr., & Srull, T. K. (1984). Category accessibility: Some theoretic and empirical issues concerning the processing of social stimulus information. In E. T. Higgins, N. A. Kuiper, & M. P. Zanna (Eds.), *Social cognition: The Ontario symposium*. Hillsdale, NJ: Erlbaum.

Yinger, J. (1991). *Housing discrimination study: Incidence of discrimination and variation in discriminatory behavior*. Washington, DC: U.S. Department of Housing and Urban Development.

Yinger, J. (1995). *Closed doors, opportunities lost: The continuing costs of housing discrimination*. New York: Russell Sage Foundation.

II

Psychological Research on Reducing Prejudice

5 Does Intergroup Contact Reduce Prejudice? Recent Meta-Analytic Findings

Thomas F. Pettigrew[1]
Linda R. Tropp
University of California, Santa Cruz

Social psychology has long held that one major means of reducing intergroup prejudice is through contact between the groups *under optimal conditions*. Explicit attention to this phenomenon was triggered after World War II by an organized effort in North America to end prejudice. Called the Human Relations Movement, it sought to correct negative stereotypes, and it took organizational form with such still-active groups as the National Conference of Christians and Jews.

The movement's controlling idea was that prejudice derived largely from ignorance. If only we could know each other better across group lines, went the reasoning, we would discover the common humanity we share. The movement, as Drake and Cayton (1945; 1962, p. 281) noted at the time, projected an "almost mystical faith in 'getting to know one another' as a solvent of racial tensions...."

To be sure, ignorance *is* a factor in intergroup relations (Stephan & Stephan, 1984), but it offers an incomplete explanation. The movement did not understand the many cognitive, affective, situational and institutional barriers to positive contact effects. Yet this effort furnished the context for social scientists to begin systematically studying intergroup contact effects.

Robin Williams (1947), followed by Gordon Allport (1954), formalized the contact hypothesis, and it has enjoyed a central place in social psychological work on intergroup relations ever since. While sharing problems found in social psychological theory generally (Pettigrew, 1986), Allport's version of the hypothesis has received considerable research attention and support.

However, unlike the naive optimism of the Human Relations Movement, Allport's contentions were conditioned by the characteristics of the contact situation.[2] He held that intergroup contact would lead to reduced intergroup prejudice *if*—and only if—the contact situation embodied four conditions: (1) equal status between the groups in the situation, (2) common goals, (3) no competition between groups, and (4) authority sanction for the contact (Allport, 1954; Pettigrew, 1971). Stressing "interdependence," Sherif (1966) focused further attention on conditions 2 and 3. Many other factors have since been proposed—some situational, such as intimacy (Amir, 1976), and some individual, such as low authoritarianism (Weigel & Howes, 1985—also discussed by Allport, 1954). A danger here is that too many factors will render the contact hypothesis meaningless; with added factors, it becomes increasingly unlikely that any situations can meet the specified conditions (Pettigrew, 1986; Stephan, 1987).

The hypothesis has inspired extensive research over the past half century (Pettigrew, 1998b). Allport's formulation has received support across a variety of societies, situations, and groups. And different research methods have yielded findings that provide support—field studies (e.g., Deutsch & Collins, 1951), archival research (e.g., Fine, 1979), survey research (e.g., Herek & Capitanio, 1996), and laboratory studies (e.g., Cook, 1978; Desforges et al., 1991).

Yet contact theory's popularity has waxed and waned. After the racial progress of the 1960s was followed by a national retreat in the 1970s and 1980s, a hardened pessimism emerged in American thinking about intergroup relations. Criticism of Allport's contentions arose in both psychology and sociology (e.g., Ford, 1986; Hewstone & Brown, 1986; Rose, 1981; Rothbart & John, 1985). Much of this criticism treated the potential of contact to reduce prejudice as purely a cognitive issue. And, as Rothbart and John (1985) made clear, there are formidable cognitive barriers that restrict positive intergroup effects of contact.

Nonetheless, research on contact expanded over recent decades to new groups and across disciplines. Going beyond the confines of ethnic and racial groups, investigators tested the theory with a diverse range of subjects and target groups. In addition to college students, children, adolescents, and adults have served as participants in contact studies, with target groups ranging from the elderly and homosexuals to the physically disabled and the mentally ill.

Past reviews of this extensive literature have been subjective and incomplete. As is often the case with such reviews, they reached sharply conflicting conclusions—in support of the hypothesis (Pettigrew, 1971, 1998b; Riordan, 1978), mixed (Stephan, 1987), and contrary to the hypothesis (Ford, 1986). Clearly, a meta-analysis is needed to evaluate this work more thoroughly. Yet, to our knowledge, no meta-analysis has been performed on this vast and rich research literature that spans several disciplines. This chapter represents the initial report on such an effort, utilizing 203 individual studies with 313 independent samples and 746 separate tests.[3] Combined, 90,000 subjects from 25 different nations participated in this body of research. While 73% of the studies are from the United States, extensive research from other nations is involved—including work from nine developing countries.

OVERVIEW OF THE META-ANALYTIC APPROACH

Because of the enormous variety of studies, a meta-analytic test of this research literature requires a clear definition as to what we mean by intergroup contact. We defined intergroup contact as *actual face-to-face interaction between members of clearly distinguishable and defined groups*. From this definition flow several inclusion criteria. All meta-analyses require specific inclusion rules, but such rules are especially critical for organizing a research literature as diverse as that of intergroup contact.

Four Inclusion Criteria

1. Because we focused on the relationship between intergroup contact and prejudice, we considered *only those empirical studies in which intergroup contact acted as a causal, independent variable for intergroup prejudice*. This requirement excluded research that treated intergroup contact as a dependent variable in explaining how and why contact occurred.

2. *Only research that involved contact between members of discrete, clearly distinguishable groups was included*. This rule allowed groups with cross-cutting categories, but only if the categories were clearly defined.

3. *To be included, the research had to involve some degree of direct intergroup interaction*. The interaction could be observed or reported, or it could occur in such focused situations as classrooms where direct contact is unavoidable. This inclusion rule eliminated a variety of studies that are sometimes cited in summaries of contact research. For example, it excluded research that utilized rough proximity or group proportions to infer intergroup interaction. Contact cannot be assumed from the opportunity for contact, such as living in an intergroup neighborhood with no report of actual interaction. Exceptions were made when the research carefully demonstrated that the intergroup proximity correlated highly with actual contact. The famous Deutsch and Collins (1951) interracial housing study is an example of such an included instance.

This rule also eliminated investigations that attempted to gauge contact with such indirect measures as knowledge about an outgroup (e.g., Taft, 1959). Studies also were excluded if they asked about attitudes toward contact unless such indicators were directly linked to prior intergroup experience (e.g., Ford, 1941). Finally, this inclusion rule also eliminated research that categorized subjects into groups that did not directly interact—as in many minimal group studies.

4. *The prejudice dependent variables had to be collected on individuals, rather than simply as a total aggregate outcome; and comparative data had to be available to evaluate any changes in prejudice*. These comparisons made use of precontact measures in within-group designs or control-group data in between-group designs.

Within these boundaries, we accepted a wide variety of prejudice indicators. This inclusive net enabled us to test whether intergroup contact had differential effects on various components and measures of prejudice. Thus, we examined studies of intergroup beliefs—the most common type of prejudice indicator. But we also included studies that had social distance, affective, stereotype, and sociometric indicators. One especially popular approach involved various forms of the semantic differential test. We distinguished between two types. One type used only adjectives that tapped Osgood, Suci, and Tannenbaum's (1957) evaluative factor; we combined these measures with other affective indicators. The other type used the semantic differential procedure to measure group stereotypes, which we combined with other studies of stereotypes.

Method

Locating Relevant Studies. To date, we have located over 200 studies that meet our inclusion rules. A wide variety of search procedures were utilized. First, we conducted computer searches of abstracts in the psychological (*PSYCHLIT*), sociological (*SOCABS* and *SOCIOFILE*), political science (*GOV*), education (*ERIC*), and general research periodical (*Current Contents*) research literature through December 1998.[4] Second, we wrote personal letters to researchers who had published especially relevant research, and we sent for pertinent unpublished conference papers. We also reviewed reference lists from previously located studies—an especially rich source. Finally, we repeatedly requested relevant materials via e-mail networks of social psychologists.

Fixed Effects Model. Rather than assuming that our collection of studies represented a random sample from a larger population of studies to which we would like to generalize (a random effects model), we treated our studies as if they were the entire population of relevant contact research (a fixed effects model—see Hedges, 1994; Raudenbush, 1994). Most meta-analytic studies have employed this model, and the varied nature of the intergroup contact literature makes it more appropriate than a random effects model. Using this model allowed us to employ Blair Johnson's (1989) extremely useful DSTAT program for fixed effects models.

This chapter is a preliminary report on our work. In the future we will add other relevant studies as we find them. Nonetheless, we are confident that the present collection represents a sizable proportion of the investigations that meet our inclusion criteria.

Variables Coded From Each Study.[5] Standard categories were recorded for each study: nation of origin, type of study (survey, field, experiment, sociometric, etc.), year of publication, type of publication (journal article, book, dissertation and other unpublished work), within- or between-subjects design, study setting (laboratory, school, work, travel, mixed, etc.), sample sizes, as well as the age, sex, and ethnicity of participants. We also rated the quality of the independent and dependent measures.

Variables recorded that were special to this effort included: the type of target group (racial, disability, laboratory groups, etc.), minority- or majority-group participants, type of control group, degree of choice in having contact, the type of contact indicator (self-report, observed, or assumed), and the type of prejudice indicator. For global tests of Allport's original hypothesis, we also rated whether intergroup friendship was used as the independent variable and whether the contact situations were structured to approximate optimal contact conditions.

Computation and Analysis of Effect Sizes. Our meta-analyses were categorical fixed effects models (Hedges, 1994; Raudenbush, 1994; Rosenthal, 1995). Effect sizes expressed as correlation coefficients were converted to the algebraically equivalent Cohen's d (Rosenthal, 1991). If no correlations were reported, effect sizes were derived from other statistics by use of the conversion formulas provided by Johnson (1989). If a relationship was merely reported as non-significant, we conservatively assigned a value of .00 for the effect size. Following Hedges and Olkin (1985), we computed all mean ds with each effect size *weighted by the reciprocal of its variance* (giving more weight to effect sizes that were more reliably estimated). In our reporting scheme, a negative mean effect size indicates that greater intergroup contact was associated with lower prejudice.

Three units of analysis were employed—studies, independent samples, and individual tests. The use of studies restricts the possibility of "laboratory effects"—i.e., any constant bias across samples and tests that might be created by a particular research environment. The use of independent samples is helpful because they are more numerous than studies and allow more detailed comparisons. Consequently, this was our primary unit of analysis. Finally, tests were especially numerous and they allowed us to compare effect sizes for such detailed factors as specific measures of contact and prejudice. But multiple tests reported for a single sample violate assumptions of independence. Therefore, we used tests as our unit of analysis only when necessary.[6]

For each category of effect sizes, we calculated the weighted mean effect size. The homogeneity of each set of effect sizes was examined by calculating the homogeneity statistic Q, which has an approximate chi-square distribution with k-1 degrees of freedom, where k is the number of effect sizes (Hedges & Olkin, 1985).

INITIAL RESULTS

Does Intergroup Contact Relate to Prejudice?

Figure 5.1 illustrates the inverse association between intergroup contact and prejudice for all studies, samples, and tests. Note that the mean estimates that were weighted for sample size were smaller than the unweighted mean estimates. This difference indicates that the less reliable studies with smaller num-

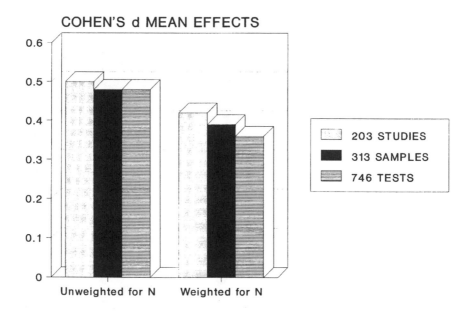

FIG. 5.1. Negative mean effect sizes for intergroup contact and prejudice.

bers of subjects yielded higher mean effect sizes. Consequently, as a conservative procedure, throughout the remainder of our analyses we employed only effect size estimates that were weighted for sample size.

The weighted mean estimate for the contact–prejudice effect size among the 203 studies was a Cohen's d of -.42 (or a mean r of -.20). For the 314 samples, the mean d was -.39 (r = -.19); and for the 746 tests, the mean d was -.36 (r = -.17). Thus, the initial answer to our query is that intergroup contact generally does relate negatively to prejudice.

Though in most empirical contexts this effect size would be considered "small" to "medium" in magnitude (Cohen, 1977, p. 25), several relevant points must be considered. First, given the large number of studies, the effect was highly significant (Z = -70.1, p <.0000001). Second, the effect sizes shown in Figure 5.1 were all enormously heterogeneous (p <.0001). Indeed, even when the one-fifth of the studies, samples, and tests that were the largest outliers were removed, significant heterogeneity remained. Such great heterogeneity is, of course, precisely what intergroup contact theory predicts. These 203 studies were highly diverse as to subjects, targets, measures, and situational variables—all of which are potential moderators and mediators of the link between contact and prejudice. As with most meta-analyses, the basic thrust of our analysis is not the gross effect sizes, but rather the mediating variables that suggest when, how, and why intergroup contact does or does not reduce prejudice. Before we turn to this topic, however, we first must explore several alternative explanations for the findings shown in Figure 5.1.

The Causal Sequence Problem

Potential selection bias limits the interpretation of many studies of intergroup contact and consequently the effects shown in Figure 5.1 (Pettigrew, 1998b). Instead of optimal contact reducing prejudice, the opposite causal sequence could be operating. That is, prejudiced people may avoid contact with outgroups. Three basic methods can overcome this limitation.[7]

1. Longitudinal designs offer the best approach. Yet such research is rare in intergroup research—with Sherif's (1966) Robbers' Cave study being a striking exception. This famous study revealed optimal contact as the cause of reduced prejudice while eliminating the possibility of selection bias.

2. Statistical methods borrowed from econometrics allow researchers to compare the reciprocal paths (contact lowers prejudice versus prejudice decreases contact), using cross-sectional data. As in other research (Herek & Capitanio, 1996), these methods reveal that prejudiced people do indeed avoid intergroup contact. But the path from contact to reduced prejudice is even stronger (Pettigrew, 1997; Powers & Ellison, 1995). Thus, these methods suggest that, while both sequences operate, the more important effect is intergroup contact reducing prejudice.

3. A final method consists of finding intergroup situations that severely limit choice. By eliminating the possibility that initial attitudes caused differential contact, such research provides a clearer indication of how intergroup contact alters prejudice. We were able to use this method by rating the degree of choice available to each study's participants as to whether or not to engage in intergroup contact. Figure 5.2 provides the results.

Surprisingly, the no-choice studies ($N = 30$) and samples ($N = 44$) provided by far the largest effect sizes between intergroup contact and prejudice. These mean *d*'s of -.72 and -.69 approach the size that is usually considered a "large" effect (Cohen, 1977, p. 25). More in line with expectations, the full-choice studies ($N = 105$) and samples ($N = 166$) yielded larger mean negative effect sizes than those studies ($N = 65$) and samples ($N = 98$) in which there was some limited choice for the subjects to interact with the outgroup. All comparisons between the three types of studies and samples were highly significant (p <.0000001).

Why would the studies that allowed no choice of contact yield higher average negative effect sizes? At least three explanations arise. First, this subset of 30 studies tended to be of somewhat higher quality than the other studies—containing more experiments and better controls.[8] But these differences alone are only part of the answer.

Two additional and interrelated possible explanations are: fewer ceiling effects and more cognitive dissonance. No-choice contact situations necessarily involve a wider range of initial prejudice scores, and thus they are less constrained by ceiling effects than are choice situations. In other words, no-choice contact settings allow for potentially greater prejudice reduction. Moreover, if the

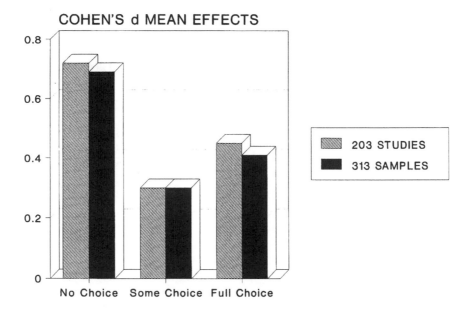

FIG. 5.2. Negative mean effect sizes for contact and prejudice by level of choice.

contact occurs under optimal conditions, initially prejudiced individuals in no-choice situations should experience considerably greater cognitive dissonance than less prejudiced ones. That is, their prior bigotry and present intergroup behavior are in conflict, and this dissonance sets the scene for potentially greater reduction in prejudice. In any event, in agreement with other methods, these data indicate that contact as the cause of reduced prejudice is more important than the selection-bias possibility that prejudiced people avoid contact.

The File Drawer Problem

A second threat to our interpretation of Figure 5.1's basic results pertains to the "file drawer problem" that besets all literature reviews (Rosenthal, 1991, pp. 103-109). It holds that reviews of all types suffer from a retrieval bias. Published studies may form a biased subset of the relevant studies actually conducted, because the statistical significance of a study's results may influence its probability of being published. Hence, studies with large effects may typically be published while studies with small effects may go unpublished. In turn, reviews may over-estimate effect sizes since they rely largely on published work.

Two sets of data suggest that this issue did not seriously bias the present results. First, following Rosenthal (1991), we calculated fail-safe indices. These in dices reveal how many missing studies and samples having no relationship whatsoever between contact and prejudice ($Z = .00$) would be required to raise the significance levels above the .05 level of confidence. For the results shown in Figure 5.1, 1,604 studies and 1,251 samples with no effects would be required to erase the significance of the association between intergroup contact and prejudice.

Also, we compared the negative mean effect sizes between intergroup contact and prejudice for studies and samples from three types of publications—journal articles, books, and unpublished work (73% of which were unpublished doctoral dissertations). For both studies and samples, the three types differed significantly in their negative effect sizes. Books yielded the smallest mean effect size. But the findings from unpublished studies were not what the file drawer bias would predict. The 11 studies and 20 samples whose results had not been published actually had the largest mean effects (studies: $d = -.52$, $r = -.25$; samples: $d = -.51$, $r = -.25$). Thus, the potential file drawer selection bias does not appear to threaten the present results.

The Generalization of Effects Problem

A third issue raised by Figure 5.1's summary results concerns the generalization problem—an issue not directly addressed by Allport (1954; Pettigrew, 1998b). It is possible that these gross results mask contrasting effects at different levels of generalization. Critics of intergroup contact theory generally concede that intergroup contact often leads to improved attitudes among the participants. But the critical question is whether these altered attitudes generalize to new situations, to the entire outgroup, or even to outgroups not involved in the contact (Pettigrew, 1998b).

With few exceptions (e.g., Nesdale & Todd, 1998), research has not focused on the generalization of effects to different situations. Of the 746 tests in our meta-analysis, 124 of them examined effects solely involving the participants in the contact. Their average d was -.31 ($r = -.15$). Most of the tests concerned generalized effects of reduced prejudice toward the entire outgroup. These 519 tests yielded an average d of -.34 ($r = -.17$)—slightly *higher* than the ungeneralized effects ($p < .025$). Fourteen additional tests checked on contact effects on prejudice toward outgroups *not* involved in the contact.[9] This rarely considered form of generalization also occurred (mean $d = -.34$; $r = -.17$), and these tests formed a homogeneous subset. Quite contrary to current theory, then, these data suggest a far wider generalization of contact effects than commonly thought. Indeed, there appears to be a sharp disconnection between the theory on this subject and the relevant research over recent decades.

PREDICTORS OF THE STRENGTH OF RELATIONSHIP
BETWEEN INTERGROUP CONTACT AND PREJUDICE

Participant Predictors

The age of participants was unrelated to the contact–prejudice link. Children, adolescents, college students, and adults all displayed similar average effect sizes across samples (mean ds ranged from -.37 to -.40), although there was great heterogeneity within each age category. Similarly, the national origin of the research was minimally related to effect sizes. The 149 American and 7 South African studies provided the highest average ds (-.43), followed by 10 studies from Australia, Canada, and New Zealand (mean d = -.40), 20 European studies (mean d = -.35), 9 studies from developing countries (e.g., Bangladesh, India, Zambia, Zimbabwe; mean d = -.33), and 8 Israeli samples (mean d = -.31).

However, as Figure 5.3 shows, minority versus majority-group status proved to be important. The 14 studies with only minority participants rendered a mean d of only -.29, compared with -.45 for the 139 studies with only majority participants. Similarly, the 64 minority samples obtained a mean effect (mean d = -.27, r = -.13) far below that of the 226 majority samples (mean d = -.46, r = -.22).[10] These sharp discrepancies invite speculation. In future work, we shall test the possibility that minority and majority group members often have divergent perceptions of such critical situational conditions as equal status.

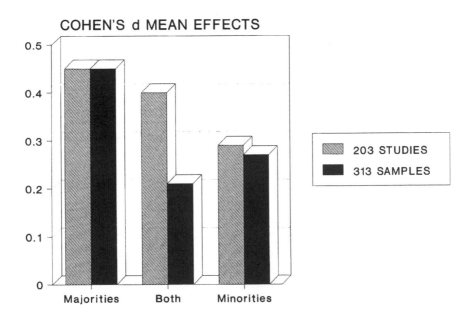

FIG. 5.3. Negative mean effect sizes for contact and prejudice by group status.

Study Predictors

Numerous research characteristics were related to the magnitude of the effects between contact and prejudice. Sample size was negatively related; larger samples, usually from surveys, tended to produce smaller effects (p <.000001). The date of the study was curvilinearly related. The 39 samples tested prior to 1960 (mean d = -.49, r = -.24) and the 83 samples studied during the 1990s (mean d = -.59, r = -.28) both yielded significantly larger mean effects than those measured during the 1960s, 1970s, and 1980s (mean ds ranged from -.30 to -.32).

Samples tested with within-subjects designs (i.e., 1-group pre-post comparisons) produced smaller effects (mean d = -.36, r = -.18) than those with between-group designs (i.e., experimental vs. control group comparisons; mean d = -.43, r = -.21). While this difference was not large, it was highly significant (p <.000001). Moreover, the 12 experiments typically yielded strong effects (mean d = -.77, r = -.36). But there were no significant differences between samples that used surveys, quasi-experiments, and research in natural settings utilizing interviews and observation (mean ds ranged from -.38 to -.40).

The type and quality of measures for both the independent and dependent variables also shaped the effect sizes. Figure 5.4 shows that when the contact was directly observed (mean d = -.48, r = -.23), the effects were significantly larger than when it was reported by the participants (mean d = -.38, r = -.18) or assumed by the investigators (mean d = -.38, r = -.19).

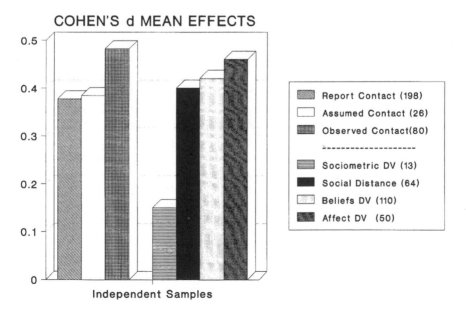

FIG. 5.4. Negative mean effect sizes for contact and prejudice by IV and DV types across independent samples.

Figure 5.4 also shows major differences in effect sizes for contrasting types of prejudice measures across samples. In addition, more detailed analyses using individual tests revealed the same trends. Samples tested with measures of affect (mean d = -.47, r = -.23) and belief (mean d = -.42, r = -.20) yielded significantly stronger effects than other measures. The affect dependent variables included items on strong emotions, favorability, and the evaluative dimension of the semantic differential scale. Moreover, the stronger the affect measured, the larger was the mean effect: for the 15 samples with strong emotions, mean d = -.54; for the 27 samples with favorability ratings, mean d = -.45; and for the 6 samples with evaluative semantic differential scores, mean d = -.42. The importance of beliefs was the original emphasis of intergroup contact theory, while the importance of affect is a more recent emphasis (Pettigrew, 1997, 1998b; Stephan & Stephan, 1985).

Social distance measures, mostly versions of Bogardus-like instruments, also provided substantial effect sizes (mean d = -.40, r = -.20). Samples that utilized sociometric choice as dependent variables typically showed small effects (mean d = -.15, r = -.07).[11] Not shown in Figure 5.4 are the results of samples using stereotypes as dependent variables. Overall, these samples provided a small average effect size (mean d = -.22, r = -.11), but this masked a sharp difference due to measurement. The 36 samples that used direct indicators of group stereotypes displayed meaningful effects (mean d = -.41, r = -.20). By contrast, the 23 samples that employed a semantic differential test of stereotypes provided the only instance in our analysis where intergroup contact was on average associated with *greater* negativity toward the outgroup (d = +.08, r = +.04). Yet the evaluative factor of the semantic differential measure (part of the affect category) yielded a sizable mean effect (mean d = -.42). These results suggest that semantic differential items from Osgood, Suci, and Tannenbaum's (1957) potency and activity factors are questionable measures of stereotypes.

Figure 5.5 presents the findings on the quality ratings of the contact and prejudice indicators across the 313 samples. For independent variables, multiple-item measures having adequate reliabilities (alphas at least .70) produced significantly larger effect sizes (mean d = -.70; N = 18) than did multiple-item measures with lower or unknown reliabilities (mean d = -.30; N = 80). Similarly, for dependent variables, multiple-item measures with adequate reliabilities also displayed significantly larger effect sizes (mean d = -.50; N = 90) than did multiple-item measures with low or unknown reliabilities (mean d = -.32; N = 183).

Indeed, single-item indicators of both contact (N = 87) and prejudice (N = 20)—which seldom tapped stereotypes—led to significantly stronger effects than the multiple-item measures of dubious reliability. Finally, the "other" categories in Figure 5.5—which refer to experimental measures of contact or to dependent-variable ratings with high rater reliability—as expected, displayed larger mean effects (respectively, mean d = -.59; N = 32; and mean d = -.58; N = 12).

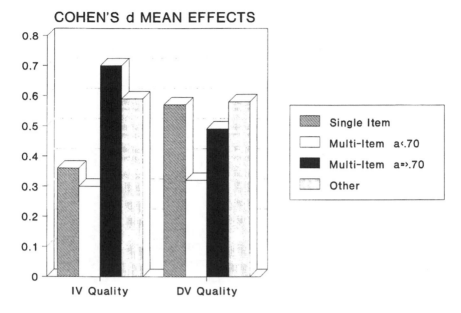

FIG. 5.5. Negative mean effect sizes for contact and prejudice by IV and DV quality across independent samples.

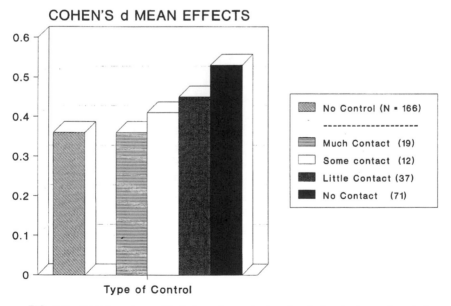

FIG. 5.6. Negative mean effect sizes for contact and prejudice by type of control across independent sample.

The final study predictor concerns control groups. In addition to the frequent absence of control groups in this research literature, we noted that many of the control groups themselves had some degree of contact with the outgroup. Figure 5.6 reveals how this influenced the effect sizes. Samples without control groups provided the smallest mean effects ($d = -.36$, $r = -.18$). And among those with control groups, the less contact the control group had with the outgroup, the larger were the mean effect sizes ($ds = -.36, -.41, -.45,$ and $-.53$).

In short, the study predictors indicate that greater research rigor leads to larger effect sizes. This general finding reassures us that the inverse association between intergroup contact and prejudice is a solid one, which becomes stronger as the research that tests it becomes stronger.

Situational Predictors

Additional predictors involve the contact situation. Figure 5.7 shows the average effect sizes for various contact settings. Investigations conducted in work and other organizational contexts achieved the largest effects across samples (mean $d = -.70$, $r = -.33$); and those conducted in the laboratory and in mixed settings

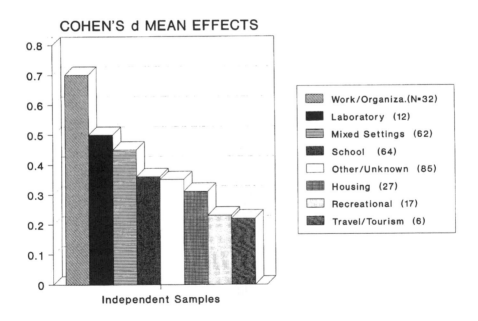

FIG. 5.7. Negative mean effect sizes for contact and prejudice by contact setting across independent samples.

also obtained larger than average effects (mean ds = -.49 and -.45). By contrast, samples studied in recreational and travel contexts had significantly lower effect sizes (mean ds = -.23 and -.22). There are probably differences in both intensity and duration of contact between these types of settings. And the contrasting effects also may reflect Allport's fourth condition for optimal intergroup contact– authority sanction. Organizational settings may benefit from explicit authority support, while recreational and travel settings may not. We plan to investigate this possibility further.

Figure 5.8 presents the mean effect sizes for the many types of outgroups studied in the contact literature. Easily the largest effects were those found for the 27 samples whose attitudes toward gay men and lesbians improved after contact (mean d = -.56, r = -.27). The most-studied outgroups, ethnic and racial ones, provided the next-largest average effect size (mean d = -.41, r = -.20), whereas contact studies with other outgroups attained below-average effects. The research literatures on contact with the disabled and the elderly are relatively recent. These studies involved such issues as "mainstreaming" disabled children in school classrooms with non-disabled students, and giving young children systematic contact with the elderly.

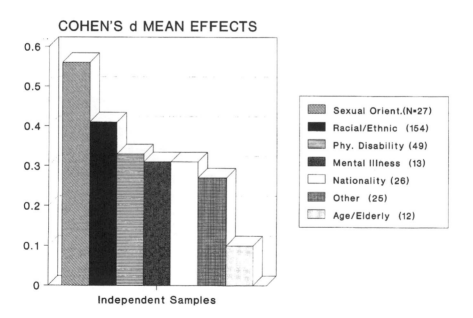

FIG. 5.8. Negative mean effect sizes for contact and prejudice by type of outgroup across independent samples.

GLOBAL MODELS

Intergroup Friendship

As a broader means of testing Allport's theory, we inspected just those tests that used intergroup friends as the contact measure. Here we assumed that friendship requires the operation of conditions that approach Allport's specifications for optimal contact. For 64 tests, having outgroup friends was quite highly associated with less intergroup prejudice (mean $d = -.53$, $r = -.26$)—markedly more so than contact in the 680 tests that did not specify friendship (mean $d = -.32$, $r = -.16$; $p < .0000001$). Still, the 64 tests with friends did not form a homogeneous subset. To attain homogeneity, 25 tests (39%) had to be removed. But, when finally attained, this homogeneous subset of 39 tests yielded essentially the same mean d (-.52).

Structured Optimal Contact

Another global predictor involves whether the intergroup contact consisted of a structured program that maximized most or all of Allport's optimal conditions for reducing prejudice. Consistent with Allport's contentions, the 44 samples with optimal contact conditions yielded significantly higher reductions of prejudice (mean $d = -.60$) than did other samples (mean $d = -.38$; $\chi 2 = 37.4$, $p < .0000001$). Moreover, these samples provided consistent effects. Their effect sizes became homogeneous after six outliers (14%) were trimmed; and the average effect size for these 38 samples comprising 2,200 subjects remained significantly larger ($d = -.57$, $r = -.27$) than that for samples experiencing unstructured contact ($\chi 2 = 16.5$, $p < .00005$).

Is this result largely a function of Allport's optimal conditions? Or does it merely reflect other aspects of this subset of contact studies? It is true that the homogeneous subset of 38 programmed samples contained mostly majority samples, and in all but one the contact was directly observed. These characteristics, we noted earlier, are associated with larger effects. But these features cannot account for the large mean effect. Moreover, this special subset of 38 samples included a wide variety of targets and settings.[12]

THEORETICAL AND EMPIRICAL IMPLICATIONS

When all relevant studies that can be attained have been collected, we shall construct both categorical and continuous models of the link between intergroup contact and prejudice. Yet even at this preliminary stage of analysis, robust trends have emerged that hold significant theoretical and empirical implications. Seven points deserve emphasis.

1. *Overall, face-to-face interaction between members of distinguishable groups is importantly related to reduced prejudice.* Of the 203 studies, 94% found an inverse relationship between contact and prejudice. This basic finding is consistent with other, more general formulations of familiarity, such as those of Homans (1950) and Zajonc (1968). Further, this solid link cannot be explained by selection and retrieval biases. Bigoted people do avoid contact with the scorned outgroup, but the causal sequence from contact to diminished prejudice is stronger (Pettigrew, 1997). In fact, the mean effect size of research which studied intergroup contact situations that eliminated choice was significantly larger than that of other research.

Two different assessments make it unlikely that a publishing bias for significant results accounts for the significant inverse relationship between contact and prejudice. In addition to large fail-safe indices, our meta-analytic data found the largest average effect size for unpublished work. Consequently, we conclude that subjective reviews that have cast doubt on contact theory were too restricted in their coverage.

2. *The association between contact and reduced prejudice casts a wide net of generalization.* Few studies have tested the generalization of effects across different situations, but most of the relevant research has firmly demonstrated the generalization of effects from immediate participants to the entire outgroups. Indeed, a few studies show significant generalization of effects to outgroups not even involved in the contact. These robust results conflict with the theoretical criticism of contact theory that holds that generalization to the group level is unlikely and rare. In later work, we shall pursue this issue further. At present, we suspect that these critiques are correct from a strictly cognitive perspective, but fail to consider the central role of affect in the generalization process.

3. *One major mediator of the size of contact–prejudice effects involves whether the participants are from a majority group or a stigmatized minority group.* Majority participants reveal much larger mean effects than do minority participants. This strong result indicates that we should regard contact theory's specified optimal conditions not as intrinsic features of the situation itself, but rather as conditions that can be perceived in contrasting ways by members of the interacting groups. Equal status in the situation, for example, may be perceived by majority group members in situations where many minority group members perceive group status to be unequal.

4. *The more rigorous the study, the larger the negative contact–prejudice effects.* Research employing control groups with no outgroup contact, experimental designs, and more reliable measures of both the independent and dependent variables all yielded larger mean effects. This consistent finding lends further credence to contact theory.

5. *Intergroup contact relates to a wide range of prejudice measures.* Early versions of contact theory concentrated on such cognitive effects as learning more about the outgroup and altering biased beliefs and stereotypes. But our

meta-analytic results suggest that the changes wrought by optimal contact are much broader. While belief, social distance, and stereotype measures showed changes, affective indicators revealed especially large effects. Affect has gained greater attention by contact researchers in recent years, just as it has in many areas of psychology. These results strongly suggest that this is a fruitful direction for further empirical and theoretical work.

6. *The outgroup that is involved influences the size of the negative contact–prejudice effects.* Contact appears to have different effects with different types of outgroups. Contact with homosexuals, for instance, produced, on average, large effects, while contact with the disabled yielded smaller effects. These sharp differences suggest that different dynamics are involved—perhaps both in the nature of these prejudices and in the typical types of contact with these groups.

7. *Global indicators of Allport's optimal conditions lead to relatively large effect sizes between contact and prejudice.* Intergroup friendship implies Allport's key conditions; it also implies long-term contact over a variety of settings. Thus, when investigators employed intergroup friendship as their indicator of contact, the mean effect size was considerably larger. Moreover, those samples that experienced carefully structured intergroup contact situations that met most or all of the optimal conditions achieved a markedly higher mean effect size than other samples. And, after minor trimming of extreme outliers, these samples provided one of the few homogeneous subsets in our analysis. Further use of, and research on, such carefully structured contact situations is strongly indicated.

IMPLICATIONS FOR REDUCING PREJUDICE

These meta-analytic data support the contention that optimal intergroup contact should be a critical component of any successful effort to reduce prejudice. Our findings suggest six points relevant to the practical problem of achieving optimal contact.

1. Programs to reduce prejudice should be carefully structured to incorporate Allport's four key situational conditions and to foster cross-group friendship.

2. But Allport's conditions must not be viewed as simply abstract features of a particular intergroup context. The perspectives of both groups—especially that of lower-status groups—must be carefully considered in fashioning the optimally structured contact situation.

3. Optimal intergroup contact has the potential to improve a variety of the components of prejudice—affect, beliefs, social distance, and stereotypes. Thus, structured contact should not focus on just one or two of these components, as many informational programs do. Of special importance is the power of optimal intergroup contact to influence affect—a realm often untouched by less intrusive remedies for prejudice.

4. Contact in work and organizational settings has far stronger effects than those typical of travel and tourism settings. This consistent finding probably re-

flects differences in the length and intensity of contact as well as whether the contact is sanctioned by an authority. Yet intergroup contact through travel is often cited as a major remedy for prejudice and provincialism. Our results do not support such claims for the types of travel that have been most studied.

5. The smaller effect sizes of contact that were found for reducing prejudice against the elderly and the disabled underline the importance of creating situations that counter prevailing negative stereotypes. In contrast, several studies in our review involved brief contact with severely senile or handicapped groups. Not surprisingly, such contact reinforced fears and stereotypes and did not reduce prejudice.

6. But how can we create optimal contact situations? This is the point where social psychology and sociology meet. Social-structural changes in our institutions are necessary to provide opportunities for optimal intergroup contact on a scale sweeping enough to make a societal difference. Such changes are typically resisted by powerful majorities. As one example, American university campuses, with their revival of intergroup conflict and discrimination in recent years, illustrate what can happen when institutions do not make the necessary structural changes to adapt to a more diverse community (Pettigrew, 1998a). By contrast, despite some distressing instances of racism, many intergroup situations in the United States Army show what can be achieved when an institution is willing to make the systematic structural alterations that are necessary for optimal intergroup contact to become a routine way of life within the institution (Moscos & Butler, 1996).

NOTES

1. This research was supported by the National Science Foundation (SBR-9709519) with the first author and Stephen Wright as co-investigators. For their invaluable assistance we are indebted to Wright and to our dedicated research assistants over the past two years: Rebecca Boice, Kimberly Lincoln, Peter Moore, Danielle Murray, Neal Nakano, Rajindra Samra, and Amanda Stout. We are grateful for the persistent and competent help of the McHenry Library staff at U.C.S.C. in tracking down hundreds of relevant journal articles in a wide assortment of specialized journals. Particular thanks are also due to Professor Blair Johnson of Syracuse University for his helpful advice on using his DSTAT software. We also express our deep appreciation to the many researchers who answered our repeated queries. Professors Rupert Brown of the University of Kent, Samuel Gaertner of the University of Delaware, Miles Houston of the University of Wales, Jean Phinney of California State University at Los Angeles, and Daniel Powers of the University of Texas were especially helpful, by digging into their old records to find the detailed data needed to compute effect sizes.

2. This basic point is often misunderstood. The erroneous notion that the hypothesis holds that intergroup contact "will of itself produce better relations between...groups" still appears in the literature (McGarty & de la Haye, 1997, p. 155; see also Ray, 1983).

3. The complete list of references used in the meta-analysis is available from the authors.

4. These searches used 42 different search terms that ranged from single words (e.g., "acculturation," "interracial") to combined terms (e.g., "age + intergroup contact," "disabled + contact"). Across the various databases, we conducted three types of searches with these terms—by "title words," "key words," and "subject."

5. Two independent judges made the ratings. The interrater agreement for the 16 rated variables ranged from 85% to 100%. The average agreement was 91.2% compared to a chance level of 28.3%. Thus, kappa = .88.

6. Those studies and samples with large numbers of tests tended to report smaller average effect sizes. This result suggests that using tests as the level of analysis in these data was a conservative method for estimating the strength of intergroup contact effects.

7. Innovative researchers have tried other ways to address the problem. Link and Cullen (1986), for example, compared intergroup contact that was chosen with contact that was not chosen. Irish (1952) tried a screening question and retained in his analysis only those subjects who reported that they had made no effort either to seek or to avoid contacts with the target group. Using national survey data, Wilson (1996) utilized a measure of diffuse prejudice toward many minorities as a proxy for the tendency to avoid contact. All three of these methods found that controlling for selection did not eliminate the link between intergroup contact and prejudice.

8. For example, 21 of the 30 studies directly observed the intergroup contact. We shall shortly see that this procedure on average, yields higher effect sizes.

9. Actually, 14 other tests—all from one study (Pettigrew, 1997)—also tested for this uninvolved-outgroup generalization and attained larger effects (mean d = -.69, r = -.33). But these tests are excluded here because they used "intergroup friends" as their contact measure, which we later note is an especially powerful independent variable.

10. "Majority" was defined in this context as the less stigmatized group. For example, in studies that measured the effects on children of having contact with the elderly, we considered the children as the "majority." This particular approach, however, is not artificially shaping the results shown in Figure 5.3. When we analyzed only the subset of samples involving racial, ethnic, and nationality groups, a slightly larger difference emerged: for the 61 all-minority samples, d = -.27; for the 124 all-majority samples, d = -.48.

11. This smaller effect size may reflect a recurrent problem in sociometric measurement. As Schofield and Whitley (1983) first pointed out, and was later replicated by Schwartzwald, Laor, and Hoffman (1986) in Israel, the nomination technique of asking for most-preferred classmates exaggerates intergroup cleavage. The rating method involving all classmates is more sensitive and reveals greater intergroup contact effects.

12. Thus, 18 of these samples provided no choice to their subjects, 10 gave some choice, and 10 gave full choice. Also, 11 of these special samples involved racial and ethnic groups, 9 disabilities, 6 age, and 3 mental illness. Their contact settings included 13 in schools, 8 in recreational areas, 7 in laboratories, and 4 in mixed settings.

REFERENCES

Allport, G. W. (1954). *The nature of prejudice*. Reading, MA: Addison-Wesley.
Amir, Y. (1976). The role of intergroup contact in change of prejudice and race relations. In P. Katz (Ed.), *Towards the elimination of racism* (pp. 245-308). New York: Pergamon.
Cohen, J. (1977). *Statistical power analysis for the behavioral sciences*. New York: Academic Press.

Cook, S. W. (1978). Interpersonal and attitudinal outcomes in cooperating interracial groups. *Journal of Research and Development in Education, 12,* 97-113.

Desforges, D. M., Lord, C. G., Ramsey, S. L., Mason, J. A., Van Leeuwen, M. D., West, S. C., & Lepper, M. R. (1991). Effects of structured cooperative contact on changing negative attitudes toward stigmatized social groups. *Journal of Personality and Social Psychology, 60,* 531-544.

Deutsch, M., & Collins, M. (1951). *Interracial housing: A psychological evaluation of a social experiment.* Minneapolis: University of Minnesota Press.

Drake, St. C., & Cayton, H. R. (1962). *Black metropolis.* (rev. ed., Vol. I.). New York: Harper & Row.

Fine, G. A. (1979). The Pinkston settlement: An historical and social psychological investigation of the contact hypothesis. *Phylon, 40,* 229-242.

Ford, R. N. (1941). Scaling experience by a multiple-response technique: A study of White-Negro contacts. *American Sociological Review, 6,* 9-23.

Ford, W. S. (1986). Favorable intergroup contact may not reduce prejudice: Inconclusive journal evidence, 1960-1984. *Sociology and Social Research, 70,* 256-258.

Hedges, L. V. (1994). Fixed effects models. In H. Cooper & L. V. Hedges (Eds.), *The handbook of research synthesis* (pp. 285-299). New York: Russell Sage Foundation.

Hedges, L. V., & Olkin, I. (1985). *Statistical methods for meta-analysis.* New York: Academic Press.

Herek, G. M., & Capitanio, J. P. (1996). "Some of my best friends": Intergroup contact, concealable stigma, and heterosexuals' attitudes toward gay men and lesbians. *Personality and Social Psychology Bulletin, 22,* 412-424.

Hewstone, M., & Brown. R. (Eds.). (1986). *Contact and conflict in intergroup encounters.* Oxford, UK: Blackwell.

Homans, G. C. (1950). *The human group.* New York: Harcourt, Brace & World.

Irish, D. P. (1952). Reactions of Caucasian residents to Japanese-American neighbors. *Journal of Social Issues, 8*(1), 10-17.

Johnson, B. T. (1989). *DSTAT: Software for the meta-analytic review of research literatures.* Hillsdale, NJ: Erlbaum.

Link, B. G., & Cullen, F. T. (1986). Contact with the mentally ill and perceptions of how dangerous they are. *Journal of Health and Social Behavior, 27,* 289-303.

McGarty, C., & de la Haye, A. M. (1997). Stereotype formation: Beyond illusory correlation. In R. Spears, P. J. Oakes, N. Ellemers, & S. A. Haslam (Eds.), *The social psychology of stereotyping and group life* (pp. 144-170). Oxford, UK: Blackwell.

Moscos, C. C., & Butler, J. S. (1996). *All that we can be: Black leadership and racial integration the army way.* New York: Basic Books.

Nesdale, D., & Todd, P. (1998). Intergroup ratio and the contact hypothesis. *Journal of Applied Social Psychology, 28,* 1196-1217.

Osgood, C. E., Suci, G. J., & Tannenbaum, P. H. (1957). *The measurement of meaning.* Urbana: University of Illinois Press.

Pettigrew, T. F. (1971). *Racially separate or together?* New York: McGraw-Hill.

Pettigrew, T. F. (1986). The contact hypothesis revisited. In H. Hewstone & R. Brown (Eds.), *Contact and conflict in intergroup encounters* (pp. 169-195). Oxford, UK: Blackwell.

Pettigrew, T. F. (1997). Generalized intergroup contact effects on prejudice. *Personality and Social Psychology Bulletin, 23,* 173-185.

Pettigrew, T. F. (1998a). Prejudice and discrimination on the college campus. In J. Eberhardt & S. T. Fiske (Eds.), *Confronting racism: The problem and the response* (pp. 263-279). Thousand Oaks, CA: Sage.

Pettigrew, T. F. (1998b). Intergroup contact theory. *Annual Review of Psychology, 49,* 65-85.

Powers, D. A., & Ellison, C. G. (1995). Interracial contact and Black racial attitudes: The contact hypothesis and selectivity bias. *Social Forces 74*, 205-226.

Raudenbush, S. W. (1994). Random effects models. In H. Cooper & L. V. Hedges (Eds.), *Handbook of research synthesis* (pp. 301-321). New York: Russell Sage Foundation.

Ray, J. J. (1983). Racial attitudes and the contact hypothesis. *Journal of Social Psychology, 119*, 3-10.

Riordan, C. (1978). Equal-status interracial contact: A review and revision of the concept. *International Journal of Intercultural Relations, 2*, 161-185.

Rose, T. L. (1981). Cognitive and dyadic processes in intergroup contact. In D. L. Hamilton (Ed.), *Cognitive processes in stereotyping and intergroup behavior* (pp. 145-181). Hillsdale, NJ: Erlbaum.

Rosenthal, R. (1991). *Meta-analytic procedures for social research* (rev. ed.). Newbury Park, CA: Sage.

Rosenthal, R. (1995). Writing meta-analytic reviews. *Psychological Bulletin, 118*, 183-192.

Rothbart, M., & John, O. P. (1985). Social categorization and behavioral episodes: A cognitive analysis of the effects of intergroup contact. *Journal of Social Issues, 41*(3), 81-104.

Schofield, J. W., & Whitley, B. E., Jr. (1983). Peer nomination vs. rating scale measurement of children's peer preferences. *Social Psychology Quarterly, 46*, 242-251.

Schwartzwald, J., Laor, T., & Hoffman, M. (1986). Impact of sociometric method and activity content on assessment of intergroup relations in the classroom. *British Journal of Educational Psychology, 56*, 24-31.

Sherif, M. (1966). *In common predicament.* Boston: Houghton Mifflin.

Stephan, W. G. (1987). The contact hypothesis in intergroup relations. In C. Hendrick (Ed.), *Review of personality and social psychology: Group processes and intergroup relations* (Vol. 9, pp. 13-40). Newbury Park, CA: Sage.

Stephan, W. G., & Stephan, C. W. (1984). The role of ignorance in intergroup relations. In N. Miller & M. B. Brewer (Eds.), *Groups in contact: The psychology of desegregation* (pp. 229-256). Orlando, FL: Academic Press.

Stephan, W. G., & Stephan, C. W. (1985). Intergroup anxiety. *Journal of Social Issues, 41*(3), 157-175.

Taft, R. (1959). Ethnic stereotypes, attitudes, and familiarity: Australia. *Journal of Social Psychology, 49*, 177-186.

Weigel, R. H., & Howes, P. W. (1985). Conceptions of racial prejudice. *Journal of Social Issues, 41*(3), 117-138.

Williams, R. M., Jr. (1947). *The reduction of intergroup tensions.* New York: Social Science Research Council.

Wilson, T. C. (1996). Prejudice reduction or self-selection? A test of the contact hypothesis. *Sociological Spectrum, 16*, 43-60.

Zajonc, R. B. (1968). Attitudinal effects of mere exposure. *Journal of Personality and Social Psychology, 9* (Monograph supplement, No. 2, part 2), 1-27.

6 Interdependence and the Reduction of Prejudice

Susan T. Fiske
University of Massachusetts at Amherst

A national retail chain, known for warehouse merchandising, employed roughly 90% men as its sales force and roughly 90% women as its cashiers. Sales positions pay better and lead to managerial positions. When women brought a class action suit against the company, it came to light that qualified women were ignored or discouraged for sales positions. Given the ethnic diversity of the company's customer base, management had worked actively to recruit more ethnic diversity into its sales force. However, the company's customer base was about evenly split between men and women, but the company failed to recognize that its economic dependence on women similarly suggested gender integration of its sales associates. Recognizing and building on economic interdependence would have created more successful contacts between genders in its sales efforts.

Similarly, during school desegregation programs of the mid-century, exponents of intergroup contact, following Gordon Allport's (1954) lead, concluded that necessary conditions included equal-status, authority-sanctioned, and common-goal interdependence. Building on interdependence was essential for successful intergroup contact. When two previously segregated groups collide, successful interaction requires that they recognize their mutual need for each other.

I and my colleagues' research addresses the psychology of interdependence—that is, how needing another person (who happens to come from an outgroup) creates the conditions for seeing that person as an individual and an ally. Our research over the last 20 years underscores the interplay between macro, social-relations analyses and micro, social-cognition analyses, in explaining the individual psychology that underlies successful intergroup contact.

SOCIAL RELATIONS INFLUENCE SOCIAL COGNITION

Social cognition, the way people think about other people, is conditioned on its emphatically interpersonal context, according to a range of theorists from Bruner and Tagiuri (1954) onwards (Heider, 1958; Higgins, Kuiper, & Olson, 1981; Krauss, 1981; Schneider, Hastorf, & Ellsworth, 1979; Tagiuri & Petrullo, 1958; for a review, see Fiske & Taylor, 1991). When people think about other people, including outgroup members, they hold a complex naive theory that includes the following beliefs: (a) People cause events—most of the meaningful and important episodes in our lives are initiated and influenced by the behavior of others. (b) People's dispositions predict their behavior—personality, attitudes, and other stable internal predispositions predict their actions (which in turn cause events that matter to us). (c) People cohere as entities—people's dispositions are internally consistent, so discrepancies invite cognitive resolution, in the service of perceived consistency and prediction of behavior and important events. (d) Accuracy matters—if people's coherent dispositions cause important events, then we will struggle to understand those people who affect us; and in particular, we will focus on any disturbing discrepancies.

Given the acknowledged importance of understanding others, how do people attempt to do so, especially to understand their inconsistencies? Social cognition, according to the Continuum Model (Fiske & Neuberg, 1990; see Fiske, Lin, & Neuberg, 1999, for an update), relies on a series of processes, ranging from initial categorization to the fuller incorporation of other individuating attributes. People prioritize categories such as gender, age, and race, using them initially and automatically, particularly to classify people who matter little to them (for a review of automaticity in stereotyping, see Fiske, 1998). Two major factors move perceivers from the category-based (e.g., race-based) to the attribute-based (i.e., individual trait-based) end of the continuum. These catalyzing factors are information and motivation. If the initial stereotypic category, on closer inspection, simply fails to fit information about other accompanying attributes (appearance, personality, attitudes, roles, behavior), then impressions result from a combination of category and attributes. Attention—to the attributes that go beyond the category—is necessary as a mediator of perceived fit. This is a key process. Because, on careful scrutiny, few people exactly match their group's stereotype, attention promotes individuation.

More relevant here, motivation also affects the continuum, in three primary ways. First, motivation can stem from the self, as when a person's values dictate careful decision-making that goes beyond stereotypic categories (Fiske & Von Hendy, 1992). When their egalitarian values are salient, people scrutinize another person carefully. Second, motivation can likewise stem from third parties, to whom the perceiver is accountable (Lerner & Tetlock, 1999). In situations of accountability to third parties with unknown values, people scrutinize and use more information. Finally, motivation can stem from the other person, the person being perceived. That is, the relationship between two people may matter, in which case, again, perceivers should be more careful and thorough. In all three cases, attention to additional information beyond the initial category mediates the effects of motivation on a perceiver's use of the continuum of category-to-attribute impression formation.

Our research has focused on one kind of relationship with the other person—namely interdependence. Defined as outcome contingency (e.g., Kelley & Thibaut, 1978; Thibaut & Kelley, 1959), interdependence simply means that people need each other to achieve goals that matter. Interdependence is the core fact of social life: It glues together dyadic relationships (Kelley et al., 1983), defines psychological groups (Forsyth, 1990), structures organizations (Pfeffer, 1998), predicts the content of group stereotypes (Fiske, Xu, Cuddy, & Glick, in press), and determines intergroup relations (Brewer & Brown, 1998). In all these domains, who depends on whom determines who attends to whom. Having outcomes contingent on another person motivates understanding that other person, in the service of prediction and control. An implication of this is that more attention is directed up the hierarchy in organizations, as each person attends to people at the next level up—those who control their outcomes. Bosses receive more individuating attention than subordinates do.

HYPOTHESIZED INTERDEPENDENCE EFFECTS

From the principles of interdependence and from the naive theories of social perceivers, several clear-cut hypotheses follow. Outcome dependency predicts (a) attention to inconsistent attributes. That is, with heightened motivation to understand another person, in order to predict and possibly control one's own outcomes, a perceiver will attend to additional information beyond initial category membership. Moreover, attention will be directed to the most informative attributes, namely those that contradict the stereotypic category. Two other kinds of information would be less useful: Irrelevant information certainly is not diagnostic, and consistent information is not especially diagnostic, in that it may reinforce the category but not contradict it. Inconsistent information potentially threatens the category membership classification, and therefore the perceived coherence of the other person, disrupting a sense of accuracy. Hence, motivated perceivers will selectively focus on category-inconsistent, counter-stereotypic attributes. They will try to understand what sets this person apart from other people in that race, gender, or age category.

Outcome dependency predicts also that (b) people will make dispositional inferences about category-inconsistent attributes. Having attended to inconsistent, counter-stereotypic information, motivated people will attempt to make coherent sense of the other person by incorporating the inconsistencies into a unified personality impression. The dispositional inferences provide the possibility of prediction, influence, and even control over outcomes influenced by the other person. They also serve to individuate the other person. If the category is contradicted, then a more specific impression will provide more sense of control.

From this, it follows that (c) evaluations of another person, upon whom the perceiver depends, will be driven more by individual attributes than will those of people irrelevant to the perceiver's outcomes. By these processes, then, interdependence provides the possibility of going beyond category-based stereotypes to more individually oriented impressions. Our program of research has focused on testing these hypotheses, thereby documenting the individual psychological processes that make interdependence work.

INDIVIDUAL-LEVEL INTERDEPENDENCE

Mutual Interdependence?

Our first foray into these hypotheses asked whether mutual outcome dependency indeed would create individuating processes of impression formation. In effect, we created a microcosm simulating real-world interdependence between people with category-based expectations about each other (Erber & Fiske, 1984). Explaining this paradigm in a little detail will illustrate the template for some of the following studies.

Undergraduate participants undertook to create educational games with wind-up toys, in collaboration with student teachers. The best games would win a cash prize, and the conditions of cooperation for the prize determined the degree of interdependence. All participants worked on ideas alone and then discussed ideas jointly with the student teacher. Half of the participants were eligible for the prize based on their solo work, in competition with other participants, but not with any of the student teachers, so they were independent of their partner. Half of the participants were eligible for the prize based on their joint work with the student teacher, in competition with other student-teacher/participant pairs; these participants thus were interdependent with their partner.

In the guise of obtaining information about their future partners, participants read their partner's expectations about his or her own performance on the task. The expectancy manipulation focused on a dimension prominent in the contents of most stereotypes, namely competence (Fiske, Xu, Cuddy, & Glick, in press). The student-teacher partner expected to do well or badly at the task of making up educational games, based on previous experiences.

Participants then read additional, more-specific attributes of the person, in the form of peer evaluations written about the student teacher. Each comment, written on a separate card, consisted of a trait adjective embedded in a single sentence, for example: "I think what impressed me most about your teaching style is that you presented the material quite thoroughly" or "I found the technique you used to be an inefficient means of conveying important concepts of the subject." Half of the comments fit an expectation of competence and half fit an expectation of incompetence. Because all participants received the same set of comments, all read comments that were mixed, half consistent and half inconsistent, with regard to their expectancy about their partner.

To test the three hypotheses, we measured, first, attention to consistent and inconsistent comments, by timing how long participants spent reading and thinking about each comment. (The experimenter concealed a stopwatch in each jacket pocket. Negative comment cards were written in blue ink and positive in black ink—or vice versa, half the time—so the experimenter could remain blind to the nature of the comments he or she was timing.)

We also measured dispositional inferences to each type of comment. In one study, we measured only attention, but in another one, we measured both attention and think-aloud protocols. In thinking aloud, participants voiced their reactions to each comment into a tape-recorder, and the transcribed comments were later coded for a variety of reactions, including dispositional inferences—that is, comments about enduring personality, attitudes, or skills.

Finally, participants evaluated their partner on an impression questionnaire that asked about initial liking and disliking responses.

The attention results nicely supported our first hypothesis (see Figure 6.1). Attention to inconsistent information was higher under cooperative interdependence than in the condition where participants were independent of each other. Attention to consistent information, in comparison, did not differ significantly. Outcome-dependent participants selectively focused on the most diagnostic, expectancy-inconsistent information, in accord with the attention hypothesis.

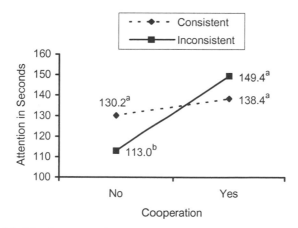

FIG. 6.1. Attention to consistent and inconsistent information as a function of one-on-one cooperative interdependence. Means not sharing a superscript differ at $p < .05$. Reprinted from Erber and Fiske (1984, p. 717) by permission of the publisher. Copyright 1984 by the American Psychological Association.

Results also supported the second hypothesis (see Figure 6.2). Dispositional inferences to expectancy-inconsistent information were higher for cooperatively interdependent participants, compared to independent participants. Dispositional inferences to consistent information did not differ significantly, nor did any other type of reaction to the partner information. Moreover, attention and dispositional inferences were correlated in the outcome dependency condition ($r = .61$, $p < .01$), but not in the independent condition ($r = .17$, ns)—a finding which is consistent with the idea that motivated attention enabled the dispositional inferences.

The third hypothesis—that, under interdependence, evaluations would be more individuated, that is, more attribute-based and less category-based—fared less well. The target person was liked moderately well, regardless of expectancy or outcome dependency. Nevertheless, we did have the impression from the protocol data that some participants were using the inconsistent attributes to contradict the expectancy, as predicted, whereas others were mangling their meaning and using them to justify the expectancy.

Two out of three hypotheses about mutual outcome dependency received ample support, showing that interdependence can create attentional vigilance and individuated dispositional thinking about one's partner. However, the evaluation results proved elusive. A subsequent study (Neuberg & Fiske, 1987) showed that both attention and evaluation changed as a function of interdependence. These effects were found in a situation where the supposed teacher belonged to a more extreme category—namely being a recently discharged schizophrenic, whom the participant met in the context of a "patient reintegration program," designed to help long-term hospitalized patients to practice social interactions.

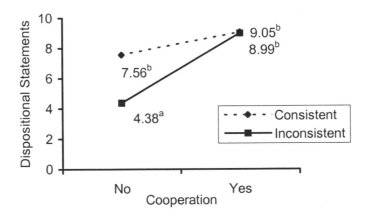

FIG. 6.2. Dispositional inferences to consistent and inconsistent information as a function of one-on-one cooperative interdependence. Means not sharing a superscript differ at $p < .05$. Reprinted from Erber and Fiske (1984, p. 717) by permission of the publisher. Copyright 1990 by the American Psychological Association.

Even Negative Interdependence?

Like earlier studies, both of the above studies had a flaw—they did not attempt to disentangle interdependence per se from cooperation. If the effects of interdependence spring from people needing to predict and possibly influence important outcomes controlled by other people, then any kind of correlated outcomes should produce the same effects. Under cooperative interdependence, one person's outcomes are positively correlated with the other's. But under competition—that is, negative interdependence—one person's outcomes are still correlated with the other's, although negatively. Under one-on-one competition, people should behave as they would under any kind of outcome dependency—selectively attend to expectancy-inconsistent information, make dispositional inferences about it, and evaluate their opponent accordingly. Note that these hypotheses, while congruent with our interdependence predictions, fly in the face of the intergroup contact hypothesis. Contact research specifies cooperative contact, not competitive contact, as a basis for over-riding stereotypes (for reviews, see Brewer & Brown, 1998; Pettigrew, 1998). Yet that research deals with group-on-group competition, in which one person's outcomes are only indirectly correlated with those of any other person from the outgroup, whereas our hypothesis deals with one-on-one competition, in which outcomes are directly (negatively) correlated. This difference turns out to matter.

In another experiment, using a similar cover story (Ruscher & Fiske, 1990), undergraduates expected to make up children's creativity games with wind-up toys, working simultaneously with another student. Half of the participants expected that their prize was contingent on creating the biggest gap between themselves and the other student (their opponent), compared to all the other pairs of opponents. The other half of the participants expected that their prize was contingent on performing better than all the other participants who had sat in their chair, and that likewise the other student had to beat all the other participants who had sat in his or her chair. Thus, in both cases, the participant was competing, but in one case against the target, and in the other case against unknowable other people.

The expectancy manipulation, as well as the consistent and inconsistent attributes, resembled those in the previous study, but a set of irrelevant attributes was added. Attention, think-aloud protocols, and evaluations were measured as before.

Results showed that, even under negative interdependence, outcome dependency produced greater attention to expectancy-inconsistent attributes, compared to no dependency, and this difference did not occur for the less-informative consistent or irrelevant attributes (see Figure 6.3). Thus, in the situation of one-on-one competition, the first hypothesis was confirmed. It is interdependence per se, not cooperation or teamwork, that underlies individuating attention.

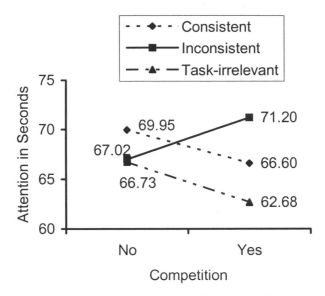

FIG. 6.3. Attention to consistent, inconsistent, and irrelevant information as a function of one-on-one competitive interdependence. A contrast ($p < .05$) indicated that competitors attended longer to inconsistent than consistent information, whereas noncompetitors did not. Reprinted from Ruscher & Fiske (1990, p. 839) by permission of the publisher. Copyright 1990 by the American Psychological Association.

Again, dispositional inferences mimicked the attention data, with a greater number of dispositional inferences being found to inconsistent attributes, but not to consistent or irrelevant attributes, under (negative) interdependence (Figure 6.4). Under competition, people tried to make sense of their opponents, in a coherent fashion.

Evaluations of the other student again showed no effect of interdependence on average ratings. However, interdependence did significantly increase the variability of the impression ratings. That is, when participants were not outcome-dependent on the target, their ratings tended to agree substantially (i.e., in the direction of the expectancy). But under competition, their ratings spread out more, becoming more idiosyncratic. Presumably some participants interpreted the inconsistency as contradicting the expectancy, whereas others used it to confirm the expectancy. This significant difference in homogeneity of variance, then, reflected individuation of a sort, though not exactly in the predicted form.

Overall, this study showed that one-on-one competition works exactly as does one-on-one cooperation, increasing attention and dispositional inferences to inconsistency, and apparently making impressions more idiosyncratic, if not explicitly less category-based (Ruscher & Fiske, 1990).

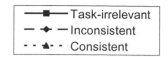

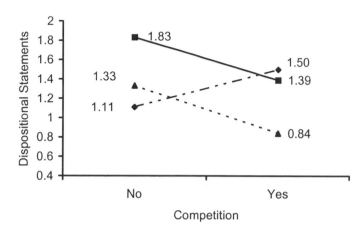

FIG. 6.4. Dispositional inferences to consistent, inconsistent, and irrelevant in-formation as a function of one-on-one competitive interdependence. A contrast ($p <$ .05) indicated that competitors made more dispositional inferences to inconsistent than consistent information, whereas noncompetitors did not. Reprinted from Ruscher and Fiske (1990, p. 839) by permission of the publisher. Copyright 1990 by the American Psychological Association.

Degrees of Asymmetrical Dependency?

Both sets of studies discussed so far possessed a confound. The effects of the perceiver's dependency on the target were not separated from the effects of the target's dependency on the perceiver. Logically, it is at least possible that the higher attention, dispositional inferences, and evaluation variability could result from perceivers realizing that the target is contingent on them, and feeling in-creased responsibility (although that argument is hard to make for competitive interdependence). If this logical alternative possibility were true, the psychology of interdependence would differ considerably from the portrait painted here—namely, impression formation motivated by needs for prediction and control over one's own outcomes. To address this confound, we designed studies in which participants depended on targets but not vice versa—that is, situations in which perceivers were relatively powerless (Dépret & Fiske, 1999). Moreover, we com-pared low and high dependency, because, if motivation is a function of out-come dependency, it should increase with degrees of increased dependency, not merely occur when dependency contrasts with no dependency.

In this study, participants expected to simulate working around noisy house-mates; they had to complete a mundane task (writing down multiples of 3, as fast and accurately as possible) in the presence of a set of distractor individuals who would "speak loudly to each other in order to distract you from your work." Participants who completed the most work were eligible for a cash prize. Under high dependency, in addition, the distractors could decide whether the participant had concentrated especially well, awarding extra points, or had been especially distracted, making the participant start over again. Thus, participants had different degrees of asymmetrical outcome dependency.

Before the alleged encounter with the distractors, participants had the opportunity to learn about one distractor, who happened to be an art major or a math major. These categories represented two outgroups for the psychology-major participants. Moreover, art- and math-major stereotypes complement each other (respectively, they are: creative, emotional, individualistic, and impulsive vs. studious, logical, traditional, and conventional). This meant that attributes consistent with the one were inconsistent with the other, a fact that was convenient for the experimental design. The attributes were presented in the context of sentences—for example, "I try to be very logical in all that I do." Participants' attention was registered on a hidden microphone that recorded the sounds of pages turning in a notebook, where a set sequence of consistent and inconsistent attributes was presented, one per page. Instead of using think-aloud protocols, we obtained their dispositional inferences as responses to the question, "According to you, what other personality characteristics may characterize this person?" Finally, in an attempt to fine-tune the impression ratings, we asked participants to rate their impressions not only of that one distractor, but also of the outgroup category (math or art) as a whole, as well as of the ingroup category (psychology students). This methodological decision was made on the conceptual grounds that many prejudice effects stem from ingroup favoritism, rather than outgroup derogation.

Our first two hypotheses again received support (Dépret & Fiske, 1999). Attention to expectancy-inconsistent information was greater in the condition with a greater degree of asymmetrical outcome dependency, but attention to consistent information did not differ across conditions. Similarly, dispositional inferences were higher as dependency increased (the dispositional measure that we used in this study did not distinguish between inferences based on consistent and inconsistent information). The third hypothesis, about evaluations of the distractor individuals, again proved to be unsupported, in this paradigm as well.

Finely-Tuned Evaluations Under Outcome Dependency

Feeling thoroughly frustrated with the contrast between the dependable findings for attention and dispositional inferences, on one hand, and the undependable findings for evaluations, on the other, we further calibrated the impression measures (Goodwin, Gubin, Fiske, & Yzerbyt, in press, Study 4). In this study, psychology majors arrived to participate in an unspecified joint task, in which half would serve as bosses and half as assistants, the assignment to be determined by a test of management aptitude. Bosses (who were not outcome-dependent) would be paid 6 lottery tickets, and during the task would "figure out what needs to be done and then implement it...be the leader." Assistants (who were outcome-dependent) could be paid 2 to 6 lottery tickets, depending on how well they and their boss together completed the task, so the boss partly controlled their chances of winning a cash prize. Expectancies once again were manipulated based on college majors, but in this case there were three, with simply non-overlapping stereotypes that nonetheless all differed from psychology—sociology, pre-medical, and early childhood education.

The new, improved impression measures, based on techniques used earlier in our lab (Fiske, Neuberg, Beattie, & Milberg, 1987; Pavelchak, 1989),were obtained as follows: At the session's outset, participants rated 24 academic majors and 46 personality traits on likability. During the experiment, each participant rated three stimulus people (a sociology, pre-med, and education major), each of whom was described with some consistent and some inconsistent traits. For example, the pre-med student was described by two consistent adjectives (self-disciplined, efficient) and two inconsistent adjectives (content, sociable). Given the prior ratings, we were able to compare each participant's rating of a target person with that participant's own prior rating of the target's category and own prior average rating of the target's attributes. The two primary dependent measures, then, were the correlation of the overall rating of the target with the rating of the category, and the correlation of the overall rating of the target with the average rating of the attributes—respectively indicating more category-based or individuating impressions. These correlations were compared under high and no outcome dependency. Given the complexity of the design, procedure, and measures, and the reliability of the results of previous studies, we decided to forgo measuring attention and dispositional inferences in this experiment.

Figure 6.5 shows that, as predicted, the outcome-dependent assistants based their impressions primarily on the attribute information and very little on the category information. In contrast, the bosses, who were not contingent, based their impressions on both, but slightly more on the category information. Thus, with a carefully calibrated measure, outcome dependency resulted in clearly more attribute-oriented impressions, in accord with our hypotheses.

Individual-Level Interdependence:
Summary and Implications for Prejudice Reduction

Our findings show that outcome dependency reliably predicts attention to expectancy-inconsistent attributes, dispositional inferences, and (if measured carefully) attribute-driven evaluations. These results hold robustly for one-on-one

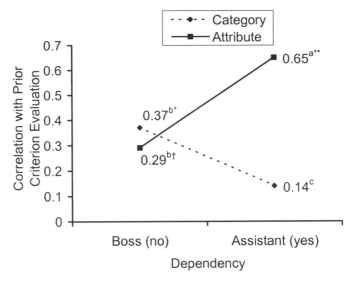

FIG. 6.5. Correlations of target evaluations with prior evaluations of their category and their attributes, as a function of asymmetrical dependency. Correlations not sharing a superscript differ at $p < .05$; correlations with additional marks differ from zero as follows: $^{t}p < .10.$ $^{*}p < .05.$ $^{***}p < .001.$ Source: Goodwin, Gubin, Fiske, and Yzerbyt (in press), *Group Processes and Intergroup Relations.* Reprinted by permission of Sage Publications, Inc.

dependence that is mutual and asymmetrical, dichotomous and graded, cooperative and competitive. These findings demonstrate an individual psychology underlying the success of the contact hypothesis. When individuals from mutual outgroups collide, if they must cooperate to achieve a common goal, they scrutinize each other more carefully than otherwise, making sense of each other as individual personalities, not ignoring the group-membership category, but still forming individuated impressions. The results fit a theory of motivated impressions—i.e., that individuals form impressions of others in a search for predictive ability and for potential control over their own outcomes.

Although our hypotheses pertain to all kinds of social categories, of which the Big Three (race, gender, and age) are of central interest, our research strategies have focused on more mundane types of categories: college majors, and competence versus incompetence. These categories appear in our research because college student participants are less reactive, less defensive, and more spontaneous in their use of these types of expectancies, compared to those involving race, gender, and age. However, when we have run studies that used more loaded categories, such as ethnicity or mental-patient status, the results have replicated.

Overall, for situations of individual-level interdependence, the implications for prejudice-reduction are straightforward. When individuals from mutual outgroups

encounter each other, they will be most likely to overcome their mutual stereotypes and prejudice if they need each other to accomplish some goal that matters
to them. Interventions that include that mainstay of intergroup contact, cooperation, work via three individual processes: attention, dispositional inferences, and
attribute-based impressions. If two people from mutual outgroups cooperate (or if
they compete, one-on-one), they will heed, interpret, and appreciate each other's
individual characteristics. They may or may not like each other, but at least their
impression of the other will be based more on individual than on group characteristics. Our results also indicate that the same processes hold if one person
depends on the other, but not vice versa. For instance, when one individual from
an under-represented group attains a position of power in an organization, that
individual, at least, will be understood as an individual to a greater extent than
will such a person in an irrelevant or subordinate role.

GROUP-LEVEL INTERDEPENDENCE

While the individual psychological portrait described above provides some answers, it does not completely explain the effects of intergroup contact, as in the
opening example of male and female sales associates in the national retail corporation. Similarly, it does not explain the results of group-level contact, as in the
other opening example of school desegregation. Group-level interdependence
raises the ante of complexity, for each person's outcomes depend positively on
the ingroup and also (perhaps negatively) on the outgroup. We predicted that
people would give priority to the ingroup dependency, attending to ingroup members as individuals, inferring their dispositions, and evaluating them by attributes.
Without knowing the ingroup first, one cannot possibly function as a group vis-à-
vis the outgroup.

The outgroup, in contrast, may presumptively block one's goals (Fiske &
Ruscher, 1993). The outgroup—by definition a group differing from one's ingroup—contains individuals who will be novel, unfamiliar, and unpredictable. An
interacting person's mere membership in the outgroup introduces elements of
strangeness that can inherently interfere with smoothly achieving one's own outcomes. But more than merely having membership on the basis of distinct categories, psychological groups also exist because of their goals. Even noninteracting
groups, such as broad demographic categories (race, gender, or age) are presumed to share certain values, which imply similar goals for individuals within
that group. Thus, outgroup members, by virtue of belonging to the category, presumably possess different and perhaps competing goals, compared to those of
the ingroup. People generally assume the presence of competition in intergroup
interaction (e.g., Insko, Schopler, Hoyle, Dardis, & Graetz, 1990). Moreover, an
outgroup is not expected to yield easily to influence, for a group is seen as a cohesive, impermeable entity, and one that mutually reinforces its members. Even

several separate individuals from a large demographic category are more easily seen as conspiring together for shared goals than are a heterogeneous collection of individuals. For all these reasons, we have proposed that people would see a cohesive outgroup as difficult to influence and would abandon attempts to learn about it, because they had little hope of prediction, less of influence, and none of control. In contrast, therefore, to the situation with interdependent individuals, and with ingroup members, another person's membership in an outgroup should eliminate attentional, dispositional, and evaluative individuation of them.

Interpersonal Versus Intergroup Competition

Although one-on-one competition individuates interacting persons, as indicated earlier (Ruscher & Fiske, 1990), group-on-group competition should not, for the reasons just outlined. To test this hypothesis, we conducted another experiment (Ruscher, Fiske, Miki, & Van Manen, 1991, Study 1). In the context of a creativity game with wind-up toys, participants found themselves on a three-person team playing against another three-person team for a cash prize. We manipulated interpersonal (one-on-one) versus intergroup (group-on-group) competition by explaining that the participant's team competed against the other team in a series of one-on-one matches, as in a singles tennis team, or they competed as an entire team, as in basketball. Expectancy was manipulated by portraying the other team as likely to be superior or inferior.

Participants then learned about one of the opponents, who had mixed positive and negative (i.e., consistent and inconsistent) attributes. We measured individuating attention, dispositional inferences, and evaluations, under situations of interpersonal and intergroup competition. As predicted, attention and dispositional inferences were greater under interpersonal, compared to intergroup, competition—but only for inconsistent (not consistent) information. Thus, group-level negative interdependence did not create individuating processes.

Ingroup Priority Over Outgroup?

One of our proposed mechanisms of interdependence is assigning priority to the ingroup, compared to the outgroup. However, the previous study assessed reactions only to the outgroup. So in a second study (Ruscher et al., 1991, Study 2), we compared reactions to ingroup and outgroup members. In the same creativity game, with the same expectancies and the same information, but with two-person teams, participants learned about their two opponents and one teammate, and they provided the usual roster of measures. As predicted, both attention and dispositional inferences to inconsistency (not consistency) were higher for the ingroup teammate, compared to the outgroup competitors. Recall that the research reviewed above has shown that these individuating processes are not a function of team-versus-opponent status or positive-versus-negative interdependence. The remaining explanation is ingroup-versus-outgroup interdependence. In this study, because the evaluations were not individually calibrated, we obtained no average effects, but idiosyncratic variability in the ratings of competence was also reliably higher for ingroup teammates.

Group Versus Aggregate Dependence?

We have argued that it is the quality of groupness or entitativity (e.g., differences from the ingroup, shared goals, cohesiveness, impermeability) that makes the outgroup seem difficult to influence and that discourages the individuating effects of interdependence when it occurs at the group level. In a direct test of the effects of psychological group entitativity, we added a condition to one of the experiments described previously. The Dépret-Fiske (1999) study, with the noisy-housemates cover story, had tested degrees of asymmetrical dependency on art- or math-major outgroup distractors, and had shown the predicted effects on attention and dispositional inferences. The results previously described came from a condition in which the distractors comprised an aggregate of outgroup individuals—i.e., math, art, and business majors. Another condition in the same study increased the entitativity of the group by making it homogeneous—either all art majors or all math majors. Then, as in the other condition, participants learned about one sample distractor individual, either an art or a math major.

As predicted, the already reported attention effects, obtained when participants were outcome-dependent on individuals, disappeared in the other condition, when participants were outcome-dependent on a homogeneous group. That is, perceivers did not bother to attend to a psychological group that held power over them, perhaps because they viewed influence or control as unlikely. Similarly, also as predicted, the dispositional inference effects, previously obtained regarding an aggregate of individuals, disappeared in the situation of a homogeneous outgroup, presumably for the same reasons.

Moreover, recall that this study assessed impressions of the ingroup as well as the outgroup, on the premise that ingroup favoritism can be a more sensitive measure of intergroup impressions than is outgroup derogation. Here again, results for the aggregate differed from those for the psychological group. In a rally-round-the-flag or circle-the-wagons effect, participants contingent on a homogeneous outgroup liked the ingroup decidedly better, on a variety of measures (Figure 6.6). Although impressions of the outgroup did not differ, they suffered relative to the more positive ratings of the ingroup, in the condition of increased ingroup contingency on the outgroup. Thus, the Dépret-Fiske (1999) study showed one more version of impression effects under outcome dependency.

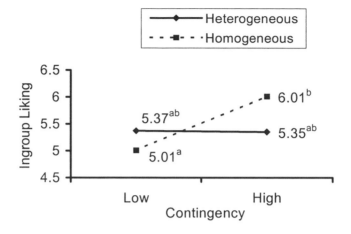

FIG. 6.6. Ingroup liking, as a function of asymmetrical dependency and outgroup homogeneity. Data from Dépret and Fiske (1999). Means not sharing a superscript differ at $p < .05$.

Generalization From Individuated Individual to the Group?

The final puzzle for our research to date has been the challenge to show interdependence effects beyond the immediate target person. The Dépret-Fiske (1999) dataset goes some distance in that direction, but does not resolve the issue, for it shows broadened effects on perceptions of the ingroup, not the out-group. An outcome-dependency study that has just been completed (Guinote & Fiske, 1999) addressed this issue. In it, individual participants who were dependent on a powerful group majority perceived more variability among them than did similarly situated participants who were not outcome-dependent. That is, participants who were contingent on the outgroup saw the outgroup members as more dissimilar, less stereotypic, and divided into more subgroups. This study gives a first indication of the kinds of generalization that can occur, from an isolated intergroup encounter, to perceptions of the larger outgroup beyond the individuals involved in the interaction.

DISCUSSION AND CONCLUSIONS

Research on the individual psychology of intergroup contact paints a portrait of a worried person, contingent on an outgroup individual, and seeking prediction, influence, and/or control over outcomes that matter. The motivated person scrutinizes the most diagnostic information available, attributes it to enduring personal dispositions, and bases some forms of evaluation on this process; and all of these processes render a more individuated portrait of the outgroup person than would otherwise be the case. When people need other people, they start to pay attention to them as individuals. In contrast, intergroup interdependence interferes with these individuating processes—instead fostering stereotypic attention, inferences, and impressions.

The interplay of interdependence and social cognition implies several levels of conclusions. At the immediate theoretical level, it supports the Continuum Model's predictions that impressions range from more individuated to more category-based, as a function of information and motivation. The Model also holds that people go beyond their initial category-based impressions, by attending to additional information, when they are motivated by factors such as outcome dependency.

At the purely interpersonal level, outcome dependency also determines individual behavior, not just cognitive processes and impression judgments. In a study by Neuberg (1989), applicants depended on an interviewer for a $50 prize, which was based on performing well in an interview to be the student manager of a hypothetical travel agency. Some interviewers had a specific goal to be accurate (similar to our outcome-dependent perceivers—Neuberg & Fiske, 1987). Accuracy-oriented interviewers altered their information-gathering behavior (listening, encouragement, questions), which in turn affected applicant performance. In a similar study, applicants dependent on an interviewer for a possible RA job adjusted their behavior according to their perceptions of the interviewer's goals, and those applicants did influence the interviewers' judgments, though the domain of influence (competence or sociability) depended on the interviewer's interpersonal dominance (Operario & Fiske, 1999).

At the interpersonal level, the goal of reducing prejudice and discrimination suggests strategies for both powerholders such as interviewers and outcome-dependent individuals such as job applicants. Interviewers need to be reminded (or to remind themselves) that their outcomes are in a sense contingent on the applicants. For instance, interviewers must make a good impression on the applicants in order to represent the organization most favorably. Interviewers need to have the applicants provide the most honest and complete information possible, in order to create the best fit between applicants and the organization. Interviewers might also be evaluated by applicants, in some instances, to assess their competence as interviewers. Interviewers may be given the goal of encouraging members of under-represented groups to join the organization in appropriate jobs, and to promote this outcome they need to develop rapport with applicants. Interviewers' own outcomes may be made contingent on their ability to select good applicants and, importantly, not to reject good ones. All these possible interventions emphasize and make use of the interviewers' often-unrecognized dependency on the applicants.

In a reciprocal fashion, applicants can stress the ways that the interviewer may depend on them (for more detail, see Eberhardt & Fiske, 1996). For instance, the applicant can stress their common interests in assessing and creating a good fit to the organization, the credit that the interviewer will receive for hiring an excellent new employee, and the positive impression that can be communicated by the applicant to other potential applicants. All these interpersonal interventions again stress interdependence—the extent to which the interviewer and applicant are on the same team. Of course, once a new employee is on the job, interpersonal relations become part of an established social structure.

At the social-structural level, outcome dependency, or its lack, predicts power relations (Fiske, 1993). Broadly, outcome dependency prescribes the direction of attention in traditional organizations—people attend up the hierarchy more than down. For example, undergraduates attend to their TAs, who attend to the faculty, who attend to the Chair, who attends to the Dean, who attends to the Provost, who attends to the President or Chancellor, who attends to the trustees, who perhaps listen only to their creator—giving "higher power" a new meaning.

At a minimum, people who control other people's outcomes are by definition less contingent, so by default they are less motivated to individuate others. Moreover, perhaps by design, people who control others' outcomes may sometimes attend to stereotype-confirming information that justifies their position (Goodwin et al., in press, Studies 1-3). Implications emerge for interventions in organizational hierarchies in cases where abuse of power occurs in the form of stereotyping, either by default or by design. In such situations leaders should be alerted to their possible biases, to their contingencies on their subordinates, and to the organization as an interdependent community. Powerful people who are exchange-oriented show more stereotype-confirming bias than those who are more communal (Chen, Lee-Chai, & Bargh, 1998), so a focus on communal needs rather than on a hierarchy of exchange relationships should reduce bias. To the extent that leaders view themselves as part of a network where people's needs matter, rather than just keeping track of who got what outcome, they will be more responsive to their subordinates as individuals. Our findings suggest that powerful people who are aware of their contingency on peers, or even on subordinates, will be less vulnerable to stereotyping and other category-based biases than those who are not so aware. The best leaders are probably those who are aware of their interdependence with their subordinates, and who therefore individuate those subordinates.

On a societal level, perceived interdependence predicts the content of stereotypes (Fiske, Xu, Cuddy, & Glick, in press; Fiske, Glick, Cuddy, & Xu, 1999; Glick & Fiske, in press). In our research, when people are asked what groups depend on their group, they perceive those groups who depend on their group (e.g., disabled people, housewives, elderly people) to be low-status and incompetent, whereas those groups on whom they say they must depend (e.g., rich people, business women, Asians, Jews) are perceived to be high-status and competent. Members of high-status groups that compete with the ingroup are seen as not warm, whereas the low-status noncompetitors are perceived as warm. These dynamics result in two primary clusters of outgroups—those subject to paternalistic prejudice (dependent, incompetent, low-status, but maybe warm) and those subject to envious prejudice (independent, competent, high-status, but not warm). Interventions to reduce prejudice toward both kinds of groups might focus on increasing group-level positive interdependence, and on reducing the sense of differential status at the group level. On the first point, to the extent that groups realize that they are not in direct competition, but in fact need each other, they share overarching goals—long a prescription in intergroup relations. On the second point, to the extent that groups can be persuaded that no group as a whole utterly dominates any other group as a whole, they will be less resentful upward and less paternalistic downward. Becoming aware of the variability of outcomes within any given group and the overlapping distributions of outcomes across groups may undermine some of the group-status effects.

Finally, also at the societal level, and most relevant to this volume, the principles of interdependence explain effective intergroup contact that undercuts people's spontaneous, default, category-based impressions. Returning to the vignette at the beginning of this chapter, just as the national warehouse chain had recognized its dependence on ethnic minorities as customers and therefore employed them as sales staff, so it also came to realize its comparable need for women in sales. We may hope that, over time, in educational settings, both majorities and minorities will realize that they need to learn from each other, in order to function competently and comfortably in the diverse population of the 21st century (cf. Johnson & Johnson, this volume). Recognition of the role of interdependence in reducing prejudice dates back nearly 50 years (e.g., Allport, 1954; see Pettigrew, 1998, for a review), but our research program has helped to explain some individual psychological processes that underlie intergroup contact, making it more effective in reducing prejudice. That is the goal we hope to reach.

REFERENCES

Allport, G. (1954). *The nature of prejudice*. Reading, MA: Addison-Wesley.

Brewer, M. B., & Brown, R. J. (1998). Intergroup relations. In D. T. Gilbert, S. T. Fiske, & G. Lindzey (Eds.), *The handbook of social psychology* (4th ed., Vol. 2, pp. 554-594). New York: McGraw-Hill.

Bruner, J. S., & Tagiuri, R. (1954). The perception of people. In G. Lindzey (Ed.), *The handbook of social psychology* (Vol. 2, pp. 634-654). Reading MA: Addison-Wesley.

Chen, S., Lee-Chai, A. Y., & Bargh, J. A. (1998). *Does power always corrupt? Relationship orientation as a moderator of the effects of social power*. Unpublished manuscript, New York University.

Dépret, E. F., & Fiske, S. T. (1999). Perceiving the powerful: Intriguing individuals versus threatening groups. *Journal of Experimental Social Psychology, 35,* 461-480.

Eberhardt, J., & Fiske, S. T. (1996). Motivating individuals to change: What is a target to do? In N. Macrae, M. Hewstone, & C. Stangor (Eds.), *Foundations of stereotypes and stereotyping* (pp. 369-415). New York: Guilford.

Erber, R., & Fiske, S. T. (1984). Outcome dependency and attention to inconsistent information. *Journal of Personality and Social Psychology, 47*, 709-726.

Fiske, S. T. (1993). Controlling other people: The impact of power on stereotyping. *American Psychologist, 48*, 621-628.

Fiske, S. T. (1998). Stereotyping, prejudice, and discrimination. In D. T. Gilbert, S. T. Fiske, & G. Lindzey (Eds.) *The handbook of social psychology* (4th ed., Vol. 2, pp. 357-411). New York: McGraw-Hill.

Fiske, S. T., Glick, P., Cuddy, A. C., & Xu, J. (1999). *Ambivalent content of stereotypes, predicted by social structure: Status and competition predict competence and warmth.* Unpublished manuscript, University of Massachusetts at Amherst.

Fiske, S. T., Lin, M. H., & Neuberg, S. L. (1999). The Continuum Model: Ten years later. In S. Chaiken & Y. Trope (Eds.) *Dual process theories in social psychology* (pp. 231-254). New York: Guilford.

Fiske, S. T., & Neuberg, S. L. (1990). A continuum model of impression formation, from category-based to individuating processes: Influence of information and motivation on attention and interpretation. In M. P. Zanna (Ed.), *Advances in experimental social psychology* (Vol. 23, pp. 1-74). New York: Academic Press.

Fiske, S. T., Neuberg, S. L., Beattie, A. E., & Milberg, S. J. (1987). Category-based and attribute-based reactions to others: Some informational conditions of stereotyping and individuating processes. *Journal of Experimental Social Psychology, 23*, 399-427.

Fiske, S. T., & Ruscher, J. B. (1993). Negative interdependence and prejudice: Whence the affect? In D. M. Mackie & D. L. Hamilton (Eds.), *Affect, cognition, and stereotyping: Interactive processes in group perception* (pp. 239-268). New York: Academic Press.

Fiske, S. T., & Taylor, S. E. (1991). *Social cognition* (2nd ed.). New York: McGraw-Hill.

Fiske, S. T., & Von Hendy, H. M. (1992). Personality feedback and situational norms can control stereotyping processes. *Journal of Personality and Social Psychology, 62*, 577-596.

Fiske, S. T., Xu, J., Cuddy, A. C., & Glick, P. S. (in press). (Dis)respect versus (dis)liking: Status and interdependence underlie ambivalent stereotypes of competence and warmth. *Journal of Social Issues.*

Forsyth, D. R. (1990). *Group dynamics* (2nd ed.). Pacific Grove CA: Brooks-Cole.

Glick, P., & Fiske, S. T. (in press). Ambivalent stereotypes as legitimizing ideologies: Differentiating paternalistic and envious prejudice. In J. Jost & B. Major (Eds.) *The psychology of legitimacy.* New York: Cambridge University Press.

Goodwin, S. A., Gubin, A., Fiske, S. T., & Yzerbyt, V. (in press). Power can bias impression processes: Stereotyping subordinates by default and by design. *Group Processes and Intergroup Relations.*

Guinote, A. P. S., & Fiske, S. T. (1999). *Outcome dependency increases perceived group variability.* Unpublished manuscript, University of Massachusetts at Amherst.

Heider, F. (1958). *The psychology of interpersonal relations.* New York: Wiley.

Higgins, E. T., Kuiper, N. A., & Olson, J. M. (1981). Social cognition: A need to get personal. In E. T. Higgins, C. P. Herman, & M. P. Zanna (Eds.), *Social cognition: The Ontario symposium* (Vol. 1, pp. 395-420). Hillsdale NJ: Erlbaum.

Insko, C. A., Schopler, J., Hoyle, R. H., Dardis, G. J., & Graetz, K. A. (1990). Individual-group discontinuity as a function of fear and greed. *Journal of Personality and Social Psychology, 58,* 68-79.

Kelley, H. H., Berscheid, E., Christiansen, A., Harvey, J. H., Huston, T. L., Levinger, G., McClintock, E., Peplau, L. A., & Peterson, D. R. (Eds.) (1983). *Close relationships.* San Francisco: Freeman.

Kelley, H. H., & Thibaut, J. W. (1978). *Interpersonal relations: A theory of interdependence.* New York: Wiley-Interscience.

Krauss, R. M. (1981). Impression formation, impression management, and nonverbal be-
  haviors. In E. T. Higgins, C. P. Herman, & M. P. Zanna (Eds.), *Social cognition: The
  Ontario symposium* (Vol. 1, pp. 323-341). Hillsdale, NJ: Erlbaum.
Lerner, J. S., & Tetlock, P. E. (1999). Accounting for the effects of accountability. *Psycho-
  logical Bulletin, 125,* 255-275.
Neuberg, S. L. (1989). The goal of forming accurate impressions during social interaction:
  Attenuating the effects of negative expectancies. *Journal of Personality and Social Psy-
  chology, 56,* 374-386.
Neuberg, S. L., & Fiske, S. T. (1987). Motivational influences on impression formation: Out-
  come dependency, accuracy-driven attention, and individuating processes. *Journal of
  Personality and Social Psychology, 53,* 431-444.
Operario, D., & Fiske, S. T. (1999). *Effects of trait dominance on powerholders' judgments
  of subordinates.* Unpublished manuscript, University of Massachusetts at Amherst.
Pavelchak, M. A. (1989). Piecemeal and category-based evaluation: An idiographic analy-
  sis. *Journal of Personality and Social Psychology, 56,* 354-363.
Pettigrew, T. F. (1998). Intergroup contact theory. *Annual Review of Psychology, 49,* 65-85.
Pfeffer, J. (1998). Understanding organizations: Concepts and controversies. In D. T.
  Gilbert, S. T. Fiske, & G. Lindzey (Eds.), *The handbook of social psychology* (4th ed..,
  Vol. 2, pp. 733-777). New York: McGraw-Hill.
Ruscher, J. B., & Fiske, S. T. (1990). Interpersonal competition can cause individuating
  processes. *Journal of Personality and Social Psychology, 58,* 832-843.
Ruscher, J. B., Fiske, S. T., Miki, H., & Van Manen, S. (1991). Individuating processes in
  competition: Interpersonal versus intergroup. *Personality and Social Psychology Bulle-
  tin, 17,* 595-605.
Schneider, D. J., Hastorf, A. H., & Ellsworth, P. C. (1979). *Person perception.* Reading MA:
  Addison-Wesley.
Tagiuri, R., & Petrullo, L. (Eds.).(1958). *Person perception and interpersonal behavior.* Palo
  Alto, CA: Stanford University Press.
Thibaut, J. W., & Kelley, H. H.(1959). *The social psychology of groups.* New York: Wiley

7 Reducing Contemporary Prejudice: Combating Explicit and Implicit Bias at the Individual and Intergroup Level[1]

John F. Dovidio
Colgate University

Kerry Kawakami
University of Nijmegen

Samuel L. Gaertner
University of Delaware

Due in part to changing norms and to the Civil Rights Act and other legislative interventions that have made discrimination not simply immoral but also illegal, overt expressions of prejudice have declined significantly in the U.S. over the past 35 years (Dovidio & Gaertner, 1986, 1998; Schuman, Steeh, Bobo, & Krysan, 1997). Prejudice and discrimination, however, continue to exist and to affect the lives of people of color and women in significant ways (Dovidio & Gaertner, 1998; see also Stephan & Stephan's chapter in this volume). Many current approaches to prejudice based on race, ethnicity, or sex acknowledge the persistence of overt, intentional forms of prejudice, but they also recognize the role of more subtle, unintentional, and, possibly, unconscious forms of bias. These approaches often also consider the role of automatic or unconscious processes and the consequent indirect expressions of bias.

In contrast to "old-fashioned" racism, which is open and blatant, *aversive racism* represents a subtle, often unintentional, form of bias that is characteristic of many White Americans who possess strong egalitarian values and who believe that they are nonprejudiced (Gaertner & Dovidio, 1986; Kovel, 1970). The work on aversive racism primarily considers Whites' attitudes toward Blacks, although elsewhere we have demonstrated the generalizability of these processes to attitudes toward Latinos (Dovidio, Gaertner, Anastasio, & Sanitioso, 1992) and women (Dovidio & Gaertner, 1983). We propose that understanding the nature of contemporary forms of bias, such as aversive racism, can inform the development of strategies and interventions designed to reduce prejudice.

Prejudice is an unfair negative attitude toward a social group or a person perceived to be a member of that group. Like other attitudes, prejudice is conceived of as having cognitive (belief), affective (emotional), and conative (behavioral predisposition) components. Stereotypes have often been identified as the belief component of prejudice. A stereotype is a set of characteristics associated with a cognitive category, and these characteristics are used by perceivers to process information about the group or members of the group (Dovidio, Brigham, Johnson, & Gaertner, 1996). The present chapter examines how prejudice and stereotyping can be reduced by focusing on individual and intergroup processes that underlie contemporary forms of bias, such as aversive racism.

AVERSIVE RACISM

According to the aversive racism perspective, many people who consciously and sincerely support egalitarian principles and believe themselves to be non-prejudiced also unconsciously harbor negative feelings and beliefs about Blacks (as well as about other historically disadvantaged groups). In contrast to traditional research that focused on the psychopathology of prejudice, we suggest that biases involved in normal human functioning may predispose a person to develop racial prejudice. In particular, racial biases may be based in part on almost unavoidable cognitive processes (e.g., the categorization of people into ingroups and outgroups—Hamilton & Trolier, 1986; see also Brewer's chapter in this volume), motivational factors (needs for power and status for one's group—Tajfel & Turner, 1979; see also Sidanius and Veniegas' chapter in this volume), and socio-cultural experiences (e.g., involving the internalization of racially biased values and beliefs, often automatically and unconsciously—Devine, 1989; see also Devine et al.s chapter in this volume).

There are, however, also strong forces that promote racial equality. Norms of fairness and equality have had great social, political, and moral impact on the history of many countries. The operation of these egalitarian norms has been clearly demonstrated in U.S. experimental research (e.g., Roese & Jamieson, 1993) and survey research (e.g., Schuman et al., 1997). The conflict between these consciously endorsed and internalized egalitarian principles and unconscious negative feelings creates the ambivalence that aversive racists experience.

The aversive racism framework helps to identify when discrimination against Blacks and other minority groups will or will not occur. Because aversive racists consciously recognize and endorse egalitarian values—they truly want to be fair and just people—they will not discriminate in situations in which they recognize that discrimination would be obvious to others and themselves. Specifically, we propose that when people are presented with a situation in which the appropriate response is unambiguous—in which right and wrong are clearly defined—aversive racists will not discriminate against Blacks. However, because aversive racists still possess negative feelings, these negative feelings may eventually be expressed, but they will be expressed in subtle, indirect, and rationalizable ways. Discrimination will occur when it is not obvious what constitutes appropriate or inappropriate behavior, or when an aversive racist can justify or rationalize a negative response on the basis of some factor other than race. Under these circumstances, aversive racists may discriminate, but usually in a way that insulates them from having to acknowledge the possibility that their behavior was racially motivated.

Other theories of contemporary prejudice, such as symbolic racism (Sears, 1988), modern racism (McConahay, 1986), and modern sexism (Swim, Aikin, Hall, & Hunter, 1995), similarly hypothesize that bias is currently expressed more subtly than in the past. Across a number of paradigms, we have found consistent empirical support for this framework (Dovidio & Gaertner, 1998; Gaertner & Dovidio, 1986). For instance, regarding helping behavior in emergency situations, we have found that Whites do not discriminate against Black victims relative to White victims when they are the only witness and bear the entire responsibility for helping. However, when Whites believe that there are other witnesses who are available to help, they are substantially less likely to take *personal* responsibility for intervention to help Black victims than White victims. This bias occurs primarily when Whites can rationalize their nonintervention on the basis of some factor other than race—the belief that *someone else* would intervene. In the area of attitude expression, the bias of aversive racists is not shown in more negative attributions about Blacks than Whites. Aversive racists are very guarded about appearing prejudiced, to other people and to themselves. Instead, their bias is expressed in terms of more positive attributions about Whites than about Blacks. Whereas the traditional form of racial prejudice is primarily anti-Black, aversive racism (as well as other contemporary forms of bias) is largely pro-White (Gaertner et al., 1997).

On the Nature of Prejudice

Although the aversive racism framework has its historical roots in psychodynamic principles (see Kovel, 1970), as do related theories of racial ambivalence (e.g., Katz & Hass, 1988), we have also conceptualized it within a more cognitive framework—in terms of dual attitudes, one explicit and conscious and the other implicit and unconscious (Dovidio, Kawakami, Johnson, Johnson, & Howard, 1997). Previous work has clearly established that attitudes and beliefs can exist both at implicit levels (often measured by response latency techniques) and at explicit levels (usually assessed by self-reports), and that these types of attitudes do not necessarily coincide (Dovidio, Kawakami, & Beach, 1999; Greenwald & Banaji, 1995). A dissociation between response latency measures of implicit attitudes and self-reported attitudes is likely to be observed for socially sensitive issues in general (Dovidio & Fazio, 1992), and for racial attitudes in particular.

Devine (1989; see also Devine et al.'s chapter in this volume), for example, proposes that high- and low-prejudiced people are equally knowledgeable about cultural stereotypes about minority groups, and that they similarly activate these stereotypes automatically when in the real or symbolic presence of a member of that group. Low- and high-prejudiced individuals differ, however, in their personal beliefs and their motivations to control the potential effects of the automatically activated cultural stereotypes. Lower prejudiced people, because they consciously endorse egalitarian values, are more motivated to suppress and counteract their initial, automatic, biased reactions. Thus unconscious associations, which are culturally shared and automatically activated, may be disassociated from expressions of personal beliefs that are expressed on self-report measures of prejudice, and these two types of measures may vary systematically.

As noted earlier, understanding the causes, dynamics, and consequences of contemporary forms of bias can help to identify effective strategies for combating bias. Based on the factors contributing to aversive racism, these strategies may focus on either individual-level or intergroup processes. Individual-level strategies involve intraindividual processes (e.g., social cognitive processes) and interpersonal relations, in which personal identity is salient. Intergroup strategies emphasize the importance of group membership and social identity and focus on collective needs, values, and motivations. We consider both approaches in this chapter.

INDIVIDUAL PROCESSES AND PREJUDICE REDUCTION

Approaches directed at combating individual-level processes in prejudice and stereotyping can be aimed either at explicit expressions or implicit beliefs. Traditional prejudice-reduction techniques have been concerned with overt expressions, but as evidence continues to accumulate on the influential role of unconscious biases, it is also important to target implicit attitudes and stereotypes.

Explicit Attitudes and Stereotypes

Attempts to reduce the direct, traditional form of racial prejudice have typically involved educational strategies to enhance knowledge and appreciation of other groups (e.g., multicultural education programs), or they have emphasized norms that prejudice is wrong (Stephan & Stephan, 1984). These approaches may involve direct attitude change techniques (e.g., mass media appeals) or indirect ones (e.g., dissonance reduction—Leippe & Eisenstadt, 1994). Other techniques are aimed at changing or diluting stereotypes by presenting counterstereotypic or nonstereotypic information about group members (Rothbart & John, 1985; Scarberry, Ratcliff, Lord, Lanicek, & Desforges, 1997; Weber & Crocker, 1983). Providing stereotype disconfirming information is more effective when it is dispersed among a broad range of group members who are otherwise typical of their group rather than concentrated in one person who is not a prototypical representative of the group. In the latter case, people are likely to maintain their overall stereotype of the group while subtyping group members who disconfirm the general group stereotype (e.g., Black athletes—Hewstone, 1996).

Approaches for dealing with the traditional form of prejudice are generally less effective for combating the consequences of contemporary forms. For example, Whites already consciously endorse egalitarian, nonprejudiced views and disavow traditional stereotypes. Moreover, the traditional approach of emphasizing social norms that proscribe the avoidance of negative behavior toward Blacks and other people of color is not likely to be effective for addressing aversive racism. People possessing this type of bias have already internalized these norms and are very guarded about overtly discriminating against people of color. Thus, contemporary forms of bias have to be combated at implicit, as well as explicit, levels.

Implicit Attitudes and Stereotypes

Whereas strategies for addressing the traditional forms of prejudice have focused on conscious racial attitudes and values (e.g., egalitarianism), attempts to change contemporary forms need to be directed at changing implicit, unconscious attitudes as well. Just because they are unconscious and automatically activated does not mean that implicit negative attitudes are immutable and inevitable. There is considerable empirical evidence that, when sufficiently motivated and when using sufficient cognitive resources, people can avoid the influence of stereotypes in their conscious evaluations of others (Bargh, 1999; Devine, 1989; Fiske, 1989). In addition, there is some evidence that people might be able to moderate the activation of unconscious negative attitudes and stereotypes, at least temporarily (Blair & Banaji, 1996; cf. Bargh, 1999). Because automaticity develops through repeated occurrence, practice, and ultimately overlearning (Wyer & Hamilton, 1998), individual differences in the personal endorsement and application of negative attitudes and stereotypes can, over time, lead to systematic differences in their automatic activation. For example, Kawakami, Dion, and Dovidio (1998) found that Whites high in prejudice personally endorsed stereotypes about Blacks more strongly than did those low in prejudice. Moreover, presumably as a consequence of differences in their application of these stereotypes, high-prejudiced Whites showed automatic activation of these stereotypes whereas low-prejudiced Whites did not (see also Lepore & Brown, 1997). If implicit attitudes and stereotypes can be learned, we propose that they can also be unlearned or inhibited by equally well-learned countervailing influences through extensive retraining. Devine and Monteith (1993) observed, "Although it is not easy, and clearly requires effort, time, and practice, prejudice appears to be a habit than can be broken" (p. 336).

Retraining Research

We conducted a series of studies (Kawakami, Dovidio, Moll, Hermsen, & Russin, in press) to examine if and how automatic stereotype activation can be reduced. Current research and theory suggest that people are able to inhibit automatic stereotype activation if they are goal-directed in their efforts not to stereotype (Devine & Monteith, 1993; Stangor, Thompson, & Ford, 1998). Although attempts to suppress stereotypes can initially produce a "rebound effect," reflecting an unintended hyperaccessibility of these thoughts (cf. Wegner, 1994), individuals can develop "auto-motive" control of their actions through frequent and persistent pursuit of a goal, such as one not to stereotype (Bargh, 1990). Monteith, Sherman, and Devine (1998) noted, "Practice makes perfect. Like any other mental process, thought suppression processes may be proceduralized and become relatively automatic" (p. 71).

The first study in this set (Kawakami et al., in press, Study 1) represented our initial test of the hypothesis that automatic stereotype activation can be eliminated by repeatedly and consistently implementing a simple act of negating category-stereotype combinations. In this study, college students in the Netherlands first performed a primed Stroop color-naming task to test for initial automatic activation of stereotypes associated with skinheads and with the elderly. In this process, participants were presented with a category label (e.g., "skinheads") followed by a stereotypic trait (e.g., "aggressive") that was printed in one of four colors. Their task was to read the first word to themselves and subsequently state as quickly as possible the *color* of the second word. For participants to succeed at this task, they must direct their attention toward the naming of ink-colors and away from the semantic meaning of the target words. If semantic stereotypes are automatically activated, they will interfere with the color-naming response and produce longer latencies (MacLeod, 1991).

In the second phase of this study, participants received extensive training (480 trials) in negating either skinhead or elderly stereotypic associations. Specifically, participants were instructed to "not activate cultural associations" when presented with a picture of a member of a particular category (e.g., skinheads) on a computer screen. Upon seeing these stereotypic combinations (e.g., a skinhead picture with the word "aggressive"), they were asked to "just say no."

In the third phase of this study, participants were once again given the Stroop task. It is important to note that participants did *not* receive instructions at this time to negate either skinhead or elderly stereotypic associations, and none of the traits used in this training task were the ones used in the first two phases. We predicted that individuals who received extensive training in negating specific stereotype associations would show a decrease in automatic stereotype activation compared to individuals who were not trained in this way.

Tests of responses on the initial Stroop task revealed evidence of automatic activation for skinhead stereotypes but not for elderly stereotypes. Specifically, participants responded slower to skinhead stereotypic words following a skin-head prime than following an elderly prime (M = 624 vs. 609 msec, p < .001), but their response times to elderly stereotypic words were not slower following an elderly prime than following a skinhead prime (M = 609 vs. 617 msec). Because these pretest results (as well as the results of subsequent studies) did not reveal evidence of automatic activation of elderly stereotypes, the findings for negation training in this and in subsequent studies focused only on skinhead stereotypes.

Responses in the second, training phase of the study reflected the effects of practice on learning and performance. Although it initially took much longer for participants to respond "no" to category-stereotype combinations (e.g., skinhead words and pictures) than to respond "yes" to these combinations, by the end of 480 trials the "no" responses were just as fast. Of central importance, however, was the effect of negation training on automatic activation of skinhead stereo-types. As illustrated in Figure 7.1, the pattern of results supported the predic-tions. Participants trained to negate skinhead stereotypes had previously taken longer on the pretest to name the color of skinhead words following a skinhead prime than following an elderly prime (M = 618 vs. 601 msec, p < .01). However, with 480 trials of negation training this difference was no longer significant prime (M = 598 vs. 600 msec, p > .70). In contrast, participants not trained to negate skinhead stereotypes showed similar levels of automatic activation of skinhead stereotypes in the pretest and the posttest. These findings support of the hy-pothesis that extensive retraining can inhibit previously automatically activated stereotypes. We have since conceptually replicated these effects with gender stereotypes in the Netherlands and with racial stereotypes in the U.S. (Kawa-kami et al., in press, Study 4). In addition, in other research we have demon-

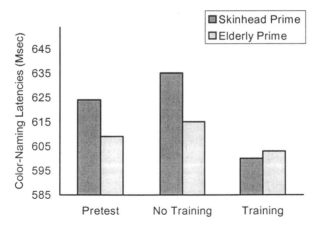

FIG. 7.1. Effects of retraining on automatic activation of stereotypes: Retraining eliminates interference of skinhead primes for color-naming of skinhead traits. The pretest data are for training and no-training conditions combined. Source: Data from Kawakami et al., in press.

strated, consistent with our theoretical framework, that extensive retraining is needed to "break the habit" that produces automatic stereotype activation. Instruction to negate stereotypes with only limited training (80 trials) is not sufficient (Kawakami et al., in press, Study 2).

Further research in this series (Kawakami et al., in press, Study 3) was designed to replicate the findings that extensive training in stereotype negation can result in the reduction of spontaneous stereotype activation and to explore the durability of this effect. Half of the participants were presented with the Stroop task upon beginning the first session and the other half of the participants received the Stroop task only after completing 480 trials in negating skinhead stereotypes. To examine the durability of the training effect, participants trained to negate skinhead stereotypes were presented with the Stroop task on three additional occasions—2 hours, 6 hours, and 24 hours subsequent to the first session.

As predicted, retraining was effective at reducing automatic activation of skinhead stereotypes on the Stroop task. Specifically, participants who did not receive extensive retraining at negating skinhead stereotypes consistently demonstrated evidence of automatic stereotype activation; they were slower at responding to skinhead associations following a skinhead prime than an elderly prime (M = 599 vs. 589 msec, $p < .05$). In contrast, participants who had 480 trials of negation training consistently demonstrated no difference in color-naming of skinhead stereotypes as a function of skinhead prime (M = 611 msec) versus elderly prime (M = 612 msec, $p > .90$). Furthermore, there were no differences as a function of the prime either 2 hours, 6 hours, or 24 hours after the training phase. Thus, in general, when participants have received sufficient training in stereotype negation, stereotype activation is diminished and no longer interferes with the color-naming task, and this effect appears to be relatively enduring—at least for 24 hours.

Although such direct stereotype-change strategies appear to be promising, such intensive and time-consuming approaches may be limited in their general applicability. Alternative strategies, however, may be possible that take advantage of aversive racists' genuine interest in being nonprejudiced in order to motivate significant and enduring change.

Good Intentions and Motivation to Change

Because aversive racists consciously endorse egalitarian values and truly want to be nonprejudiced, it may be possible to capitalize on their good intentions— enlisting them to motivate efforts to reduce their implicit biases once they become aware of them. Techniques that lead aversive racists to discover, apparently without much external pressure, inconsistencies among their self-images, values, and behaviors may arouse cognitive dissonance (Leippe & Eisenstadt, 1994) or other negative emotional states (Rokeach, 1973), and these can produce more favorable attitudes toward specific race-related issues and duce more favorable attitudes toward specific race-related issues and toward Blacks in general. In Rokeach's (1973) value confrontation procedure, for example, Whites are guided to recognize contradictions between their core value of equality and other core values (e.g., freedom), and to see the potential impact of this conflict on their racial attitudes. This discovery of contradictions among self-conceptions, values, and attitudes arouses a state of dissatisfaction that motivates participants to increase the importance of equality as a core value and to behave in ways that are more consistent with their nonprejudiced self-concept (Grube, Mayton, & Ball-Rokeach, 1994). These effects may be quite enduring and can influence even subtle interracial behaviors. Penner (1971), for instance, demonstrated increases in participants' eye contact with a Black confederate three months after the procedure, and Altemeyer (1994) demonstrated increased support for Canadian Native land claims seven months following value confrontation.

Other evidence suggests that inducing low-prejudiced people to become aware of inconsistencies among their self-images, values, and behaviors can motivate changes even in implicit attitudes and stereotypes. People who consciously endorse nonprejudiced attitudes but whose behaviors may reflect racial bias commonly experience feelings of guilt and compunction when they became aware of discrepancies between their potential behavior toward minorities (i.e., what they *would* do) and their personal standards (i.e., what they *should* do). These emotional reactions, in turn, can motivate people to control subsequent spontaneous stereotypical responses and behave more favorably in the future (Devine & Monteith, 1993; see also Devine et al.'s chapter in this volume).

This process of self-regulation, extended over time, may produce changes even in previously automatic, implicit negative responses. In their process model of prejudice reduction, Devine and Monteith (1993) suggested that individuals who are committed to maintaining egalitarian standards learn to reject old stereotypical ways of responding and to adopt new nonprejudiced ways. Over time and with practice, these people learn to reduce prejudicial responses to category members and to respond in ways that are consistent with their nonprejudiced personal standards.

We directly investigated whether the type of self-regulatory processes outlined in the Devine and Monteith (1993) model may apply to personally motivated changes in implicit stereotypes (Dovidio, Gaertner, & Kawakami, 1998). White participants first completed, in counterbalanced orders, an explicit measure of prejudice (Brigham, 1993); an implicit, response-latency measure of stereotyping (Dovidio & Gaertner, 1993); and an implicit measure of attribution of stereotypically Black characteristics to another person after being subliminally primed with racially stereotypic characteristics (Devine, 1989). Participants then completed a task, modeled after the procedures of Devine and Monteith (1993), that made them aware of discrepancies between what they *would* do and what they *should* do (i.e., personal standards) in interracial situations. Finally, we administered a measure of emotional reactions. Three weeks later, participants returned to the laboratory and performed the two implicit stereotyping tasks (response latency and attribution), and completed another measure of "would-should" discrepancy. We hypothesized, on the basis of Devine and Monteith's (1993) model, that initial discrepancies between one's actions (what one would do) and personal standards (what one should do) would produce stronger feelings of guilt and compunction and produce more self-initiated efforts at change among low-prejudiced participants, but not necessarily among high-prejudiced participants. The effects of this self-regulatory process were expected to be reflected in decreases in discrepancies and implicit stereotyping.

As anticipated, in the first session, greater discrepancies between what one would do and should do produced higher levels of guilt ($r = .25$), and this relationship occurred primarily for low-prejudiced participants ($r = .50$) but not for high-prejudiced participants ($r = .04$). These findings indicate the potential initiation of self-regulatory processes for low- but not high-prejudiced participants. When participants returned three weeks later, we found an overall decrease in the reported discrepancies between what one would and should do ($p < .01$). In addition, this decrease was greater among participants who had larger initial discrepancies ($r = -.66$)—and this relationship was comparable for low- ($r = -.70$) and high- ($r = -.72$) prejudiced Whites. Thus, awareness of discrepancies between one's actions and standards seemed to motivate changes by Whites in general toward greater adherence to personal standards, at least in terms of their public displays. However, as hypothesized, low- and high-prejudiced Whites differed in terms of the extent to which they internalized these changes. Low-prejudiced Whites who had larger initial discrepancies showed greater reductions in implicit stereotyping on both the attribution measures ($r = -.51$) and the response latency measure ($r = -.56$). In contrast, for high-prejudiced Whites the relationships were weaker ($r = -.25$ and $-.07$) and nonsignificant. These results thus support Devine and Monteith's (1993) model and suggest that the good intentions of low-prejudiced people who inadvertently express racial bias—i.e., aversive racists—can be harnessed to produce self-initiated change, if given appropriate awareness, effort, and practice over time.

Although they may be effective, strategies that focus on the interpersonal and intrapersonal aspects of contemporary forms of prejudice—such as making people sensitive to their racial biases—may not be sufficient for combating bias at all levels. Social Identity Theory (Tajfel & Turner, 1979) and Self-Categorization Theory (Turner, Hogg, Oakes, Reicher, & Wetherell, 1987) view the distinction between personal identity and social identity as a critical one. When personal identity is salient, a person's individual needs, standards, beliefs, and motives primarily determine behavior. In contrast, when social identity is salient, "people come to perceive themselves as more interchangeable exemplars of a social category than as unique personalities defined by their individual differences from others" (Turner et al., 1987, p. 50). Under these conditions, collective needs, goals, and standards are primary. Illustrating the dynamics of this distinction, Verkuyten and Hagendoorn (1998) found that when individual identity was primed, individual differences in authoritarianism were the major predictor of the prejudice of Dutch students toward Turkish immigrants. In contrast, when social identity (i.e., national identity) was made salient, ingroup stereotypes and standards primarily predicted prejudiced attitudes. Thus, whether personal or collective identity is more salient critically shapes how a person perceives, interprets, evaluates, and responds to situations and to others (Kawakami & Dion, 1993). Consequently, strategies that emphasize intergroup processes, such as intergroup contact and social categorization and identity, are alternative approaches that can complement interventions which focus on the individual.

INTERGROUP PROCESSES AND PREJUDICE REDUCTION

Studies of intergroup processes and stereotype reduction have commonly involved either direct or symbolic contact with one or more representatives of another group. Actual intergroup contact, under specified conditions, can be a powerful way of reducing intergroup biases (Pettigrew, 1998; see also Pettigrew's chapter in this volume). In this section of the chapter, we explore when and how intergroup contact can reduce prejudice.

Intergroup Contact

Over the past half-century, the Contact Hypothesis has been a guiding framework for strategies designed to reduce intergroup bias and conflict (Pettigrew, 1998). This hypothesis proposes that simple contact between groups is not sufficient to improve intergroup relations. Rather, to reduce bias, the contact situation must reflect certain conditions—including, for example, equal status between the groups, cooperative intergroup interactions, opportunities for personal acquaintance with outgroup members, and supportive egalitarian norms. Cooperative learning and jigsaw classroom interventions (Aronson & Patnoe, 1997) are designed to increase interdependence between members of different groups and to enhance appreciation for the resources they bring to the task. Cooperation is most effective at reducing bias when the outcomes are successful, group contributions are seen as different or complementary, and positive and rewarding interaction is involved.

Recent approaches have extended research on the Contact Hypothesis by attempting to understand theoretically what common processes and mechanisms these diverse factors engage, that help to reduce bias. Participating in joint activities to achieve common, superordinate goals, for instance, changes the functional relations between groups from actual or symbolic competition to cooperation. Through psychological processes to restore cognitive balance or reduce dissonance, attitudes toward members of the other group and toward the group as a whole may improve to be consistent with the positive nature of the interaction. Also, the rewarding properties of achieving success may become associated with members of other groups, thereby increasing attraction (Gaertner et al., 1999).

Social Categorization and Identity

The factors specified by the Contact Hypothesis may also reduce bias through the process of reducing the salience of the intergroup boundaries, that is, through *decategorization*. According to this perspective, under the conditions specified by the Contact Hypothesis, intergroup interaction can individuate members of the outgroup by revealing variability in their opinions (Wilder, 1986) or can produce personalizing interactions with the exchange of more intimate information (Brewer & Miller, 1984). Making people aware of multiple, cross-cutting group memberships can also reduce the salience of group boundaries and lead to decategorization (see Brewer's chapter in this volume). Alternatively, intergroup contact may be structured to maintain group boundaries but alter their nature—that is to produce *recategorization*. Increasing the salience of a second, cross-cutting group membership (as opposed to multiple group memberships) can facilitate recategorization of individuals on that dimension and thereby improve intergroup attitudes (Urban & Miller, 1998). Another recategorization strategy, represented by our own work on the Common Ingroup Identity Model, involves interventions to change people's conceptions of their membership from being in different groups to being in one more-inclusive group (Gaertner, Dovidio, Anastasio, Bachman, & Rust, 1993).

The Common Ingroup Identity Model

The Common Ingroup Identity Model is rooted in the social categorization perspective of intergroup behavior, and it recognizes the central role of social categorization in reducing as well as in creating intergroup bias (Tajfel & Turner, 1979). Specifically, if members of different groups are induced to conceive of themselves more as a single, superordinate group rather than as two separate groups, attitudes toward former outgroup members will become more positive through processes involving pro-ingroup bias.

Categorization of a person as an ingroup member rather than as an outgroup member has been demonstrated to produce more positive evaluations and stronger affective connections, as well to influence how information about people is processed. Upon mere categorization, people value ingroup members more than outgroup members (e.g., Tajfel, Billig, Bundy, & Flament, 1971). With respect to affective responses, ingroup categorization facilitates greater empathy in response to others' needs (Piliavin, Dovidio, Gaertner, & Clark, 1981). In terms of information processing, people retain information in a more detailed fashion for ingroup members than for outgroup members (Park & Rothbart, 1982), have better memory for information about ways that ingroup members are similar to the self and outgroup members are dissimilar to the self (Wilder, 1981), and remember more positive information about ingroup than about outgroup members (Howard & Rothbart, 1980). Positive behaviors of ingroup members and negative behaviors of outgroup members are encoded at more abstract rather than concrete levels, representing schemas that are more resistant to change (Maass, Salvi, Arcuri, & Semin, 1989). These effects on information processing further reinforce pro-ingroup biases in evaluations. For instance, perhaps as a consequence of the development of these different schemas, people are more generous and forgiving in their explanations for the behaviors of ingroup members than of outgroup members (Hewstone, 1990). Cognitive and affective pro-ingroup biases can also promote more positive behaviors. Identifying others as ingroup members elicits greater helping (Dovidio et al., 1997) and cooperation (Kramer & Brewer, 1984). Thus, changing the basis of categorization from race to an alternative dimension can alter who is considered a member of "we" and who is a "they." And this process can undermine a contributing force to contemporary forms of racism, such as aversive racism.

The Common Ingroup Identity Model is presented schematically in Figure 7.2. On the left, situational factors and interventions, such as interdependence and group similarities or differences, are hypothesized to influence, either independently or jointly, cognitive representations of the memberships (center). These cognitive representations may be as one group (recategorization), two subgroups in one group or "on the same team" (recategorization with a dual identity), as two groups (categorization), or as separate individuals (decategorization). Within the model, intergroup cognition involved in social categorization is the critical mediator of subsequent intergroup attitudes and behavior. The model recognizes that recategorization and decategorization strategies can both reduce prejudice, but in different ways. Recategorization, either in terms of a one-group or dual-identity representation, reduces bias by extending the benefits of ingroup favoritism to former outgroup members. Attitudes and behaviors toward these former outgroup members thus become more favorable, approaching those directed toward ingroup members. Decategorization, in contrast, reduces favoritism toward original ingroup members as they become perceived as separate individuals rather than members of one's own group.

Recategorization and the Reduction of Bias

Consistent with the Common Ingroup Identity Model, we have found evidence that key aspects of intergroup contact identified by the Contact Hypothesis decrease bias, in part through changing cognitive representations of the groups. Cooperative interaction is one of the most powerful and robust aspects of inter-

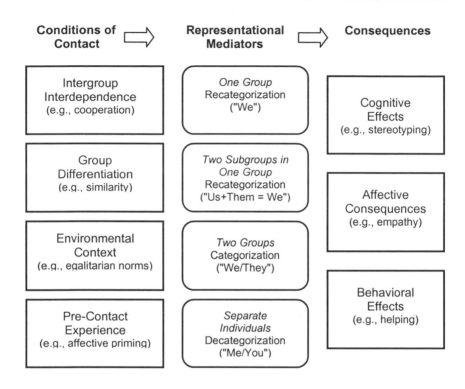

FIG. 7.2. Within the Common Ingroup Identity Model, elements of an intergroup contact situation (e.g., intergroup interdependence) influence cognitive representations of the groups as one superordinate group (recategorization), as two subgroups in one group (recategorization involving a dual identity), as two groups (categorization), or as separate individuals (decategorization). Both recategorization and decategorization, in turn, can reduce cognitive (e.g., beliefs), affective (e.g., feelings of empathy), and behavioral (e.g., helping) biases, but they do so in different ways. Source: Dovidio & Gaertner (1999, p. 104), reprinted by permission.

group contact for reducing bias (Sherif & Sherif, 1969). From our perspective, cooperative interaction may enhance positive evaluations of outgroup members (an affective consequence listed on the right of Figure 7.2), because cooperation transforms members' representations of the memberships from separate groups to one group.

To test this hypothesis directly, we conducted a laboratory experiment that brought two three-person laboratory groups together under conditions designed to vary both the members' representations of the aggregate as one group or two groups (by varying factors such as seating arrangement) and, independently, the presence or absence of intergroup cooperative interaction (Gaertner, Mann, Dovidio, Murrell, & Pomare, 1990). Both the groupness and the cooperation manipulations independently reduced intergroup bias. Moreover, in the absence of cooperative interaction, participants induced to feel like one group (compared to those whose separate group identities were reinforced) reported that the aggregate did feel more like one group. They also had lower degrees of intergroup bias in their evaluations of ingroup and outgroup members. Consistent with our hypothesis about how cooperation reduces bias among participants induced to feel like two groups, the introduction of cooperative interaction increased their perceptions of one group and also reduced their bias in evaluative ratings (compared to those who did not cooperate during the contact period). Also supportive of the Common Ingroup Identity Model, reduced bias associated with introducing cooperation was due to enhanced favorable evaluations of outgroup members.

More direct support for the hypothesized mediating role of cognitive representations was revealed by a multiple regression mediation analysis, a form of path analysis. Its results indicated that the influence of cooperation on more positive evaluations of outgroup members was substantially reduced when the mediating effects of group representations and perceptions of cooperation and competition were considered. Furthermore, consistent with our model, among these potential mediators, only the "one group" representation related independently to evaluations of outgroup members. That is, cooperation improved attitudes toward the outgroup, and thereby reduced intergroup bias, but it did this primarily indirectly by producing more-inclusive, one-group representations.

The advantage of this experimental design is that cooperation preceded changes in participants' representations of the aggregate from two groups to one group and also changes in intergroup bias. Also, because we manipulated the cognitive representations of the aggregate in the absence of cooperation, the development of a one-group representation preceded changes in intergroup bias. Thus, we can be confident about the directions of causality in this study (Gaertner et al., 1990).

In a second series of studies, we utilized survey techniques under more naturalistic circumstances. The advantage of this type of study is that it can provide more externally valid evidence concerning enduring and meaningful groups— often ones with histories of conflict. One of these studies involved a survey of 1,357 Black, Chinese, Hispanic, Japanese, Korean, Vietnamese, and Caucasian students attending a multiethnic high school in the northeastern United States (Gaertner et al., 1994, 1996). The primary theoretical question in this study was whether students' perceptions of the student body as one group, as different groups "playing on the same team," or as separate groups would mediate the hypothesized relationship between their perceptions of the favorableness of the conditions of intergroup contact and their degrees of intergroup bias. The favorability of conditions of contact was assessed using Green, Adams, and Turner's (1988) survey of school intergroup climate, which includes items related to four key dimensions identified by the Contact Hypothesis: equal status among groups, cooperative interdependence, interpersonal interaction, and supportive norms. One index of intergroup bias included items designed to assess feelings toward one's own ethnic group (e.g., good, uneasy, badly, respectful) in comparison to each of the other ethnic groups. Another index involved rating each ethnic/racial group on a modified "feelings thermometer" (see Esses, Haddock, & Zanna, 1993).

The findings were consistent with the processes we hypothesized in the Common Ingroup Identity Model. More favorable perceptions of the conditions of intergroup contact predicted stronger representations of the student body as one group and as different groups on the same team, but weaker representations as separate groups. These cognitive representations, in turn, predicted bias. The more the student body was perceived to be one group or different groups on the same team, the lower was the bias in intergroup affective reactions. The more the student body was perceived as different groups, the greater was the bias toward unfavorable views of outgroups. Overall, these results are consistent with those of our laboratory study, and they indicate the applicability of the Common Ingroup Identity Model to naturalistic settings. Two additional survey studies conducted in natural settings and across different intergroup contexts—banking mergers (Bachman, 1993), and blended families from remarriage (Banker & Gaertner, 1998)—offered converging evidence that the features specified by the Contact Hypothesis improve evaluations of outgroup members and decrease intergroup bias by changing members' representations of the groups.

Dual Identities

As the findings regarding the "different groups on the same team" representation in the high school survey study suggest, the development of a common ingroup identity does not necessarily require groups to forsake their original identities. Recognizing both different and common group membership—a more complex form of a common ingroup identity than a simple one-group representation—may also reduce prejudice. Furthermore, the results demonstrate that the beneficial effects of intergroup contact can generalize toward outgroups as a whole, for members of both majority and minority groups. The development of a common ingroup identity contributes to more positive attitudes toward members of other groups who are present in the contact situation, and in addition, recognition of the separate group memberships provides the associative link by which these more-positive attitudes may generalize to other members of the groups who are not directly involved in the contact situation.

The dual identity representation is also compatible with the Mutual Intergroup Differentiation Model (Hewstone, 1996; Hewstone & Brown, 1986), which proposes that introducing a cooperative relationship between groups without degrading the original ingroup-outgroup categorization scheme is an effective way to change intergroup attitudes and to have these attitudes generalize to additional outgroup members. From the perspective of the Common Ingroup Identity Model, Hewstone and Brown's proposal would keep earlier group identities salient while simultaneously providing a superordinate connection between the groups. If people continue to regard themselves as members of different groups but also as part of the same superordinate entity, intergroup relations between these "subgroups" should be more positive than if members only consider themselves as "separate groups."

The benefits of a dual identity may be particularly relevant to interracial and interethnic group contexts. Racial and ethnic identities are fundamental aspects of individuals' self-concepts and esteem and thus are unlikely to be readily abandoned. In addition, attempts to produce a single superordinate identity at the expense of one's racial or ethnic group identity may ultimately be detrimental to intergroup relations. Threats to important personal identities or the "positive distinctiveness" of one's group can, in fact, exacerbate intergroup prejudices (Dovidio, Gaertner, & Validzic, 1998). The development of a dual identity (two subgroups in one group), in which original and superordinate group memberships are simultaneously salient, is explicitly considered in the Common Ingroup Identity Model. Indeed, the development of a dual identity, in terms of a bicultural or multicultural identity, is not only possible, but it can contribute to the social adjustment, psychological adaptation, and overall well-being of minority group members (LaFromboise, Coleman, & Gerton, 1993).

Not only does the development of a common ingroup identity *not* require people to forsake their racial or ethnic identities, but there is evidence that intergroup benefits of a strong superordinate identity can be achieved for both majority and minority group members when the strength of the subordinate identity is equivalently high. For example, in a survey study of White adults, Smith and Tyler (1996, Study 1) found that respondents with a strong superordinate American identity, regardless of how strongly they identified with being White, were more likely to base their support for affirmative action on the fairness of the policy than on whether these policies would increase or decrease their personal well-being. This pattern of findings suggests that a strong superordinate identity (such as being American) allows individuals to support policies that would benefit members of other racial subgroups without giving primary consideration to their own group's instrumental needs. Among people of color, even when racial or ethnic identity is strong, perceptions of a superordinate connection enhance interracial trust and acceptance of authority within an organization (Huo, Smith, Tyler, & Lind, 1996).

We found converging evidence in our multiethnic high school survey study (Gaertner et al., 1996). In particular, we compared students who identified themselves on the survey using a dual identity (e.g., indicating they were Korean and American) with those who used only a single, subgroup identity (e.g., Korean). Supportive of the role of a dual identity, students who described themselves as *both* American and as a member of their racial or ethnic group had less bias toward other groups in the school than did those who described themselves only in terms of their subgroup identity.

Not only do Whites and people of color bring different values, identities, and experiences to intergroup contact situations, but in addition these different perspectives can shape perceptions of and reactions to the nature of the contact. Recent U.S. surveys, for example, reveal that Blacks show higher level of distrust and greater pessimism about intergroup relations than do Whites (Dovidio & Gaertner, 1998; Hochschild, 1995). Majority group members tend to perceive intergroup interactions as more harmonious and productive than do minority group members (Gaertner et al., 1996; Islam & Hewstone, 1993). In addition, majority and minority group members have different preferences for the ultimate outcomes of intergroup contact. Whereas many minority group members want to retain their cultural identity, majority group members typically favor the assimilation of minority groups into one single culture (a traditional "melting pot" orientation)—i.e., the dominant culture (Horenczyk, 1996).

Berry (1984; Berry, Poortinga, Segall, & Dasen, 1992) has described four forms of cultural relations in pluralistic societies that represent the four possible combinations of "yes–no" responses to two relevant questions: (1) Are cultural identity and customs to be retained? (2) Are positive relations with the larger society of value, and to be sought? These combinations reflect four adaptation strategies for intergroup relations: (1) integration, when cultural identities are retained and positive relations with the larger society are sought; (2) separatism, when cultural identities are retained but positive relations with the larger society are not sought; (3) assimilation, when cultural identities are abandoned and positive relations with the larger society are desired; and (4) marginalization, when cultural identities are abandoned and are not replaced by positive identification with the larger society.

Although this framework has been applied primarily to the ways in which immigrants acclimate to a new society (van Oudenhoven, Prins, & Buunk, 1998), we propose that it can be applied to intergroup relations between majority and minority groups more generally. An adaptation of this framework, substituting the strengths of the subgroup and subordinate group identities for the answers to Berry's (1984) two questions, appears in Figure 7.3. These combinations map onto the four main representations considered in the Common Ingroup Identity Model, as shown in the figure. For instance, cell (1) represents the same team (subgroup and superordinate group identities are high, like integration), while cell (2) represents different groups (subgroup identity is high and superordinate identity is low, like separatism).

Research in the area of immigration suggests that immigrant groups and majority groups have different preferences for these different types of group relations. In the Netherlands, van Oudenhoven et al. (1998) found that Dutch majority group members preferred an assimilation of minority groups (in which minority group identity was abandoned and replaced by identification with the dominant Dutch culture), whereas Turkish and Moroccan immigrants most strongly endorsed integration (in which they would retain their own cultural iden-

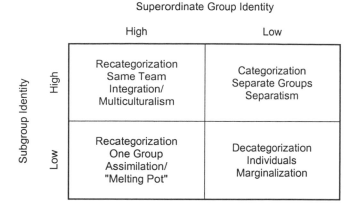

FIG. 7.3 Strategies for intergroup relations as a function of superordinate and sub-group identities and their cognitive representations.

tity while also valuing the dominant Dutch culture). This pattern also applies to the preferences of Whites and of people of color about racial and ethnic group relations in the United States. We have found that Whites most prefer assimilation, whereas Blacks and Hispanics favor pluralistic integration (Dovidio & Kafati, 1999, Study 1). Moreover, we proposed that these preferred types of intergroup relations for majority and minority groups—i.e., a one-group representation for Whites and a same-team representation for people of color—may differentially mediate the consequences of intergroup contact for the different groups.

To explore this possibility, we examined how different types of cognitive representations might mediate the relationship between more positive perceptions of intergroup contact and higher levels of student satisfaction for White college students and for students of color. Satisfaction was chosen as the main outcome variable for this study because attrition rate is a serious issue for students of color on college campuses (Steele, 1997), and satisfaction is an important predictor of retention (Bennett & Okinaka, 1990). Perceptions of favorable intergroup contact were measured in the same way as in our multiethnic high school study (Gaertner et al., 1996) and included ratings on the dimensions of equal status, supportive norms, personal interaction, and intergroup interdependence. Satisfaction included items about the academic and social climate (e.g., "I am satisfied with the social climate at _____"), as well as about intentions to complete one's education at the institution and willingness to recommend the institution to others. The cognitive representations were the four identified within the Common Ingroup Identity Model and hypothesized to represent different models of intergroup relations (see Figure 7.3). In addition, participants' identification with their racial or ethnic group was assessed. We hypothesized that the positive relation between perceptions of more favorable intergroup contact and satisfac-

White Students

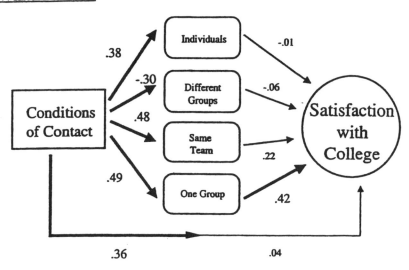

Students of Color

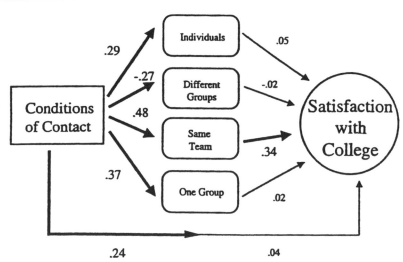

FIG. 7.4. Intergroup relations and satisfaction at college for White students and for students of color.

tion would be mediated by different representations for the different groups. Whereas we expected that the relation for Whites would be mediated by one-group representations, reflecting an assimilation perspective, we anticipated that the relation for people of color would be mediated by same-team representations—a multicultural perspective that recognizes both one's racial or ethnic group identity and a superordinate identity—a dual identity.

The results confirmed these hypotheses. For Whites, more positive perceptions of intergroup contact related to stronger perceptions of students as consisting of one group, different groups on the same team, and separate individuals, as well as weaker perceptions of different groups. More positive perceptions of intergroup contact also related directly to satisfaction with the college (beta = .36). However, when the representations were considered simultaneously, only the one-group representation was significantly related to satisfaction (see Figure 7.4, top panel). As evidence of mediation, conditions of contact no longer predicted satisfaction in this equation (illustrated by the change in beta from .36 to .04). Conditions of contact were also significantly related to each of the representations for students of color. In contrast to the pattern for Whites, the same-team representation—but not the one-group representation—predicted satisfaction with college (see Figure 7.4, bottom panel); but, as with Whites, it mediated the effect of the conditions of contact. In general, these effects were stronger for people higher in racial/ethnic identification, both for Whites and for people of color.

These findings have practical as well as theoretical implications. Although correlational data should be interpreted cautiously, it appears that, for both Whites and people of color, favorable intergroup contact conditions may contribute to their satisfaction with their institution. However, strategies and interventions designed to enhance satisfaction need to recognize that Whites and people of color may have different ideals and motivations. Because White values and culture have been the traditionally dominant ones in the United States, American Whites are likely to see an assimilation model—in which members of other cultural groups are absorbed into the "mainstream"—as the most comfortable and effective strategy. For people of color, this model, which denies the value of their culture and traditions, is likely to be perceived as less desirable but also as threatening to their personal and social identity—particularly for people who strongly identify with their group. Thus, efforts to create a single superordinate identity, although well-intentioned, may threaten people's social identity, which in turn can intensify intergroup bias and conflict (Dovidio, Gaertner, & Validzic, 1998).

CONCLUSION

Prejudice can exist in many forms. The traditional form of prejudice is blatant and conscious. In contrast, contemporary forms often involve dissociations between underlying negative feelings and beliefs (which may be unconscious and automatic) and conscious expressions of egalitarian values and principles. Whereas the traditional form of prejudice may be combated by using direct and conventional attitude change and educational techniques, addressing contemporary forms requires alternative strategies. Individual-level strategies engage the genuine motivations of people to be nonprejudiced. Revealing inconsistencies between individuals' nonprejudiced self-images and their underlying feelings (which are not necessarily conscious), or their intergroup behaviors, can produce negative emotional reactions (e.g., guilt), which then motivate people to alter their beliefs, feelings, and actions to be more truly egalitarian.

Because intergroup biases are also based on realistic group conflict, as well as on the psychological effects of categorizing people into ingroups and outgroups, strategies for reducing bias can additionally focus on intergroup processes. The benefits of appropriately structured intergroup contact can occur through many routes, one of which is producing more individualized perceptions of outgroup members and more personalized relationships. Intergroup contact can also produce more inclusive, superordinate representations of the groups. Transforming members' representations of the groups to recognize a common ingroup identity can harness the psychological forces that contribute to intergroup bias and redirect them, thus improving attitudes toward people who would otherwise be recognized only as outgroup members. However, intervention strategies should consider the different identities, values, and experiences that groups bring to contact situations. Majority and minority groups frequently have different objectives and perspectives, and effective strategies for change must accommodate the needs of both groups. Thus, understanding the processes that contribute to the nature of prejudice can guide, both theoretically and pragmatically, interventions that can effectively reduce both traditional and contemporary forms of prejudice.

NOTE

1. Research presented in this chapter and preparation of the manuscript were supported by NIMH Grant MH 48721.

REFERENCES

Altemeyer, B. (1994). Reducing prejudice in right-wing authoritarians. In M. Zanna & J. Olson (Eds.), *The psychology of prejudice: The Ontario symposium* (Vol. 7, pp. 131-148). Hillsdale, NJ: Erlbaum.

Aronson, E., & Patnoe, S. (1997). *The jigsaw classroom*. New York: Longman.

Bachman, B. A. (1993). *An intergroup model of organizational mergers*. Unpublished Ph.D. dissertation, University of Delaware, Newark.

Banker, B. S., & Gaertner, S. L. (1998). Achieving stepfamily harmony: An intergroup relations approach. *Journal of Family Psychology, 12*, 310-325.

Bargh, J. (1990). Auto-motives: Preconscious determinants of thought and behavior. In E. Higgins & R. Sorrentino (Eds.), *Handbook of motivation and cognition* (Vol. 2, pp. 93-130). New York: Guilford.

Bargh, J. (1999). The cognitive monster: The case against controllability of automatic stereotype effects. In S. Chaiken & Y. Trope (Eds.), *Dual process theories in social psychology*. New York: Guilford.

Bennett, C., & Okinaka, A. M. (1990). Factors related to persistence among Asian, Black, Hispanic and White undergraduates at a predominantly White university: Comparisons between first and fourth year cohorts. *Urban Review, 22,* 33-60.

Berry, J. W. (1984). Cultural relations in plural societies. In N. Miller & M. B. Brewer (Eds.), *Groups in contact: The psychology of desegregation* (pp. 11-27). Orlando, FL: Academic Press.

Berry, J. W., Poortinga, Y. H., Segall, M. H., & Dasen, P. R. (1992). *Cross-cultural psychology: Research and applications*. Cambridge, England: Cambridge University Press.

Blair, I., & Banaji, M. R. (1996). Automatic and controlled processes in gender stereotyping. *Journal of Personality and Social Psychology, 70,* 1142-1163.

Brewer, M. B., & Miller, N. (1984). Beyond the contact hypothesis: Theoretical perspectives on desegregation. In N. Miller & M. B. Brewer (Eds.), *Groups in contact: The psychology of desegregation* (pp. 281-302). Orlando FL: Academic Press.

Brigham, J. C. (1993). College students' racial attitudes. *Journal of Applied Social Psychology, 23,* 1933-1967.

Brown, R. J., & Wade, G. (1987). Superordinate goals and intergroup behavior: The effect of role ambiguity and status on intergroup attitudes and task performance. *European Journal of Social Psychology, 17,* 131-142.

Devine, P. G. (1989). Stereotypes and prejudice: The automatic and controlled components. *Journal of Personality and Social Psychology, 56,* 5-18.

Devine, P. G., & Monteith, M. J. (1993). The role of discrepancy-associated affect in prejudice reduction. In D. M. Mackie & D. L. Hamilton (Eds.), *Affect, cognition, and stereotyping: Interactive processes in intergroup perception* (pp. 317-344). Orlando, FL: Academic Press.

Dovidio, J. F., Brigham, J., Johnson, B. T., & Gaertner, S. L. (1996). Stereotyping, prejudice and discrimination. In N. Macrae, C. Stangor, & M. Hewstone (Eds.), *Foundations of stereotypes and stereotyping* (pp. 276-319). New York: Guilford.

Dovidio, J. F., & Fazio, R. H. (1992). New technologies for the direct and indirect assessment of attitudes. In J. Tanur (Ed.), *Questions about survey questions: Meaning, memory, attitudes, and social interaction* (pp. 204-237). New York: Russell Sage Foundation.

Dovidio, J. F., & Gaertner, S. L. (1983). The effects of sex, status, and ability on helping behavior. *Journal of Applied Social Psychology, 13,* 191-205.

Dovidio, J. F., & Gaertner, S. L. (1986). Prejudice, discrimination, and racism: Historical trends and contemporary approaches. In J. F. Dovidio & S. L. Gaertner (Eds.), *Prejudice, discrimination and racism* (pp. 1-34). Orlando, FL: Academic Press.

Dovidio, J. F., & Gaertner, S. L. (1993). Stereotypes and evaluative intergroup bias. In D. M. Mackie & D. L. Hamilton (Eds.), *Affect, cognition, and stereotyping: Interactive processes in intergroup perception* (pp. 167-193). Orlando, FL: Academic Press

Dovidio, J. F., & Gaertner, S. L. (1998). On the nature of contemporary prejudice: The causes, consequences, and challenges of aversive racism. In J. Eberhardt & S. T. Fiske (Eds.), *Confronting racism: The problem and the response* (pp. 3-32). Newbury Park, CA: Sage.

Dovidio, J. F., & Gaertner, S. L. (1999). Reducing prejudice: Combating intergroup biases. *Current Directions in Psychological Science, 8,* 101-105.

Dovidio, J. F., Gaertner, S. L., Anastasio, P. A., & Sanitioso, R. (1992). Cognitive and motivational bases of bias: The implications of aversive racism for attitudes toward Hispanics. In S. Knouse, P. Rosenfeld, & A. Culbertson (Eds.), *Hispanics in the workplace* (pp. 75-106). Newbury Park, CA: Sage.

Dovidio, J. F., Gaertner, S. L., & Validzic, A. (1998). Intergroup bias: Status, differentiation, and a common in-group identity. *Journal of Personality and Social Psychology, 75,* 109-120.

Dovidio, J. F., Gaertner, S. L., Validzic, A., Matoka, K., Johnson, B., & Frazier, S. (1997). Extending the benefits of re-categorization: Evaluations, self-disclosure and helping. *Journal of Experimental Social Psychology, 33,* 401-420.

Dovidio, J. F., & Kafati, G. (1999). *Intergroup contact between majority and minority group members.* Unpublished manuscript, Colgate University, Hamilton, NY.

Dovidio, J. F., Kawakami, K., & Beach, K. R. (1999). Implicit and explicit attitudes: Examination of the relationship between measures of intergroup bias. In R. Brown & S. L. Gaertner (Eds.), *Blackwell handbook of social psychology, Vol. 4: Intergroup Processes.* Oxford, England: Blackwell.

Dovidio, J., Kawakami, K., Johnson, C., Johnson, B., & Howard, A. (1997). The nature of prejudice: Automatic and controlled processes. *Journal of Experimental Social Psychology, 33,* 510-540.

Esses, V., Haddock, G., & Zanna, M. (1993). Values, stereotypes, and emotions as determinants of intergroup attitudes. In D. Mackie & D. Hamilton (Eds.), *Affect, cognition, and stereotyping: Interactive processes in group perception* (pp. 137-166). San Diego, CA: Academic Press.

Fiske, S. (1989). Examining the role of intent: Toward understanding its role in stereotyping and prejudice. In J. Uleman & J. Bargh (Eds.), *Unintended thought* (pp. 75-123). New York: Guilford.

Gaertner, S. L., & Dovidio, J. F. (1986). The aversive form of racism. In J. F. Dovidio & S. L. Gaertner (Eds.), *Prejudice, discrimination, and racism* (pp. 61-89). Orlando, FL: Academic Press.

Gaertner, S. L., Dovidio, J. F., Anastasio, P. A., Bachman, B. A., & Rust, M. C. (1993). The common ingroup identity model: Recategorization and the reduction of intergroup bias. In W. Stroebe & M. Hewstone (Eds.), *European Review of Social Psychology* (Vol. 4, pp. 1-26). London: Wiley.

Gaertner, S. L., Dovidio, J. F., Rust, M. C., Nier, J., Banker, B., Ward, C. M., Mottola, G. R., & Houlette, M. (1999). Reducing intergroup bias: Elements of intergroup cooperation. *Journal of Personality and Social Psychology, 76,* 388-402.

Gaertner, S. L., Mann, J. A., Dovidio, J. F., Murrell, A. J., & Pomare, M. (1990). How does cooperation reduce intergroup bias? *Journal of Personality and Social Psychology, 59,* 692-704.

Gaertner, S. L., Rust, M. C., Dovidio, J. F., Bachman, B. A., & Anastasio, P. A. (1994). The contact hypothesis: The role of a common ingroup identity on reducing intergroup bias. *Small Groups Research, 25(2),* 224-249.

Gaertner, S. L., Rust, M. C., Dovidio, J. F., Bachman, B. A., & Anastasio, P. A. (1996). The contact hypothesis: The role of a common ingroup identity on reducing intergroup bias among majority and minority group members. In J. L. Nye & A. M. Brower (Eds.), *What's social about social cognition?* (pp. 230-360). Newbury Park, CA: Sage.

Green, C. W., Adams, A. M., & Turner, C. W. (1988). Development and validation of the School Interracial Climate Scale. *American Journal of Community Psychology, 16,* 241-259.

Greenwald, A. G., & Banaji, M. R. (1995). Implicit social cognition: Attitudes, self-esteem, and stereotypes. *Psychological Review, 102,* 4-27.

Grube, J. W., Mayton, D. M., II, & Ball-Rokeach, S. J. (1994). Inducing change in values, attitudes, and behaviors: Belief system theory and the method of value self-confrontation. *Journal of Social Issues, 50* (4), 153-173.

Hamilton, D. L., & Trolier, T. K. (1986). Stereotypes and stereotyping: An overview of the cognitive approach. In J. F. Dovidio & S. L. Gaertner (Eds.), *Prejudice, discrimination, and racism* (pp. 127-163). Orlando, FL: Academic Press.

Hewstone, M. (1996). Contact and categorization: Social psychological interventions to change intergroup relations. In N. Macrae, M. Hewstone, & C. Stangor (Eds.), *Foundations of stereotypes and stereotyping* (pp. 323-368) New York: Guilford.

Hewstone, M., & Brown, R. J. (1986). Contact is not enough: An intergroup perspective on the "contact hypothesis." In M. Hewstone & R. Brown (Eds.), *Contact and conflict in intergroup encounters* (pp. 1-44). Oxford, England: Blackwell.

Hochschild, J. L. (1995). *Facing up to the American dream: Race, class, and the soul of the nation.* Princeton, NJ: Princeton University Press.

Horenczyk, G. (1966). Migrant identities in conflict: Acculturation attitudes and perceived acculturation ideologies. In G. Breakwell & E. Lyons (Eds.), *Changing European identities: Social psychological analyses of social change* (pp. 241-250). Oxford, England: Butterworth-Heinemann.

Hornstein, H. A. (1976). *Cruelty and kindness: A new look at aggression and altruism.* Englewood Cliffs, NJ: Prentice Hall.

Howard, J. M., & Rothbart, M. (1980). Social categorization for in-group and out-group behavior. *Journal of Personality and Social Psychology, 38,* 301-310.

Huo, Y. J., Smith, H. H., Tyler, T. R., & Lind, A. E. (1996). Superordinate identification, subgroup identification, and justice concerns: Is separatism the problem. Is assimilation the answer? *Psychological Science, 7,* 40-45.

Islam, M. R., & Hewstone, M. (1993). Dimensions of contact as predictors of intergroup anxiety, perceived outgroup variability, and outgroup attitude: An integrative model. *Personality and Social Psychology Bulletin, 19,* 700-710.

Katz, I., & Hass, R. G. (1988). Racial ambivalence and value conflict: Correlational and priming studies of dual cognitive structures. *Journal of Personality and Social Psychology, 55,* 893-905.

Kawakami, K., & Dion, K. L. (1993). The impact of salient self-identities on relative deprivation and action intentions. *European Journal of Social Psychology, 23,* 525-540.

Kawakami, K., Dion, K., & Dovidio, J. F. (1998). Racial prejudice and stereotype activation. *Personality and Social Psychology Bulletin, 24,* 407-416.

Kawakami, K., Dovidio, J. F., Moll, J., Hermsen, S., & Russin, A. (in press). Just say no (to stereotyping): Effects of training in trait negation on stereotype activation. *Journal of Personality and Social Psychology.*

Kovel, J. (1970). *White racism: A psychohistory.* New York: Pantheon.

Kramer, R. M., & Brewer, M. B. (1984). Effects of group identity on resource utilization in a simulated commons dilemma. *Journal of Personality and Social Psychology, 46,* 1044-1057.

LaFromboise, T., Coleman, H. L. K., & Gerton, J. (1993). Psychological impact of biculturalism: Evidence and theory. *Psychological Bulletin, 114,* 395-412.

Leippe, M. R., & Eisenstadt, D. (1994). Generalization of dissonance reduction: Decreasing prejudice through induced compliance. *Journal of Personality and Social Psychology, 67,* 395-413.

Lepore, L., & Brown, R. (1997). Category and stereotype activation: Is prejudice inevitable? *Journal of Personality and Social Psychology, 72,* 275-287.

Maass, A., Salvi, D., Arcuri, L., & Semin, G. R. (1989). Language use in intergroup contexts: The linguistic intergroup bias. *Journal of Personality and Social Psychology, 57,* 981-993.

MacLeod, C. (1991). Half a century of research on the Stroop effect: An integrative review. *Psychological Bulletin, 109,* 163-203.

McConahay, J. B. (1986). Modern racism, ambivalence, and the modern racism scale. In

J. F. Dovidio & S. L. Gaertner (Eds.), *Prejudice, discrimination, and racism* (pp. 91-125). Orlando, FL: Academic Press.

Monteith, M., Sherman, J., & Devine, P. (1998). Suppression as a stereotype control strategy. *Personality and Social Psychology Review, 1,* 63-82

Park, B., & Rothbart, M. (1982). Perception of out-group homogeneity and levels of social categorization: Memory for the subordinate attributes of in-group and out-group members. *Journal of Personality and Social Psychology, 42,* 1051-1068.

Penner, L. A. (1971). Interpersonal attraction to a Black person as a function of value importance. *Personality: An International Journal, 2,* 175-187.

Pettigrew, T. F. (1998). Intergroup contact theory. *Annual Review of Psychology, 49,* 65-85.

Piliavin, J. A., Dovidio, J. F., Gaertner, S. L., & Clark, R. D., III. (1981). *Emergency intervention.* New York: Academic Press.

Roese, N. J., & Jamieson, D. W. (1993). Twenty years of bogus pipeline research: A critical review and meta-analysis. *Psychological Bulletin, 114,* 363-375.

Rokeach, M. (1973). *The nature of human values.* New York: Free Press.

Rothbart, M., & John, O. P. (1985). Social categorization and behavioral episodes: A cognitive analysis of the effects of intergroup contact. *Journal of Social Issues, 41*(3), 81-104.

Scarberry, N. C., Ratcliff, C. D., Lord, C. G., Lanicek, D. L., & Desforges, D. M. (1997). Effects of individuating information on the generalization part of Allport's contact hypothesis. *Personality and Social Psychology Bulletin, 23,* 1291-1299.

Schuman, H., Steeh, C., Bobo, L., & Krysan, M. (1997). *Racial attitudes in America: Trends and interpretations* (2nd ed.). Cambridge, MA: Harvard University Press.

Sears, D. O. (1988). Symbolic racism. In P. A. Katz & D. A. Taylor (Eds.), *Eliminating racism: Profiles in controversy* (pp. 53-84). New York: Plenum.

Sherif, M., & Sherif, C. W. (1969). *Social psychology.* New York: Harper & Row.

Smith, H. J., & Tyler, T. R. (1996). Justice and power: When will justice concerns encourage the advantaged to support policies which redistribute economic resources and the disadvantaged to willingly obey the law? *European Journal of Social Psychology, 26,* 171-200.

Stephan, W. G., & Stephan, C. W. (1984). The role of ignorance in intergroup relations. In N. Miller & M. B. Brewer (Eds.), *Groups in contact: The psychology of desegregation* (pp. 229-257). Orlando, FL: Academic Press.

Stangor, C., Thompson, E., & Ford, T. (1998). An inhibited model of stereotype inhibition. In R. Wyer (Ed.), *Stereotype activation and inhibition: Advances in social cognition* (Vol. 11, pp. 193-210). Mahwah, NJ: Erlbaum.

Steele, C. M. (1997). A threat in the air: How stereotypes shape intellectual identity and performance. *American Psychologist, 52,* 613-629.

Swim, J., Aiken, K., Hall, W., & Hunter, B. (1995). Sexism and racism: Old-fashioned and modern prejudices. *Journal of Personality and Social Psychology, 68,* 199-214

Tajfel, H., Billig, M. G., Bundy, R. F., & Flament, C. (1971). Social categorisation and intergroup behavior. *European Journal of Social Psychology, 1,* 149-177.

Tajfel, H., & Turner, J. C. (1979). An integrative theory of intergroup conflict. In W. G. Austin & S. Worchel (Eds.), *The social psychology of intergroup relations* (pp. 33-48). Monterey, CA: Brooks/Cole.

Turner, J. C., Hogg, M. A., Oakes, P. J., Reicher, S. D., & Wetherell, M. S. (1987). *Rediscovering the social group: A self-categorization theory.* Oxford, England: Blackwell.

Urban, L. M., & Miller, N. (1998). A theoretical analysis of crossed categorization effects: A meta-analysis. *Journal of Personality and Social Psychology, 74,* 894-908.

van Oudenhoven, J. P., Prins, K. S., & Buunk, B. (1998). Attitudes of minority and majority members towards adaptation of immigrants. *European Journal of Social Psychology, 28,* 995-1013.

Verkuyten, M., & Hagendoorn, L. (1998). Prejudice and self-categorization: The variable role of authoritarianism and in-group stereotypes. *Personality and Social Psychology Bulletin, 24,* 99-110.

Weber, R., & Crocker, J. (1983). Cognitive processes in the revision of stereotypic beliefs. *Journal of Personality and Social Psychology, 45,* 961-977.

Wegner, D. (1994). Ironic processes of mental control. *Psychological Review, 101,* 34-52.

Wilder, D. A. (1981). Perceiving persons as a group: Categorization and intergroup relations. In D. L. Hamilton (Ed.), *Cognitive processes in stereotyping and intergroup behavior* (pp. 213-257). Hillsdale, NJ: Erlbaum.

Wilder, D. A. (1986). Social categorization: Implications for creation and reduction of intergroup bias. In L. Berkowitz (Ed.), *Advances in experimental social psychology* (Vol. 19, pp. 291-355). Orlando, FL: Academic Press.

Wyer, N., & Hamilton, D. (1998). The balance between excitation and inhibition in stereotype use. In R. Wyer (Ed.), *Stereotype activation and inhibition: Advances in social cognition* (Vol. 11, pp. 227-242). Mahwah, NJ: Erlbaum.

8 Reducing Prejudice Through Cross-Categorization: Effects of Multiple Social Identities

Marilynn B. Brewer
Ohio State University

For the past two decades, social psychological research on intergroup relations has been guided by the synthesis of two major theoretical perspectives. The first of these had its origin in the study of race relations in the U.S. and is best represented by the so-called "contact hypothesis," the idea that intergroup prejudice and discrimination can be reduced by interpersonal contact between members of the respective social groups under conditions that promote equal-status, cooperative, and personalized interaction (see Pettigrew & Tropp, this volume). The second perspective had its origin in European research and the development of social identity theory. In brief, social identity theory, as articulated by Tajfel (1978) and Turner (1975, 1985), represents the convergence of two traditions in the study of intergroup attitudes and behavior—social categorization, as seen in work by Doise (1978; Doise & Sinclair, 1973), Tajfel (1969), and Wilder (1986), and social comparison, as exemplified by Pettigrew (1967; Vanneman & Pettigrew, 1972) and Lemaine (1974).

The social identity theoretical perspective rests on two basic premises:

1. Individuals organize their understanding of the social world on the basis of categorical distinctions that transform continuous variables into discrete classes. Such categorization has the effect of minimizing perceived differences *within* categories and accentuating intercategory differences.

2. Since individuals are themselves members of some social categories and not others, social categorization carries with it implicit *ingroup-outgroup* (we-they) distinctions. Because of the self-relevance of social categories, the ingroup-outgroup classification is a superimposed category distinction with affective and emotional significance.

These two premises provide a framework for conceptualizing any social situation in which a particular ingroup-outgroup categorization is made salient. In effect, the theory posits a basic *intergroup schema* with the following character- istic features:

(a) assimilation within category boundaries and contrast between categories, such that all members of the ingroup are perceived to be more similar to the self than are members of the outgroup (the *intergroup accentuation* principle),
(b) positive affect (trust, liking) selectively generalized to fellow ingroup members but not to outgroup members (the *ingroup favoritism* principle),
(c) intergroup social comparison associated with perceived negative interde- pendence between ingroup and outgroup (the *social competition* princi- ple).

The affective and behavioral consequences of this schema lead to intergroup situations characterized by preferential treatment of ingroup members, mutual distrust between ingroup and outgroup, and intergroup competition. According to this theoretical perspective, *the starting point for intergroup discrimination and prejudice is a cognitive representation of the social situation in which a particular categorical distinction is highly salient.*

One advance toward an integrative theory of intergroup relations was achieved when intergroup contact research was combined with concepts of so- cial categorization and social identity theory to provide a theoretical framework for understanding the cognitive mechanisms by which cooperative contact is presumed to work (see Brewer & Miller, 1984; Hewstone & Brown, 1986; Hew- stone, 1996; Wilder, 1986). From the social categorization perspective, the issue to be addressed in reducing prejudice is how intergroup contact and cooperation can be structured so as to alter cognitive representations in ways that would eliminate one or more of the basic features of the negative intergroup schema.

Based on the premises of social identity theory, three alternative models for contact effects have been developed and tested in experimental and field set- tings. (These models have been described at length in Dovidio, Kawakami, and Gaertner's chapter in this volume, so they will be only briefly listed here.) One model recommends a process of *decategorization,* based on personalized inter- action between members of the respective social groups (Brewer & Miller, 1984). A second model focuses on *recategorization*—i.e., uniting groups in a common (superordinate) ingroup identity (Gaertner et al., 1993). Both decategorization and recategorization share a basic assumption that reducing the salience of the original ingroup-outgroup category distinctions is a critical factor in reducing in- tergroup prejudice. As such, these models are often associated with assimila- tionist philosophies of improving intergroup relations. By contrast, the third model, *mutual differentiation*, recommends maintaining social category distinc- tions in the context of mutual interdependence (Hewstone & Brown, 1986)—a model which comes closer to pluralistic philosophies of intergroup relations.

Although all three models of cooperative contact have received empirical support in both laboratory and field research contexts, each has its limitations as a method for long-term social integration (Brewer & Brown, 1998). More recent approaches recommend combining aspects of each of the models to meet needs for social identity and social integration (e.g., Gaertner et al., in press; Hewstone, 1996; Pettigrew, 1998). Dovidio et al. (this volume) have presented the case for a *dual identity* model, in which mutual group differentiation is combined with a common ingroup identity to promote positive intergroup attitudes and respect. In this chapter, I will use the dual identity model as a starting point, consider both its strengths and potential weaknesses, and then describe yet another approach which extends the dual identity model to the case of multiple social identities.

DUAL IDENTIFICATION: WITH THE PART AND THE WHOLE

The idea of dual identification is based on the recognition that social identities with different groups at different levels of inclusiveness need not be mutually exclusive. More specifically, it assumes that individuals can have strong attachment to a specific subgroup and at the same time identify with a superordinate group or social category that includes their ingroup and other subgroups (which are outgroups at the subgroup level)—for instance, they can live in different communities but also be citizens of the same country. Dual identification is presumed to mitigate the negative effects of ingroup-outgroup comparisons at the subgroup level, when both groups are viewed as complementary parts of a larger whole. Dual identities in this sense have been promoted as an appropriate model for multiethnic societies, allowing for preservation of ethnic differentiation and ethnic identity on the one hand, and integration at the national level on the other (e.g., Berry, 1984; Huo, Smith, Tyler, & Lind, 1994).

There are certainly many group contexts in which the dual identity model applies well. Teams, for instance, are often differentiated into specialized subgroups (e.g., offense and defense) which work together in complementary, interdependent ways on behalf of a common superordinate team identity. Many organizational structures are also characterized by differentiation into functional departments or regional subgroups that unite under a common organizational umbrella. In these kinds of organizational structures, identification with subgroup units is presumed to promote the interests of the collective as a whole. But even in organizational settings (where interdependence, complementarity of functions, and common goals are highly salient), intergroup rivalries at the departmental or other subgroup levels often operate in ways that undermine organizational interests at the collective level. If ingroup-outgroup distinctions can create antagonism even within the context of strong superordinate entities, maintaining loyalty to superordinate groups is likely to be problematic when the subgroups are more autonomous and antagonistic to begin with.

There are at least three reasons why dual identifications at both subgroup and superordinate group levels are likely to be unstable. First, the very existence of a common superordinate categorization creates conditions for invidious intergroup comparisons. Social comparison requires a common frame of reference—some relevant standard against which both groups can be evaluated. Common identity implies the existence of some common norms or standards that apply to all group members. Through a process of ethnocentric projection, subgroups are likely to generalize their *own* values and perspectives to the superordinate level, placing any differences between the ingroup and other subgroups in a negative light and promoting perceived ingroup superiority (Mummendey & Wenzel, in press). When all of the groups within a system are jockeying for this kind of ingroup advantage, the collective is undermined by social competition for positive valuation or value dominance.

Second, when dual identities involve social groups at different levels of inclusion, there are both cognitive and motivational reasons why subgroup identities are stronger and more stable than identification at the superordinate level. Subgroups have more cognitive immediacy and salience; ingroup-outgroup distinctions at the subgroup level are more frequently encountered than are shared group boundaries at the superordinate level. At the same time, subgroups are more likely to meet individual needs for inclusion and differentiation, thereby providing more optimal social identities (Brewer, 1991). This differential strength of identification is not necessarily problematic if the goals and interests of the subgroup and the collective interests of the superordinate group are generally compatible or mutually promotive. But under conditions where collective interests require some sacrifice by the subgroup (or advantage an outgroup over the ingroup at the subgroup level), subgroup loyalties are likely to override collective welfare at the superordinate level.

Finally, the problems with dual identification are exacerbated when there are asymmetries of size or status or power among the subgroups within the superordinate context. Given the combined forces of ingroup bias and ethnocentric projection, groups that are larger or have more access to resources or political control will be in a position to dominate the value system and the collective identity of the superordinate group. For dominant subgroups, dual identification at the subgroup and the superordinate levels will appear to be relatively unproblematic. For disadvantaged or nondominant subgroups, however, superordinate identity may imply acceptance of domination by an outgroup, and thus be perceived as being in conflict with identification at the subgroup level (Brewer, von Hippel, & Gooden, 1999; Sidanius, Feshbach, Levin, & Pratto, 1997).

For all of these reasons, one may accept the concept of dual identities as an ideal that can be achieved under some circumstances, but be pessimistic about its potential as a stable solution for reducing prejudice and intergroup discrimination. This does not mean, however, that the only alternative to continued intergroup conflict is assimilation to a single, undifferentiated common ingroup.

There may be other forms of pluralism that hold more promise for maintaining distinctive social identities within a common superordinate structure.

MULTIPLE IDENTITIES AND CROSS-CUTTING CATEGORIES

The dual identity model implies an embedded hierarchy of social groupings in which a superordinate category is divided into subgroups on the basis of a *single* dimension of differentiation. Examples of such embedded hierarchies would be regions or states within a federation, ethnic and religious groups within a nation, or academic departments within a university. In such a system, subgroup identities are mutually exclusive and each group member belongs to one and only one subgroup—all other groups at that level in the hierarchy being outgroups. In this case, the only choices of identity are at different levels of inclusiveness (e.g., individual, sub-subgroup, subgroup, or superordinate levels).

Large, complex organizations or societies, however, are rarely characterized by such a simple hierarchical structure of embedded groupings. Instead, societies are differentiated along a number of different dimensions of social identity—ethnicity, religion, region, occupation, gender—each of which subdivides the whole into different subgroupings with overlapping memberships. In such a system, individuals may belong to, and identify with, multiple ingroups *at the same level of inclusion*. Further, other individuals, who are outgroup members in one category distinction, may be fellow ingroup members in another.

Societies or social systems that are differentiated along a single line of fission are the ones that are most susceptible to the subgroup conflicts and strife discussed above. Cross-cutting categorizations (and associated multiple identities) may diffuse or prevent the more invidious consequences of ingroup-outgroup differentiation and intergroup comparison. This insight that complex, cross-cutting patterns of social differentiation increase social stability and tolerance has been independently generated by anthropologists (e.g., Gluckman, 1955; Murphy, 1957), sociologists (e.g., Blau, 1977; Coser, 1956; Flap, 1988), and political scientists (e.g., Almond & Verba, 1963; Lipset, 1959). Coser (1956) hypothesized, for instance:

> In flexible social structures, multiple conflicts crisscross each other and thereby prevent basic cleavages along one axis. The multiple group affiliations of individuals make them participate in various group conflicts so that their total personalities are not involved in any single one of them. Thus segmental participation in a multiplicity of conflicts constitutes a balancing mechanism within the structure....(pp. 153-154)

Similarly, Lipset (1959) identified role differentiation and cross-cutting ties as essential structural preconditions for the development of stable democracies. Social psychologists, however, are just beginning to recognize the potential importance of cross-cutting group memberships for the reduction of prejudice and discrimination, and to subject these political-sociological hypotheses to experimental test.

EFFECTS OF CROSS-CATEGORIZATION

Theoretical Principles

From a social psychological perspective, the question to be asked is whether ingroup bias and intergroup discrimination based on a particular ingroup-outgroup distinction are reduced when another cross-cutting ingroup-outgroup category distinction is introduced. There are a number of theoretical reasons why multiple cross-cutting social identities might reduce discrimination along any one dimension.

First, cross-cutting distinctions make social categorization more complex and reduce the magnitude of ingroup-outgroup distinctions. According to social categorization theory (Deschamps & Doise, 1978; Doise, 1978; Vanbeselaere, 1991) processes of intracategory assimilation and intercategory contrast counteract each other when categories are cross-cutting. Thus, the effects of intercategory accentuation are reduced or eliminated, and differences between groups are minimized (or are no greater than perceived differences within groups). This undermines the cognitive basis of ingroup bias.

Second, partially overlapping group memberships reduce the evaluative significance for the self of intergroup comparisons (Brown & Turner, 1979), thereby undermining the motivational base for intergroup discrimination (Vanbeselaere, 1991).

Third, multiple group memberships reduce the importance of any one social identity for satisfying an individual's need for belonging and self-definition (Brewer, 1991), again reducing the motivational base for ingroup bias.

Finally, principles of cognitive balance (Heider, 1958; Newcomb, 1963) are also brought into play when ingroups and outgroups have overlapping membership. When another person is an ingroup member on one category dimension but belongs to an outgroup on another categorization, cognitive inconsistency is introduced if that individual is evaluated positively as an ingroup member but is also evaluated negatively as an outgroup member and associated with other outgroup members who are evaluated negatively. In an effort to resolve such inconsistencies, interpersonal balance processes should lead to greater positivity toward the outgroup based on overlapping memberships.

All of these factors that would mitigate intergroup bias when categories are crossed would operate to *enhance* bias if two different bases of categorization are convergent (i.e., ingroup-outgroup distinctions on one category overlap perfectly with ingroup-outgroup distinctions on a second category, as when distinctions based on ethnicity and religion correspond). To take the simplest possible case, consider the possible relationships between one two-group categorization (designated as A vs. B) and a second two-group categorization (designated as 1 vs. 2). In the convergent category case, all members of group A are also members of group 1 while all members of group B are also members of group 2. Thus, the only existing category distinction is A1 vs. B2 and intergroup differentiation would be strengthened by this combination of two superimposed category distinctions (Arcuri, 1982).

In the cross-cutting categorization case, membership in A vs. B and membership in 1 vs. 2 would be orthogonal. Thus, individuals could fall into any one of four classifications: A1, A2, B1, B2. For a member of group A, some members of outgroup B would be fellow ingroup members on the other dimension. In this case, we would predict that intergroup bias on the A-B dimension would be lowered compared to the degree of A-B bias in the convergent category situation.

Experimental Evidence

This prediction was tested experimentally in a laboratory paradigm designed by Marcus-Newhall, Miller, Holtz, & Brewer (1993). In this experiment, participants were first divided into arbitrary social categories, based (ostensibly) on the results of a dot-estimation judgment task. Each experimental session was run with 8 same-sex participants, four of whom were told they were "underestimators" and four of whom were assigned to the "overestimators" category. All were given large colored ID buttons to wear that clearly signified their estimator category membership. Overestimators and underestimators were then segregated for a brief discussion period which served as an ingroup formation consolidation phase. In the next phase of the experiment, participants were reassigned to four-person teams, each team consisting of two underestimators and two overestimators. The teams then engaged in a cooperative task which provided the opportunity for the introduction of a crossed category manipulation.

The cooperative task that teams undertook was to reach consensus, through team discussion, on a list of the seven most critical traits that should be considered in selection of NASA astronauts. Prior to engaging in the group discussion, each team-member was given a set of preliminary materials to read that would establish their "expertise" regarding the stresses and demands faced by astronauts in preparing for and experiencing space travel. Two of the team-members were given materials that provided information on the cognitive and skill demands of the astronaut role, and the other two were given information on the emotional and social demands of the job. Thus, two members shared the role of "cognitive expert" and two shared the role of "emotional expert" for the upcoming team task. In the *convergent categorization* experimental condition, both overestimators were assigned to the same expert role and both underestimators were assigned to the other role, so that estimator category and role were redundant differentiations. In the *cross-cutting* condition, on the other hand, two members of the same category were assigned to different roles, so that the estimator category and role were orthogonal.

After individually receiving their role assignment and reviewing their information packets, all four team-members were brought together, and they engaged in
free discussion until they had agreed upon a list of seven emotional and cognitive requirements for the selection of astronauts. Once the team handed in their
consensual list to the experimenter, members were again separated and asked
to complete a number of postdiscussion measures. The critical measures were
evaluations of each of the fellow team-members and a point assignment wherein
the rater allocated up to 100 "chips" to each of the team-members as recognition
for their contributions to the group product. From these measures, estimator
category bias scores were computed by subtracting the average rating and allocation assigned to the outgroup category members on the team from those assigned to the ingroup category member. This made it possible to assess how
intercategory discrimination (for supposed underestimators vs. overestimators)
had been affected by intergroup cooperation and the assignment of role categories.

As expected, Marcus-Newhall et al. (1993, Experiment 1) found that the convergent role assignment condition produced significant bias based on category
membership on the point-allocation measure. In the cross-categorization condition, however, this category-based bias was completely eliminated. Since this
initial study was published, two replication experiments have been conducted
that demonstrate that the cross-categorization effect on bias reduction is robust
also for natural (as opposed to artificial) social categories, including ones that
are asymmetric in terms of size or status. Bettencourt and Dorr (1998) formed 6-
person teams composed of Republicans and Democrats where one group was
in the minority (2 members on the team) and the other group was in the majority
(4 members on the team), and role assignment either converged with or cross-
cut political group membership. In another context, Rust (1996) created 4-person
teams consisting of two university sophomores (higher status group) and two
freshmen (lower status group), again with cross-cutting or convergent role assignments on the team task. Both of these experiments replicated the Marcus-
Newhall et al. findings, showing significant differences for the effect of role assignment on ingroup bias, both in evaluations and in point allocation.

A summary of the mean bias results for convergent and cross-cutting category conditions from all three of these studies is provided in Table 8.1. As can
be seen from the pattern of findings, in all three experiments cross-cutting role
assignments eliminated any significant ingroup bias based on the original ingroup-outgroup category distinctions, and they did so on both evaluative and allocation measures. On the allocation measure, ingroup bias was significant under the convergent role assignment condition in all three experiments. (Evidence
of ingroup bias on the evaluative ratings was generally low, but when it did appear under convergent role assignment conditions, it disappeared with cross-
cutting categorization.) These differences as a function of task assignment occurred even though all conditions involved high levels of face-to-face contact

TABLE 8.1
Summary of Laboratory Experimental Findings on
Cross-Cutting Categorization and Ingroup Bias

	Task Assignment Condition	
Study and Measure	Convergent	Cross-Cutting
Marcus-Newhall et al. (1993, Study 1)		
Evaluative bias	+0.17	+0.11
Allocation bias	+3.27	+0.06 **
Bettencourt & Dorr (1998, Study 1)		
Evaluative bias	+0.25	-0.02 **
Allocation bias	+4.84	-1.76 **
Rust (1996)		
Evaluative bias	+0.74	+0.43 **
Allocation bias	+1.16	+0.05 **

** condition means are significantly different (p < .01).

under cooperative goal conditions—the very conditions specified by the contact hypothesis to reduce intergroup discrimination and prejudice. The results from these experiments suggest that cooperative contact will not necessarily eliminate category-based biases unless the contact situation makes other social identities salient and meaningful.

Generalizing Beyond the Laboratory

These laboratory experiments are promising with respect to the potential for cross-cutting category membership to reduce intergroup bias and discrimination, but they do have their limitations as a general model of prejudice reduction. The intergroup situation in the laboratory paradigm involves a great deal of interpersonal contact between members of the two social categories, and bias assessments have been obtained only for group members who have participated in the team task. Given the demands of the discussion task, the cross-cutting role assignment promotes more personalization of team-members across category boundaries and, indeed, there is evidence that this personalization mediates the effects of role assignment, and that the effectiveness of cross-categorization in reducing bias is diminished when there is less opportunity for personalized interaction (Marcus-Newhall et al., 1993, Experiment 2; Bettencourt & Dorr, 1998, Experiment 2). Thus, although the positive results of the cross-cutting role assignment experiments do have direct implications for work teams in organizational settings (Brewer, 1995), generalization of these effects for large-scale social categories whose members are not involved in close intergroup interaction has yet to be established.

In the society at large, social categories tend to constrain social contact, so that individuals have most interpersonal interactions with others who share one or more ingroup category memberships. Thus, even though individuals may belong to multiple relatively inclusive categories with overlapping memberships, their *cognitive representations* of those ingroup categories may be limited by their range of experience with category members with whom they interact (Blau, 1977).

The first issue to be confronted in real-world contexts is whether two or more social categorizations are equally salient in a given social situation. If a single dimension of social differentiation dominates the definition of social identities in a given context, the presence of cross-cutting group identities will be largely ignored and cannot be expected to influence intergroup discrimination based on the dominant category. In some cases, category dominance may be chronic, as when a single line of social fission (e.g., race or religion) comes to have pervasive social and political significance across all domains of social life. In other cases, category dominance may be situation-specific. Some social differentiations are particularly meaningful in one social setting (e.g., occupation in the workplace) while different category distinctions are more meaningful in another setting (e.g., ethnicity in a school setting). When ingroup memberships are situationally or psychologically isolated, individuals will classify themselves and others according to the single category distinction that is relevant in a particular situation, ignoring the fact that some ingroup members would be considered outgroupers in a different situation and vice versa.

In order for crossed categories to have psychological effects, two or more category distinctions must have *functional significance within the same social context*. That is, individuals must confront the fact that their different ingroup-outgroup categories have overlapping memberships. The experimental situation designed by Marcus-Newhall et al. (1993) was structured so as to insure that both social distinctions (overestimation category and role expertise) would be salient and functionally significant within the cooperative task context. The salience and importance of the overestimator-underestimator distinction was established by the alleged purpose of the experiment itself (to study the effects of this difference between people) and by the salience of visual cues to category membership throughout the experimental session. Classification on the basis of role assignment was made important by virtue of its relevance to success on the assigned task, since the final product of the group discussion required integration of information from both domains of expertise. The effectiveness of role assignment cross-categorization in reducing discrimination based on category membership may have depended on this high degree of simultaneous salience and relevance of the two category distinctions. If one category distinction had dominated the social interaction, overall bias might not have been reduced even though a crossed categorization was present (Pepels, 1999).

Even when two or more categories are made simultaneously salient and meaningful, the effects of crossed category memberships may not be sufficient to reduce intergroup discrimination. The outcome will depend on how the individual construes his or her multiple group memberships. To take the simple 2 (A-B) x 2 (1-2) crossed categorization considered earlier, an individual who belongs simultaneously to category A and category 1 may construe those combined ingroups in a number of different ways. Figure 8.1 presents three different cognitive representations that vary in terms of the *degree of inclusiveness* of the psychological ingroup.

In the representation depicted by Figure 8.1(a), the individual is aware that his/her ingroup A contains some members of category 2, and that ingroup 1 contains some persons who are members of category B, and all of these persons are considered to be ingroup members. Thus, the combined psychological ingroup is *more* inclusive than either category A or category 1 considered alone. However, persons who are members of neither ingroup category still constitute a distinct outgroup (the "double outgroup"), and are subject to intergroup discrimination and prejudice.

Figure 8.1(b) depicts a very different representation of dual category memberships, in which only persons who share *both* ingroup memberships are considered as the ingroup. In this case, the combined psychological ingroup is *less* inclusive than either ingroup A or ingroup 1. Only the overlapping portions of the

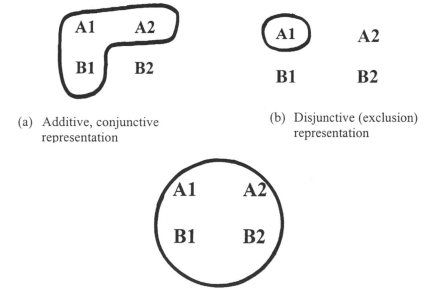

(a) Additive, conjunctive
    representation

(b) Disjunctive (exclusion)
    representation

(c) Inclusive (equivalence) representation

FIG. 8.1. Alternative representations of multiple group memberships.

two categories are defined as the ingroup, and individuals who share only one category membership are part of the outgroup.

Finally, Figure 8.1(c) depicts the most inclusive representation of combined categories, where the presence of crossed categories eliminates discrimination based on either category distinction. In this case, overlapping memberships reduce the psychological distances between ingroup and outgroup in both dimensions, including even those who do not share membership with the perceiver in either category A or category 1. Through their connections with members of the overlapping ingroups, B2 individuals become members of the expanded psychological ingroup.

To make the alternatives represented in Figure 8.1 more concrete, let's consider the example of an individual who is both a female and an African American, i.e., has social identities that derive from gender categorization on the one hand and from her ethnicity on the other. Objectively, gender and ethnicity are cross-cutting social distinctions. Thus, when the individual considers her gender ingroup, the group includes females of various ethnicity, some Black and some non-Black. Conversely, when she considers her ethnic ingroup, it includes male as well as female African Americans. As long as the individual embraces *both* ingroup identities inclusively, her psychological ingroup includes at least some ethnic outgroupers and some gender outgroupers, as in Figures 8.1(a) and 8.1(c).

Imagine, however, that when our individual thinks about her female ingroup, she is aware that she represents an ethnic minority within that gender category and hence feels socially differentiated from White females. Similarly, when she thinks about her ethnic ingroup, she is aware of the implications of her gender identity vis-a-vis African American males. Under these circumstances, she may categorize herself as an African American woman, and only those who share this combined category membership may constitute her psychological ingroup, as in Figure 8.1(b). In this case, African Americans who are males, and females who are White, represent outgroup categories rather than shared social identities.

WHEN DO MULTIPLE IDENTITIES REDUCE PREJUDICE?

The different cognitive representations depicted in Figure 8.1 demonstrate that the relationship between multiple social identities and intergroup discrimination and prejudice is not a simple straightforward one, even when the categories involved are objectively cross-cutting or overlapping. The patterns of inclusiveness represented by 1(a) and 1(c) should reduce (or eliminate) intergroup discrimination based on either category distinction, as expected from the sociological literature on cross-cutting social structures (Coser, 1956). However, if multiple category distinctions serve to differentiate a society into a greater number of exclusive subcategories, as represented in 1(b), the consequence may be an increase in ingroup bias and intergroup conflict, rather than a decrease. Thus, the issue for those interested in the reduction of prejudice and conflict is to understand when (or under what conditions) multiple identities will be defined *inclusively* rather than exclusively.

One way to think of the difference between inclusive and exclusive identity patterns is in terms of social and cognitive complexity. Although the representation depicted in 1(b) results in a greater number of differentiated groups at the societal level, 1(a) and 1(c) reflect more complex representations of the ingroup because they involve both differentiation and integration (Schroder, 1971). Thinking about it in this way provides a conceptual framework for speculating as to what situational and individual difference factors may promote inclusive vs. exclusive representations of multiple category identities.

Generalizing from the literature on cognitive complexity (e.g., Hunsberger et al., 1992; Tetlock, 1983, 1986), we would expect that exclusive definitions of the ingroup would be promoted when individuals have a high need for certainty or cognitive simplification. If multiple, overlapping ingroup-outgroup distinctions increase uncertainty about whether to classify others as ingroup members or not, a simplifying strategy that limits ingroup membership to those who clearly meet all criteria for shared identity reduces that uncertainty. This strategy has parallels to the "ingroup overexclusion effect" (Leyens & Yzerbyt, 1992; Yzerbyt, Leyens, & Bellour, 1995) whereby an individual decides by the rule "when in doubt, assume the other is *not* an ingroup member."

Need for certainty has been studied as an individual difference variable, with a focus largely on the development of measures to assess individual dispositions to seek certainty or avoid uncertainty (e.g., Huber & Sorentino, 1996; Neuberg & Newsom, 1993; Webster & Kruglanski, 1994), rather than on the antecedents or causes of these differences in cognitive style. However, high need for certainty can also be situationally induced, particularly by conditions that generate high stress or perceived threat. Thus, we would predict that when individuals, or social systems, are threatened by psychological, economic, or political loss, social identities will be defined more exclusively (less complexly) than under low threat conditions. Exclusiveness should also be associated with high levels of conservatism and resistance to change.

Another factor that may influence the propensity toward exclusive ingroup representations can be derived from the optimal distinctiveness theory of social identification (Brewer, 1991). This theory holds that social identification with groups is motivated by two opposing needs or social drives. On the one hand, individuals have a need for inclusion with others in social units larger than the individual self, and on the other hand, they have a need for differentiation from others. These two drives hold each other in check. As individuals begin to feel highly individuated, distinct, and separate from others, the need for inclusion is aroused; but when they feel immersed in very large and highly inclusive groups, the need for differentiation is activated. As a consequence, individuals are most satisfied by identification with distinctive social groups or categories that meet both needs simultaneously; the need for inclusion is met by assimilation *within* such groups, while the need for differentiation is met by distinctions *between* the ingroup and other groups.

The motivation to define ingroups exclusively rather than inclusively should be related to the strength of activation of the need for differentiation (relative to the need for inclusion). Thus, when individuals feel immersed in a nonoptimally large or amorphous social unit ("just a number"), or are experiencing a loss of the sense of boundary for social obligations and relationships, they should seek more exclusive ingroup category memberships and be less willing to tolerate overlapping group memberships. Social status differentials can also combine to motivate exclusive subgroup identifications. Individuals who belong to multiple groups who are disadvantaged or relatively low in social status (e.g., African American females), or are relatively high-status (e.g., White males), may be more likely to define their psychological ingroup exclusively (based on shared status) than are individuals whose ingroup memberships confer differential status positions (i.e., where high and low status is an additional crossed category).

Factors that would be predicted to promote more inclusive multiple identities include high cognitive complexity and tolerance for uncertainty, as well as secure social identity or strong activation of the need for inclusion (relative to the need for differentiation). In addition, general positive affect should be associated with inclusive representations of multiple ingroups. Positive mood has been found to affect cognitive style in the direction of greater category breadth (e.g., Isen & Daubman, 1984), and to encourage more inclusive social categorization (Isen, 1987). Consistent with this expectation, a review of the research literature on evaluations of stimulus persons who vary in combined category memberships indicates that positive affect predicts more positive attitudes toward others who share ingroup membership on any dimension (Urban & Miller, 1998).

There are also a number of external conditions or situational factors that might encourage more inclusive cross-category representations. Social mobility and increased contact across group boundaries reduce provincialism (Pettigrew, 1997) and expose the individual to direct experiences with cross-cutting group memberships. Such experience increases awareness that an ingroup category includes others who are diverse with respect to alternative category memberships. If this exposure takes place in the context of positive, shared ingroup experiences, the consequence should be a more inclusive conceptualization of ingroups in general (cf. Pettigrew & Tropp, this volume). Similarly, pluralistic cultural norms and social values that favor tolerance and openness to change should also encourage more inclusive ingroup representations (Roccas & Schwartz, 1997).

Finally, the undifferentiated acceptance of all combinations of crossed categories depicted in Figure 8.1(c) may be facilitated by the presence of a salient, attractive superordinate category that encompasses all of the subcategory combinations (Crisp & Hewstone, in press). Thus, if A-B and 1-2 are cross-cutting subdivisions of the same superordinate group (e.g., a nation), identification at the more inclusive level solves the problems of achieving cognitive balance in the face of overlapping ingroups and outgroups. If this is the case, then there will be a reciprocal relationship between superordinate category identification and the presence of multiple cross-cutting subgroups. That is, a superordinate category identity facilitates acceptance of overlapping ingroup-outgroup memberships; and at the same time, multiple cross-cutting social identities contribute to motivation to sustain identification at the superordinate level. Thus, cross-cutting social structures may provide the context in which relationships between subgroup and superordinate levels of identification can be both positive and stable.

SOCIAL IDENTITY COMPLEXITY AND PREJUDICE REDUCTION

This conceptual analysis of the causes and consequences of the cognitive representation of multiple identities focuses on the *phenomenological* rather than the objective categorization structure. In order to understand when cross-cutting categories will be effective in reducing prejudice, we need to know how the individual perceives his or her ingroups. To study social identity complexity and prejudice requires some method for assessing the subjective meaning of crossed category memberships at the individual level.

At this stage, our own research on assessing social identity complexity is still very preliminary, but some of our preliminary efforts have produced promising results. In questionnaire surveys of undergraduate college students, we have asked respondents to check various social categories to which they belong (from a lengthy list of ethnic, religious, political, organizational, demographic, and geographical social groups), and to indicate which of these group memberships are particularly important to them. The vast majority of college students list at least 4 or 5 different social identities as important to them, and most of these represent objectively cross-cutting social distinctions (e.g., Catholic religion and Ohio citizen). Thus, the raw material of cross-cutting multiple social identities is prevalent even among this relatively young population.

In a subsequent questionnaire, we have reminded respondents of their individual social group identities and asked them a series of questions about the relationships they perceive between different pairs of their ingroups (e.g., Catholics and Ohioans). One question assesses (on a 10-point rating scale) their subjective impression of the extent of overlap in membership between the two ingroups (e.g., "Of persons who are Catholic, how many are also Ohioans?" "Of persons who are Ohioans, how many are also Catholic?"). In general, the lower the degree of overlap between different ingroups, the more inclusively the individual is defining each ingroup separately (i.e., if the number of Ohioans who are also Catholic is perceived to be low, then the Ohio ingroup must include many non-Catholics; if the number of Catholics who are Ohioans is low, then the Catholic ingroup must include non-Ohioans, etc.). On the other hand, if the overlap between ingroups is perceived to be high, the categories are subjectively convergent rather than cross-cutting (i.e., the ingroup is conceptualized exclusively—as Catholic *and* Ohioan).

Based on this logic, a relatively crude index of the complexity of multiple category representations can be generated by averaging the overlap ratings across all possible pairings of the person's mentioned ingroups. Low values on this index signify relatively *high* complexity (ingroup inclusiveness), while high values represent low complexity (exclusiveness). An initial assessment of the psychometric properties of this index (based on pairings of nationality, religion, ethnicity, and university ingroup identities) revealed a reasonable distribution of scores (M = 3.17, sd = 1.03, N = 198) (Roccas & Brewer, 1999). Further, scores on the index were correlated in a predictable manner with respondents' important social values. Using Schwartz's (1992) circumplex model of value classification, we found that the overlap index (where higher scores indicate less complexity—greater exclusiveness) correlated positively with Conservation (r = .13, N = 151) and Self-Enhancement (individualism) (r = .25), and negatively with Openness to Change (r = -.18) and Universalism (r = -.25).

As a further exploration of the construct validity of the perceived overlap index of identity complexity, some respondents rated (on a 7-point scale of feelings of closeness) a series of target persons described by category memberships that either corresponded to the respondents' ingroups or to contrasting outgroups. Respondents who were classified as high in identity complexity (low index scores) did not differ from low complexity respondents in their evaluations of ingroup targets, but they rated the multiple outgroup targets significantly more positively. The difference between ratings of the ingroup targets and outgroup targets was significantly smaller for high complexity respondents (M = .40, N = 31) than for low complexity respondents (M = 1.22, N = 32). Thus, there is preliminary evidence that complexity, or inclusiveness, of ingroup representations is associated with greater tolerance and acceptance of outgroup members.

At this point, the development of our measure of ingroup inclusiveness is still rather crude, and the data are very preliminary. But if these findings are replicated with more refined measures and larger samples, they will provide support for our thesis that having a cross-cutting category structure and multiple social identities with awareness of ingroup diversity will contribute to reduced intergroup prejudice. If this is the case, then the next step in a program of prejudice reduction will be to understand the conditions under which membership in multiple social categories will be accompanied by a complex and inclusive cognitive representation of those ingroups. From this perspective, what we will need is a comprehensive theory involving the dynamic interactions between individual differences, social structure, and social cognition, as the foundation of a social psychologically informed approach to prejudice reduction.

REFERENCES

Almond, G. A., & Verba, S. (1963). *The civic culture: Political attitudes in five nations.* Princeton, NJ: Princeton University Press.

Arcuri, L. (1982). Three patterns of social categorization in attribution memory. *European Journal of Social Psychology, 12,* 271-282.

Berry, J. W. (1984). Cultural relations in plural societies: Alternatives to segregation and their sociopsychological implications. In N. Miller & M. Brewer (Eds.), *Groups in contact: The psychology of desegregation* (pp. 11-27). New York: Academic Press.

Bettencourt, B. A., & Dorr, N. (1998). Cooperative interaction and intergroup bias: Effects of numerical representation and cross-cut role assignment. *Personality and Social Psychology Bulletin, 24,* 1276-1293.

Blau, P. M. (1977). *Inequality and heterogeneity: A primitive theory of social structure.* New York: Free Press.

Brewer, M. B. (1991). The social self: On being the same and different at the same time. *Personality and Social Psychology Bulletin, 17,* 475-482.

Brewer, M. B. (1995). Managing diversity: The role of social identities. In S. Jackson & M. Rudderman (Eds.), *Diversity in work teams* (pp. 47-68). Washington, DC: American Psychological Association.

Brewer, M. B., & Brown, R. (1998). Intergroup relations. In D. Gilbert, S. Fiske, & G. Lindzey (Eds.), *Handbook of social psychology* (Vol. 2, pp. 554-594). Boston: McGraw-Hill.

Brewer, M. B., & Miller, N. (1984). Beyond the contact hypothesis: Theoretical perspectives on desegregation. In N. Miller & M. Brewer (Eds.), *Groups in contact: The psychology of desegregation* (pp. 281-302). New York: Academic Press.

Brewer, M. B., von Hippel, W., & Gooden, M. (1999). Diversity and organizational identity: The problem of entrée after entry. In D. Prentice & D. Miller (Eds.). *Cultural divides: Understanding and overcoming group conflict* (pp. 337-363). New York: Russell Sage Foundation.

Brown, R., & Turner, J. C. (1979). The criss-cross categorization effect in intergroup discrimination. *British Journal of Social Psychology, 18,* 371-383.

Coser, L. A. (1956). *The functions of social conflict.* New York: Free Press.

Crisp, R. J., & Hewstone, M. (in press). Multiple categorization and social identity. In D. Capozza & R. Brown (Eds.), *Social identity processes: Trends in theory and research.* London, England: Sage.

Deschamps, J-C., & Doise, W. (1978). Crossed category membership in intergroup relations. In H. Tajfel (Ed.), *Differentiation between social groups: Studies in the social psychology of intergroup relations* (pp. 141-158). London: Academic Press.

Doise, W. (1978). *Groups and individuals: Explanations in social psychology.* Cambridge: Cambridge University Press.

Doise, W., & Sinclair, (1973). The categorization process in intergroup relations. *European Journal of Social Psychology, 3,* 145-157.

Flap, H. D. (1988). *Conflict, loyalty and violence: The effects of social networks on behaviour.* Frankfurt, Germany: Lang.

Gaertner, S. L., Dovidio, J. F., Anastasio, P. A., Bachman, B. A., & Rust, M. C. (1993). The common ingroup identity model: Recategorization and the reduction of intergroup bias. In W. Stroebe & M. Hewstone (Eds.), *European review of social psychology* (Vol. 4, pp. 1-26). London: Wiley.

Gaertner, S. L., Dovidio, J. F., Nier, J. A., Banker, B. S., Ward, C. M., Houlette, M., & Loux, S. (in press). The common ingroup identity model for reducing intergroup bias: Progress and challenges. In D. Capozza & R. Brown (Eds.), *Social identity processes: Trends in theory and research*. London, England: Sage.

Gluckman, M. (1955). *Customs and conflict in Africa*. London, England: Blackwell.

Heider, F. (1958). *The psychology of interpersonal relations*. New York: Wiley.

Hewstone, M. (1996). Contact and categorization: Social psychological interventions to change intergroup relations. In C. N. Macrae, C. Stangor, & M. Hewstone (Eds.), *Foundations of stereotypes and stereotyping* (pp. 323-368). New York: Guilford.

Hewstone, M., & Brown, R. (1986). Contact is not enough: An intergroup perspective on the "contact hypothesis." In M. Hewstone & R. Brown (Eds.), *Contact and conflict in intergroup encounters* (pp. 1-44). Oxford, England: Blackwell.

Huber, G. L., & Sorrentino, R. M. (1996). Uncertainty in interpersonal and intergroup relations: An individual-differences perspective. In R. Sorrentino & E. T. Higgins (Eds.), *Handbook of motivation and cognition* (vol. 3, pp. 591-619). New York: Guilford.

Hunsberger, B., Lea, J., Pancer, S., Pratt, M., & McKenzie, B. (1992). Making life complicated: Prompting the use of integratively complex thinking. *Journal of Personality, 60*, 95-114.

Huo, Y., Smith, H., Tyler, T., & Lind, E. A. (1994). Superordinate identification, subgroup identification, and justice concerns: Is separatism the problem; Is assimilation the answer? *Psychological Science, 7*, 40-45.

Isen, A. M. (1987). Positive affect, cognitive processes, and social behavior. In L. Berkowitz (Ed.), *Advances in experimental social psychology* (Vol. 20, pp. 203-253). San Diego, CA: Academic Press.

Isen, A. M., & Daubman, K. A. (1984). The influence of affect on categorization. *Journal of Personality and Social Psychology, 47*, 1206-1217.

Lemaine, G. (1974). Social differentiation and social originality. *European Journal of Social Psychology, 4*, 17-52.

Leyens, J-P., & Yzerbyt, V. (1992). The ingroup overexclusion effect: Impact of valence and confirmation on stereotypical information search. *European Journal of Social Psychology, 22*, 549-570.

Lipset, S. M. (1959). Some social requisites of democracy: Economic development and political legitimacy. *American Political Science Review, 53*, 69-105.

Marcus-Newhall, A., Miller, N., Holtz, R., & Brewer, M. B. (1993). Cross-cutting category membership with role assignment: A means of reducing intergroup bias. *British Journal of Social Psychology, 32*, 125-146.

Mummendey, A., & Wenzel, M. (in press). Social discrimination and tolerance in intergroup relations: Reactions to intergroup difference. *Personality and Social Psychology Review*.

Murphy, R. F. (1957). Intergroup hostility and social cohesion. *American Anthropologist, 59*, 1018-1035.

Neuberg, S. L., & Newsom, J. T. (1993). Personal need for structure: Individual differences in the desire for simple structure. *Journal of Personality and Social Psychology, 65*, 113-131.

Newcomb, T. (1963). Stabilities underlying changes in interpersonal attraction. *Journal of Abnormal and Social Psychology, 66*, 376-386.

Pepels, J. (1999). *The myth of the positive crossed categorization effect*. Amsterdam:

European Centre on Migration and Ethnic Relations.

Pettigrew, T. F. (1967). Social evaluation theory: Convergences and applications. In D. Levine (Ed.), *Nebraska symposium on motivation, 1967* (pp. 241-311). Lincoln: University of Nebraska Press.

Pettigrew, T. F. (1997). Generalized intergroup contact effects on prejudice. *Personality and Social Psychology Bulletin, 23*, 173-185.

Pettigrew, T. F. (1998). Intergroup contact theory. *Annual Review of Psychology, 49*, 65-85.

Roccas, S., & Brewer, M. B. (1999). Unpublished data.

Roccas, S., & Schwartz, S. H. (1997). Church-state relations and the association of religiosity with values: A study of Catholics in six countries. *Cross-Cultural Research, 31*, 356-375.

Rust, M. C. (1996). *Social identity and social categorization*. Unpublished doctoral dissertation, University of Delaware.

Schroder, H. M. (1971). Conceptual complexity. In H. Schroder & P. Suedfeld (Eds.), *Personality theory and information processing* (pp. 240-273). New York: Ronald.

Schwartz, S. H. (1992). Universals in the content and structure of values: Theoretical advances and empirical tests in 20 countries. In M. Zanna (Ed.), *Advances in experimental social psychology* (Vol. 25, pp. 1-65). Orlando, FL: Academic Press.

Sidanius, J., Feshbach, S., Levin, S., & Pratto, F. (1997). The interface between ethnic and national attachment: Ethnic pluralism or ethnic dominance? *Public Opinion Quarterly, 61*, 103-133.

Tajfel, H. (1969). Cognitive aspects of prejudice. *Journal of Social Issues, 25*(4), pp. 79-97.

Tajfel, H. (1978). Social categorization, social identity and social comparison. In H. Tajfel (Ed.), *Differentiation between social groups: Studies in the social psychology of intergroup relations*. London: Academic Press.

Tetlock, P. E. (1983). Accountability and complexity of thought. *Journal of Personality and Social Psychology, 45*, 74-83.

Tetlock, P. E. (1986). A value pluralism model of ideological reasoning. *Journal of Personality and Social Psychology, 50*, 819-827.

Turner, J. C. (1975). Social comparison and social identity: Some prospects for intergroup behaviour. *European Journal of Social Psychology, 5*, 5-34.

Turner, J. C. (1985). Social categorization and the self-concept: A social cognitive theory of group behavior. In E. Lawler (Ed.), *Advances in group processes* (Vol. 2, pp. 77-122). Greenwich, CT: JAI Press.

Urban, L. M., & Miller, N. (1998). A theoretical analysis of crossed categorization effects: A meta-analysis. *Journal of Personality and Social Psychology, 74*, 894-908.

Vanbeselaere, N. (1991). The different effects of simple and crossed categorizations: A result of the category differentiation process or of differential category salience? In W. Stroebe & M. Hewstone (Eds.), *European review of social psychology* (Vol. 2, pp. 247-278). Chichester, UK: Wiley.

Vanneman, R. D., & Pettigrew, T. F. (1972). Race and relative deprivation in the urban United States. *Race, 13*, 461-486.

Webster, D. M., & Kruglanski, A. W. (1994). Individual differences in the need for cognitive closure. *Journal of Personality and Social Psychology, 67*, 1049-1062.

Wilder, D. (1986). Social categorization: Implications for creation and reduction of intergroup bias. In L. Berkowitz (Ed.), *Advances in experimental social psychology* (Vol. 19, pp. 291-355). San Diego, CA: Academic Press.

Yzerbyt, V., Leyens, J-P., & Bellour, F. (1995). The ingroup overexclusion effect: Identity concerns in decisions about group membership. *European Journal of Social Psychology, 25*, 1-16.

9 Breaking the Prejudice Habit: Progress and Obstacles

Patricia G. Devine
E. Ashby Plant
Brenda N. Buswell
University of Wisconsin–Madison

The latter half of the 20th century has witnessed dramatic legislative changes (e.g., the 1954 Supreme Court ruling on school desegregation and the Civil Rights Laws of the early 1960s), which made overt discrimination based on race illegal. These laws altered the social and political landscape in fundamental ways and began to erode traditional racist norms. These changes have culminated in a rather pervasive norm that discourages overt expressions of prejudice in the United States (Blanchard, Lily, & Vaughn, 1991; Monteith, Deneen, & Tooman, 1996; Plant & Devine, 1998). In response, social scientists quickly became interested in documenting such changes and developing conceptual analyses to understand their impact.

Our major goal in this chapter is to explore the implications of these changing social norms as influences on individual-level attitudes and on the prospects for reducing prejudice. In our own research, consideration of the consequences of normative changes has led us in two directions, both of which, we believe, are critically important to understanding contemporary obstacles in combating prejudice. On one hand, evidence shows that we as a society, and some individuals personally, have made great strides in conquering this formidable foe. Indeed, some people have renounced prejudice and have embraced and internalized egalitarian norms (see Devine & Monteith, 1993). Despite the challenges inherent in personal efforts to reduce prejudice, these individuals are making progress. On the other hand, however, there is clear evidence that prejudice still exists and stubbornly resists efforts to reduce it. As a result, the answer to the age-old question of how best to change prejudiced attitudes remains elusive.

Thus, against a backdrop of substantial progress made and real reason for optimism, we must acknowledge that there are still significant challenges and obstacles that interfere with efforts to eradicate prejudice. In our contemporary society, most people comply with the nonprejudiced normative prescriptions. However, it seems clear that some do so, not because they view them as right, moral, or appropriate, but rather because to do otherwise is likely to result in disapproval or even sanctions from others (Plant & Devine, 1998). We have become increasingly interested in the attitudinal, affective, and behavioral consequences of compliance with such social pressure when it is at odds with people's privately held racial attitudes. We have found that compliance is relatively easy to elicit, but the question of "compliance at what cost?" must be taken seriously.

Our most recent work suggests that resentment of the pervasive nonprejudiced norms can lead to potentially destructive reactance, which may fuel a tendency to backlash against minority group members or against policies designed to promote minority-group rights. Indeed, some individuals have developed rather strong walls of resistance to normative pressure. However, our hope is that, by exploring the nature of resistance processes and the value structure that supports them, we may glean insights into how to break through the walls of resistance.

THE NATURE OF CONTEMPORARY PREJUDICE

Consider the following commentary on some of the challenges faced by those who have learned prejudice early in childhood, and later in life want to change or eliminate their prejudices:

> Many Southerners have confessed to me, for instance, that even though in their minds they no longer feel prejudice toward Blacks, they still feel squeamish when they shake hands with a Black. These feelings are left over from what they learned in their families as children. (Pettigrew, quoted in Golman, 1987, p. C1)

Are these Southerners prejudiced? On what does one base such a decision? Think about the two types of responses described. One represents a decision to reject previous ways of thinking. It involves control, and the decision is very much intentional and rational. The other type of response, based on a lifetime of socialization experiences, is relatively automatic, spontaneous, and unintentional, even if it is recognized as inappropriate.

What does it mean for people to say that they have renounced prejudice and yet they continue to experience negative feelings toward Black people? How can one make sense of the disparity between what these people say about their nonprejudiced beliefs and what they report as their actual reactions, which sometimes seem prejudiced? It is just this type of question that has consumed the attention of many researchers who are concerned about the nature of prejudice in the contemporary social climate, which actively discourages overt expressions of prejudice (e.g., Devine, 1989; Gaertner & Dovidio, 1986; Katz & Hass, 1988; McConahay, 1986; Sears & Kinder, 1985).

Following the legislative changes that promoted the rights of Black Americans, social scientists began to study the extent to which shifts in Whites' personal attitudes kept pace with the legal changes. The research literature reveals conflicting findings—ones that parallel the type of conflict described in Pettigrew's quotation above. On one hand, survey studies of racial and ethnic attitudes and beliefs indicate that racial prejudice is declining in the United States (e.g., Schuman, Steeh, & Bobo, 1985; Taylor, Sheatsley, & Greeley, 1978). Whereas a majority of Whites expressed overt racism in the 1950s (when it was legally sanctioned), only a minority do so today. Surveys show that, over time, White Americans' attitudes toward integration of schools, housing, and jobs have become more positive. Also, stereotypes about Blacks have become more favorable, and fewer people endorse negative characteristics about Blacks (e.g., that they are lazy, superstitious, or stupid—see Devine & Elliot, 1995; Dovidio & Gaertner, 1986). In sum, overt, direct forms of prejudice (often labeled "old-fashioned" prejudice) have declined.

Yet, despite the decline in old-fashioned prejudice shown in survey studies, a number of experimental studies have found that subtle indicators of prejudice (e.g., unobtrusive measures, nonverbal responses) continue to reveal negative reactions to Blacks, even among those who claim to have renounced prejudice (Crosby, Bromley, & Saxe 1980; Dovidio, Kawakami, Johnson, Johnson, & Howard, 1997). How should these paradoxical reactions be understood? Any model developed to understand this paradox must address why such negative responses persist in spite of changes in attitudes or beliefs.

Some theorists reject the optimistic conclusion suggested by the survey research, and argue that prejudice is *not* declining, but instead is only changing its form by becoming more subtle and disguised. According to these views, most (if not all) Americans are assumed to be racist, with only the *type* of racism differing among people (e.g., Gaertner & Dovidio, 1986). Such conclusions are based on the belief that *any* response which results in differential reactions should be taken as evidence of prejudice. However, these approaches fail to consider people's *intentions* or motives. Further, they imply that real change exists only when *all* behaviors and responses are consistent with nonprejudiced standards. Such arguments are based on the assumption that nonthoughtful or unintentional (e.g., nonverbal) responses are, by definition, more trustworthy than intentional responses (Crosby et al., 1980; Dovidio & Fazio, 1992).

In contrast, we argue that the unfortunate implications of this assumption lead to overlooking or denying real change when it is present. Rather than dismissing one response or the other as necessarily untrustworthy, our approach has been to try to understand the origin of both the intentional and unintentional responses. In the case of the Southerners in the above quotation, we seek to understand why negative feelings persist despite the fact that these people have renounced prejudice and adopted nonprejudiced values.

Automatic Versus Controlled Processes

We argue that understanding why low-prejudice people sometimes respond in prejudice-like ways requires considering the distinction between automatic and controlled cognitive processes. *Automatic processes* are those that occur unintentionally and spontaneously—basically without our awareness. Considerable evidence has shown that both low- and high-prejudice people are vulnerable to automatic activation of the cultural stereotype of Blacks (e.g., Devine, 1989; Dovidio et al., 1997; Fazio, Jackson, Dunton, & Williams, 1995; Greenwald, McGhee, & Schwartz, 1998). Indeed, avoiding the influence of stereotypes is difficult precisely because they come to mind so easily. This automatic activation of stereotypes is a legacy of people's socialization experiences in a culture that has historically promoted prejudice. The research evidence shows that renouncing prejudice and developing nonprejudiced beliefs does not eliminate stereotypes from one's mind. This is true despite the fact that low- and high-prejudice people differ in the extent to which they believe in or endorse the stereotype. That is, whereas high-prejudice people report negative beliefs that overlap substantially with the cultural stereotype of Blacks, low-prejudice people reject the stereotype and, instead, report egalitarian, nonprejudiced beliefs (Devine, 1989; Devine & Elliot, 1995; Lepore & Brown, 1997).

Controlled processes, by definition, are intentional and under the control of the individual. An important aspect of such processes is that their initiation and use requires time and sufficient cognitive capacity. If low-prejudice people are to respond consistently with their nonprejudiced beliefs and values, they need to have the time and the cognitive capacity to *inhibit* the spontaneously activated stereotype, to replace those thoughts with their nonprejudiced personal beliefs, and then to respond on the basis of those beliefs. Without sufficient time or capacity, their responses may well be stereotype-based and appear prejudiced. An important implication of the distinction between automatic and controlled processes is that if one looks *only* at the automatic responses, one may conclude that all White Americans are prejudiced. Yet, our research suggests that this is not a valid conclusion.

Personal Standards and Prejudice

Many studies in this area have measured prejudice in terms of responses to the Modern Racism Scale (MRS—McConahay, 1986). In such studies, we have found that low- and high-prejudice people have established different personal standards for how they should treat members of stigmatized groups (Devine, Monteith, Zuwerink, & Elliot, 1991; Monteith, Devine, & Zuwerink, 1993; Monteith & Viols, 1998; Zuwerink, Devine, Monteith, & Cook, 1996). In addition, they report differences in how important they believe it is to live up to these standards. To assess such differences, we have asked participants to indicate how they personally believed they should respond or behave in a variety of contact situations involving Blacks. The questions were designed to assess the extent to which respondents believed it was personally appropriate to respond in biased or negative ways, or to think in stereotypic ways.

One scenario asked participants to consider whether they *should* feel uncomfortable that the person who interviewed them for a job was Black. Another scenario asked whether they *should* feel bothered if a Black person sat next to them on a bus. Each scenario was answered on a 1-7 scale ranging from strongly agree to strongly disagree. To obtain a measure of personal standards, respondents' answers were averaged across the scenarios—scored such that lower numbers indicated less prejudiced responses. In these studies, we also assessed the extent to which respondents had internalized the standards. This measure was composed of three items asking respondents how committed they were to responding consistently with their standards. We found that low-prejudice people's personal standards permitted significantly less prejudice ($M =$ 1.20) than high-prejudiced people's personal standards ($M = 3.71$). Moreover, low-prejudice people's personal standards ($M = 6.29$) were more strongly internalized than high-prejudice people's personal standards ($M = 4.99$) (Devine et al., 1991).

In short, we have found important differences between low- and high-prejudice people based on the personal standards they hold. This is true despite the two groups' similar knowledge of and vulnerability to stereotype activation (Devine, 1989). We suggest that the distinctions between automatic and controlled processes, and between knowledge of and endorsement of cultural stereotypes, hold the key for understanding why those who have renounced prejudice may continue to experience prejudice-like thoughts and feelings. Even if one's beliefs change, stereotype-based responses continue to be automatically activated when one encounters a member of the stereotyped group (Devine, 1989). A strength of this approach is that it suggests how stereotypes can influence perception and behavior even for those who no longer feel prejudice in their minds. When given sufficient time, low-prejudice people censor responses based on the stereotype and instead respond based on their nonprejudiced standards. High-prejudice people, on the other hand, do not reject the stereotype and are not personally motivated to overcome its effect on their behavior, although they may decide to respond in nonprejudiced ways to avoid social sanctions, as we show later in the chapter.

Consequences of Violating One's Personal Standards

To more completely understand the processes involved in reducing prejudice, we examined the challenges faced by individuals who have internalized non-prejudiced standards and are trying to control their prejudiced responses, but

who sometimes fail. More specifically, we examined the personal, internal consequences of these types of failures (i.e., responding with prejudice). Such failure experiences are particularly interesting because they are likely to threaten
low-prejudice people's nonprejudiced self-concepts. That is, low-prejudice people are likely to hold themselves personally accountable for violations of their
personal standards. Indeed, to the extent that their nonprejudiced standards are
internalized, they should feel guilty (Ausubel, 1955; Higgins, 1987; Hoffman,
1975; Schwartz, 1977). Because high-prejudice people do not have strongly internalized standards, violations of these standards should not be as personally
distressing, and thus should not result in much guilt nor self-criticism.

To test these ideas, we explored how people feel when they fail to inhibit
their negative intergroup responses—that is, when they report a discrepancy
between their personal standards and their enduring negative reactions. After
reporting their personal standards for how they *should* feel, using the procedure
described previously, low- and high-prejudice people were presented with the
same interpersonal scenarios and were asked to indicate how they actually
would feel. In addition, immediately after completing the "should" and "would"
scenarios, the respondents indicated how they were feeling at that moment—
specifically, the extent to which they were currently feeling guilty, self-critical,
positive, sad, angry at others, bothered, etc. These items were designed to tap a
variety of different affective reactions (e.g., global discomfort, and positive
affect), but for this study we were particularly interested in the *guilt* measure (i.e.,
negative affect directed toward the self).

These measures allowed us to examine the relationship between failures to
respond consistently with one's standards and the affective consequences of
such failures. First we examined the findings for the "should" and "would" measures. As can be seen in Table 9.1, low-prejudice people's "should" standards
permitted less prejudice than did those of high-prejudice people (Monteith et al.,
1993). Also, on average, both groups' "would" responses were higher (i.e., revealed more prejudice) than their "should" responses. As a measure of failure to
follow one's standards, we calculated the discrepancy between each person's
"should" and "would" responses for each scenario, and then summed the differences. Positive discrepancy scores indicated that people had responded with
more prejudice than they believed they should.

In a large number of studies, we have found that the magnitude of this discrepancy score is systematically related to the level of guilt reported (Devine et
al., 1991; Monteith et al., 1993; Monteith & Viols, 1998; Plant & Devine, 1998;
Zuwerink et al., 1996). As can be seen in Figure 9.1, when discrepancies were
small, neither high- nor low-prejudice people reported particularly high levels of
guilt.[1] However, when discrepancies were large, low-prejudice people reported
much higher levels of guilt and self-criticism than high-prejudice people. This
pattern of findings has been replicated, whether we examined discrepancies
from standards about Blacks as the target group (e.g., Zuwerink et al., 1996), or

TABLE 9.1
Mean Ratings of Feelings That One Personally Should and Would
Have in Specific Intergroup Interactions, as a Function of Prejudice Level

	Prejudice Level	
Feelings	Low	High
Should have	1.53_A	3.61_B
Would have	2.43_A	5.04_B

Note. Should α = .86; Would α = .84; different subscripts on the same line indicate differences at the .05 level. (Source: Monteith, Devine, & Zuwerink,
1993, *Journal of Personality and Social Psychology, 64*, p. 204. Copyright
1993 by the American Psychological Association. Reprinted with permission.)

about homosexuals (e.g., Devine et al., 1991), or about women (e.g., Pressly &
Devine, 1992); and also whether the discrepancies were imagined (as in the
"should"–"would" studies) or real behavioral transgressions (e.g., Amodt &
Devine, 1994).

Breaking the Prejudice Habit

At this point in our program of research, it was crucial to determine what role, if
any, guilt plays in helping low-prejudice people overcome unwanted prejudiced
responses. The accumulating evidence on this point provides reason for optimism—it shows that progress can be made and that people can learn to regulate
their responses so as to avoid responding with prejudice (Devine & Monteith,
1993; Monteith, 1993; Monteith, Ashburn-Nardo, Voils, & Kephart, 1999). More
specifically, the evidence suggests that failures to live up to internalized personal standards, along with the guilt that such failures engender, can actually

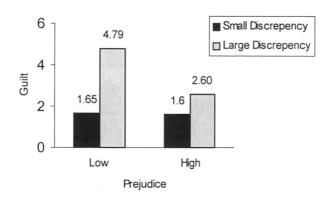

FIG. 9.1. Guilt as a function of prejudice and discrepancy between "should" and
"would" responses (based on data from Devine et al., 1991, p. 823).

help people learn to live up to their standards more effectively in the future (Monteith, 1993). A theoretical basis for this process is that the guilt associated with failure to live up to one's nonprejudiced standards is aversive and serves as a psychological signal that something has gone wrong and needs attention (Monteith, 1993). More specifically, discrepancy experiences and their associated guilt produce consequences that should facilitate control over future discrepancy responses. The first consequence is that people become highly self-focused. Second, a set of self-regulatory processes is engaged, the goal of which is to accomplish discrepancy-reduction. Monteith (1993) suggested that these reactions to failure experiences help low-prejudice people to use controlled processes to inhibit the automatically activated, yet personally unacceptable, responses and to replace them with responses that are based on their nonprejudiced beliefs.

Monteith's (1993) research provided strong evidence in support of these ideas. Low-prejudice participants who had recently violated their nonprejudiced standards (e.g., rated a law school applicant low because of his sexual orientation), and therefore felt guilty, showed evidence of self-focused attention and self-regulation. In addition, low-prejudice people who had experienced a prejudice-relevant discrepancy changed their future behavior to make it less prejudiced and, thus, more consistent with their personal standards (i.e., they were less likely to violate their standards on a subsequent occasion). High-prejudice people showed none of the signs of self-regulation, and activating a prejudice-relevant discrepancy had no effect on their subsequent behavior. In summary, it appears that low-prejudice people not only feel guilty about violating their nonprejudiced personal standards, but that this guilt facilitates their prejudice-reduction efforts. It appears that these people are learning from their mistakes.

Based on this program of research, we have come to see the importance of characterizing prejudice reduction as a *process* that is like breaking a habit. The process begins with the renunciation of prejudice and stereotype-based responses. That is, people must decide for themselves that prejudice is an inappropriate way of relating to people around them. Next, they must *internalize* the new nonprejudiced beliefs, so that they will be motivated to continue their efforts to change. Finally, people must learn to inhibit automatic, prejudice-like responses and replace them with belief-based (nonprejudiced) controlled responses. Although prejudice reduction is not easy and clearly requires effort, time, and practice, prejudice appears to be a habit that can be broken. In contrast to many authors' opinion that little progress is being made toward the alleviation of prejudice, we believe that these research findings suggest that many people are embroiled in the arduous task of overcoming their prejudices. Indeed, evidence is accumulating which shows that some people can be quite effective at regulating prejudiced responses and can successfully inhibit or avoid any prejudiced responses (e.g., Kawakami, Dion, & Dovidio, 1998; Lepore & Brown, 1997; Moskowitz & Solomon, in press; Wittenbrink, Judd, & Park, 1997; for a review, see Blair, in press).

COUNTER-INTENTIONAL EFFECTS OF NORMS—BACKLASH

Although Devine and Monteith's work on the intrapersonal processes involved in overcoming prejudice provides reason for considerable optimism, it is important to acknowledge that their analysis focuses mostly on the experience of low-prejudice people and on the role of self-imposed standards (but see Monteith et al., 1993). Thus, their analysis does not speak to the experiences of those who *have not* renounced prejudice, but who need to function in a social world that actively discourages expressions of prejudice. Because high-prejudice people's personal standards permit rather high levels of prejudice, their *self-imposed* standards are at odds with the pervasive normative, or other-imposed, standards that oppose prejudice. Legal sanctions and public censure are the potential costs of violating these standards. Indeed, in recent years many organizations have adopted a proliferation of policies and programs designed to promote intergroup understanding. In view of these other-imposed pressures against prejudice, it is important to understand reactions to them and the experiences of high-prejudice people. Research on these topics will provide a more complete picture of the challenges associated with avoiding prejudice responses in the contemporary social climate.

As an example, consider Texaco's 1995 annual report, which stated: "Our commitment to diversity is an inclusive process, grounded in our core values of respect for the individual and in our long-standing policies of equal opportunity for all employees" (cited in Page, 1996, p. A22). However, as dramatically illustrated in the widely publicized "Texaco scandal," such public statements supporting egalitarian norms are no guarantee that members of the organization privately endorse the policies. The sentiments expressed in the annual report stand in stark contrast to the malicious and hostile statements that were secretly recorded during a 1994 private meeting of top Texaco executives during a discussion of a lawsuit against the company filed by Black middle managers. The tape recording revealed both feelings of hostility and strong resistance to the idea of Blacks' ascension into upper management positions. Moreover, the negative comments also revealed opposition toward corporate efforts to provide employees with diversity training. The executives conveyed their views by jokes about the metaphor of jelly beans that had been used by a diversity trainer (e.g., they noted that the black jelly beans always seemed to be glued to the bottom of the bag).

It seems clear that such behaviors contradicted the intention of the corporation's normatively imposed nonprejudiced or egalitarian norms. This example highlights the likelihood that some people, when not under the watchful eyes of others, will freely express and act upon their prejudice. In our research we have

begun to explore the possibility that the cumulative effects of normative pressures could lead those who resent the pressure to lash out in some way against
the nonprejudiced norms.

Research on Motivation to Respond Without Prejudice

Recently, we have argued that, in the context of strong social norms discourag-
ing prejudice (e.g., Blanchard et al., 1991; Monteith et al., 1996), it is important
to consider both *whether* individuals are motivated to respond without prejudice
and the reasons *why* they are so motivated (Plant & Devine, 1998). For example, we have demonstrated that people can be motivated to respond without
prejudice toward Black people for personal (i.e., internal) or for normative (i.e.,
external) reasons. The key distinction between these alternative sources of motivation is the evaluative audience that sets the standards for appropriate behavior. When the motivation to respond without prejudice derives from internal
standards, the self is the important evaluative audience. In contrast, when the
motivation derives from external standards, significant others constitute the important evaluative audience.

We have developed and validated separate scales of internal motivation to
respond without prejudice (IMS) and external motivation to respond without
prejudice (EMS) (Plant & Devine, 1998). The IMS includes items such as, "I am
personally motivated because of my beliefs to be nonprejudiced toward Blacks"
and "Because of my personal values, I believe that using stereotypes about
Black people is wrong." This measure was found to be closely related to traditional measures of racial prejudice such as Brigham's (1993) Attitude Toward
Blacks (ATB) scale ($r = .79$). This strong relationship indicates that low-prejudice
people report high levels of internal motivation to respond without prejudice,
whereas high-prejudice people report comparatively low levels of internal motivation. This finding is consistent with our previous research, which demonstrated
that low-prejudice people report that their attitudes are highly internalized and
part of their self-concepts (e.g., Devine et al., 1991; Zuwerink et al., 1996). The
EMS includes items such as, "I attempt to appear nonprejudiced toward Black
people because of pressure from others" and "If I acted prejudiced toward Black
people, I would be concerned that others would be angry with me." Because the
EMS focuses on concern over how others will react to prejudiced responses, we
examined the relationship between the EMS and measures of self-presentation
and social desirability. We found that the EMS was only modestly related to
measures of self-presentation (e.g., Leary, 1983; $r = .16$) and unrelated to
measures of social desirability (e.g., Crowne & Marlowe, 1960; $r = -.11$). Thus,
the EMS appears to assess something beyond a general concern with social
appearance.

Further, we demonstrated that the IMS ($\alpha = .81$) and EMS ($\alpha = .80$) were reliable, and we provided compelling evidence regarding the scales' convergent,

discriminant, and predictive validity (Plant & Devine, 1998). We also found that the IMS and EMS scales were largely independent of each other (average r in 4 samples = -.14).[2] Thus, individuals can be motivated to respond without prejudice primarily for internal reasons, primarily for external reasons, for both internal and external reasons, or they may not be much motivated to respond without prejudice at all.

In two additional studies, Plant and Devine (1998) provided evidence concerning the consequences of self-imposed and other-imposed standards for prejudice-relevant behavior. In one study, for example, we found that responding in a prejudiced manner was associated with different affective consequences, depending on the evaluative audience imposing the nonprejudiced standard (i.e., self vs. other) and the motivation underlying a person's desire to respond without prejudice (i.e., internal vs. external). This study used methods very similar to the should–would measures described previously. As can be seen in Figure 9.2, larger violations of self-imposed nonprejudiced standards were associated with more guilt and self-criticism, particularly for high-IMS participants. This pattern is consistent with the findings discussed previously for low-prejudiced people (e.g., Zuwerink et al., 1996). Larger violations of other-imposed nonprejudiced standards, however, were associated with greater threatened affect (e.g., feeling threatened, fearful, afraid), particularly for high-EMS participants (see Figure 9.3). These findings are consistent with theories that link guilt-related affect to self-punishment and threat-related affect to anticipated punishment from others (Higgins, 1987). We argue that this fear of sanctions or punishment from others may lead people who hold it to curtail their expressions of prejudice, at least in public settings.

This general expectation was verified in a second study, in which we found that people's reported racial beliefs varied as a function of both the source of their

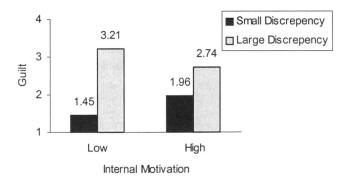

FIG. 9.2. Guilt as a function of internal motivation to respond without prejudice and discrepancies from self-imposed standards (based on data from Plant & Devine, 1998, p. 821).

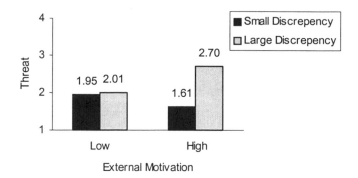

FIG. 9.3. Threatened affect as a function of external motivation to respond without prejudice and discrepancies from other-imposed standards (based on data from Plant & Devine, 1998, p. 822).

motivation to respond without prejudice and the social context in which they reported their beliefs (Plant & Devine, 1998). In this study, participants indicated the extent to which they endorsed the stereotype of Blacks (e.g., as being lazy, hostile, or athletic). They responded either privately (anonymously) or publicly (directly to the experimenter). The data were combined in an index, with larger numbers indicating stronger endorsement of the stereotype. The findings are shown in Figure 9.4.

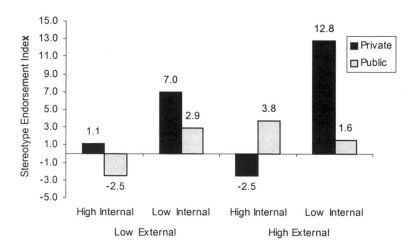

FIG. 9.4. Stereotype endorsement as a function of internal and external motivation to respond without prejudice and private versus public reporting condition. (Adapted from Plant & Devine, 1998, *Journal of Personality and Social Psychology, 75,* p. 825. Copyright 1998 by the American Psychological Association. Reprinted with permission.)

As Figure 9.4 indicates, high-IMS participants reported low levels of stereo-type endorsement, and their responses did not differ significantly as a function of whether they gave their responses privately or publicly, nor whether they were low or high in EMS. Among those low in IMS, however, their level of EMS mattered greatly for the level of stereotype endorsement reported. For example, among low-IMS, low-EMS participants, stereotype endorsement scores did not differ significantly across the public and private reporting conditions. In contrast, low-IMS, high-EMS participants (those who had no personal convictions against expressing prejudice but who were very sensitive to external norms) showed a dramatic difference in their stereotype endorsement in the public versus private conditions—they reported much stronger endorsement of the stereotype when they reported their beliefs in private. It seems that making public responses cued the potential to be evaluated by an external audience and prompted low-IMS, high-EMS participants to strategically alter their responses to meet the other-imposed nonprejudiced standard. These findings suggest that, although these people may avoid responding with prejudice when under the scrutiny of a non-prejudiced audience, when they are not in the public eye they will respond with prejudice—much like the Texaco executives.

Consequences of Avoiding Prejudiced Responses

It seems clear that individuals who are sensitive to normative pressure to avoid prejudice, but who also have prejudiced attitudes, will conceal their prejudice from others. Although curtailing of immediate expressions of prejudice may be desirable, it is possible that such compliance may lead to deleterious outcomes, and thus the short-term gains may be outweighed by long-term negative out-comes. To investigate this possibility, we have recently explored the impact of blatant versus subtle forms of social influence to respond without prejudice. If responses to other-imposed nonprejudiced norms were found to be benign, es-tablishing and enforcing nonprejudiced norms would be an effective way to re-duce prejudice (or at least expressions of it). However, our recent work suggests that the consequences may be far from benign, at least for some people (Plant & Devine, 1999). In this work, we examined a variety of affective, behavioral, and attitudinal consequences of being exposed to normatively imposed pressure to respond without prejudice. The cumulative evidence we have collected suggests that compliance with nonprejudiced norms imposed on one by others can, at least in some cases, fuel prejudice and lead to backlash.

In one study, for example, we examined the impact of a *blatant* influence at-tempt, which was a persuasive communication designed to change participants' negative attitudes regarding a race-based affirmative action policy (Plant & Devine, 1999). Exposure to the communication resulted in positive change among high-IMS participants, but led to very different outcomes for low-IMS par-ticipants. Specifically, following the communication, high-IMS participants reported favorable attitudes toward the policy, and their behavior showed support for it. In contrast, low-IMS participants responded to the communication with elevated angry affect, less favorable attitudes toward the policy, and behavioral backlash against the policy. Overall, their reactions suggested strong resistance to this blatant effort to change their attitudes toward the policy.

In trying to account for these different reactions between high- and low-IMS participants, we suggested that low-IMS participants' reactions were not determined simply by their specific pretest attitudes, which were opposed to affirmative action. These specific attitudes were inevitably embedded in their broader system of attitudes and values regarding prejudice. According to Rokeach (1973), beliefs, attitudes, and values are arranged in a hierarchy, with those that are more central and general being the most resistant to change. For participants high in IMS, the intent of the communication was consistent with their general nonprejudiced beliefs and values (e.g., Devine, 1989; Katz & Hass, 1988; Plant & Devine, 1998), and this fact enabled them to be receptive to the communication. In contrast, for individuals low in IMS, the intent of the communication clashed with both their specific negative attitude toward the affirmative action policy and their more general prejudiced beliefs and values. For them, the persuasive communication served as an attack on both their specific and general attitudes. Under these circumstances, the effects of the communication were clearly counter-intentional. Specifically, these participants responded with anger, which facilitated their resistance to the communication both attitudinally and behaviorally and, thus, appeared to shore up their walls of resistance to the influence attempt. Their response fit the classic mold described by reactance theory (Brehm, 1966).

In another study, we examined the impact of a more subtle influence tactic— one that may be less inclined to elicit anger and resentment, at least among some low-internal-motivation participants. This technique has been commonly used by dissonance theorists to encourage people to advocate a position that runs counter to their beliefs (e.g., Festinger, 1957; Harmon-Jones & Mills, 1999). It is a rather subtle form of social influence, which maintains the illusion that respondents have freely chosen to behave in a counterattitudinal fashion. Specifically, in this study we induced people to write an essay supporting the same race-related affirmative action recruiting policy as in the previous study (i.e., recruiting more African Americans to the University by offering them more scholarships—Plant & Devine, 1999). The participants were students who had previously reported being opposed to the policy, but who had varying levels of IMS and EMS. Half of the participants were induced to freely choose to prepare an essay supporting the new recruiting policy; the other half were assigned to advocate the counterattitudinal position. The participants were led to believe that the essays they prepared would be sent to the university committee considering the recruitment policy. Most people complied with the request to write the essay.

As in the previous study, we were interested in the attitudinal, affective, and behavioral reactions of our participants. As an attitude change measure, we

asked participants, after they wrote the essay, to report their current attitude toward the policy, using the same measure on which they had initially indicated
their opposition to the policy. As an affective measure, we asked them how they
felt about writing the essay. Our interest here concerned the extent to which
complying with the request led to elevated feelings of anger (e.g., feeling angry,
irritated, annoyed, and resentful). Finally, participants completed a behavioral
measure of support or opposition to the affirmative action policy. Specifically, we
gave participants the opportunity to fill out cards stating their support for or opposition to the recruiting policy, which would be sent to the committee considering the policy. We gave them a packet of 20 cards and told them they could fill
out as many or as few as they wished. This measure assessed the extent to
which participants would show backlash (i.e., take direct action against the policy), thereby reasserting their negative attitudes.

The findings from this study indicated that, although some people responded
positively, regardless of whether they were induced or assigned to prepare the
counterattitudinal essay, others responded in quite negative ways (Plant &
Devine, 1999). Consider first the attitude data, and recall that all participants
were initially opposed to the policy. Consistent with findings from the previous
study, participants' final attitudes toward the recruitment policy were determined
primarily by their level of IMS. High-IMS participants reported relatively positive
attitudes toward the policy, suggesting a change in their attitudes, but low-IMS
participants maintained their negative attitudes toward the policy.

However, examination of the affect and behavior data revealed that the picture was considerably more complex. The findings for the angry affect measure
indicated that people's affective reaction to preparing the counterattitudinal essay was jointly determined by their levels of IMS and EMS. As shown in Figure
9.5, for high-IMS participants, regardless of their level of EMS, writing the essay
resulted in low levels of angry affect. For low-IMS participants, however, whether
they became angry after preparing the essay depended on their level of EMS.

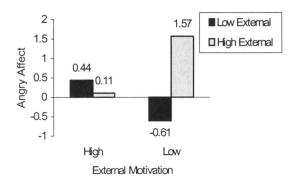

FIG. 9.5. Angry affect as a function of internal and external motivation to respond
without prejudice, controlling for initial attitude (from Plant & Devine, 1999).

Those who were also low in EMS did not become angered by writing the essay, but those who were high in EMS became quite angered by writing the essay. We believe that this anger resulted because these people, owing to their high level of *external* motivation to respond without prejudice, are constantly on the lookout for pressures imposed on them by others and have grown to resent such restrictions, as posited by reactance theory (Brehm, 1966).

Participants' responses on the behavioral card measure, displayed in Figure 9.6, mirrored those for angry affect. That is, their responses were determined jointly by their levels of IMS and EMS. Participants high in IMS, regardless of their level of EMS, showed similar levels of support for the recruitment policy after writing the essay. In contrast, the behavior of low-IMS participants depended on their level of EMS. The low-IMS, low-EMS participants' behavior indicated moderate support for the policy, whereas the low-IMS, high-EMS participants' behavior displayed strong opposition to it. This latter group appeared to be lashing out against being "forced" to endorse a policy they did not favor.

Our research strategy enabled us to explore the processes underlying these differential reactions to writing the essay. A series of mediational analyses (cf. Baron & Kenny, 1986; Judd & Kenny, 1981a, 1981b) highlighted the role of anger in promoting attitudinal resistance and behavioral backlash. Specifically, participants' anger mediated the attitudinal and behavioral outcomes. These findings suggest that positive responses to other-imposed nonprejudiced norms are only likely to occur if such anger can be mitigated.

Antiprejudice Normative Pressure: Reasons for Optimism and Pessimism

Taken together, the studies provide some reason for optimism regarding the role of norms in eliciting favorable changes regarding prejudice-relevant issues. In both studies, favorable changes were elicited among people high in internal mo-

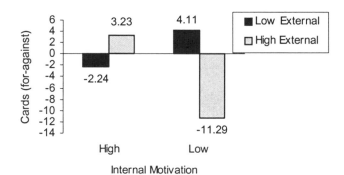

FIG. 9.6. Number of cards filled out for or against a proposed affirmative action policy, as a function of internal and external motivation to respond without prejudice, controlling for initial attitude (from Plant & Devine, 1999).

tivation to respond without prejudice. These participants' general nonprejudiced values provided a context that made the positive features of the recruitment policy salient and prevented resistance processes from being engaged. Second, it is worth noting that it was not sensitivity to normative prescriptions per se that led to anger. Participants who were high in internal motivation, but who were also high in external motivation to respond without prejudice—and hence were sensitive to normative prescriptions—neither reported being angry nor showed any tendency toward backlash. The social pressure against prejudice was, after all, consistent with their internalized personal standards.

Third, in the final study, favorable outcomes were displayed by a subset of the low-internal participants—those who were also low in external motivation to respond without prejudice. That is, although the low-internal, low-external participants did not show positive attitude changes, they reported low levels of anger, and their immediate behavior, rather then showing backlash, revealed support for the policy. The fact that they were not angered by the subtle influence strategy may permit later long-term change. Indeed, if their favorable behavioral responses continue, over time these individuals may come to see themselves as the type of people who support such policies and may shift their attitude to be in line with their behavior (cf. Bem, 1972). Further, in promoting long-term change, it may be possible to capitalize on the fact that these people perceived that their behavior was freely chosen (cf. Festinger, 1957). To the extent that we can develop interventions that draw attention to their freely chosen behavior, consistency pressures, perhaps combined with self-perception processes, may encourage long-term change.

However, these studies also provide reason for caution, or even pessimism, about the potentially harmful consequences of normative social influence attempts. That is, for some types of people, the influence attempts led to counterintentional and destructive outcomes (i.e., polarization of negative attitudes, and behavioral backlash). These concerns are important because nonprejudiced norms are both salient and pervasive in our contemporary social and political climate.

REDUCING PREJUDICE IN THE CONTEMPORARY SOCIAL CLIMATE

Over the last 50 years in the U.S., the norms regarding the acceptability of prejudice have changed quite dramatically. Whereas prejudice in this country was once not only normatively accepted but also legally sanctioned, today the norms opposing prejudice are very well understood and often enforced in subtle and not so subtle ways. The hope of many civil rights activists was that imposing normative standards against discrimination would curtail overt expressions of prejudice and that, over time, attitude change would follow. And, as our previous work suggests, for many individuals this has been the outcome. It is noteworthy, however, that other individuals have not only maintained negative racial attitudes but appear to resent the pressure from others to curtail expressions of prejudice.

Our findings suggest that the effects of imposing nonprejudiced norms are more complex and, in some cases, less benign than had been hoped.

Specifically, our recent research suggests that merely imposing nonprejudiced norms on people is not always sufficient to overcome prejudice, and may lead to an exacerbation of its effects, at least for some people under some circumstances (Plant & Devine, 1999). Our findings suggest that compliance with norms opposing prejudice is rather easy to elicit. However, the findings also emphasize that focusing only on immediate outcomes can be misleading regarding the efficacy of norms to control expressions of prejudice. In situations where succumbing to the pressure imposed on one by others can be construed as a restriction on one's freedom, it appears to create resentment and reactance. The findings from our recent studies suggest that these feelings may actually fuel prejudice and increase the tendency to lash out against nonprejudiced norms or against policies designed to promote the opportunities of minority group members.

We hasten to add, however, that we do not favor abandoning the legal and normative prohibitions against expressing prejudice. Their goals are important and their impact on many people has been beneficial (e.g., sincere attitude change). Nevertheless, it is necessary to acknowledge that the effects of these restrictions are not uniformly positive and, indeed, can be counterproductive for some people (i.e., those who resent the imposition of the norms). Only when these possibilities are acknowledged and a theoretical analysis of the sources of resistance to such normative pressure is developed, can these potential unintended effects be combated.

We believe that, in order to combat prejudice effectively, researchers need to take seriously the nature of the challenges and dilemmas that different people face in their everyday dealings with prejudice. For example, the dilemma faced by low-prejudice people who fail in their efforts to control their prejudiced tendencies is very different from that of high-prejudice people who possess no personal motivation to respond without prejudice but feel compelled to do so nevertheless. In what follows, we consider recommendations about how to further reduce prejudice and its ill effects. A key implication of our research is that strategies to reduce prejudice should be tailored to the specific needs and potential pitfalls that people experience in the prejudice-reduction process.

Breaking the Prejudice Habit: Developing the Ability
To Respond Without Prejudice

For low-prejudice people who already possess the requisite internal motivation to overcome prejudice, the challenge is to learn the skills necessary to respond consistently with their nonprejudiced beliefs. The task of the social scientist is to develop strategies to assist them in their efforts to eliminate negativity and respond in nonprejudiced ways. Currently the clearest recommendation is to practice frequently (i.e., to interact with members of stigmatized groups—Monteith, Sherman, & Devine, 1998). For example, people who appear to be most effective in regulating their prejudiced tendencies (Devine, Plant, & Brazy, 1999) report having more experience interacting with Blacks and feeling less anxiety during intergroup interactions (Devine & Plant, 1998).

For these low-prejudice people, the goal is to become skilled at bringing to mind their standards, rather than stereotypes, to serve as the basis for their responses to stigmatized others. Building on Monteith's (1993) work, it seems clear that one essential element in combating prejudice is to learn to identify the cues that signaled previous failure (Monteith et al., 1999). To the extent that people can successfully identify these cues, they may be better able to take steps proactively to avoid transgressions of their personal standards and, over time, to bring their behavior in line with their beliefs.

Cracking the Walls of Resistance: Creating Internal Motivation

Now let us consider the more daunting challenge of creating internal motivation to avoid prejudice among people who currently have no such motivation. There is a large literature demonstrating that changing prejudiced attitudes is notoriously difficult (Monteith, Zuwerink, & Devine, 1994). Techniques as wide-ranging as education, persuasion, propaganda, insight therapy, and intergroup contact have achieved, at best, mixed success. Moreover, conclusions regarding why and for whom the strategies were (in)effective have not been clear. Monteith et al. (1994) argued that a serious limitation of the previous work was its atheoretical nature. Our hope is that focusing on individual differences in the sources of motivation to respond without prejudice, together with an analysis of resistance processes, will put us in a better position to combat these resistances and to promote positive change.

Because the evidence concerning these issues is limited, our comments here are speculative, but they grow out of factors studied in our research. For example, we have learned that creating external motivation is not always sufficient to change prejudiced attitudes and may, in fact, have counterintentional effects that exacerbate the problem (i.e., that enhance resistance). A theme that cuts across each of the approaches we propose is that any effective strategy will have to mitigate anger, which we believe is a primary impediment to prejudice reduction.

One possibility worth considering is whether normative pressure can be effectively harnessed in the service of creating internal motivation to respond without prejudice. Maximizing the utility of social pressure for promoting prejudice reduction will require striking a delicate balance between exerting sufficient external force to encourage desired responses, but not so much pressure as to provide a clear external justification for one's behavior (cf. Festinger & Carlsmith, 1959). As dissonance theory suggests, to the extent that there is not sufficient external justification to explain one's nonprejudiced behavior, some internal justification will be sought. Thus, consistency pressures may encourage attitude change, particularly if the behavior is freely chosen and perceived to be irrevocable (Brehm & Cohen, 1962; Festinger 1957).

Another approach would be to attend to the characteristics of those who impose nonprejudiced pressure. For example, if the norms are imposed by highly credible or well-liked others, resistance to them may be lessened (e.g., Hovland & Weiss, 1951; Roskos-Ewoldsen & Fazio, 1992; see McGuire, 1985 for a review). Also, in keeping with Kelman's (1958) analysis of identification, to the extent that the targets of social influence identify with the source of the external pressure, attitude change may be forthcoming.

Although it may be possible to create changed standards through norms and social influence, a more productive approach may be to couple the positive effects of norms with other efforts explicitly designed to encourage internal change. Below, we outline two potentially promising strategies for promoting internal change, both of which involve mitigating the type of anger and resentment elicited by external influence attempts. The first strategy focuses on creating feelings of empathy for members of the stigmatized outgroup. The logic of the strategy is that feelings of empathy are fundamentally incompatible with feelings of anger and resentment. To the extent that empathy can be effectively elicited, it may prevent the resistance processes that serve to bolster people's prejudice. Recently, Batson and his colleagues (1997) provided empirical support for the role of empathy in improving attitudes toward a number of social groups (e.g., AIDS victims, homeless persons, and murderers). Of course, attitudes toward these social groups may well differ in important ways from racial attitudes (e.g., in importance, extremity, etc.—cf. Batson et al., 1997), and the norms opposing negative reactions to these groups are not as clear as in the case of racial attitudes. However, to the extent that inducing empathy for Blacks can mitigate anger, it is possible that people's walls of resistance to change may be cracked. As a result, respondents who typically resent other-imposed antiprejudice influence may be more open and, possibly, more receptive to information and attitude change. Thus, empathy may pave the way for development of internal changes and reduction of negative intergroup attitudes.

A possible alternative approach is one that appeals to people's more general values, as opposed to directly attacking their specific beliefs (cf. Rokeach, 1973). Both classic and contemporary scholars of prejudice have posited that most Americans have egalitarian ideals and self-conceptions (Allport, 1954; Devine, 1989; Gaertner & Dovidio, 1986; Katz & Hass, 1988; Monteith & Walters, 1998; Myrdal, 1944; Rokeach, 1973). Monteith and Walters (1998) recently demonstrated that people across *all* levels of prejudice toward Blacks consider themselves to be egalitarian persons who believe in the principles of democracy. Following in the tradition of Rokeach's (1973) classic work on value self-confrontation, highly prejudiced people could be encouraged to consider the implications of their responding with more prejudice than their egalitarian values indicate is appropriate. Acknowledging the inconsistency between their egalitarian ideals and their specific responses toward Blacks should, according to Rokeach, lead to self-dissatisfaction, and may instigate self-regulatory processes aimed at reducing such inconsistencies (Monteith, 1993).

Applying the value self-confrontation technique successfully with high-prejudice people may require an additional step. Monteith and Walters (1998) found that low-prejudice individuals were more likely than their high-prejudice counterparts to construe egalitarianism in terms of equal opportunity and protection of the rights of all people. In contrast, high-prejudice individuals construed egalitarianism in terms of the Protestant Work Ethic (i.e., getting only what one works for). Moreover, construing egalitarianism as equal opportunity led to a sense of moral obligation to live up to one's personal standards regarding how to respond to Blacks. Such feelings of moral obligation may be necessary to promote long-term change. Thus, changing the way high-prejudice people view egalitarianism, so that they see it as meaning equal opportunity for all, may be critical for Rokeach's procedure to be maximally effective.

Rokeach's value self-confrontation procedure is interesting because it does not explicitly challenge people's specific prejudiced attitudes, but instead it provides a condition under which people can discover for themselves the implications that their values have for their reactions to Black people. It may be the subtlety of the technique that produces its effectiveness—and also the fact that it allows people to consider privately the possibility that their prejudiced attitudes may be unfair. The privacy of this technique may circumvent the kind of anger and resentment displayed by individuals who are highly sensitive to antiprejudice social pressure and who do not privately embrace those views (i.e., low-internal, high-external individuals).

Although the challenges associated with reducing prejudiced attitudes remain daunting, we are optimistic that such changes can be created. By understanding the importance of anger in the process of resistance and backlash, we may be better able to harness normative pressure and combine it with efforts designed to help develop internalized nonprejudiced beliefs. Our hope is that, over time, these efforts will be successful in encouraging high-prejudice people to renounce prejudice and join their internally motivated counterparts in trying to break the prejudice habit.

NOTES

1. All analyses were conducted using hierarchical regression. To determine low and high levels of discrepancies, we used one standard deviation below and above the mean respectively.

2. Scales of internal and external motivation to respond without prejudice have been developed for the areas of sexism (Klonis & Devine, 1999), homophobia (Lemm & Banaji, 1999), and prejudice toward fat people (Buswell & Devine, 1999). In all cases the internal and external scales were independent.

REFERENCES

Allport, G. W. (1954). *The nature of prejudice.* Reading, MA: Addison-Wesley.

Amodt, I. J., & Devine, P. G. (1994, May). *When personal standards collide with social pressure: Competing motivations and affective consequences.* Paper presented at Midwestern Psychological Association meeting, Chicago.

Ausubel, D. P. (1955). Relationships between shame and guilt in the socializing process. *Psychological Review, 62,* 378-390.

Baron, R. M., & Kenny, D. A. (1986). The moderator–mediator variable distinction in social psychological research: Conceptual, strategic, and statistical considerations. *Journal of Personality and Social Psychology, 51,* 1173-1182.

Batson, D. C., Poplycarpou, M. P., Harmon-Jones, E., Imhoff, H. J., Mitchener, E. C., Bednar, L. L., Klein, T. R., & Highberger, L. (1997). Empathy and attitudes: Can feeling for a member of a stigmatized group improve feelings toward the group? *Journal of Personality and Social Psychology, 72,* 105-118.

Bem, D. (1972). Self-perception theory. In L. Berkowitz (Ed.), *Advances in experimental social psychology* (Vol. 6, pp. 1-62). San Diego, CA: Academic Press.

Blair, I. (in press). Implicit stereotypes and prejudice. In G. Moskowitz (Ed.), *Cognitive social psychology: On the tenure and future of social cognition.* Mahwah, NJ: Erlbaum.

Blanchard, F. A., Lilly, T., & Vaughn, L. A. (1991). Reducing the expression of racial prejudice. *Psychological Science, 2,* 101-105.

Brehm, J. W. (1966). *A theory of psychological reactance.* New York: Academic Press.

Brehm, J. W., & Cohen, A. R. (1962). *Explorations in cognitive dissonance.* New York: Wiley.

Brigham, J. (1993). College students' racial attitudes. *Journal of Applied and Social Psychology, 23,* 1933-1967.

Buswell, B. N., & Devine, P. G. (1999). [Internal and external motivations to respond without prejudice to fat people]. Unpublished raw data, University of Wisconsin–Madison.

Crosby, F., Bromley, S., & Saxe, L. (1980). Recent unobtrusive studies of Black and White discrimination and prejudice: A literature review. *Psychological Bulletin, 87,* 546-563.

Crowne, D. P., & Marlowe, D. (1960). A new scale of social desirability independent of psychopathology. *Journal of Consulting Psychology, 24,* 349-354.

Devine, P. G., & Plant, E. A. (1998). [Controlling prejudice: Approach and avoidance motives]. Unpublished raw data, University of Wisconsin–Madison.

Devine, P. G. (1989). Stereotypes and prejudice: Their automatic and controlled components. *Journal of Personality and Social Psychology, 56,* 5-18.

Devine, P., & Elliot, A. (1995). Are racial stereotypes really fading? The Princeton trilogy revisited. *Personality and Social Psychology Bulletin, 21,* 1139-1150.

Devine, P. G., & Monteith, M. J. (1993). The role of discrepancy-associated affect in prejudice reduction. In D. M. Mackie & D. L. Hamilton (Eds.), *Affect, cognition, and stereotyping: Interactive processes in group perception* (pp. 317-344). San Diego: Academic Press.

Devine, P. G., Monteith, M. J., Zuwerink, J. R., & Elliot, A. J. (1991). Prejudice with and without compunction. *Journal of Personality and Social Psychology, 60,* 817-830.

Devine, P. G., Plant, E. A., & Brazy, P. (1999). *Challenges in the understanding of racial prejudice.* Manuscript in preparation, University of Wisconsin–Madison.

Dovidio, J. F., & Fazio, R. H. (1992). New technologies for direct and indirect assessment of attitudes. In J. M. Tanur (Ed.), *Questions about questions: Inquiries into the cognitive bases of surveys* (pp. 203-237). New York: Russell Sage Foundation.

Dovidio, J. F., & Gaertner, S. L. (1986). Prejudice, discrimination, and racism: Historical trends and contemporary approaches. In J. F. Dovidio & S. L. Gaertner (Eds.), *Prejudice, discrimination, and racism* (pp. 1-34). San Diego: Academic Press.

Dovidio, J., Kawakami, K., Johnson, C., Johnson, B., & Howard, A. (1997). On the nature of prejudice: Automatic and controlled processes. *Journal of Experimental Social Psychology, 33*, 510-540.

Fazio, R. H., Jackson, J. R., Dunton, B. C., & Williams, C. J. (1995). Variability in automatic activation as an unobtrusive measure of racial attitudes: A bona fide pipeline? *Journal of Personality and Social Psychology, 69*, 1013-1027.

Festinger, L. (1957). *A theory of cognitive dissonance.* Stanford, CA: Stanford University Press.

Festinger, L., & Carlsmith, J. M. (1959). Cognitive consequences of forced compliance. *Journal of Abnormal and Social Psychology, 58*, 203-210.

Gaertner, S. L., & Dovidio, J. F. (1986). The aversive form of racism. In J. F. Dovidio & S. L. Gaertner (Eds.), *Prejudice, discrimination, and racism* (pp. 61-89). San Diego: Academic Press.

Golman, D. (1987, May 12). "Useful" models of thinking contribute to the power of prejudice. *New York Times,* p. C1.

Greenwald, A., McGhee, D., & Schwartz, J. (1998). Measuring individual differences in implicit cognition: The implicit association test. *Journal of Personality and Social Psychology, 74*, 1464-1480.

Harmon-Jones, E., & Mills, J. (1999). *Cognitive dissonance: Progress on a pivotal theory in social psychology.* Washington, DC: American Psychological Association.

Higgins, E. T. (1987). Self-discrepancy: A theory relating self and affect. *Psychological Review, 94*, 319-340.

Hoffman, M. L. (1975). Sex differences in moral internalization and values. *Journal of Personality and Social Psychology, 32*, 720-729.

Hovland, C. I., & Weiss, W. (1951). The influence of source credibility on communication effectiveness. *Public Opinion Quarterly, 15*, 635-650.

Judd, C. M., & Kenny, D. A. (1981a). *Examining the effects of social interactions.* Cambridge, England: Cambridge University Press.

Judd, C. M., & Kenny, D. A. (1981b). Process analysis: Estimating mediation in treatment evaluations. *Evaluation Review, 5*, 602-619.

Katz, I., & Hass, R. G. (1988). Racial ambivalence and American value conflict. *Journal of Personality and Social Psychology, 55*, 893-905.

Kawakami, K., Dion, K., & Dovidio, J. (1998). Racial prejudice and stereotype activation. *Personality and Social Psychology Bulletin, 24*, 407- 416.

Kelman, H. C. (1958). Compliance, identification, and internalization: Three processes of attitude change. *Journal of Conflict Resolution, 2*, 51-60.

Klonis, S., & Devine, P. G., (1999). *Internal and external motivations to respond without sexism.* Unpublished manuscript, University of Wisconsin–Madison.

Leary, M. R. (1983). A brief version of the Fear of Negative Evaluation Scale. *Personality and Social Psychology Bulletin, 9*, 371-375.

Lemm, K., & Banaji, M. R. (1999). Unpublished raw data. Yale University.

Lepore, L., & Brown, R. (1997). Category and stereotype activation: Is prejudice inevitable? *Journal of Personality and Social Psychology, 72*, 275-287.

McConahay, J. B. (1986). Modern racism, ambivalence, and the modern racism sale. In J. F. Dovidio & S. L. Gaertner (Eds.), *Prejudice, discrimination, and racism* (pp. 91-126). San Diego: Academic Press.

McGuire, W. J. (1985). Attitudes and attitude change. In G. Lindzey & E. Aronson (Eds.), *Handbook of Social Psychology* (3rd ed., Vol. 2, pp. 233-346). New York: Random House.

Monteith, M. J. (1993). Self-regulation of prejudiced responses: Implications for progress in prejudice-reduction efforts. *Journal of Personality and Social Psychology, 65*, 469-485.

Monteith, M. J., Ashburn-Nardo, L., Voils, C. I., & Kephart, C. M. (1999). *Putting the brakes* on prejudice: Toward understanding how stereotyping may be deautomatized. Unpublished manuscript.

Monteith, M. J., Deneen, N. E., & Tooman, G. D. (1996). The effect of social norm activation on the expression of opinions concerning gay men and Blacks. Basic and Applied Social Psychology, 18, 267-288.

Monteith, M. J., Devine, P. G., & Zuwerink, J. R. (1993). Self-directed versus other-directed affect as a consequence of prejudice-related discrepancies. Journal of Personality and Social Psychology, 64, 198-210.

Monteith, M. J., Sherman, J. W., & Devine, P. G. (1998). Suppression as a stereotype control strategy. Personality and Social Psychology Review, 2, 63-82.

Monteith, M. J., & Viols, C. I. (1998). Proneness to prejudiced responses: Toward understanding the authenticity of self-reported discrepancies. Journal of Personality and Social Psychology, 75, 901-916.

Monteith, M. J., & Walters, G. L. (1998). Egalitarianism, moral obligation, and prejudice-related personal standards. Personality and Social Psychology Bulletin, 24, 186-199.

Monteith, M. J., Zuwerink, J. R., & Devine P. G. (1994). Prejudice and prejudice reduction: Classic challenges, contemporary approaches. In P. G. Devine, D. L. Hamilton, & T. M. Ostrom (Eds.), Social cognition: Impact on social psychology (pp. 323-346). New York: Academic Press.

Moskowitz, G., & Salomon, A. (in press). Implicit control of stereotype activation through the preconscious operation of chronic goals. Social Cognition.

Myrdal, G. (1944). An American dilemma. New York: Harper & Row.

Page, C. (1996, November 11). Texaco, a reason for affirmative action. Houston Chronicle, p. A22.

Plant, E. A., & Devine, P. G. (1998). Internal and external motivation to respond without prejudice. Journal of Personality and Social Psychology, 75, 811-832.

Plant, E. A., & Devine, P. G. (1999). Responses to nonprejudiced standards imposed by others: Acceptance or backlash? Manuscript under review.

Pressly, S. L., & Devine, P. G. (1992, May). Sex, sexism, and compunction: Group membership or internalization of standards? Paper presented at Midwestern Psychological Association meeting, Chicago.

Rokeach, M. (1973). The nature of human values. New York: Free Press.

Roskos-Edoldsen, D. R., & Fazio, R. H. (1992). The accessibility of source likability as a determinant of persuasion. Personality and Social Psychology Bulletin, 18, 19-25.

Schuman, H., Steeh, C., & Bobo, L. (1985). Racial attitudes in America: Trends and interpretations. Cambridge, MA: Harvard University Press.

Schwartz, S. (1977). Normative influences on altruism. In L. Berkowitz (Ed.), Advances in experimental social psychology (Vol. 10, pp. 221-279). San Diego, CA: Academic Press.

Sears, D. O., & Kinder, D. R. (1985). Whites' opposition to busing: On conceptualization and operationalization of group conflict. Journal of Personality and Social Psychology, 48, 1141-1147.

Taylor, D. G., Sheatsley, P. B., & Greeley, A. M. (1978). Attitudes towards racial integration. Scientific American, 238, 42-49.

Wittenbrink, B., Judd, C., & Park, B. (1997) Evidence for racial prejudice at the implicit level and its relationship with questionnaire measures. Journal of Personality and Social Psychology, 72, 262–274.

Zuwerink, J. R., Devine, P. G., Monteith, M. J., & Cook, D. A. (1996). Prejudice towards Blacks: With and without compunction? Basic and Applied Social Psychology, 18, 131-150.

III

Applications in Social Settings

10 Reducing Prejudice: The Target's Perspective

Brenda Major
Wendy J. Quinton
Shannon K. McCoy
Toni Schmader
University of California, Santa Barbara

In all societies, some individuals are stigmatized—they possess attributes or identities that are socially devalued and denigrated, and that subject them to prejudice and discrimination in some contexts (Crocker, Major, & Steele, 1998). The ubiquity and devastating consequences of prejudice, both for the stigmatized and for society more broadly, have led to a tremendous amount of theory and research on the origins of prejudice. Social psychologists, for example, have theorized that prejudice results from group conflict (e.g., Sherif, Harvey, White, Hood, & Sherif, 1961), negative stereotypes (e.g., Hamilton & Sherman, 1994); ingroup/outgroup differences (e.g., Turner, Hogg, Oakes, Reicher, & Wetherell, 1987), threats to the self (Pyszczynski, Greenberg, Solomon, & Hamilton, 1991), and attempts to justify unequal distributions of power and resources (Sidanius & Pratto, 1993), among other factors.

Theory and research addressing ways to reduce prejudice, in contrast, are far less common. And theory and research addressing the role that the stigmatized themselves may play in reducing prejudice are almost nonexistent (for exceptions, see Eberhardt & Fiske, 1996; Kirk & Madsen, 1989). The current chapter ventures into this uncharted territory by considering prejudice reduction from the perspective of the stigmatized. Our goal is to present a conceptual framework for thinking about how targets of prejudice might help to reduce prejudice. This framework is grounded in theories of stress and coping as well as social psychological theories of the origins of prejudice.

We believe that psychologists have ignored the target's potential role in prejudice reduction for several reasons. First, it is often more difficult to study prejudice from the perspective of the stigmatized than it is to study it from the perspective of members of the dominant group—in part because members of stigmatized groups tend to be less accessible to researchers than are members of the dominant group. Second, we suspect that many psychologists find this perspective politically incorrect, if not downright distasteful. To ask what a target can do to reduce prejudice raises the specter of "blaming the victim"—after all, prejudice is not the victim's fault, so he or she should not be expected to take any responsibility for reducing it. Third, many psychologists probably believe there is nothing much that targets can do to reduce prejudice directed against them. Because victims of prejudice generally have less power and resources than those who are intolerant of them, they are not regarded as influential agents of interpersonal or social change.

However, the stigmatized are frequently in positions where they must contend with, and can potentially act on, prejudice. The stigmatized also are most directly and negatively affected by prejudice; hence, they have the most to gain by reducing it. For these reasons, targets of prejudice are likely to be highly motivated to reduce prejudice. Furthermore, contrary to traditional views of social interaction that portray targets as passive victims of perceivers' expectations, stereotypes, and prejudices (e.g., Merton, 1948; Rosenthal & Jacobsen, 1968), more contemporary views emphasize the impact of the target's self-views, goals, and motives on their interactions (e.g., Deaux & Major, 1987; Swann, 1984). For example, when targets have strongly held self-conceptions, they are unlikely to behave in ways that confirm perceiver expectancies, or to change their self-beliefs as a result of perceiver expectancies, and they may even alter perceivers' erroneous beliefs about them (e.g., Major, Cozzarelli, Testa, & McFarlin, 1988; Swann & Ely, 1984; Testa & Major, 1988). Contemporary views of the target's role emphasize resilience to stereotypes and prejudice, rather than powerlessness (Crocker & Major, 1989). These perspectives portray targets as active agents who play a role in shaping their interactions with prejudiced perceivers. Thus, despite the obstacles to research that were mentioned above, we believe that the absence of attention to the target's perspective on prejudice reduction has left important theoretical and practical questions ignored.

A COPING PERSPECTIVE ON TARGETS' RESPONSES TO PREJUDICE

In this chapter we use psychological models of stress and coping (e.g., Bandura, 1982; Lazarus & Folkman, 1984) as a framework for understanding how targets may reduce prejudice in their interactions with prejudiced perceivers (see also Miller & Major, in press). These models view people as active agents who attempt to manage stressful life events and the emotions associated with those events. In these models, two central mediators of how individuals respond to potentially stressful events are *cognitive appraisals* and *coping*.

Bandura (1982) conceptualized cognitive appraisals as self-efficacy beliefs—beliefs an individual holds about whether he or she can achieve mastery or control over the environment. These self-efficacy beliefs are hypothesized to direct the ways that individuals attempt to cope with potentially stressful events. Two types of cognitive appraisals are central in Lazarus and Folkman's (1984) theory. Primary appraisal involves the individual's evaluation of whether he or she has anything at stake in an encounter—for example, whether there is a potential for harm, benefit, or loss. Secondary appraisal involves the individual's evaluation of his or her coping resources (e.g., perceived control, social support) and of options for overcoming or preventing harm or improving the prospects for benefit. Events are appraised as stressful when primary appraisals of threat exceed secondary appraisals of coping abilities (Folkman, Lazarus, Dunkel-Schetter, DeLongis, & Gruen, 1986).

Coping is defined as a person's "constantly changing cognitive and behavioral efforts to manage specific external and/or internal demands that are appraised as taxing or exceeding the resources of the person" (Lazarus & Folkman, 1984, p. 141). Coping efforts are process-oriented and context-specific, and are distinguished from the outcomes of coping efforts (i.e., whether or not they are successful in achieving their goal). A key assumption of these models is that there is no one "best" coping strategy that is effective for all people in all situations. Rather, the effectiveness of different coping strategies differs, depending upon the person, the situation, and the person's goals. These goals may be to alter or eliminate the problem that is creating the perceived stress (i.e., problem-focused coping), or to regulate stressful emotions (i.e., emotion-focused coping—Folkman et al., 1986). Although these forms of coping are often treated as if they are mutually exclusive strategies, research indicates that people often engage in problem-focused and emotion-focused coping efforts simultaneously (Folkman et al., 1986).

We believe that theories of coping with stressful life events provide a fruitful framework for analyzing prejudice reduction from the target's point of view. A schematic diagram of our proposed framework is shown in Figure 10.1. This model starts with an individual who is objectively the target of prejudice because of possessing some devalued attribute or social identity. This target individual is exposed to someone who expresses derogatory social attitudes or cognitive beliefs, exhibits negative affect, or displays hostile or discriminatory behaviors toward him or her (Brown, 1995). We propose that the likelihood that a stigmatized target will be motivated, and able, to reduce the prejudice of a perceiver depends upon the target's appraisals of the prejudice to which he or she is exposed, and the types of coping efforts he or she employs. These appraisals and coping efforts are shaped by a variety of factors, including characteristics of the target, characteristics of the perceiver, and characteristics of the situation, as well as the target's goals in the situation.

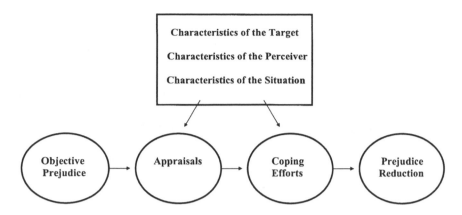

FIG. 10.1. A coping perspective on a target's responses to prejudice.

In this chapter, we first discuss the role of appraisals in targets' responses to prejudice, and then discuss specific problem-focused coping strategies that targets might use to reduce prejudice. Within this discussion of coping strategies, we consider five major theories of prejudice and ask what each theory offers to targets as potential prejudice-reduction coping strategies. We next discuss factors that moderate how targets appraise prejudice and the coping strategies they use to reduce it. We conclude with a discussion of the costs and benefits of various strategies of prejudice reduction from the target's point of view.

Appraisals of Prejudice

Imagine a situation in which an African American customer shopping in a department store is put under extra surveillance by the store manager because the manager believes that African Americans are likely to steal merchandise. Can the customer reduce the prejudice of the store manager, and if so, how?

Before making any attempt at prejudice reduction, our customer must first perceive himself as a target of prejudice, that is, he must appraise the store manager's scrutiny as indicative of prejudice. Although some scholars suggest that the stigmatized are vigilant to signs of prejudice and discrimination in others (Allport, 1954; Goffman, 1963), several sources of evidence suggest that this is often not the case. Members of oppressed social categories often fail to see injustice in their personal situations (Crosby, 1984; Jost & Banaji, 1994; Major, 1994), and they typically perceive less discrimination directed against themselves personally than against their group as a whole (e.g., Crosby, 1982; Guimond & Dube-Simard, 1983; Major, Levin, Schmader, & Sidanius, 1999; Taylor, Wong-Reiger, McKirnan, & Bercusson, 1982).

There are several reasons why the stigmatized may not see themselves as targets of prejudice. First, prejudice is often ambiguous. Although blatant displays of "old-fashioned" prejudice (i.e., hostility and hate) do still occur, the more common modern forms of prejudice are subtle (e.g., Gaertner & Dovidio, 1986; Kinder & Sears, 1981; McConahay, 1986), making it difficult for targets to decipher whether or not negative outcomes involve prejudice (Crocker & Major, 1989). Second, because of social comparison biases, especially tendencies to compare themselves with similar, or ingroup, others, the stigmatized are often unaware that they are being treated worse than members of other groups (Major, 1994). Third, even when the stigmatized become aware that they or their group are disadvantaged relative to others, endorsement of ideologies that justify the social hierarchy may preclude them from labeling their disadvantaged treatment as due to prejudice (see Major, 1994). For example, Crocker, Cornwell, and Major (1993) found that overweight women who were rejected by a male partner blamed their rejection on their weight but did not blame it on the partner's prejudice. Finally, labeling oneself as a target of prejudice has intrapsychic costs, including acknowledging that one is a victim and not in control of one's outcomes (Crocker & Major, 1994; Crosby, 1984; Major, 1987). Thus, returning to our example above, there are various reasons why our African American customer may not appraise his treatment by the store manager as due to prejudice.

Even when the stigmatized do appraise themselves as having been a target of prejudice, this will not necessarily result in efforts to reduce this prejudice. Primary and secondary appraisals of the prejudicial event are critical. In our example above, the responses of the customer (assuming he perceives himself as a target of the store manager's prejudice) depend upon his primary appraisals of the personal significance and gravity of the encounter (i.e., "Is this prejudicial act harmful enough to me that it warrants me putting forth effort to change it?"), and his secondary appraisals of the options available to him (e.g., "I could confront the manager...write a letter to the company...organize a protest in front of the store"), and his resources for implementing those options. These primary and secondary appraisals are shaped by several factors. For example, prejudice is more likely to be appraised as a threat if the perceiver has power over the target, or controls important resources that the target desires or needs, or the prejudice occurs in a domain that is central to the target (Paterson & Neufeld, 1987). Targets are more likely to feel they have the resources to cope if they perceive they have some control in the situation and have social support from others (e.g., Cohen & Wills, 1985; Lazarus & Folkman, 1984). We will return to a discussion of factors that moderate cognitive appraisals, as well as coping efforts, later in the chapter.

Coping with Prejudice

Assuming our hypothetical customer perceives the store manager's actions as prejudicial and appraises those actions as a threat, what can he do to reduce the manager's prejudice? Research on coping indicates that people use a variety of strategies to cope with situations they appraise as threatening. As noted above, these include strategies focused on reducing the problem that is causing the stress (the perceived prejudice), as well as strategies focused on managing stress-related emotions. Which type of strategy our customer is likely to use depends upon his secondary appraisals—i.e., his appraisals of his coping options, abilities, and resources.

Problem-Focused Coping. The target may engage in two forms of problem-focused coping. First, he can engage in coping efforts aimed directly at reducing or destroying the prejudicial attitudes, beliefs, or behaviors of others. This type of prejudice reduction, if successful, has more global and enduring results for the target. Examples of such strategies might include directly confronting the store manager with evidence of her bigotry, or writing letters to the newspaper about the evils of racial profiling. These strategies aimed at *prejudice destruction* are what come to mind for most of us when we think of what it means to reduce prejudice.

Targets' efforts to reduce the problem of prejudice, however, can also be more situation- and relationship-specific. In particular, a second way a target may reduce prejudice is by trying to reduce the likelihood that he or she will be treated in a prejudicial way by a particular perceiver in a particular encounter. Examples of such strategies might include portraying oneself to a prejudiced perceiver in a counter-stereotypical manner (e.g., our customer could whistle Mozart while he shops), or attempting to forge a common identity with a prejudiced perceiver that will override prejudicial tendencies (e.g., our customer could comment to the store manager that based on their attire, they both appear to be Buffalo Bills fans). These are strategies of *prejudice deterrence*, for their aim is to deter others from treating the target in a prejudicial way. Although these strategies may be successful for a target in a particular relationship and situation, they are likely to leave the prejudiced perceiver relatively unchanged in her interactions with other members of the target's group.

Emotion-Focused Coping. Targets can also attempt to reduce prejudice by diminishing the emotional impact of prejudice. These strategies can be thought of as strategies of *prejudice deflection*, because they aim not to reduce prejudice directly, but rather to deflect its impact on the self. Examples might include devaluing the importance of a domain in which one has experienced prejudice, dismissing the significance of others who have acted in a prejudicial way, or discounting the validity of their opinions, all of which can maintain self-esteem in the face of prejudice (see Crocker & Major, 1989). Because emotion-focused coping with prejudice has been considered in depth elsewhere (e.g., Crocker & Major, 1989; Crocker et al., 1998; Major & Crocker, 1994), and because it does not reduce the problem of prejudice, we limit our discussion in this chapter to the problem-focused strategies of prejudice destruction and prejudice deterrence.

Two important factors that determine the type of problem-focused coping strategies that targets will attempt are their goals in the interaction, and their theories of the origins of prejudiced responses in a given perceiver and/or relationship. These two factors are discussed next.

Individual Versus Collective Goals and Coping Strategies

One important determinant of targets' coping strategies is whether their prejudice reduction goals are individual or collective. If targets' goals are largely individual, they are more likely to engage in coping strategies that aim to reduce prejudice and discrimination directed against themselves personally. If targets' goals are collective, they are more likely to engage in coping strategies that aim to reduce prejudice directed against their group. Reducing prejudice on an individual basis is often essential for individual advancement, yet individually-oriented strategies have many shortcomings. Most notably, individually oriented strategies have limited utility in changing prejudicial attitudes and behaviors toward a group as a whole, and thus must be repeated time and time again with different prejudiced perceivers and in different situations. Collective attempts at prejudice reduction, in contrast, allow perceivers to generalize more tolerant attitudes to the group as a whole, and are more effective at changing institutionalized prejudice and discrimination—often the most difficult and impactful type of change to achieve. Thus, targets' most effective and enduring route to reducing prejudice is to use collective problem-focused strategies.

Nevertheless, collective efforts to reduce prejudice are rare. For example, when asked what actions they would take against sex discrimination, the majority of women say that collective action (e.g., participating in a protest) is the type of action that should be taken, but the majority also say that individual action (e.g., filing a personal complaint) is what they actually would do (Taylor & Dubé, 1986). Collective actions to reduce sex discrimination are rare even among women who are high in the belief that women as a group are discriminated against (Foster & Matheson, 1998). Even when they are made aware that gaining access to higher status groups is severely restricted for members of their group, members of low status groups still prefer to engage in individual action strategies (Wright, Taylor, & Moghaddam, 1990).

One reason that targets of prejudice so rarely engage in collective action is that it typically requires immense personal sacrifices of money, time, and relationships on their part. Women who file sexual harassment or sex discrimination charges, for example, often report experiencing tremendous interpersonal rejection and personal costs as a result (Fitzgerald, Swan, & Fischer, 1995). Thus, although collective efforts yield many advantages for the group and are most likely to result in enduring reduction of prejudice, individual efforts aimed at reducing prejudice directed against the self are the most common way in which targets attempt to reduce prejudice.

INDIVIDUAL COPING STRATEGIES FOR REDUCING PREJUDICE

In this section we consider various types of strategies that individual targets might employ to reduce prejudice directed against themselves personally in encounters with prejudiced perceivers. In particular, we consider five major theoretical perspectives on prejudice and what each suggests as the best strategies that targets can use to reduce prejudice against them personally. As will become apparent, these theories make very different predictions as to what a target should do.

Prejudice Results from Negative Stereotypes

Many theories suggest that negative stereotypes held about social groups form the foundation of prejudice and discrimination (Fiske & Taylor, 1991; Hamilton & Sherman, 1994). These theories thus imply that reducing prejudice requires altering stereotypes. One approach is for targets to try to eliminate (destroy) the negative stereotypes that others hold about their group. Alternatively, the target might attempt to prevent (deter) prejudiced perceivers from applying their negative stereotypes about the target's group to the individual target. Attacking the expression of prejudice at the level of stereotypes, however, is a daunting task. Stereotypes are largely automatic in their occurrence (Hamilton & Sherman, 1994) and, as such, often are not under the control of the perceiver, can occur without the conscious awareness of the perceiver, and require little investment of cognitive resources (Devine, 1989). Stereotypes also serve a cognitive efficiency function (Fiske & Taylor, 1991), and are highly resistant to change (for a relevant review, see Hamilton & Sherman, 1994). Consequently, attempting to reduce prejudice by destroying others' stereotypes is a formidable task.

Deterring prejudiced perceivers from applying their negative stereotypes to oneself is potentially a more promising route. Brewer (1996) argued that application of a stereotype to an individual has two necessary steps. The first requirement is that a stereotype must exist in the mind of a perceiver, and the second is that the individual must be placed in the stereotyped category. Therefore, although the stereotype itself may be largely unchangeable, the target may attempt to reduce prejudice by avoiding placement into a stereotyped category. There are three options suggested by the literature that may reduce either the activation of the stereotype, the categorization of the target, or the application of the stereotype to the target in a dyadic interaction. These are: activate a more positive subtype, highlight cross-cutting category memberships, and reduce one's fit to the stereotype mold.

Arguably, the least optimal of these three stereotype-based strategies is the use of positive subtype categories. Many negatively stereotyped groups contain subgroups that have a more positive stereotype, for example: the African American athlete or musician. These subcategories are as stereotyped as the superordinate category, but by activating this positive subgroup stereotype, and encouraging the perceiver to categorize him or her in the subgroup, the target may be able to avoid the prejudice and discrimination that results from the negative stereotype about the superordinate category. The interaction with the perceiver would still be based on stereotypes, but the outcome might be less negative for the target. Toward this end, targets could, for example, display identity symbols associating themselves with respected or well-liked subgroups of their superordinate category. By highlighting their similarity to, and aligning themselves with, a positive subgroup, targets might remove themselves from association with many negative attributions.

This strategy, however, is less than appealing. By creating exceptions to the rule, subcategories can serve to maintain the overarching category stereotype (Weber & Crocker, 1983). In using this strategy, the target may induce the perceiver to treat him or her as an exception, and may achieve a specific positive outcome. However, the target will probably fail to alter the overarching stereotype and the prejudice of the perceiver. Thus, while this strategy may be useful for an individual target in a specific interaction to reduce prejudice directed against him or her, it is not apt to be effective in changing the stereotype or reducing the prejudice of the perceiver towards the target's group.

A second strategy for the target is to create cross-cutting category memberships (Doise, 1978). This involves the simultaneous activation of two categories, the second of which crosses group boundaries—e.g., simultaneous activation of one's ethnicity and one's occupation. If these categories are equally salient, then the perceiver may not react to the target based on the negative stereotype of one category. Research indicates that cross-cutting category memberships do have the potential to reduce expressed prejudice (Deschamps & Doise, 1978). However, only certain types of alternative categories may elicit the desired effect of prejudice reduction (Brewer, Ho, Lee, & Miller, 1987). Optimally, the target should attempt to make salient a cross-cutting category of which the perceiver is also a member. In this manner the target can be assured that the category has some positive valence for the perceiver and may be a dominant or higher status category for the perceiver. Again, this strategy reduces the target's personal experience of prejudice in particular interactions with particular perceivers, but does not eliminate the perceiver's prejudice toward the target's group.

Perhaps the most ideal of the stereotype-based strategies is for the target to avoid categorization altogether, thereby forcing the perceiver to process him or her in terms of individuating information rather than on the basis of group membership. Although there is potential for this strategy to result in subtyping, its goal is for the target to be treated as an individual rather than as a category member. However, because categorization is a basic cognitive function, this may be difficult to achieve.

Strategies aimed at reducing prejudice through reducing categorization, utilizing positive subtypes, or emphasizing cross-cutting category memberships are

all strategies of prejudice deterrence. These strategies do not destroy the prejudice of the perceiver; however, they may allow an individual target to achieve a
desired outcome in a particular circumstance.

Prejudice Results from Threat

A second set of theories argues that prejudice stems from the need to maintain
self-esteem (Pyszczynski et al., 1991) or, more broadly, the integrity of the self-
concept (Steele, 1988). According to these theories, threats to self-esteem or the
self-concept result in defensive derogation of outgroup members. For example,
social identity theory (Tajfel & Turner, 1979) and terror management theory
(Pyszczynski et al., 1991) posit that derogation of outgroups serves to maintain
the value of the ingroup and thus, through our group identification, our own self-
value. In a similar vein, self-affirmation theory (Steele, 1988; Steele & Liu, 1983;
Steele, Spencer, & Lynch, 1993) holds that individuals faced with threats to the
self can restore positive self-evaluation by affirming central values through the
derogation of different others. As well, Stephan and Stephan (1985, 1996) suggest that the perception of threat in intergroup interactions (either realistic
threats or threats to values) gives rise to anxiety, which in turn results in increased stereotyping and prejudice.

Consistent with these theories, research has shown that perceivers exhibit
an increased propensity to derogate or stereotype lower-status others following
a threat to the self (Fein & Spencer, 1997; Greenberg, Pyszczynski, Solomon, &
Rosenblatt, 1990), and that this outgroup derogation can protect self-esteem
(Chin & McClintock, 1993; Lemyre & Smith, 1985). In contrast, affirming the self
through writing about important values (Fein & Spencer, 1997), or by having important values validated by a member of the outgroup (Greenberg et al., 1990),
reduces the expression of prejudice toward outgroups.

These theories suggest two strategies for reducing a perceiver's prejudice:
affirming central values of the perceiver, and/or raising the self-esteem of the
perceiver. By opening up a discussion with a prejudiced perceiver about important self-affirming values, or by expressing agreement with important self-
affirming aspects of his or her world view, a target may effectively deter a perceiver from prejudice or discrimination in a given situation. The target may also
attempt to bolster the perceiver's self-esteem—for example, by praising or com-
plimenting him or her—thereby negating the need for the perceiver to derogate
the target to maintain self-value. In short, threat-based theories of prejudice
suggest that, by providing prejudiced perceivers with the opportunity for self-
affirmation, or by boosting their self-esteem, a stigmatized target may be able to
reduce the likelihood of experiencing prejudice in interactions with that perceiver.
Although these strategies sound repugnant, they are time-honored self-
presentation strategies for gaining power and influencing others (Carnegie,
1937; Jones & Pittman, 1982). By using them, a stigmatized person may be able

to take control of the interaction and get what he or she needs, at least in the short-term.

Prejudiced Perceivers Feel Ambivalence and Conflict

A third theoretical perspective on the origins of prejudice is that it arises out of ambivalence and conflicting belief systems (Devine, 1989; Gaertner & Dovidio, 1986; Katz & Hass, 1988; also see chapters by Devine et al. and Dovidio et al. in this volume). Theories relevant to this view all posit that modern forms of racism and prejudice are characterized by holding both positive and negative feelings toward members of other groups. For example, Devine's (1989) dissociation model of prejudice distinguishes between stereotypes, which are activated automatically when one encounters an outgroup member, and the attitudes or evaluations that are intentionally brought to mind either to support or refute the content of the stereotype. Thus, low prejudiced individuals are differentiated from high prejudiced individuals, not by the content or possession of negative stereotypes, but by the beliefs that are called forth to counteract that stereotypic information.

A similar model based on ambivalence is Gaertner and Dovidio's (1986) notion of aversive racism. Aversive racism, they maintain, is an attitudinal ambivalence resulting from deeply ingrained negative attitudes toward ethnic minority groups, combined with beliefs about egalitarianism. Whereas Devine and Gaertner and Dovidio would suggest that negative attitudes toward other groups are derived from the activation of negative stereotypes, Katz and Hass (1988) assert that White Americans' negative attitudes toward African Americans, in particular, are derived from deeply held beliefs about individualism that conflict with social policies and programs aimed at compensating Blacks for past social transgressions. They suggest that many White Americans possess ambivalent attitudes toward racial minority groups such as African Americans, because American culture breeds attitudes about equality for all people as well as a firm conviction that those who work hard deserve better rewards.

These three views are similar in that they all suggest that one coping strategy that targets might use in an effort to destroy or deter prejudice is to take advantage of ambivalence by reminding perceivers of their egalitarian beliefs so that those beliefs will then direct their behavior with the stigmatized target. This process of prejudice reduction can also be construed in terms of cognitive dissonance theory (Festinger, 1957), because the intent is to induce attitude change (or compensatory behaviors) by revealing to the perceiver the discrepancy between her prejudicial attitudes or behaviors and her deeply held beliefs about egalitarianism and humanity. As Devine (1989) has demonstrated, even low prejudiced individuals may make prejudicial judgments about a target under conditions that prevent egalitarian beliefs from overriding the automatic activation of negative stereotypes. Because prejudiced behaviors are sometimes automatic, this sort of prejudice may not be consciously recognizable as such by the perceiver. The target, however, may be more likely to appraise the action as prejudicial and may communicate this appraisal to the perceiver. Thus, targets may help to destroy a person's prejudicial behaviors, or at least to deter prejudice within a given situation, by inducing dissonance for the perceiver who considers herself to be nonprejudiced. Gaertner and Dovidio (1986) also posit that making people aware of subtle forms of prejudice can be a useful strategy for reducing their occurrence.

Although we are not aware of research examining how perceivers respond when targets of their prejudice confront them with discrepancies in their belief systems (e.g., a stigmatized person making a perceiver aware that her negative attitudes towards gays do not mesh with her belief that she is nonprejudiced), there is evidence that this strategy is effective when used by an ingroup authority figure. Specifically, Rokeach (1973) demonstrated in a series of studies that college students who initially reported having negative attitudes toward African Americans developed more positive attitudes after a college instructor made them aware of a discrepancy between their views of themselves as fair and democratic individuals and their more global views about the relative importance of the values of individual freedom versus equality for all. Furthermore, Kirk and Madsen (1989) pointed out that this strategy may be particularly effective at destroying and deterring prejudice because it leads to an association between acting prejudicially and feeling shame or guilt. Indeed, work by Monteith and Devine demonstrates that people who are low or moderate in prejudiced beliefs do experience feelings of guilt when they are reminded of how their behavior disagrees with their beliefs (Devine, Monteith, Zuwerink, & Elliot, 1991; Monteith, 1993). Those who hold highly prejudiced beliefs, however, do not experience those same feelings of compunction, suggesting that this strategy may be ineffective with them.

Prejudice Results from Perceived Differences

A fourth theoretical perspective on the origins of prejudice is that it is a consequence of perceiving others as different from oneself or one's group. According to self-categorization theory (Turner et al., 1987), for example, people define the boundaries of ingroups and outgroups by seeing those who share similar characteristics as belonging to the same group. Social identity theory builds on this description of how groups are defined by asserting that intergroup conflict is born out of a need to differentiate one's ingroup from outgroups in a favorable direction (Tajfel, 1978).

These theories imply that prejudice can be destroyed or deterred if the perceived differences between people can be minimized or overshadowed by perceived similarities. If a target of prejudice can be seen as part of the perceiver's ingroup, the target will benefit from ingroup biases and be perceived in a more favorable manner. Dovidio and Gaertner (1993) use the term *recategorization* to refer to the process whereby two distinct groups are recategorized into one larger group, which may have superordinate goals that supplant the goals of the two separate groups. For example, in Sherif et al.'s (1961) classic Robber's Cave study, more positive intergroup perceptions were elicited when two rival teams of boys were faced with situations that required them to combine their efforts to overcome obstacles. Recent research confirms that perceiving two groups as combining under one inclusive group identity is an important mechanism in reducing intergroup biases (Dovidio, Gaertner, & Validzic, 1998; also see Dovidio et al., this volume).

Given these benefits of recategorization, one prejudice-reduction coping strategy that targets might use is to highlight a superordinate goal that is shared by themselves and by prejudiced perceivers. For example, a female police officer who is having difficulties with prejudiced male coworkers might reduce their prejudice by reminding them that they and she share a similar concern for fighting crime. As discussed earlier, this strategy also creates cross-cutting categorizations that might reduce the extent to which negative stereotypes are used in evaluating a target.

Another way that these theories suggest for targets to attempt to reduce prejudice is by displaying signs and symbols that emphasize or create a shared identity between the target and the prejudiced perceiver, because this shared identity will minimize perceived differences. Bourhis and Giles (1977; Bourhis, 1979; Giles & Powesland, 1975), for example, assert that language is often used strategically by groups of individuals who adopt and maintain idiosyncratic modes of communication as a way to differentiate themselves from other groups. Intergroup interactions often lead members of one group to differentiate their communication patterns from those of other groups (Taylor & Royer, 1980). In contrast to this pattern, individuals who are motivated to do so can create a shared identity in a given intergroup encounter by converging their mode of speech and non-verbal behavior to that of the outgroup (Giles, Mulac, Bradac, & Johnson, 1987). Thus, in individual encounters with prejudiced perceivers, targets might be able to reduce their experience of prejudice by matching their own communication styles to those of their perceivers (e.g., by using a regional accent or terminology). There is some evidence that such a strategy may be effective at deterring and perhaps even destroying prejudice. For example, Gallois and Callan (1988) found that Australians perceived immigrants to their country more favorably to the extent that the immigrants used nonverbal behaviors that are prototypical of Anglo-Australians. In addition, perceptions of ethnic outgroup members are further enhanced when perceivers believe that outgroup members' attempts at communication convergence are motivated by a desire to break down barriers between the groups (Simard, Taylor, & Giles, 1976).

These coping strategies suggest that, for a target to deter or destroy prejudice, she may have to give up or set aside the identity of her ingroup in order to
assimilate to the majority outgroup. However, recent research on majority group
perceptions of ethnic minority group members suggests that this may not be
necessary. van Oudenhoven, Prins, and Buunk (1998) asked members of minority (Turkish and Moroccan immigrants) and majority groups in the Netherlands to read descriptions of minority group individuals who had adopted one of
four modes of cultural adaptation outlined by Berry (1980). These four modes
constituted the four possible combinations of being identified versus not identified with one's own ethnic minority group and being identified versus not identified with the ethnic majority group. The research results revealed that most of
the minority participants saw themselves as persons who had integrated themselves into Dutch society while also maintaining their minority identification.
Furthermore, members of the Dutch majority held as favorable opinions of immigrants who adopted this coping strategy as they did of those who had given up
their minority heritage and completely assimilated themselves into Dutch society.
Majority group members had the least favorable opinions of ethnic immigrants
who retained their minority identity and eschewed majority culture. Unfortunately,
however, the findings also showed that majority group members overestimated
the extent to which immigrants adopted this separatist approach. Thus, as difficult as it may be, maintaining identification both with one's own group and an
outgroup may be an adaptive coping technique for deterring or destroying prejudicial attitudes held by outgroup members, although getting the outgroup to perceive one's identification with their group may be a challenge.

Most of the coping strategies described so far to create a common identity
should help foster more favorable opinions of a specific target in the mind of a
specific perceiver during an isolated interaction. They are thus more beneficial
for deterring specific acts of prejudice than for destroying prejudice more
broadly. There is an additional coping strategy that might have the further benefit
of extending positive opinions of an individual target to other members of the
target's group as a whole. Specifically, targets may be able to aid in the destruction of prejudicial attitudes against their group by seeking out friendships and al-
liances with outgroup members (Wright, Aron, McLaughlin-Volpe, & Ropp,
1997). By doing so, they create real shared identities that cross-cut group
boundaries (cf. Brewer, this volume). Furthermore, when prejudiced individuals
find themselves liking individual members of a disliked outgroup, they are faced
with an imbalance in their relationships that may be reconciled by developing
more positive opinions of the group as a whole (Heider, 1946, 1958). Recent research provides support for this hypothesis by demonstrating that attitudes toward an outgroup do become more favorable when perceivers observe friendships forming between members of the ingroup and the outgroup (Wright, et al.,
1997).

Prejudice Results from Unequal Distribution
of Power and Resources

A fifth theoretical perspective on the origins of prejudice is that it results from the unequal distribution of resources and status within society, and in particular from a need to justify or legitimize that inequality (Allport, 1954; Hegel, 1807/1966; Fanon, 1968). This approach is consistent with research on the need for belief in a just world (Lerner, 1980), on outcome biases (Allison, Mackie, & Messick, 1996), and on cognitive dissonance theory (Festinger, 1957). For example, the need to believe in a just world is hypothesized to lead people to assume that those who have less power, wealth, and status than others must have done something bad, or have some negative attribute, that leads them to deserve their lower status. Likewise, those who have more than others must have done something good, or have some positive attribute, that causes them to deserve their position of relative advantage. According to cognitive dissonance theory, rationalizations and stereotypes resolve the dissonance aroused by the inequality of resource allocation.

More recent theories that share this perspective on prejudice include system justification theory (Jost & Banaji, 1994) and social dominance theory (Pratto, Sidanius, Stallworth, & Malle, 1994). According to Jost and Banaji (1994), group stereotypes develop to rationalize and legitimize inequality and discrimination. These stereotypes are endorsed by those lower in the status hierarchy, as well as those higher up, and hence they maintain the status quo. Social dominance theory proposes that social hierarchy and inequality are inevitable, and that oppression and prejudice result from societal attempts to diffuse and prevent group conflict (Sidanius & Pratto, 1993). Legitimizing myths (e.g., belief in a meritocracy; belief in a just world) are created to ensure that the social hierarchy is widely accepted by all social groups, and with this acceptance comes stability and perpetuation of the status quo.

These theories imply that in order for stigmatized targets successfully to reduce prejudice against them, they must first redistribute resources by gaining positions of power and status. Because of perceivers' needs to justify the (new) status hierarchy, they will shift to more favorable opinions of stigmatized targets who have successfully gained more power and resources. That is, perceptions of inputs will be revised upwards to justify or explain attained outcomes. For example, a perceiver who encounters a target in a relative position of power will be inclined, due to outcome biases or the need to justify the status hierarchy, to attribute her achievement to her merits. The successful use of this strategy by an individual target involves gaining positions of power and status—clearly a formidable task since the target must contend with prejudice and discrimination in order to do so. Nevertheless, according to theories of prejudice that focus on justification of status positions in society, those who gain positions of higher status may reduce others' prejudice directed against themselves, and potentially, against other members of their group.

Summary

In summary, different theories of the origins of prejudice lead to different recommendations for ways that a target might destroy or deter prejudice in others. Theories that prejudice results from stereotypes offer the possibilities of activating a positive subtype or a cross-cutting category membership. Theories that prejudice results from threats to the self make the discomforting recommendation to praise or affirm the perceiver. If prejudice results from perceivers' ambivalence or conflict, reminding perceivers of their egalitarian values may be the best route for prejudice reduction. If perceived differences are the root of prejudice, then emphasizing similarity with the perceiver, through signs and symbols and shared goals, is probably the strategy of choice. Finally, theories that suggest that prejudice results from justification of the status quo propose the daunting strategy of gaining a position of relative power and status.

MODERATORS OF PREJUDICE APPRAISALS AND COPING EFFORTS

Thus far, we have outlined several different strategies that targets might use to destroy, deter, or deflect prejudice. The likelihood that a target will employ any of these coping strategies, as well as the probable effectiveness of those strategies, depends upon how prejudice is appraised by the target. These appraisals are shaped by several factors that can be roughly organized under characteristics of the target, the perceiver, and the situation. We briefly discuss some of these moderating variables in the following section.

Characteristics of the Target

Perceived Control over the Problem. An important moderator of targets' appraisals and coping efforts is the extent to which targets perceive themselves as having some control over the problem of prejudice. Perceived control is a key component of self-efficacy and secondary appraisals (Bandura, 1982; Lazarus & Folkman, 1984), and it directs the extent to which individuals adopt either problem-focused or emotion-focused coping strategies (Folkman et al., 1986). Thus, targets who believe that they have some control over a perceiver's level of prejudice or expression of prejudice are more likely to engage in strategies that aim directly to destroy that prejudice or deter its expression. Targets who perceive themselves as having little control, in contrast, are more likely to engage in emotion-focused strategies of prejudice deflection. To return to our example of the African American shopper, if he perceives that he has control over the manager's application of a negative stereotype, he may alter his dress, speech, or other salient signs and symbols to avoid being viewed stereotypically.

Perceived Control over the Stigma. Targets of prejudice also differ in the extent to which they perceive themselves as having control over their stigmatizing attribute. People whose stigma is perceived as controllable are held more responsible for it, both by others and by themselves (Crandall & Martinez, 1996; Weiner, Perry, & Magnusson, 1988). The perceived controllability of a stigma can prevent members of stigmatized groups from seeing themselves as targets of prejudice, in part because they view their negative treatment as legitimate (Crocker et al., 1993; Crocker & Major, 1994; Major & Schmader, in press). Thus, people who believe that their stigmatizing condition is under their own control are more likely to try to reduce prejudice by using strategies that focus on changing themselves (e.g., losing weight, having plastic surgery, becoming more educated), rather than on reducing prejudice in others (see Miller & Major, in press). If successful, these strategies should allow individuals to avoid being categorized as part of a stigmatized group, and thus to avoid being negatively stereotyped as well.

Targets who do not perceive their stigma to be controllable, on the other hand, may try to destroy prejudice in others by convincing them that the stigma is uncontrollable. For example, some members of the lesbian and gay male community try to fight homophobia by educating the public about the possible genetic origins of homosexuality and downplaying the view that it is a lifestyle choice. Reducing the perceived controllability of a stigma in perceivers' eyes can lead them to respond to the target with less anger and more compassion (Weiner et al., 1988).

Stigma Concealability. In addition to variation in the extent to which stigmas can be controlled, there is also variation in the extent to which they can be concealed. An individual who is unable to change her status as a member of a stigmatized group might, if feasible, attempt to hide that group membership from others. Concealing a stigma from a prejudiced perceiver can reduce exposure to prejudice by maintaining the illusion of perceived similarity to the perceiver, evading being negatively stereotyped by the perceiver, and avoiding direct acts of discrimination in social interactions.

Interestingly, for those who possess a concealable stigma, the decision to conceal or reveal it achieves very different goals. For example, take a man who is gay. Obviously, one way for him to avoid direct prejudice and discrimination from others is to avoid disclosing his sexual orientation. Because concealing a stigma can be effective on the individual level, this strategy will often be adopted. Concealing one's stigma, however, will not destroy prejudice more broadly. Concealing one's sexual orientation, for example, may even have unfavorable effects on prejudice reduction toward gays and lesbians as a group, because the larger consequence of concealment is an under-representation of the frequency of people in the population who are gay and lesbian. The resulting be-lief that the stigma is rare may exacerbate the perception that possessing that mark is somehow deviant and undesirable. Consequently, for those who share the same concealable stigma, one collective approach to reducing prejudice against their group is to encourage people possessing that stigma to reveal themselves to others. In fact, this strategy has been adopted by the gay and les-bian community to demonstrate to straights, and to gays, that homosexuality is not an unusual lifestyle adopted by only a rare "type" of person.

In addition to reducing the perceived deviance of a stigma, revealing con-cealable stigmas can also work to change attitudes toward stigmatized groups in general, by increasing the perceived similarity among diverse people. This can occur both by creating imbalances between current relationships and existing group attitudes and by making perceivers aware of cross-categorizations that they did not know existed. For example, when a person who is prejudiced against Jews learns that one of her most liked colleagues is Jewish, the disso-nance produced by that imbalance of evaluations may lead her to reevaluate her opinion of Jews. Furthermore, the content of the perceiver's already-formed and favorable impression of her colleague, and the positive stereotype of their shared ingroup, might enter into and adjust the content of the stereotype held about the stigmatized group more generally—in this example, Jews might now be perceived as good workers and friends.

Collective Identity. Another important characteristic of the target that affects appraisals and choice of coping strategy is the extent to which the target has a sense of group, or collective, identity. Stigmatized individuals differ in the extent to which they have a sense of themselves as a member of a stigmatized group. Some stigmas are strongly associated with a group or collectivity, whereas oth-ers are not. For example, African Americans and gay males and lesbians are usually viewed as members of a collective group, whereas the facially disfigured and the overweight are not. Targets of prejudice also differ in their attachment to the group upon which prejudice is based. The perception that one has a com-mon fate with members of one's group (i.e., that one's own individual outcomes are linked to the outcomes of others) is an essential component of a collective identity (Gurin & Townshend 1986; Rabbie & Horwitz, 1988; Rabbie, Schot, & Visser, 1989). Those who have a highly developed collective identity are more likely to adopt collective efforts at prejudice reduction than are those who do not. Indeed, many scholars argue that a collective identity is a necessary component for collective action (Gamson, Fireman, & Rytina, 1982; Melucci, 1989). Thus, targets who are high in collective identity may appraise prejudice against their group as more personally significant than targets who do not feel a strong sense of collective identification.

Collective identity is more likely to lead to collective action if it is accompa-nied by a sense of collective efficacy. Collective efficacy refers to the belief that problems can be solved and lives can be improved through concerted effort (Bandura, 1982), and it has been shown to relate positively and consistently to social activism (Forward & Williams, 1970; Marsh, 1977; Muller, 1972, 1979). Gamson et al. (1982) argued that targets of prejudice who adopt what they called a "collective action frame" will view collective action as a more viable and desirable option. Collective action frames consist of the concepts of injustice (others' intention to bring about harm to you or members of your group), identity (the definition of a "we" in conflict with "they"), and agency (belief in the possibility of improving conditions through collective action).

Characteristics of the Perceiver

Targets' appraisals and coping efforts, and the effectiveness of those efforts, also will vary depending on the nature of the prejudiced perceiver. Three different types of perceivers have been identified by Kirk and Madsen (1989): "intransigent bigots," "ambivalent skeptics," and "well-meaning friends." Intransigent bigots are individuals who have malicious and deeply held prejudicial attitudes. These "old-fashioned" or "redneck" racists are unlikely to change their prejudicial beliefs. Thus, strategies aimed at altering stereotypes, increasing perceived similarity, or inducing ambivalence in belief systems are likely to be ineffective with this type of perceiver. Ingratiation or activating a positive subtype might be more viable strategies, but they too are unlikely to result in a change of attitude or improved treatment. Some of these attempts to destroy or deter prejudice among perceivers who hold highly prejudicial attitudes can actually backfire, resulting in increased prejudice among these individuals (Devine et al., this volume; Myers & Bishop, 1970). Consequently, targets may be reluctant to try to reduce prejudice among these types of perceivers, and may resort instead to emotion-focused coping strategies when forced to interact with such individuals. Collective strategies of prejudice reduction may be the only way to reduce prejudice among intransigent bigots.

"Well-meaning friends" are low prejudiced individuals who are sensitive to the predicament faced by specific targets of prejudice, and who are likely to feel compunction (Devine et al., 1991) when discrepancies between their strongly held egalitarian values and the uncontrolled influence of stereotypes become apparent. Thus, strategies aimed at making egalitarian beliefs salient should be most effective with this group. Well-meaning friends, according to Kirk and Madsen, should be mobilized and encouraged to support the target group's efforts. Because people's attitudes and behaviors are most influenced by members of their same reference group (Merton, 1957), well-meaning friends can be a strong source of influence in prejudice reduction appeals aimed at others in their same group.

The third group of perceivers identified by Kirk and Madsen (1989) are "ambivalent skeptics." Ambivalent skeptics display modern forms of prejudice—

aversive racism (Gaertner & Dovidio, 1986) and ambivalence (Katz, 1979; Katz & Hass, 1988)—wherein they hold negative feelings toward certain target groups but at the same time subscribe to egalitarian values that conflict with these negative emotions. Research by Katz and his colleagues (Katz & Hass, 1988; Katz, Wackenhut, & Hass, 1986) has shown that the ambivalence these types of individuals feel leads to extreme, unstable, and highly variable responses to targets. Ambivalent skeptics have the capacity for change, and targets should appraise prejudice reduction efforts aimed at these individuals as well worth the effort. Unlike well-meaning friends, however, skeptics do hold negative attitudes. Therefore, by directing prejudice reduction efforts toward these skeptics, targets do not waste their efforts on those who are already sympathetic to their cause. Targets may be able to make the greatest strides in prejudice reduction by appealing to ambivalent skeptics, reminding them of their egalitarian beliefs, and emphasizing similarities between their respective groups. In fact, this approach may even work with some prejudiced individuals whom targets view as intransigent bigots, but who nonetheless subscribe to some egalitarian values.

Characteristics of the Situation

Several important aspects of the situation can affect targets' appraisals of prejudice and their efforts to cope with it. First, the power of a prejudiced perceiver over the target is likely to be a critical determinant of the target's appraisals and coping efforts. Targets who are in a low-power position relative to a perceiver should be particularly likely to appraise the prejudice as threatening and should be particularly motivated to try to reduce prejudice in their interactions with the perceiver. However, they may be in the weakest position to do so. Direct attempts to destroy prejudice in a perceiver are potentially risky for a target who depends upon that perceiver for necessary outcomes. For example, it is likely to be highly desirable, yet also highly risky, for a female manager to attempt to directly reduce her male boss's sexism. In contrast, there is less risk, but also less motivation, for an African American shopper to attempt to directly reduce the prejudice of a store manager if the store manager has no power over him. An implication of this reasoning is that, for targets who are in a low-power position relative to the prejudiced perceiver, the most effective strategies for deterring prejudice may be indirect strategies such as validating the perceiver's beliefs, values, and self-esteem.

A second situational factor that affects targets' appraisals and coping efforts is the anticipated duration of the relationship between the target and the perceiver. Targets are likely to be more motivated to reduce the prejudice of perceivers with whom they expect to have a relationship of some duration than when they expect the relationship to be brief. For example, targets are more likely to be motivated to reduce the prejudice of their coworkers than of strangers. However, because directly confronting another person's prejudice may damage the relationship with that person, targets may be more likely to adopt indirect strategies with someone they interact with regularly than with someone they interact with only briefly. For example, strategies aimed at emphasizing superordinate goals or cross-cutting relationships might be more effective for destroying or deterring prejudice in prejudiced colleagues with whom the target must interact frequently.

A third situational factor that can affect targets' appraisals of various prejudice reduction efforts are perceived opportunities for change in the situation. If the differences between target and perceiver groups are perceived as unstable, targets will be more likely to appraise the benefits of prejudice reduction attempts as outweighing the costs (Tajfel & Turner, 1979) and to have a sense of efficacy that change can be achieved. This sort of instability in the status hierarchy is likely to facilitate collective action among members of stigmatized groups.

COSTS AND BENEFITS OF PREJUDICE REDUCTION STRATEGIES FOR THE TARGET OF PREJUDICE

In this chapter, we have distinguished between strategies geared toward deflecting, deterring, or destroying prejudice. Prejudice deflection strategies aim, not to reduce prejudice directly, but merely to diminish its negative emotional impact on oneself. Prejudice reduction strategies try to reduce or destroy the prejudiced beliefs, attitudes, or behaviors of others; while prejudice deterrence strategies attempt to deter others from treating oneself prejudicially. These strategies may be used in the service of different goals, but they may also be employed simultaneously in the service of a single goal.

These different strategies have different costs, as well as different benefits, for the target of prejudice. Prejudice deflection, which primarily involves emotion-focused coping strategies, avoids the possible personal and social costs of attempting to change the attitudes, beliefs, or behaviors of other individuals. Such strategies, however, are unlikely to have the potential benefit of improving the treatment of oneself or one's group by prejudiced others. Nevertheless, in some situations, targets may only be able to cope with prejudice in emotion-focused ways. Such situations, we have argued, are especially likely to be those in which the target feels that he or she has little control relative to a powerful perceiver.

Prejudice destruction and deterrence strategies are both problem-focused methods of coping, aimed at reducing the occurrence of prejudice. They also have differences in their risks and rewards—differences that center on the impact and scope of prejudice reduction. Targets who attempt to destroy prejudice focus on eliminating the occurrence of prejudice broadly. The benefits of this approach include the potential for improved treatment of the target *and* of his or her stigmatized group—not only in a specific encounter or with a specific perceiver, but also *across a variety of situations and perceivers*. Although the benefits of attempting to destroy prejudice are high, so are the costs. Prejudice destruction requires a high level of effort, often prolonged over time, and also the possible sacrifice of personal safety if one is faced with extremely prejudiced perceivers.

Attempting to deter prejudice, on the other hand, has fewer costs. When a target attempts to deter prejudice, he or she tries to reduce the likelihood that a perceiver will treat him or her in a prejudicial way in a specific encounter. This approach is unlikely to be as dangerous as the prejudice destruction approach. The potential benefits, however, are also unlikely to be as high. Because prejudice deterrence strategies do not directly challenge the attitudes, values, and beliefs of the perceiver, but rather work around them to achieve a temporary positive outcome, the resulting benefits may be unlikely to generalize to other perceivers or situations.

Costs and benefits also differ based on whether the target's goal in a prejudice reduction strategy is individual or collective. One key benefit of individually focused efforts is the possibility of individual advancement. It is almost always easier for an individual target to reduce prejudice against himself or herself than to change attitudes toward their stigmatized group as a whole. Yet, when targets advance individually, especially through methods that separate them from their stigmatized ingroup (e.g., recategorization, positive subtyping), prejudice against their group remains intact. In contrast, by participating in collective action, targets can not only improve their personal situation, but also reduce the plight of others who share their stigma. Collective action often has high costs, such as the need for organization, resources, commitment, communication, personal sacrifice, and effort over time. Nevertheless, it may be the best way to combat institutionalized prejudice and discrimination, and to create more tolerant attitudes that will generalize to the group as a whole.

CONCLUSIONS

We have attempted to describe in this chapter strategies that targets of prejudice might use to reduce prejudice against themselves or their group—strategies of prejudice deflection, deterrence, and destruction. Our approach has been guided by theory and research on coping with stressful life events, and informed by theories of the origins of prejudice. We have described prejudice reduction strategies that are logically derived from social psychological theories of prejudice, and we have done so without regard to their palatability or feasibility.

Any type of prejudice reduction effort has risks. Certain strategies we have outlined here (e.g., boosting a prejudiced perceiver's self-esteem, avoiding categorization altogether, assimilation to the perceiver's group) carry a high risk to the integrity and self-esteem of targets. Other strategies (e.g., gaining status and power so as to induce a revision of attributions or stereotypes about oneself or one's group) are neither easily implemented nor highly feasible. Nonetheless, we believe that each of these strategies is likely to be employed at some time in some situations by targets of prejudice who are attempting to cope with their predicament.

Our intent here has been to outline what social psychological theories predict that targets can do to combat prejudice in prejudicial interactions, rather than to endorse a particular type or set of strategies. The risks and benefits of these various approaches to prejudice reduction are ultimately borne by the targets.

REFERENCES

Allison, S. T., Mackie, D. M., & Messick, D. M. (1996). Outcome biases in social perception: Implications for dispositional inferences, attitude change, stereotypes, and social behavior. *Advances in Experimental Social Psychology, 28,* 53-93.

Allport, G. W. (1954). *The nature of prejudice.* Cambridge, MA: Addison-Wesley.

Bandura, A. (1982). Self-efficacy mechanism in human agency. *American Psychologist, 37,* 122-147.

Berry, J. W. (1980). Psychology of acculturation: Understanding individuals moving between cultures. In R. Brislin (Ed.), *Applied cross-cultural psychology* (pp. 232-253). Beverly Hills, CA: Sage.

Bourhis, R. Y. (1979). Language and ethnic interaction: A social psychological approach. In H. Giles & B. Saint-Jacques (Eds.), *Language and ethnic relations* (pp. 117-141). Oxford, England: Pergamon.

Bourhis, R. Y., & Giles, H. (1977). The language of intergroup distinctiveness. In H. Giles (Ed.), *Language, ethnicity, and intergroup relations* (pp. 119-135). London: Academic Press.

Brewer, M. B. (1996). When contact is not enough: Social identity and intergroup cooperation. *International Journal of Intercultural Relations, 20,* 291-303.

Brewer, M. B., Ho, H., Lee, J., & Miller, N. (1987). Social identity and social distance among Hong Kong schoolchildren. *Personality and Social Psychology Bulletin, 13,* 156-165.

Brown, R. (1995). *Prejudice: Its social psychology.* Cambridge, MA: Blackwell.

Carnegie, D. (1937). *How to win friends and influence people.* New York: Simon & Schuster.

Chin, M. G., & McClintock, C. G. (1993). The effects of intergroup discrimination and social values on level of self-esteem in the minimal group paradigm. *European Journal of Social Psychology, 23,* 63-75.

Cohen, S., & Wills, T. A. (1985). Stress, social support, and the buffering hypothesis. *Psychological Bulletin, 98,* 310-357.

Crandall, C. S., & Martinez, R. (1996). Culture, ideology, and antifat attitudes. *Personality and Social Psychology Bulletin, 22,* 1165-1176.

Crocker, J., & Major, B. (1989). Social stigma and self-esteem: The self-protective properties of stigma. *Psychological Review, 96,* 608-630.

Crocker, J., Cornwell, B., & Major, B. (1993). The stigma of overweight: Affective consequences of attributional ambiguity. *Journal of Personality and Social Psychology, 64,* 60-70.

Crocker, J., Major, B., & Steele, C. (1998). Social stigma. In D. T. Gilbert & S. T. Fiske (Eds.), *Handbook of social psychology* (4th ed., Vol. 2, pp. 504-553). Boston, MA: McGraw-Hill.

Crosby, F. (1982). *Relative deprivation and working women.* New York: Oxford University Press.

Crosby, F. (1984). The denial of personal discrimination. *American Behavioral Scientist, 27,* 371-386.

Deaux, K., & Major, B. (1987). Putting gender into context: An interactive model of gender-related behavior. *Psychological Review, 94,* 369-389.

Deschamps, J. C., & Doise, W. (1978). Crossed category memberships in intergroup relations. In H. Tajfel (Ed.), *Differentiation between social groups: Studies in the social psychology of intergroup relations* (pp. 141-158). London: Academic Press.

Devine, P. G. (1989). Stereotypes and prejudice: Their automatic and controlled components. *Journal of Personality and Social Psychology, 56,* 5-18.

Devine, P. G., Monteith, M. J., Zuwerink, J. R., & Elliot, A. J. (1991). Prejudice with and without compunction. *Journal of Personality and Social Psychology, 60,* 817-830.

Doise, W. (1978). *Groups and individuals: Explanations in social psychology.* New York: Cambridge University Press.

Dovidio, J. F., & Gaertner, S. L. (1993). Stereotypes and evaluative intergroup bias. In D. M. Mackie & D. L. Hamilton (Eds.), *Affect, cognition, and stereotyping: Interactive processes in group perception* (pp. 167-193). San Diego, CA: Academic Press.

Dovidio, J. F., Gaertner, S. L., & Validzic, A. (1998). Intergroup bias: Status, differentiation, and a common in-group identity. *Journal of Personality and Social Psychology, 75,* 109-120.

Eberhardt, J. L., & Fiske, S. T. (1996). Motivating Individuals to change: What is a target to do? In C. N. Macrae, C. Stangor, & M. Hewstone (Eds.), *Stereotypes and stereotyping.* New York: Guilford.

Fanon, F. (1968). *Black skin, white masks.* New York: Grove.

Fein, S., & Spencer, S. J. (1997). Prejudice as self-image maintenance: Affirming the self through derogating others. *Journal of Personality and Social Psychology, 73,* 31-44.

Festinger, L. (1957). *A theory of cognitive dissonance.* Stanford, CA: Stanford University Press.

Fiske, S. T., & Taylor, S. E. (1991). *Social cognition* (2nd ed.). New York: McGraw-Hill.

Fitzgerald, L. F., Swan, S., & Fischer, K. (1995). Why didn't she just report him? The psychological and legal implications of women's responses to sexual harassment. *Journal of Social Issues, 51*(1), 117-138.

Folkman, S., Lazarus, R. S., Dunkel-Schetter, C., DeLongis, A., & Gruen, R. J. (1986). Dynamics of a stressful encounter: Cognitive appraisal, coping, and encounter outcomes. *Journal of Personality and Social Psychology, 50,* 992-1003.

Forward, J. R., & Williams, J. R. (1970). Internal-external control and black militancy. *Journal of Social Issues, 26,* 75-92.

Foster, M. D., & Matheson, K. (1998). Perceiving and feeling personal discrimination: Motivation or inhibition for collective action? *Group Processes and Intergroup Relations, 1,* 165-174.

Gaertner, S. L., & Dovidio, J. F. (1986). The aversive form of racism. In J. F. Dovidio & S. L. Gaertner (Eds.), *Prejudice, discrimination, and racism* (pp. 361-89). Orlando, FL: Academic Press.

Gallois, C., & Callan, V. J. (1988). Communication accommodation and the prototypical speaker: Predicting evaluations of status and solidarity. *Language and Communication, 8,* 271-283.

Gamson, W. A., Fireman, B., & Rytina, S. (1982). *Encounters with unjust authority.* Homewood, IL: Dorsey.

Giles, H., & Powesland, P. F. (1975). *Speech style and social evaluation.* London: Academic Press.

Giles, H., Mulac, A., Bradac, J., & Johnson, P. (1987). Speech accommodation theory: The first decade and beyond. In M. L. McLaughlin (Ed.), *Communication yearbook 10* (pp. 13-48). Beverly Hills, CA: Sage.

Goffman, E. (1963). *Stigma: Notes on the management of spoiled identity.* Englewood Cliffs, NJ: Prentice-Hall.

Greenberg, J., Pyszczynski, T., Solomon, S., & Rosenblatt, A. (1990). Evidence for terror management theory, II: The effects of mortality salience on reactions to those who threaten or bolster the cultural worldview. *Journal of Personality and Social Psychology, 58,* 308-318.

Guimond, S., & Dube-Simard, L. (1983). Relative deprivation theory and the Quebec nationalist movement: The cognition-emotion distinction and the personal-group deprivation issue. *Journal of Personality and Social Psychology, 44,* 526-535.

Gurin, P., & Townshend, A. (1986). Properties of gender identity and their implications for group consciousness. *British Journal of Social Psychology, 25,* 139-148.

Hamilton, D. L., & Sherman, J. W. (1994). Stereotypes. In R. S. Wyer, Jr. & T. K. Srull (Eds.), *Handbook of social cognition, Vol. 1: Basic processes* (pp. 1-68). Hillsdale, NJ: Erlbaum.

Hegel, G. W. F. (1807/1966). *The phenomenology of mind.* London: Allen & Unwin.

Heider, F. (1946). Attitudes and cognitive organization. *Journal of Psychology, 21,* 107-112.

Heider, F. (1958). *The psychology of interpersonal relations.* New York: Wiley.

Jones, E. E., & Pittman, T. S. (1982). Toward a general theory of strategic self-presentation. In J. Suls (Ed.), *Psychological perspectives on the self* (Vol. 1, pp. 231-260). Hillsdale, NJ: Erlbaum.

Jost, J. T., & Banaji, M. R. (1994). The role of stereotyping in system-justification and the production of false consciousness. *British Journal of Social Psychology, 33,* 1-27.

Katz, I. (1979). Some thoughts about the stigma notion. *Personality and Social Psychology Bulletin, 5,* 447-460.

Katz, I., & Hass, R. G. (1988). Racial ambivalence and American value conflict: Correlational and priming studies of dual cognitive structures. *Journal of Personality and Social Psychology, 55,* 893-905.

Katz, I., Wackenhut, J., & Hass, R. G. (1986). Racial ambivalence, value duality, and behavior. In J. F. Dovidio & S. L. Gaertner (Eds.), *Prejudice, discrimination, and racism* (pp. 35-59). Orlando, FL: Academic Press.

Kinder, D. R., & Sears, D. O. (1981). Prejudice and politics: Symbolic racism versus racial threats to the good life. *Journal of Personality and Social Psychology, 40,* 414-431.

Kirk, M., & Madsen, H. (1989). *After the ball: How America will conquer its fear and hatred of gays in the '90s.* New York: Doubleday.

Lazarus, R. S., & Folkman, S. (1984). *Stress, appraisal, and coping.* New York: Springer.

Lemyre, L., & Smith, P. M. (1985). Intergroup discrimination and self-esteem in the minimal group paradigm. *Journal of Personality and Social Psychology, 49,* 660-670.

Lerner, M. J. (1980). *The belief in a just world: A fundamental delusion.* New York: Plenum.

Major, B. (1994). From social inequality to personal entitlement: The role of social comparisons, legitimacy appraisals, and group membership. In M. P. Zanna (Ed.), *Advances in experimental social psychology* (Vol. 26, pp. 293-348). San Diego, CA: Academic Press.

Major, B., & Crocker, J. (1994). Reactions to stigma: The moderating role of justifications. In M. P. Zanna & J. M. Olson (Eds.), *The psychology of prejudice: The Ontario Symposium* (Vol. 7, pp. 289-314). Hillsdale, NJ: Erlbaum.

Major, B., Cozzarelli, C., Testa, M., & McFarlin, D. B. (1988). Self-verification versus expectancy confirmation in social interaction: The impact of self-focus. *Personality and Social Psychology Bulletin, 14,* 346-359.

Major, B., Levin, S., Schmader, T., & Sidanius, J. (1999). *Effects of justice ideology, group identification, and ethnic group membership on perceptions of personal and group discrimination.* Manuscript in preparation.

Major, B., & Schmader, T. (in press). From social devaluation to self-esteem: The impact of legitimacy appraisals. In J. Jost & B. Major (Eds.), *The psychology of legitimacy: Emerging perspectives on ideology, justice, and intergroup relations.* Cambridge, England: Cambridge University Press.

Marsh, A. (1977). *Protest and political consciousness.* Beverly Hills, CA: Sage.

McConahay, J. B. (1986). Modern racism, ambivalence, and the Modern Racism Scale. In J. F. Dovidio & S. L. Gaertner (Eds.), *Prejudice, discrimination, and racism* (pp. 91-125). Orlando, FL: Academic Press.

Melucci, A. (1989). *Nomads of the present: Social movements and individual needs in contemporary society.* Philadelphia: Temple University Press.

Merton, R. K. (1948). The self-fulfilling prophecy. *Antioch Review, 8,* 193-210.

Merton, R. K. (1957). *Social theory and social structure.* Glencoe, IL: Free Press.

Miller, C. T., & Major, B. (in press). Coping with stigma and prejudice. In T. Heatherton, R. Kleck, & J. G. Hall (Eds.), *Stigma.* New York: Guilford.

Monteith, M. J. (1993). Self-regulation of prejudiced responses: Implications for progress in prejudice-reduction efforts. *Journal of Personality and Social Psychology, 65,* 469-485.

Muller, E. N. (1972). A test of a partial theory of potential for political violence. *American Political Science Review, 66,* 928-959.

Muller, E. N. (1979). *Aggressive political participation.* Princeton, NJ: Princeton University Press.

Myers, D. G., & Bishop, G. D. (1970). Discussion effects on racial attitudes. *Science, 169,* 778-779.

Paterson, R. J., & Neufeld, R. W. J. (1987). Clear danger: Situational determinants of the appraisal of threat. *Psychological Bulletin, 101,* 404-416.

Pratto, F., Sidanius, J., Stallworth, L. M., & Malle, B. F. (1994). Social dominance orientation: A personality variable predicting social and political attitudes. *Journal of Personality and Social Psychology, 67,* 741-763.

Pyszczynski, T., Greenberg, J., Solomon, S., & Hamilton, J. (1991). A terror management analysis of self-awareness and anxiety: The hierarchy of terror. In R. Schwarzer & R. A. Wicklund (Eds.), *Anxiety and self-focused attention* (pp. 67-85). New York: Harwood.

Rabbie, J. M., & Horwitz, M. (1969). Arousal of ingroup-outgroup bias by a chance win or loss. *Journal of Personality and Social Psychology, 13,* 269-277.

Rabbie, J. M., Schot, J. C., & Visser, L. (1989). Social identity theory: A conceptual and empirical critique from the perspective of a behavioural interaction model. *European Journal of Social Psychology, 19,* 171-202.

Rokeach, M. (1973). *The nature of human values.* New York: Free Press.

Rosenthal, R., & Jacobson, D. (1968) *Pygmalion in the classroom: Teacher expectations and pupils' intellectual development.* New York: Holt, Rinehart & Winston.

Sherif, M., Harvey, O. J., White, B. J., Hood, W. R., & Sherif, C. W. (1961). *Intergroup conflict and cooperation: The Robbers Cave experiment.* Norman: University of Oklahoma Book Exchange.

Sidanius, J., & Pratto, F. (1993). The inevitability of oppression and the dynamics of social dominance. In P. M. Sniderman & P. E. Tetlock (Eds.), *Prejudice, politics, and the American dilemma* (pp. 173-211). Stanford, CA: Stanford University Press.

Simard, L., Taylor, D. M., & Giles, H. (1976). Attribution processes and interpersonal accommodation in a bilingual setting. *Language and Speech, 19,* 374-387.

Steele, C. M. (1988). The psychology of self-affirmation: Sustaining the integrity of the self. In L. Berkowitz, (Ed.), *Advances in experimental social psychology, Vol. 21: Social psychological studies of the self: Perspectives and programs* (pp. 261-302). San Diego, CA: Academic Press.

Steele, C. M., & Liu, T. J. (1983). Dissonance processes as self-affirmation. *Journal of Personality and Social Psychology, 45,* 5-19.

Steele, C. M., Spencer, S. J., & Lynch, M. (1993). Self-image resilience and dissonance: The role of affirmational resources. *Journal of Personality and Social Psychology, 64,* 885-896.

Stephan, W. G., & Stephan, C. W. (1985). Intergroup anxiety. *Journal of Social Issues, 41*(3), 157-175.

Stephan, W. G., & Stephan, C. W. (1996). Predicting prejudice. *International Journal of Intercultural Relations, 20,* 409-429.

Swann, W. B. (1984). Quest for accuracy in person perception: A matter of pragmatics. *Psychological Review, 91,* 457-477.

Swann, W. B., & Ely, R. J. (1984). A battle of wills: Self-verification versus behavioral confirmation. *Journal of Personality and Social Psychology, 46,* 1287-1302.

Tajfel, H. (1978). *Differentiation between social groups: Studies in the social psychology of intergroup relations.* London: Academic Press.

Tajfel, H., & Turner, J. C. (1979). An integrative theory of intergroup conflict. In W. G. Austin & S. G. Worchel (Eds.), *The social psychology of intergroup relations* (pp. 33-47). Monterey, CA: Brooks/Cole.

Taylor, D. M., & Dube´, L. (1986). Two faces of identity: The "I" and the "We". *Journal of Social Issues, 42*(2), 81-98.

Taylor, D. M., & Royer, E. (1980). Group processes affecting anticipated language choice in intergroup relations. In H. Giles, W. P. Robinson, & P. M. Smith (Eds.), *Language: Social psychological perspectives* (pp. 185-192). Oxford, England: Pergamon.

Taylor, D. M., Wong-Rieger, D., McKirnan, D. J., & Bercusson, T. (1982). Social comparison in a group context. *Journal of Social Psychology, 117,* 257-269.

Testa, M., & Major, B. (1988). Self-verification and expectancy confirmation in social interaction: Independent or interactive processes? *Representative Research in Social Psychology, 18,* 35-48.

Turner, J. C., Hogg, M. A., Oakes, P. J., Reicher, S. D., & Wetherell, M. S. (1987). *Rediscovering the social group: A self-categorization theory.* New York: Blackwell.

van Oudenhoven, J. P., Prins, K. S., & Buunk, B. P. (1998). Attitudes of minority and majority members towards adaptation of immigrants. *European Journal of Social Psychology, 28,* 995-1013.

Weber, R., & Crocker, J. (1983). Cognitive processes in the revision of stereotypic beliefs. *Journal of Personality and Social Psychology, 45,* 961-977.

Weiner, B., Perry, R. P., & Magnusson, J. (1988). An attributional analysis of reactions to stigmas. *Journal of Personality and Social Psychology, 55,* 738-748.

Wright, S. C., Aron, A., McLaughlin-Volpe, T., & Ropp, S. A. (1997). The extended contact effect: Knowledge of cross-group friendships and prejudice. *Journal of Personality and Social Psychology, 73,* 73-90.

Wright, S. C., Taylor, D. M., & Moghaddam, F. M. (1990). Responding to membership in a disadvantaged group: From acceptance to collective protest. *Journal of Personality and Social Psychology, 58,* 994-1003.

11 The Three Cs of Reducing Prejudice and Discrimination

David W. Johnson
Roger T. Johnson
University of Minnesota

Reducing prejudice and discrimination occurs most successfully when majority and minority individuals interact, have positive experiences, form personal relationships, engage in open and truthful discussions with each other, and develop a personal commitment to reducing prejudice and discrimination. While there are many ways in which prejudice and discrimination can be reduced, it is through personal relationships with diverse individuals that the most profound and lasting changes in prejudice and discrimination take place. When prejudice and discrimination become personal issues involving people one cares about, commitment to ending prejudice in oneself and others is developed. When friendships develop among diverse individuals, stereotyping, prejudice, and discrimination are reduced (Pettigrew, 1997). Through personal, one-on-one interaction, categories break down, and outgroup members are perceived in more individualized terms (Brewer & Miller, 1984; Johnson & Johnson, 1980, 1989; Johnson, Johnson, & Maruyama, 1983; Marcus-Newhall et al., 1993).

There are very few settings in which such personal relationships may be developed. Schools may be the only place where diverse children and adolescents are in proximity for long periods of time. Educators, therefore, may have a unique opportunity to create the conditions for promoting in most (if not all) children, adolescents, and young adults the types of interactions, relationships, competencies, and values that decrease stereotyping and prejudice.

For over 30 years we have been conducting a program of theory, research, and practice to teach children, adolescents, and young adults the procedures and values needed to reduce prejudice and discrimination and to further human rights (Johnson, 1970; Johnson & Johnson, 1999). To reduce prejudice and discrimination, children and adolescents must live and learn within a school culture

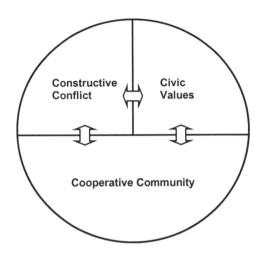

FIG 11.1 The Three Cs of Reducing Prejudice

that promotes the development of caring, personal relationships among diverse individuals, and that values diversity and human rights. Such schools are built on the Three Cs Program: Establishing a cooperative community, resolving conflicts constructively, and internalizing civic values (see Figure 11-1).

THE FIRST C: COOPERATIVE COMMUNITY

The Nature of Community and Social Interdependence

If children and youth are to develop free from ethnic and cultural prejudices and to value diversity, a cooperative school community in which they interact and form positive relationships with diverse peers must be established. Schooling should begin with establishing a learning community based on cooperation (i.e., working together to achieve mutual goals). A *community* is a group of people who live in the same locality and share common goals and a common culture. Broadly, the school community encompasses all stakeholders, including central administrators, college admission officers, and future employers; but in practice the school community is made up of the faculty and staff, the students, their parents, and members of the neighborhood.

The heart of cooperation, community, and culture is social interdependence. *Social interdependence* means that each individual's outcomes are affected by the actions of others (Deutsch, 1962; Johnson & Johnson, 1989). Social interdependence may be positive or negative. Positive interdependence (cooperation) exists when individuals work together to achieve mutual goals, whereas negative interdependence (competition) exists when individuals work against each other to achieve a goal that only one or a few may attain. Positive interdependence may be structured through mutual goals, joint rewards, shared resources, complementary roles, division of labor, and a mutual identity. *Social independence*, where the outcomes of each person are unaffected by others' actions, is characterized by individualistic actions.

Positive interdependence may be structured at all levels of school life. The heart of a cooperative school community is the predominant use of cooperative learning. *Cooperative learning* is the instructional use of small groups so that students work together to maximize their own and each other's learning (Johnson, Johnson, & Holubec, 1998a). Any assignment in any curriculum, in any subject area, for any age student can be structured cooperatively. There are three types of cooperative learning (Johnson, Johnson, & Holubec, 1998a, 1998b): formal cooperative learning, informal cooperative learning, and cooperative base groups. Table 11.1 summarizes these three types, including the key activities of the teacher in each.

Formal cooperative learning consists of students working together, for one class period to several weeks, to achieve shared learning goals and jointly complete specific tasks and assignments (such as decision making or problem solving, completing a curriculum unit, writing a report, conducting a survey or experiment, reading a chapter or reference book, learning vocabulary, or answering questions at the end of the chapter) (Johnson, Johnson, & Holubec, 1998a). Any course requirement or assignment may be structured to include formal cooperative learning.

Informal cooperative learning consists of having students work together to achieve a joint learning goal in temporary, ad-hoc groups that last from a few minutes to one class period (Johnson, Johnson, & Holubec, 1998b; Johnson, Johnson, & Smith, 1998). During a lecture, demonstration, or film, informal cooperative learning can be used to focus student attention on the material to be learned, set a mood conducive to learning, help set expectations as to what will be covered in a class session, ensure that students cognitively process and rehearse the material being taught, summarize what was learned and precue the next session, and/or provide closure to an instructional session. Informal cooperative learning groups are often organized so that students engage in three-to-five-minute focused discussions before and after a lecture and two-to-three-minute turn-to-your-partner discussions interspersed throughout a lecture.

Cooperative base groups are long-term, heterogeneous cooperative learning groups with stable membership (Johnson, Johnson, & Holubec, 1998b; Johnson, Johnson, & Smith, 1998). Base groups give the support, help, encouragement, and assistance each member needs to make academic progress (i.e., to attend class, complete all assignments, learn) and develop cognitively and so-

TABLE 11.1
Types of Cooperative Learning

Formal Cooperative Learning	Informal Cooperative Learning	Cooperative Base Groups
Students complete assignment, lesson, unit, or project to maximize own and groupmates' learning	Students discuss assigned questions for a few minutes to focus attention, organize knowledge, set expectations, create mood, ensure cognitive processing and rehearsal, summarize, pre-cue next session, or provide closure	Permanent; last for one semester, one year, or several years to ensure that all members make academic progress and develop cognitively and socially in healthy ways
Teacher Procedure	*Teacher Procedure*	*Teacher Procedure*
Make pre-instructional decisions	Conduct introductory focused discussion	Structure opening class meeting to check homework, ensure members understand academic material, complete routine tasks such as attendance, and prepare members for the day
Explain task & cooperative structure	Conduct intermittent pair discussions every ten or fifteen minutes	Structure ending class meeting to ensure all members understand the academic material, know what homework to do, and are making progress on long-term assignments
Monitor learning groups and intervene to improve task-work and teamwork	Conduct closure-focused discussion	Members help and assist each other learn in-between classes
Assess learning and process group effectiveness		Conduct semester or year-long school or class service projects

Source: Johnson, D. W., & Johnson, R. (1999).

cially in healthy ways. Base groups are permanent (lasting from one to several years) and provide the long-term, caring peer relationships necessary to influence members to work hard and consistently in school.

In addition to cooperative learning, positive interdependence can be extended through all levels of the school. *Classroom* interdependence may be created through such procedures as class goals, rewards, or celebrations, student roles (such as establishing a classroom government), or dividing resources among all class members (having the class publish a newsletter in which each cooperative group contributes one article). *Interclass* interdependence may be created through organizing several classes into a "neighborhood" and having them engage in joint projects. *School* interdependence may be structured through displaying the school's goals, organizing faculty into collegial teaching teams and study groups, using cooperative groups during faculty meetings, and conducting all-school projects. Projects with parents, such as creating a "strategic plan" or raising money, can create *school-parent* interdependence. Finally, *school-neighborhood* interdependence may be created by mutual projects, such as having neighborhood members play in the school band or having students and neighborhood members jointly clean up a park.

Effective cooperation requires that five basic elements be carefully structured into the situation (Johnson & Johnson, 1989; Johnson, Johnson, & Holubec, 1998a). First, there must be a strong sense of *positive interdependence*, in which individuals believe they are linked with others so that they cannot succeed unless the others do (and vice versa). As mentioned above, positive interdependence may be structured through mutual goals, joint rewards, divided resources, complementary roles, or a shared identity. Second, each collaborator must be *individually accountable* to do his or her fair share of the work. Third, collaborators must have the opportunity to *promote each other's success* by helping, assisting, supporting, encouraging, and praising each other's efforts to achieve. Fourth, working together cooperatively requires *interpersonal and small-group skills*, such as leadership, decision-making, trust-building, communication, and conflict-management skills. Finally, cooperative groups must engage in *group processing*, in which group members discuss how well they are achieving their goals and maintaining effective working relationships.

When interaction takes place within such a cooperative structure, the relationships that are built among diverse individuals result in both a reduction of prejudice and creation of a respect and liking for diversity. Within cooperative efforts there tends to be a process of acceptance of other individuals, whereas within competitive and individualistic efforts there tends to be a process of rejection of others.

Forming and Maintaining Positive Relationships

Building a cooperative community that includes diverse individuals does not begin at a neutral point. Many of the individuals will have preinteraction attitudes and perhaps previous experiences that will predispose them to negative interactions (Johnson & Johnson, 1980, 1989; Johnson, Johnson, & Maruyama, 1983). Positive attitudes lead to an expectation of having rewarding interactions, whereas negative attitudes lead to an expectation of nonrewarding interactions. Within a school community, physical proximity in and of itself is a necessary but not sufficient condition for the formation of caring and committed relationships.

Furthermore, proximity carries the risk of making things worse as well as the possibility of making things better. Cooperation, therefore, has to be carefully structured at all levels of the school to create an effective community.

Regardless of preexisting attitudes, physical proximity among diverse individuals is a positive opportunity, but also a potential hazard. When diverse individuals are brought into proximity, the results may be constructive, positive relationships characterized by a reduction of stereotyping and prejudice, or hostile, negative relationships characterized by increased stereotyping and prejudice. Ethnic desegregation of American schools, for example, has had all three possible outcomes—positive, negative, and neutral results (Johnson & Johnson, 1989). Prejudice may have been reduced in only a small minority of the instances. For example, in one of the most extensive study of cross-ethnic proximity, Gerard and Miller (1975) found that years after the schools were voluntarily desegregated, Black, White, and Mexican American students tended not to associate with each other, but rather to hang together in their own ethnic clusters so that relatively few cross-ethnic friendships emerged. Similar results have been found in studies of inclusion of handicapped students in regular classrooms (Johnson & Johnson, 1989).

The research findings on cross-ethnic and cross-handicap interaction are consistent. Creating constructive interaction and positive relationships requires something more than simple proximity. Placing majority and minority individuals in the same classroom or situation may be a necessary condition for promoting positive relationships, but it is not a sufficient condition. Its limitations may be due to the strength of preinteraction prejudices, negative emotions such as fear and anxiety, ambivalent feelings, the strain of interacting with members of stigmatized groups, or even a paternalistic tendency to be overfriendly. Due to these and similar factors, physical proximity can often increase prejudice and rejection, rather than result in acceptance and liking. Whether positive or negative outcomes occur from the proximity of diverse individuals depends on how the interaction is structured.

There is much research evidence that cooperative experiences, compared with competitive and individualistic ones, promote more positive, committed, and caring relationships—regardless of differences in ethnic, cultural, language, social class, gender, ability, or other characteristics (Johnson & Johnson, 1989). When people cooperate, they tend to like each other more, trust each other more, be more candid with each other, and be more willing to listen to and be influenced by each other. When people compete or work individualistically, then liking, trust, influence, and candor tend to decrease. The impact of positive interdependence is enhanced when participants have equal status and shared social norms, and when authorities promote positive relationships and friendship-formation (Allport, 1954; Watson, 1947; Williams, 1947).

Social Judgment Theory

Social judgment theory was developed to explicate the powerful effects that a cooperative context has on relationships among diverse individuals. The theory posits that a process of acceptance or rejection occurs, depending on whether interaction takes place within a context of positive, negative, or no interdependence (Johnson & Johnson, 1980, 1989).

The Process of Acceptance

The process of acceptance may be defined as relationships becoming more and more caring and committed as proximity and interaction continue (Johnson & Johnson, 1989—see Table 11.2). The process of acceptance begins with *positive interdependence*. Individuals must believe that they "sink or swim together" in striving to achieve important mutual goals. Striving for mutual benefit requires *promotive interaction*—assisting, helping, sharing, and encouraging each other's efforts to achieve. Promotive interaction may be contrasted with oppositional interaction (individuals attempting to obstruct and frustrate each other's goal achievement), and no interaction (individuals ignoring—neither facilitating nor frustrating—each other's goal achievement). More promotive interaction among individuals (as opposed to oppositional or no interaction) leads to greater resulting interpersonal attraction.

TABLE 11.2
Processes of Acceptance and Rejection

Process of Acceptance	*Process of Rejection*
Positive Interdependence	Negative or No Interdependence
⇓	⇓
Promotive interaction 　Frequent & open communication 　Understanding of other perspectives 　Inducibility 　Differentiated views of each other 　High self-esteem 　Successful achievement, productivity 　Expectations of positive and productive future interaction with others	Oppositional or no interaction 　No or inaccurate communication 　Egocentrism 　Resistance to Influence 　Monopolistic views of each other 　Low self-esteem 　Failure, lack of productivity 　Expectations of negative and unproductive future interaction with others
⇓	⇓
Positive relationships	Negative relationships

Source: Johnson, D. W., & Johnson, R. (1989).

1. The relationship between cooperative experiences and interpersonal attraction may be partially caused by the frequent and accurate communication occurring among collaborators. Frequent, accurate, and open communication (a) is required to coordinate efforts to maximize mutual benefit and gain; (b) involves giving and receiving help, assistance, encouragement, and support; and (c) results in better understanding of each other's needs, interests, perspectives, abilities, and reasoning processes. To coordinate their efforts, collaborators communicate as they encourage, support, help, and assist each other. Effective coordination and communication requires understanding of each other's conclusions, needs, interests, perspectives, abilities, and reasoning processes. This process results in realistically (a) knowing each other on a personal level and (b) seeing each other as a complex of qualities (who the person is) rather than as a complex of performances (what the person does). The coordination, mutual helping, and personal relationships result in interpersonal attraction among group members. Thus, the more frequent, accurate, and candid is the communication aimed at facilitating each other's success, the greater will be the interpersonal attraction.

2. The relationship between cooperative experiences and interpersonal attraction may be partially caused by the accurate understanding which collaborators develop of each other's perspectives. *Social perspective-taking* is the ability to understand how a situation appears to another person and how that person is reacting cognitively and emotionally to the situation. The opposite of perspective-taking is *egocentrism*—embeddedness in one's own viewpoint to the extent that one is unaware of other points of view. Egocentrism tends to accompany competitive and individualistic attitudes and efforts, while perspective-taking ability and accuracy are associated with cooperative attitudes and efforts (Johnson, 1995a, 1995b). Cooperative experiences promote greater cognitive and emotional perspective-taking abilities than do either competitive or individualistic experiences.[1] The more accurate one's perspective-taking, the greater is one's empathy with, understanding of, and altruism for others. Mutual understanding that results from efforts to enhance mutual benefit also increases liking. Understanding the perspectives of others results in viewing the world from a broader and more sophisticated personal perspective. In addition, accurate perspective-taking generally results in an awareness that one is liked and accepted by others; one then usually reciprocates, which creates a cycle of increasing liking among cooperators. Thus, within a cooperative context, the more accurate the understanding of others' perspectives, the greater will be the interpersonal attraction.

3. The relationship between cooperative experiences and interpersonal attraction may be partially caused by the mutual influence that occurs among collaborators. *Inducibility* refers to individuals being receptive to the influence attempts of others (Deutsch, 1962). Cooperation tends to increase openness to being influenced by others, whereas competitive and individualistic interactions tend to create resistance to other's influence. Being influenced to engage in more effective and efficient actions (thereby being more successful) creates appreciation and liking. Generally, we like people whom we can influence, and we like people who use "friendly" influence strategies (persuasion and problem-solving) when interacting with us. Within a cooperative context, therefore, the greater the inducibility among individuals, the greater will be the interpersonal attraction.

4. The relationship between cooperative experiences and interpersonal attraction may be partially caused by the differentiated, multidimensional views of each other formed by collaborators. If one's views of collaborators are *differentiated* (i.e., multidimensional, taking into account many different characteristics), *dynamic* (modifiable from situation to situation), and *realistic* (accurate), then one will tend to like and identify with them, and the group cohesion will be greater. A differentiated, dynamic, and realistic view of another person includes many different categories—and each category is assigned a weight indicating its importance according to the demands of any specific situation, with the weight or salience of each category changing as the requirements of the situation change. In this form of interpersonal perception, new information concerning the person is admitted to one's impression as it becomes relevant. Thus, the conceptualization of the person stays in a dynamic state, open to modification with new information and taking situational factors into account.

In contrast, the more *monopolistic* (i.e., single-dimensional) and *static* (i.e., unchanging) are one's views of others, the less one will tend to like them. A monopolistic and static view of another person focuses on only one or two dimensions and tends to be permanently fixed, regardless of new information received. Thus, unrealistic stereotypic views of others generally result. Monopolistic impressions by their very nature are static and oversimplified, due to their rigid weighting of a few characteristics that are regarded as potent, regardless of the demands of the current situation. In competitive and individualistic situations, individuals tend to organize information about others on the basis of the few characteristics that are most salient for individual high performance. The perceived distribution of ability becomes polarized, and these perceptions become shared. A person is seen as a winner or a loser, but rarely in-between.

Cooperative situations, by contrast, generate a multidimensional, dynamic, and realistic view of others. Negative stereotypes tend to lose their primary potency and to be reduced when interactions reveal enough detail that group members are seen as individuals rather than as members of an ethnic group. All collaborators become "one of us." In other words, cooperation widens the sense of who is in the group, and "they" become "we."

5. The relationship between cooperative experiences and interpersonal attraction may be partially caused by the higher self-esteem of collaborators. The better one is known, liked, and supported, the higher one's self-esteem tends to be. High self-esteem is related to self-acceptance, liking of others, and a lack of prejudices. Fein and Spencer (1997), for example, found that increases in self-esteem resulted in decreases in negative stereotyping, and decreases in self-esteem resulted in increases in negative stereotyping (aimed at shoring up self-esteem). Individuals who like themselves tend to like others. Cooperation tends to promote higher self-esteem, and healthier processes for deriving conclusions about one's self-worth, than do competitive or individualistic interactions.[2] In contrast to cooperative experiences, competitive experiences tend to be related to conditional self-esteem, and individualistic experiences tend to be related to basic self-rejection.

6. The relationship between cooperative experiences and interpersonal attraction may be partially caused by the greater productivity of collaborators. The greater one's psychological success, the more one likes those who have contributed to and facilitated that success. There is abundant evidence that cooperation tends to produce higher achievement and greater productivity than do competition or individualistic efforts.[3] In turn, liking for collaborators (including majority and minority members) generally becomes progressively greater as the group's success increases.

7. The relationship between cooperative experiences and interpersonal attraction may be partially caused by expectations for enjoyable and productive interactions in the future. The more one expects future interactions to be cooperative, positive, and productive, the more one tends to like one's collaborators (Johnson & S. Johnson, 1972; S. Johnson & Johnson, 1972).

The Process of Rejection

The process of rejection may be defined as relationships becoming more and more negative as proximity and interaction continue (see Table 11.2). It results from interaction within a context of negative or no goal interdependence. Negative goal interdependence promotes oppositional interaction, and no goal interdependence results in little or no interaction with peers. Both lead to avoidance of and/or inaccurate communication; egocentrism; resistance to influence; monopolistic, static, and stereotyped views of others; feelings of rejection and low self-esteem; psychological failure; and expectations of distasteful and unpleasant interactions with others. All of these factors promote dislike and rejection among individuals. Furthermore, diversity among individuals may amplify these outcomes once the process begins.

Each Part of the Process Elicits All Other Parts

The factors involved in the processes of acceptance and rejection are interdependent, and each influences the others. Deutsch's (1985) "crude law" states that positive interdependence creates a variety of interrelated outcomes, which, in turn, create greater positive interdependence. Any part of the process elicits all other parts of the process. For instance, frequent and open communication results in better understanding of each other's perspectives, and increased understanding of each other's perspectives leads to more frequent and open communication. The more multidimensional and dynamic are the perceptions of each other, the higher will be the self-esteem of everyone involved—which, in turn, makes it easier to have multidimensional and dynamic views of each other. The many variables related to positive interdependence are interconnected such that they can influence/cause each other, as well as promote further positive interdependence. The variables are a "gestalt," with each variable being a door through which to enter the whole process. Thus, reduction of stereotyping and prejudice can be accomplished through cooperative relationships with outgroup members.

Summary of Research Evidence

We conducted a meta-analysis of 180 studies that compared the relative impact of cooperative, competitive, and individualistic experiences on interpersonal attraction (Johnson & Johnson, 1989). The overall results are displayed in Table 11.3, which presents Cohen's (1992) d as the measure of effect size. These results demonstrate that cooperation usually promotes greater interpersonal attraction among participants than does competition ($d = .66$) or individualistic relationships ($d = .60$). These findings are strong ones. The probability that they have occurred by chance is less than one in 100,000, and it would take thousands of new studies finding exactly no difference to reduce the overall findings to statistical nonsignificance. In contrast, there is little difference between the levels of interpersonal attraction developed within competitive and individualistic situations ($d = .08$). In further tests not shown in Table 11.3, we demonstrated that cooperation promotes better relationships when *intergroup* competition is absent ($d = .77$ and $.63$, respectively).

Many of the early studies on cooperation versus other forms of relationships focused specifically on cross-ethnic relationships. Actual contact between Blacks and Whites in these studies included lectures from Black instructors in classrooms, meetings with Black professionals, school integration, joint recreational activities in integrated summer camps, voyages of White merchant seamen serving with Black seamen, and contact within combat infantry platoons, occupational and educational settings, and desegregated residential settings. The results of these studies indicated that it is the *nature* of the contact between members of different ethnic groups, not their frequency, that promotes favorable intergroup attitudes (Johnson & Johnson, 1989). Moreover, the greater the degree of cooperation between majority and minority individuals, the more likely was the development of friendly cross-ethnic relationships.

In Johnson and Johnson's (1989) meta-analysis, there were more than 50 studies that compared the relative effects of cooperative, competitive, or individualistic experiences on interpersonal attraction between ethnic majority and minority individuals. As shown in the second panel of Table 11.3, a cooperative goal structure promoted significantly better relationships between White and mi-

TABLE 11.3
Impact of Social Interdependence on
Interpersonal Attraction: Average Effect Sizes

Type of Contact and Comparison	Mean Effect Size	sd	n
Overall			
Cooperative vs. Competitive	.66	.49	93
Cooperative vs. Individualistic	.60	.58	60
Competitive vs. Individualistic	.08	.70	15
Ethnic Desegregation			
Cooperative vs. Competitive	.52	.50	40
Cooperative vs. Individualistic	.44	.51	12
Competitive vs. Individualistic	-.65	.40	3
Inclusion of Handicapped			
Cooperative vs. Competitive	.70	.35	12
Cooperative vs. Individualistic	.64	.47	25
Competitive vs. Individualistic	-.16	.68	5
Homogeneous			
Cooperative vs. Competitive	.76	.46	53
Cooperative vs. Individualistic	.64	.60	48
Competitive vs. Individualistic	.26	.64	12

Source: Johnson, D. W., & Johnson, R. (1989).

nority individuals than did competition (d = .52) or an individualistic goal structure (d = .44). There were three studies which showed that an individualistic structure promoted more positive cross-ethnic relationships than did competition (d = -.65), but the small number of studies makes this finding only suggestive.

Quite similar results were found for comparisons of the relative effects of different goal structures on interpersonal attraction between handicapped and non-handicapped individuals (Johnson & Johnson, 1989—see the third panel of Table 11.3). Again, cooperation resulted in much greater interpersonal attraction than did competition (d = .70) or individualistic goals (d = .64). In five studies, individualistic goals tended to promote greater cross-handicapped interpersonal attraction than did competition (d = -.16).

Finally, Johnson and Johnson's (1989) review found over 100 studies that compared the effect of different goal structures on interpersonal attraction between groups of participants who were homogeneous in terms of ethnic membership and/or handicap status. In these studies again, cooperative experiences promoted greater interpersonal attraction than did competitive experiences (d = .76) or individualistic ones (d = .64). However, among these homogeneous individuals, competition promoted somewhat greater interpersonal attraction than did individualistic experiences (d = .26).

Our Research on Social Interdependence
and Cross-Ethnic Relationships

In order to test our model of the processes of acceptance and rejection, we have conducted a 20-year program of research consisting of over 80 studies (cf. Johnson & Johnson, 1989). Many of those studies were highly controlled field-experimental studies of cross-ethnic relationships. The measures of interpersonal attraction used included (a) an observation system that classified student-student interactions into categories of task, relationship-maintenance, and social statements, (b) an observation system that classified student-student interactions during classroom free-time, (c) a social-schema, figure-placement measure that asked students to position all class members on a classroom diagram according to where they would be during classroom free-time, and (d) a sociometric measure of interpersonal attraction that asked students to write down the names of three students they would like to work with in a future learning group. Our studies addressed the following five questions:

1. Do cooperative, competitive, and individualistic experiences differentially affect cross-ethnic interaction and relationships? Cooper, Johnson, Johnson, and Wilderson (1980) randomly assigned 60 students to these three conditions, stratifying on sex, ethnic membership, and ability. The students were lower- and working-class students from an inner-city junior high school. The same curriculum was used in all three conditions, and teachers were rotated across all conditions. Students participated in the study for three hours a day (English, geography, and science classes) for 15 instructional days. The results indicated that cooperation promoted more positive cross-ethnic relationships than did competitive or individualistic experiences.

In a similar study, Johnson and Johnson (1982) randomly assigned 76 students to cooperative, competitive, and individualistic conditions on a stratified random basis, controlling for ethnic membership, ability, and sex. The same curriculum was used in all conditions, and teachers were rotated across all conditions. Students participated in two 45-minute instructional units a day for 15 instructional days. Both behavioral and sociometric measures of interpersonal attraction were taken, based on cross-ethnic interaction during the instructional sessions and during daily free-time periods. The authors found that cooperative learning promoted more cross-ethnic interaction and more positive cross-ethnic attitudes and relationships in both academic and free-time situations than did competitive or individualistic learning.

2. Does *intergroup* competition increase or decrease positive cross-ethnic relationships? Johnson, Johnson, Tiffany, and Zaidman (1984) randomly assigned 51 fourth-grade students to intergroup competition and intergroup cooperation conditions, stratifying within group on minority status and sex. The same curriculum was used in both conditions, and teachers were rotated across conditions. Students participated in the study for 55 minutes a day for 10 instructional

days. Both behavioral and sociometric measures of interpersonal liking were used. Though no differences were found for within-group cross-ethnic liking, there was more inclusion of minority students and greater cross-ethnic liking for members of *different* cooperating groups within the intergroup cooperation condition. In other words, the positive cross-ethnic relationships established in the cooperative groups tended to generalize to other cross-ethnic relationships more in the intergroup cooperation condition than in the intergroup competition condition.

In a follow-up study, Johnson and Johnson (1985) randomly assigned 48 sixth-grade students to intergroup cooperation and competition conditions, stratifying on minority status, ability, and sex. The same curriculum was used in both conditions, and teachers were rotated across conditions. The students participated in the study for 55 minutes a day for 10 instructional days. Both behavioral and paper-and-pencil measures of interpersonal attraction were used. In this study, more positive cross-ethnic relationships, both within and between groups, were promoted by intergroup cooperation than by intergroup competition.

3. Are minority students who achieve at a lower level than their majority classmates liked, or not? When students who are minority-group members also achieve at a lower level, they have, in essence, two strikes against them. They may be disliked because they are from a low-status minority and, additionally, because their low achievement decreases the likelihood of the group performing well. Johnson, Johnson, Tiffany, and Zaidman (1983) compared the effects of cooperative and individualistic learning experiences on the relationship between majority students and lower-achieving minority peers. Forty-eight students (20 minority and 28 majority) were assigned to conditions on a stratified random basis, controlling for ethnic membership, sex, social class, and ability level. They participated in the study for 55 minutes a day for 15 instructional days. The same curriculum was used in both conditions, and teachers were rotated across conditions. Both behavioral and sociometric measures of interpersonal attraction were used. Minority students did in fact achieve at lower levels than did their majority peers, yet more positive cross-ethnic interaction and relationships were found in the cooperative condition than in the individualistic condition.

In a different study, Johnson et al. (1984) found that intergroup competition accentuates the salience of ability and status within cooperative learning groups. Intergroup cooperation produced more participation and more inclusion of minority students than did intergroup competition. Although minority students achieved at a lower level than majority students, perceived themselves to be less able as students, and were perceived as needing more academic help, they were viewed as being equally valuable members of the learning groups in the intergroup cooperation condition. In the intergroup competition condition, they were viewed as being less valuable members.

4. Does the presence of conflict within cooperative groups create divisive cross-ethnic relationships, or not? Within cooperative groups, disagreements and

intellectual challenges occur frequently. Such conflicts are "moments of truth" that can strengthen relationships or can create divisiveness and hostility. Low-achieving students may be at a disadvantage in such academic conflicts. When low-achievers are minority students, academic conflicts could potentially increase cross-ethnic hostility and rejection, and lower the academic self-esteem of minority students. To address these issues, Johnson, Johnson, and Tiffany (1984) compared the effects of controversy, debate, and individualistic learning on cross-ethnic relationships. Seventy-two sixth-grade students were randomly assigned to conditions on a stratified random basis, controlling for sex, reading ability, and ethnic membership. The same curriculum was used in all conditions, and teachers were rotated across conditions. In all three conditions students studied a controversial issue with materials representing both pro and con views. In the controversy condition, each learning group was divided into two pairs, representing the pro and con sides. In the debate condition, each member of a learning group was assigned a pro or con position to represent, in a competition to see who could make the best presentation. In the individualistic condition, students were given all the pro and con materials and told to learn the material without interacting with other students. Both behavioral and sociometric measures of interpersonal attraction were used. The controversy condition promoted the most cross-ethnic interaction, the most supportive cross-ethnic relationships, and the greatest cross-ethnic liking. These results indicate that, despite the existing prejudices and hostility between majority and minority students, structured academic conflicts characterized by high positive interdependence promoted considerable cross-ethnic liking. Furthermore, minority students felt more successful in the controversy condition than in the debate and individualistic conditions.

5. Do the cross-ethnic relationships formed within cooperative groups generalize to post-instructional situations, or not? Even though individuals interacted constructively with peers from other ethnic groups and expressed liking for them during achievement-oriented situations, there is a need to determine whether these relationships and interaction patterns will generalize to free-choice situations in which individuals can interact with whomever they wish. A number of our studies demonstrated that when individuals were placed in post-instructional, free-choice situations, there was more cross-ethnic interaction among individuals who had been in a cooperative condition than among those who had been in a competitive or individualistic condition (Johnson & Johnson, 1981, 1982; Johnson, Johnson, Tiffany, & Zaidman, 1983). For example, Warring, Johnson, Maruyama, and Johnson (1985) surveyed 74 sixth-grade and 51 fourth-grade students in an ethnically integrated, inner-city elementary school regarding the cross-ethnic interactions they had engaged in during the academic year. An activity report scale was given to these students to determine with whom they interacted in structured class activities, unstructured class activities, school activities outside of class, and activities in their homes. The authors found that students who par-

ticipated in cooperative learning groups had more noninstructional cross-ethnic interactions within the classroom and school, as well as out-of-school, than did individuals who participated in individualistic learning situations.

In summary, the results of our research indicate that: (a) cooperative experiences promote more positive cross-ethnic relationships than do competitive or individualistic experiences, (b) intergroup cooperation increases the frequency of positive cross-ethnic relationships within a class whereas intergroup competition may reduce them, (c) positive cross-ethnic relationships form within cooperative situations even when the minority students achieve at lower levels than do the majority students, (d) intellectual conflicts between majority and minority students can increase cross-ethnic liking within cooperative groups, and (e) the cross-ethnic relationships formed within cooperative groups generalize to free-time, in-school and out-of-school situations.

Increased Sophistication and Understanding of Other Groups

Sophistication includes knowledge of how to act appropriately and courteously—in well-mannered, refined ways—within many different settings, perspectives, and cultures. In contrast, individuals who are *provincial* only know how to act appropriately with their narrow perspective. To become sophisticated, a person must be able to see the situation from the cultural perspective of the other people involved. Much of the important information about different cultural and ethnic heritages and perspectives cannot be attained through reading books or listening to lectures. Only through meeting, working with, and personally sharing viewpoints with members of diverse groups, and developing personal as well as professional relationships with them, can individuals fully learn to value diversity and understand the perspective of others from different ethnic and cultural backgrounds. Understanding diverse cultures and perspectives requires (a) actual interaction, (b) trust, so that personal reactions and opinions can be expressed, and (c) candor, so that personal opinions, feelings, and reactions are openly shared.

Summary

Establishing a cooperative community, in which diverse children and adolescents share common goals and a common culture while they are in school, requires structuring cooperative interaction at all levels of the school. Most important is the predominant use of cooperative learning, in which diverse students promote each other's academic success and contribute to the overall success of the school (i.e., the common good). There are three types of cooperative learning: formal cooperative learning, informal cooperative learning, and cooperative base groups. The use of cooperative learning approaches will not only tend to increase the academic learning of all students, but will also tend to promote positive relationships among diverse students. Social judgment theory explains the process by which this happens. Positive personal relationships tend to grow among diverse students as they communicate more frequently and openly, more accurately understand each other's perspectives, engage in mutual influence, develop differentiated and dynamic views of each other, increase their self-esteem, achieve more highly, and expect their future interactions to be cooperative and positive. Whether or not the acceptance process is maintained, and relationships among diverse individuals continue to strengthen, depends on how their conflicts are managed and what values they adopt. In the rest of this chapter, we turn to these two issues.

THE SECOND C: CONSTRUCTIVE CONFLICT RESOLUTION

Within a cooperative community, diverse individuals work together to achieve mutual goals. Within joint efforts, however, conflicts tend to occur frequently. Conflict is the moment of truth within any cooperative effort. It is almost paradoxical that conflicts are more frequent and intense when individuals are more committed to their joint goals and when their relationships are more caring and committed. When conflicts are managed destructively, they can destroy relationships and tear the community apart. In contrast, when conflicts are managed constructively, they can significantly strengthen and improve the relationships among diverse individuals. In fact, the full benefits of diversity may be unattainable unless there are frequent, constructively managed conflicts. Constructively managed conflicts can result in such positive outcomes as increased: (a) energy, curiosity, and motivation, (b) achievement, retention, insight, creativity, problem-solving, and synthesis, (c) healthy cognitive and social development, (d) clarity of own and others' identity, commitments, and values, and (e) positiveness of relationships (Johnson & Johnson, 1995a, 1995b, 1995c, 1996a).

Especially when diverse individuals, who may have negative stereotypes of each other, are involved in conflicts, it is important to engage in procedures that maximize the likelihood that constructive outcomes will result. The two most common types of conflicts are (a) *controversies,* in which the ideas and conclusions of one person contradict the ideas and opinions of others—e.g., in decision-making and problem-solving situations, and (b) *conflicts of interests,* in which the actions of one person seeking benefits within a situation prevent, block, or interfere with another person's potential benefits. For each of these types of conflict, individuals need to learn procedures for resolving the conflict constructively (see Table 11.4).

Constructive Controversies

Controversy exists when one person's ideas, opinions, information, theories, or conclusions are incompatible with those of another and the two seek to reach an agreement (Johnson & Johnson, 1979, 1989, 1995b). Controversies are resolved

TABLE 11.4
Types of Conflict

Controversies	Conflicts of Interests
One person's ideas, information, theories, conclusions, and opinions are incompatible with those of another and the two seek to reach an agreement.	The actions of one person attempting to maximize his/her own benefits prevents, blocks, or interferes with another person maximizing their benefits.
Controversy Procedure	Integrative (Problem-Solving) Negotiations
Research and prepare positions	Describe wants
Present and advocate positions	Describe feelings
Refute opposing position and refute attacks on own position	Describe reasons for wants and feelings
Reverse perspectives	Take other's perspective
Synthesize and integrate best evidence and reasoning from all sides	Invent three optional agreements that maximize joint outcomes
	Choose one and formalize agreement

Source: Johnson, D. W., & Johnson, R. (1999).

by engaging in what Aristotle called *deliberate discourse* (i.e., discussion of the advantages and disadvantages of proposed actions) aimed at synthesizing novel solutions (i.e., creative problem solving).

Constructive controversy provides a procedure for diverse individuals to engage in conflict over ideas, conclusions, and opinions. A method for teaching students how to engage in the constructive controversy process begins with randomly assigning students to heterogeneous cooperative learning groups of four members (Johnson & Johnson, 1995b). The groups are given an issue on which to write a report and then take a test. Each cooperative group is divided into two pairs. One pair is given the con position on the issue and the other pair is given the pro position. Each pair is given the instructional materials needed to define their position and point them toward supporting information. The cooperative goal of reaching a consensus on the issue (by synthesizing the best reasoning from both sides) and writing a quality group report is highlighted. Students then:

1. Research, learn, and prepare a position. Students prepare the best case possible for their assigned position by researching the assigned position, organizing the information into a persuasive argument, and planning how to advocate the assigned position effectively.
2. Present and advocate their position. Students present the best case for their assigned position to ensure it gets a fair and complete hearing.
3. Engage in an open discussion in which there is spirited disagreement. Students freely exchange information and ideas while (a) arguing force-

fully and persuasively for their position, (b) critically analyzing and refuting the opposing position, (c) rebutting attacks on their position, and (d) presenting counterarguments.

4. Reverse perspectives. Students reverse perspectives and present the best case they can for the opposing position.

5. Synthesize. Students drop all advocacy and find a synthesis on which all members can agree. They summarize the best evidence and reasoning from both sides and integrate it into a joint position that is a new and unique. They then write a group report on the group's synthesis and the supporting evidence and rationale, and take a test on both positions. Finally, they process how well their group functioned and celebrate the group's success and hard work.

Over the past 30 years, with such colleagues as Dean Tjosvold and Karl Smith, we have developed and tested a theory of controversy (Johnson, 1970; Johnson & F. Johnson, 1975; Johnson, R. Johnson, & F. Johnson, 1976; Johnson & R. Johnson, 1979, 1989, 1995b). During this time, we have conducted over 20 experimental and field-experimental studies on controversy with intermediate elementary and college students as participants. In all of these studies, participants were randomly assigned to conditions of controversy, de- bate, concurrence seeking, or individualistic learning. The studies lasted from one to thirty hours of instructional time, and all have been published in journals. In connection with our research, we have developed a series of curriculum units on energy and environmental issues structured for academic controversies. The use of academic controversy has been field-tested in schools and colleges throughout the United States, Canada, and a number of other countries. A meta-analytic summary of findings from these studies is shown in Table 11.5.

As Table 11.5 demonstrates, engaging in constructive controversy has powerful positive effects on the interpersonal attraction and social support among diverse individuals (Johnson & Johnson, 1989). The research indicates that controversy promotes greater liking among participants than does concurrence seeking (d = .24), debate (d = .72), or individualistic learning (d = .81). Two studies showed that debate within cooperative groups promoted greater interpersonal attraction among participants than did individualistic efforts (d =.46). Engaging in constructive controversies also produced greater perceptions of social support from other students than did concurrence seeking (d = .32), debate (d = .92), and individualistic learning (d = 1.52). Debate within cooperative groups promoted greater perceptions of social support than did individualistic learning (d = .85). Finally, controversy resulted in more accurate perspective- taking than concurrence seeking (d = .62), debate (d = 1.35), or individualistic learning (d = .90). Only the later finding, however, had enough studies to make it reliable. Thus, when diverse individuals are working together to achieve mutual goals, and their ideas, opinions, conclusions, and theories conflict, the disagreement can lead to

TABLE 11.5
Meta-Analysis of Controversy Studies: Average Effect Sizes

Dependent Variable and Comparison	Mean Effect Size	sd	n
Interpersonal Attraction			
Controversy vs. Concurrence Seeking	0.24	0.44	8
Controversy vs. Debate	0.72	0.25	6
Controversy vs. Individualistic Learning	0.81	0.11	3
Debate vs. Individualistic Learning	0.46	0.13	2
Perceived Social Support			
Controversy vs. Concurrence Seeking	0.32	0.44	8
Controversy vs. Debate	0.92	0.42	6
Controversy vs. Individualistic Learning	1.52	0.29	3
Debate vs. Individualistic Learning	0.85	0.01	2
Self-Esteem			
Controversy vs. Concurrence Seeking	0.39	0.15	4
Controversy vs. Debate	0.51	0.09	2
Controversy vs. Individualistic Learning	0.85	0.04	3
Debate vs. Individualistic Learning	0.45	0.17	2

Source: Johnson, D. W., & Johnson, R. (1995b).

increased liking and support for each other, if the constructive controversy procedure is followed.

In addition to the improved relationships among diverse individuals, engaging in intellectual disputes tends to create higher achievement and better retention, more frequent use of higher-level reasoning, metacognitive thought, and critical thinking, more continuing motivation to achieve and learn, and greater accuracy in interpersonal perspective taking. Moreover, engaging in constructive controversy is perceived to be fun, enjoyable, and exciting. Every time students use the constructive controversy procedure, they are learning how to view an issue from more than one perspective, and how to manage intellectual conflicts by listening to each other and working cooperatively to reach solutions that are based on the best reasoned judgment of everyone involved.

Negotiation and Mediation Training

In addition to intellectual conflicts, conflicts based on individuals' differing interests within a situation must be resolved constructively. As stated above, conflicts of interests exist when the actions of one person attempting to maximize his or her wants and benefits prevent, block, or interfere with another person maximizing his or her wants and benefits. Such conflicts are resolved through negotiation and mediation. There are two types of negotiations (Johnson & F. Johnson, 2000): *distributive* or "win-lose" (where one person benefits only if the opponent agrees to make a concession), and *integrative* or problem-solving (where disputants work together to create an agreement that benefits everyone involved). In ongoing relationships, especially among diverse individuals, distributive negotiations tend to result in destructive outcomes, whereas integrative negotiations tend to lead to constructive outcomes.

A program called *Teaching Students To Be Peacemakers,* begun in the 1960s (Johnson, 1970; Johnson & Johnson, 1995a), is aimed at teaching all students in a school how to resolve conflicts of interests constructively. All students are taught how to engage in problem-solving negotiations and to mediate their schoolmates' conflicts. The steps in using problem-solving negotiations are (Johnson & Johnson, 1995a):

1. Describing what you want. "*I want to use the book now.*" This includes using good communication skills and defining the conflict as a small and specific mutual problem.
2. Describing how you feel. "*I'm frustrated.*" Disputants must understand how they feel and communicate it openly and clearly.
3. Describing the reasons for your wants and feelings. "*You have been using the book for the past hour. If I don't get to use the book soon, my report will not be done on time. It's frustrating to have to wait so long.*" This includes expressing cooperative intentions, listening carefully, separating interests from positions, and differentiating interests before trying to integrate the two sets of interests.
4. Taking the other's perspective and summarizing your understanding of what the other person wants, how the other person feels, and the reasons underlying both. "*My understanding of you is....*" This includes understanding the perspective of the opposing disputant and being able to see the problem from both perspectives simultaneously.
5. Inventing three optional plans to resolve the conflict that maximize joint benefits. "*Plan A is..., Plan B is..., Plan C is....*" This includes inventing creative options to solve the problem in a way that is beneficial to everyone involved.
6. Choosing one plan and formalizing the agreement with a hand shake. "*Let's agree on Plan B!*" A wise agreement is fair to all disputants and has a clear rationale based on principles. It maximizes joint benefits and strengthens disputants' ability to work together cooperatively and to resolve conflicts constructively in the future. It specifies how each disputant should act in the future, and how the agreement will be reviewed and renegotiated if it does not work.

Once students have learned to negotiate to solve the problem, they are taught to mediate schoolmates' conflicts. A *mediator* is a neutral person who helps two or more people resolve their conflict, usually by negotiating an integrative agreement. In contrast, *arbitration* is the submission of a dispute to a disinterested third party (such as a teacher or principal), who makes a final and bind-ing judgment as to how the conflict will be resolved. Mediation consists of four steps (Johnson & Johnson, 1995a):

1. Ending hostilities. Breaking up hostile encounters and cooling off the disputants.
2. Ensuring disputants are committed to the mediation process. To ensure that disputants are committed to the mediation process and are ready to negotiate in good faith, the mediator introduces the process of mediation and sets the ground rules that (a) mediation is voluntary, (b) the mediator is neutral, (c) each person will have the chance to state his or her view of the conflict without interruption, and (d) each person agrees to solve the problem with no name-calling or interrupting, being as honest as they can, abiding by any agreement made, and keeping anything said in mediation confidential.
3. Helping disputants successfully negotiate with each other. The disputants are carefully taken through the problem-solving negotiation steps.
4. Formalizing the agreement. The agreement is solidified into a contract.

Once students understand how to negotiate and mediate, the Peacemakers Program is implemented. Each day the teacher selects two class members to serve as official mediators. Any conflicts that students cannot resolve themselves are referred to the mediators. The mediators wear official T-shirts, patrol the playground and lunchroom, and are available to mediate any conflicts that occur in the classroom or school. The role of mediator is rotated so that all students in the class or school serve as mediators an equal amount of time. Initially, students mediate in pairs. This ensures that shy or nonverbal students get the same amount of experience as more extroverted and verbally fluent students. Mediating classmates' conflicts is perhaps the most effective way of teaching students the need for the skillful use of each step of the negotiation procedure.

If peer mediation fails, the teacher mediates the conflict. If teacher mediation fails, the teacher arbitrates by deciding who is right and who is wrong. If that fails, the principal mediates the conflict. If that fails, the principal arbitrates. Teaching all students to mediate properly results in a schoolwide discipline program where students are empowered to regulate and control their own and their classmates' actions. Teachers and administrators are thus freed to spend more of their energies on instruction.

The Peacemakers Program is a 12-year spiral program that is retaught each year in an increasingly sophisticated and complex way. Continued practice in using the negotiation and mediation procedures is created by integrating the procedures into academic lessons and units. Almost any lesson in literature and history, for example, can be modified to include role playing situations in which the negotiation and/or mediation procedures are used.

When diverse individuals work together to achieve mutual goals, there are inevitably times when their interests will conflict. There may be conflicts over who is to exert leadership, who gets what materials, who is responsible for what aspects of the assignment, and so forth. In addition, the relationships built in cooperative learning groups extend to nonacademic situations (such as the hallways and playground), where other types of interests may conflict. If the positive relationships and the reductions of prejudice built within cooperative efforts are to be maintained and strengthened, the diverse students need to master common procedures for resolving their conflicts of interests.

We have conducted 14 studies on implementing the Peacemakers Program in schools, involving students from kindergarten through the tenth grade, and several other researchers have conducted relevant studies (Johnson & Johnson, 1995a, 1995c, 1995d, 1996a). We found that untrained students tend to manage their conflicts either by forcing the other person to concede, or by withdrawing from the relationship and the situation when forcing does not work. These strategies are especially destructive when used among diverse individuals. In addition, students from different backgrounds tend to view conflict and talk about it in different ways. Research findings showed that participating in the Peacemakers Program resulted in students and faculty developing a shared understanding of how conflicts should be managed and a common vocabulary to discuss conflicts. Students not only learned the negotiation and mediation procedures, but also: (a) retained their knowledge throughout the school year and into the following year, (b) applied the procedures to their and other people's conflicts, (c) transferred the procedures to nonclassroom settings such as the playground and lunchroom, (d) transferred the procedures to nonschool settings such as the home, and (e) when given the option, engaged in problem-solving rather than win-lose negotiations. In addition, students' attitudes toward conflict tended to become more positive, and they tended to resolve their conflicts without the involvement of faculty and administrators. The number of discipline problems that teachers had to deal with decreased by about 60% and referrals to administrators dropped about 90%. Faculty and administrators no longer had to arbitrate frequent conflicts among students; instead they spent their time maintaining and supporting the peer mediation process.

One result of the Peacemakers training was that students became more relationship-oriented in conflicts, using strategies aimed at preserving the relationship as well as achieving their goals. After training, students tended to use the integrative negotiation procedure to resolve most of their conflicts and used the forcing/aggression and withdrawing strategies very infrequently. As a result, students tended to experience increased social support and less victimization from others. This improvement in their relations with others led to increased self-esteem, decreased feelings of anxiety and depression, and more frequent positive feelings of well-being. The higher self-esteem, in turn, produced a greater sense of personal control over their own fates. Furthermore, serving as a mediator resulted in increased understanding of the perspectives of people with different views.

Finally, when integrated into academic units, the conflict resolution training tended to increase academic achievement and long-term retention of the academic material (Johnson & Johnson, 1995c, 1996a). Especially in subject areas such as literature and history, academic units can provide a setting to understand conflicts, practice how to resolve them, and use them to gain insight into the material being studied.

Summary

Cooperation, and the process of acceptance, cannot be maintained unless conflicts occur and are managed constructively. Two of the important types of conflicts are controversies and conflicts of interests. In dealing with conflicts, students must be instructed about the desirability of conflicts and the procedures that should be used to resolve conflicts. Such training is essential for maintaining the overall community. Conflicts among ideas, opinions, and conclusions are ideally managed through the constructive controversy procedure, and conflicts among interests are ideally managed through the problem-solving negotiation and peer mediation procedures. Doing this will significantly strengthen the relationships among diverse individuals. In order to resolve conflicts constructively, however, individuals from diverse backgrounds have to adopt a common set of values.

THE THIRD C: CIVIC VALUES

Why did Rome decline and fall? Was it corruption from within or conquest from without? Rome fell, it can be argued, because Romans lost their civic virtue. *Civic virtue* means that individuals meet both the letter and the spirit of their public obligations. For a community to exist and sustain itself, members must share common goals and values, which should aim at increasing the quality of life within the community (Johnson & Johnson, 1996b, 1999). The more diverse that individuals are, the more essential is a set of common values that bind them together and provide guidelines for appropriate behavior. A learning community cannot exist in schools that are dominated by (a) competition, where students are taught to value striving for their personal success at the expense of others, or (b) individualistic efforts, where students value only their own self-interests. Rather, students need to internalize values underlying cooperation and constructive conflict resolution, such as commitment to the common good and the well-being of other members, and an appreciation of diversity.

While there are many ways to inculcate values (such as direct teaching, modeling, and enactment of assigned or voluntary roles), the most important influence may be the implicit values existing in the pattern and flow of daily life. The value systems underlying competitive, individualistic, and cooperative situations are thus a hidden curriculum beneath the surface of school life. Whenever students engage in competitive efforts, for example, they learn these values: (a) what is important is winning (not mastery or excellence); (b) success depends on beating, defeating, and getting more than other people (triumphing over others and being "Number One" are valued); (c) opposing, obstructing, and sabotaging the success of others is a natural way of life (winning depends on a good offense—doing better than others—and a good defense—not letting anyone do better than you); (d) feeling joy and pride in one's wins and others' losses (the pleasure of winning is associated with others' disappointment with losing); (e) viewing others as a threat to one's success; (f) believing a person's worth (one's own and others) is conditional and contingent on his or her "wins" (a person's worth is never fixed, it depends on the latest victory); and (g) people who are different are either to be feared (if they have an advantage) or held in contempt (if they have a handicap or clearly are going to lose).

The values inherently taught by individualistic experiences are: (a) striving to maximize one's own self-interest; (b) success depends on reaching preset criteria; (c) the pleasure of succeeding is personal and relevant only to oneself; (d) other people are irrelevant (success depends only on one's own efforts); (e) a person's worth depends on possessing the few characteristics that help the person succeed (in school that is primarily reading and math ability); and (f) similar people are liked and dissimilar people are disliked.

The values inherently taught by cooperative efforts are: (a) commitment to both one's own and others' success and well-being, as well as to the common good; (b) a sense of responsibility to contribute one's fair share of the work; (c) respect for the efforts of others and for them as people; (d) behaving with integrity; (e) compassion when other members are in need; (f) one's own and other people's worth is unconditional (because there are so many diverse ways that a person may contribute to a joint effort, everyone has value all the time); (g) intrinsic motivation, based on striving to learn, grow, develop, and succeed (learning is the goal, not winning); and (h) people who are different from oneself are to be sought out and utilized, because they can make unique contributions to the joint effort.

In addition to the values inherent in cooperation, constructive ways of resolving conflicts inherently teach values. The value underlying the constructive controversy procedure include: respecting the right of others to hold beliefs and opinions different from one's own; accepting that one is fallible and may be wrong; valuing reasoned positions based on valid information and logic; believing that "truth" is derived from the clash of adverse opinions; viewing issues from all perspectives; and synthesizing disparate positions. The values underlying problem-solving negotiations and peer mediation situations include: being open and honest about one's wants and feelings; striving to understand others' wants and feelings; being concerned about others' outcomes as well as one's own; seeking agreements that are satisfying to all disputants; and maintaining effective and caring long-term relationships. Both constructive controversy and problem-solving negotiations are based on the values of human equality, nonviolence, and reciprocity (i.e., the other person is entitled to the same things that oneself is entitled to). In other words, constructive conflict resolution inherently teaches a set of civic values that help to ensure the fruitful continuation of the community.

The values that are implicitly taught by involving diverse individuals in cooperative efforts and constructive conflicts tend to unite diverse individuals into a common community identity. In the United States, for example, the superordinate identity of "American" is based on a set of common, pluralistic values specified in the Constitution, the Bill of Rights, and the Declaration of Independence. These include valuing democracy, freedom, liberty, equality, justice, the rights of individuals, and the responsibilities of citizenship. It is these values that form the American creed. All individuals are free to speak their minds and give their opinions. All individuals are considered to be of equal value. Every member has the right and responsibility to contribute his or her resources and efforts to achieving the group's goals and to take responsibility for the common good. Each member has a right to expect other individuals to be considerate of his or her needs and wants. All individuals are obligated to reciprocate good deeds. All individuals must at times put the good of the group above their own needs and desires. All individuals must participate in civic activities, including voting in elections. Americans are supposed to respect basic human rights, listen to dissenters instead of jailing them, and have a multiparty political system, a free press, free speech, freedom of religion, and freedom of assembly. Through this set of common values that promote cooperation and constructive conflict resolution, widely diverse individuals can become knit together into a community.

There is presently very little research on the development of values through (a) cooperative, competitive, and individualistic experiences, or (b) the use of constructive conflict resolution procedures. It might be argued that the more that diverse individuals cooperate to achieve mutual goals, and the more that they resolve their conflicts constructively, the less prejudiced they will become, and the more they will value human equality and the individual rights of all persons to life, liberty, and the pursuit of happiness. However, not enough research studies have been conducted to demonstrate this as a causal connection. This topic should be one of the important research agendas of the next decade.

SUMMARY

Few events have resulted in more consequences than the 1954 Supreme Court decision that ruled segregation of the public schools to be unconstitutional. Beneficial outcomes of that decision may include Rosa Parks' refusal the next year to give up her seat on a Montgomery, Alabama, bus to a White man, the first sit-ins in North Carolina in 1960, the Civil Rights Act of 1964, the Voting Rights Act of 1965, and many others. Unintended negative consequences of this chain of events may include an intensely legalistic climate (in which the concept of "rights" is used in complaints and claims of entitlement) and heightening tensions among diverse groups in our society. Social science research on interpersonal interaction has played a prominent role in this area of intergroup relations.

   This research indicates that reducing prejudice and discrimination requires more than intellectual knowledge about other groups or the desire to be accepting and appreciative, although both of these factors help. Reducing prejudice and discrimination requires the direct interaction of diverse individuals, the development of personal relationships, open and candid conversations, and commitment to human equality and the equal rights of all individuals. It takes more than proximity to create such relationships. Proximity can easily lead to increased prejudice and even to violence among members of different ethnic and cultural groups. Despite the cultural clashes and misunderstandings that inevitably occur when individuals with diverse heritages interact, positive relationships are quite possible, and they are built and maintained by three factors:

1. Working together cooperatively to achieve mutual goals.
2. Resolving conflicts in constructive ways.
3. Internalizing civic values.

   Together, these three factors provide an environment, an ebb-and-flow of daily life, that promotes the committed relationships and personal conversations that reduce prejudices and discriminatory practices. The three factors form a gestalt that should be structured in a place where children, adolescents, and young adults spend considerable time and, therefore, can be influenced by the experience. Schools may be the only such place.

   To establish a learning community, cooperation must be carefully structured at all levels in the school. Cooperation creates a structure within which diverse faculty, students, and parents work together to educate the students. The more cooperative the structure, the more committed and dedicated will faculty, students, and parents be to providing quality education. Committed cooperative activities result in greater efforts to achieve, greater psychological health, and more positive relationships, especially among diverse individuals who initially have negative stereotypes of each other.

   The more that diverse individuals are committed to the school's goals and to each other, the more frequent and intense will their conflicts tend to be with each other. When the controversy and problem-solving negotiation procedures are used skillfully, such conflicts tend to result in higher-level reasoning, the utilization of diverse perspectives, creative insights, synthesis of different positions, high-quality and novel solutions, and trusting, supportive, and caring relationships. To maintain the cooperative community, therefore, constructive conflict resolution procedures must be taught to all school members.

To guide and direct the cooperation and constructive conflict resolution, civic values must be inculcated in all school members. Civic values that highlight the need to work together toward the common good, maximize joint (not individual) benefits, and seek the "truth" through the clash of adverse positions, are the glue that holds the school together; and they define how members should act toward each other.

While each of the three Cs may be discussed and implemented separately, together they represent a gestalt in which each enhances and promotes the others. Together the three Cs may create schools where prejudices and discrimination are reduced, and children and youth learn and develop in positive and healthy ways.

NOTES

1. A meta-analysis of studies that compared the relative impact of cooperative, competitive, and individualistic experiences, using Cohen's (1992) d as the measure of effect size, showed that cooperation promotes much better perspective-taking than competition or individualistic activities (d = .61 and .44, respectively—Johnson & Johnson, 1989).

2. Meta-analytic findings showed that cooperation promotes higher self-esteem than competition (d = .58) and than individualistic experiences (d = .44) (Johnson & Johnson, 1989).

3. Meta-analysis showed that cooperation produces much greater productivity than competition (d = .67) and than individualistic activity (d = .64) (Johnson & Johnson, 1989).

REFERENCES

Allport, G. The nature of prejudice. Cambridge, MA: Addison-Wesley.

Brewer, M., & Miller, N. (1984). Beyond the contact hypothesis: Theoretical perspectives on desegregation. In N. Miller & M. Brewer (Eds.), Groups in contact: The psychology of desegregation (pp. 281-302). New York: Academic Press.

Cohen, J. (1992). A power primer. Psychological Bulletin, 112, 155-159.

Cooper, L., Johnson, D. W., Johnson, R., & Wilderson, F. (1980). The effects of cooperative, competitive, and individualistic experiences on interpersonal attraction among heterogeneous peers. Journal of Social Psychology, 111, 243-252.

Deutsch, M. (1962). Cooperation and trust: Some theoretical notes. In M. R. Jones (Ed.), Nebraska symposium on motivation (pp. 275-319). Lincoln: University of Nebraska Press.

Deutsch, M. (1973). The resolution of conflict. New Haven, CT: Yale University Press.

Deutsch, M. (1985). *Distributive justice: A social psychological perspective*. New Haven, CT: Yale University Press.

Fein, S., & Spencer, S. (1997). Prejudice as self-image maintenance: Affirming the self through derogating others. *Journal of Personality and Social Psychology, 73*, 31-44.

Gerard, H., & Miller, N. (1975). *School desegregation*. New York: Plenum.

Johnson, D. W. (1970). *Social psychology of education*. Edina, MN: Interaction.

Johnson, D. W. (1975a). Cooperativeness and social perspective taking. *Journal of Personality and Social Psychology, 31*, 241- 244.

Johnson, D. W. (1975b). Affective perspective-taking and cooperative predisposition. *Developmental Psychology, 11*, 869-870.

Johnson D. W., & Johnson, F. (1975). *Joining together: Group theory and group skills*. Boston: Allyn & Bacon.

Johnson D. W., & Johnson, F. (2000). *Joining together: Group theory and group skills* (7th ed.). Boston: Allyn & Bacon.

Johnson, D. W., & Johnson, R. (1979). Conflict in the classroom: Controversy and learning. *Review of Educational Research, 49*, 51-61.

Johnson, D. W., & Johnson, R. (1980). Integrating handicapped students into the mainstream. *Exceptional Children, 47*(2), 90-98.

Johnson, D. W., & Johnson, R. (1981). Effects of cooperative and individualistic learning experiences on interethnic interaction. *Journal of Educational Psychology, 73*(3), 454-459.

Johnson, D. W., & Johnson, R. (1982). Effects of cooperative, competitive, and individualistic learning experiences on cross-ethnic interaction and friendships. *Journal of Social Psychology, 118*, 47-58.

Johnson, D. W., & Johnson, R. (1985). Relationships between Black and white students in intergroup cooperation and competition. *Journal of Social Psychology, 125*(4), 421-428.

Johnson, D. W., & Johnson, R. (1989). *Cooperation and competition: Theory and research*. Edina, MN: Interaction.

Johnson, D. W., & Johnson, R. (1994). *Leading the cooperative school* (2nd ed.). Edina, MN: Interaction.

Johnson, D. W., & Johnson, R. (1995a). *Teaching students to be peacemakers* (3rd ed.). Edina, MN: Interaction.

Johnson, D. W., & Johnson, R. (1995b). *Creative controversy: Intellectual challenge in the classroom* (3rd ed.). Edina, MN: Interaction.

Johnson, D. W., & Johnson, R. (1995c). Teaching students to be peacemakers: Results of five years of research. *Peace and Conflict: Journal of Peace Psychology, 1*, 417-438.

Johnson, D. W., & Johnson, R. (1995d). Why violence prevention programs don't work— and what does. *Educational Leadership, 52*(5), 63-68.

Johnson, D. W., & Johnson, R. (1996a). Conflict resolution and peer mediation programs in elementary and secondary schools: A review of the research. *Review of Educational Research, 66*, 459-506.

Johnson, D. W., & Johnson, R. (1996b). Cooperative learning and traditional American values. *NASSP Bulletin, 80* (No. 579), 11-18.

Johnson, D. W., & Johnson, R. (1999). *Human relations: Valuing diversity*. Edina, MN: Interaction.

Johnson, D. W., & Johnson, R. (in press). Cooperative learning, values, and culturally plural classrooms. In M. Leicester, C. Modgil, & S. Modgil, (Eds.), *Values, the classroom, and cultural diversity*. London, UK: Cassell.

Johnson, D. W., Johnson, R., & Holubec, E. (1998a). *Cooperation in the classroom* (7th ed.). Edina, MN: Interaction.

Johnson, D. W., Johnson, R., & Holubec, E. (1998b). *Advanced cooperative learning* (3rd ed.). Edina, MN: Interaction.

Johnson, D. W., Johnson, R., & Johnson, F. (1976). Promoting constructive conflict in the classroom. *Notre Dame Journal of Education, 7*, 163-168.

Johnson, D. W., Johnson, R., & Maruyama, G. (1983). Interdependence and interpersonal attraction among heterogeneous and homogeneous individuals: A theoretical formulation and a meta-analysis of the research. *Review of Educational Research, 53*, 5-54.

Johnson, D. W., Johnson, R., & Smith, K. (1998). *Active learning: Cooperation in the college classroom* (2nd ed.). Edina, MN: Interaction.

Johnson, D. W., & Johnson, R., & Tiffany, M. (1984). Structuring academic conflicts between majority and minority students: Hindrance or help to integration. *Contemporary Educational Psychology, 9*, 61-73.

Johnson, D. W., Johnson, R., Tiffany, M., & Zaidman, B. (1983). Are low achievers disliked in a cooperative situation? A test of rival theories in a mixed-ethnic situation. *Contemporary Educational Psychology, 8*, 189-200.

Johnson, D. W., Johnson, R., Tiffany, M., & Zaidman, B. (1984). Cross-ethnic relationships: The impact of intergroup cooperation and intergroup competition. *Journal of Experimental Education, 78*(2), 75-79.

Johnson, D. W., & Johnson, S. (1972). The effects of attitude similarity, expectation of goal facilitation, and actual goal facilitation on interpersonal attraction. *Journal of Experimental Social Psychology, 8*, 197-206.

Johnson, S., & Johnson, D. W. (1972). The effects of others' actions, attitude similarity, and race on attraction towards others. *Human Relations, 25*, 121-130.

Marcus-Newhall, A., Miller, N., Holtz, R., & Brewer, M. (1993). Cross-cutting category membership with role assignment: A means of reducing intergroup bias. *British Journal of Social Psychology, 32*, 124-146.

Pettigrew, T. (1997). Generalized intergroup contact effects on prejudice. *Personality and Social Psychology Bulletin, 23*, 173-185.

Warring, D., Johnson, D. W., Maruyama, G., & Johnson, R. (1985). Impact of different types of cooperative learning on cross-ethnic and cross-sex relationships. *Journal of Education Psychology, 77*, 53-59.

Watson, G. (1947). *Action for unity*. New York: Harper.

Williams, R. (1947). *The reduction of intergroup tensions*. New York: Social Science Research Council.

12 Interventions to Reduce Prejudice and Discrimination in Children and Adolescents

Frances E. Aboud
McGill University

Sheri R. Levy
SUNY Stony Brook

For many years, people have thought that prejudice and discrimination were relatively minor problems in children. In part, this may have been based on the reports of parents and teachers, who typically do not witness racial conflicts and name-calling. While it is probably the case that the prejudice of children is not as hostile and intentionally hurtful as that of adolescents and adults, it is nonetheless harmful to the children who possess it, and even more so to those who are its targets. As with adults, prejudice and exclusion vary with the child, and they also vary with the child's developmental level and social world. Children are not as cognitively, emotionally, and verbally sophisticated as adults. Consequently, their understanding of racial differences may be simpler and may lead to false dichotomies. Their emotional reactions to people who differ may be wariness rather than hostility, and their name-calling may be hollow imitations, rather than heartfelt. Nonetheless, prejudice and discrimination isolate children from others in a society that is becoming increasingly diverse.

Also, the belief that prejudice is a minor problem in children was in part due to theories of prejudice development. The learning theory of prejudice asserted that children gradually acquired prejudice from parents, peers, and the media. Most psychologists assumed that the learning curve was a gradual one. While it is probably true that children are not born prejudiced, we now know that they do not simply imitate others' prejudice. Social-cognitive capabilities initially constrain their processing of social information into dichotomous categories and evaluations, which only later become more flexible. Consequently, interventions are likely to be effective only if they take into account whether particular children already have a bias or not, and whether they are cognitively able to integrate the new message.

While there are many pitfalls in designing and conducting prejudice-reduction interventions with children and adolescents, there are also potential benefits. Children and adolescents undergo a great deal of change in their cognitive, social, and emotional skills. So there is reason to hope that their racial attitudes and behaviors are modifiable. Also, they spend a great deal of time in adult-directed structured activities at school. Interventions can therefore be directed at large groups of children and adolescents, and can be evaluated and modified appropriately. We will not elaborate here on the pitfalls, as many will become apparent later in the chapter. However, a common pitfall in interventions has been difficulty in involving basic researchers, who are the leaders in testing theories and evaluating laboratory analogue studies of attitude and behavior change. In their absence, to keep pace with the demand for school programs, professionals in the field of education have relied on their own creative talents and their expertise in pedagogy to produce interventions. By highlighting the strengths as well as the limitations of these interventions, we hope to engage all those who have a stake in this endeavor.

If the goal of an intervention is to reduce prejudice, stereotyping, and/or discrimination, there must be adequate ways to measure these constructs. Brown's (1995) definition of prejudice provides a conceptual basis for the measurement of all three constructs: "the holding of derogatory social attitudes or cognitive beliefs, the expression of negative affect, or the display of hostile or discriminatory behavior towards members of a group on account of their membership of that group" (p. 8). Prejudice is usually measured as a negative evaluation of members from an outgroup, and prominent measures of it are the Preschool Racial Attitude Measures (PRAM—Williams, Best, Boswell, Mattson, & Graves, 1975), the Katz-Zalk Projective Technique (Katz & Zalk, 1978), the Multi-response Racial Attitude measure (MRA—Doyle & Aboud, 1995), spontaneous descriptors about cross-race encounters (Aboud, 1999), and facial affect (Carol Martin, personal communication, June 1999). Stereotyping is often assessed in terms of the belief that most, not just some, members of the outgroup possess negative attributes, and that few ingroup members possess these attributes (Bigler & Liben, 1993; Levy & Dweck, in press). Peer relations are measured in terms of the presence or exclusion of cross-race friends, generally indexed by friend nominations or chumship networks (Cairns, Leung, Buchanan, & Cairns, 1995; Graham, Cohen, Sbikowski, & Secrist, 1998). Researchers have come to realize that children do not necessarily show consistency among their attitudes, beliefs, and peer relationships. Consequently, an intervention that aims to improve peer contact may not necessarily reduce prejudice, and vice versa.

In this chapter, we describe and critically evaluate five types of interventions that attempt to reduce prejudice and discrimination, particularly in White children, and to encourage friendship and cooperation between children from different racial and ethnic groups. Some of the programs have been implemented at the classroom and school level, and others at the individual student level. Rather than cover the broad spectrum of extant approaches, we have chosen to describe a few interventions from each type to illustrate current practices. For each, we will point out the target of change in terms of who, what, and how much change is intended by the intervention. We will then provide the rationale underlying the intervention from the theoretical and empirical literature. Finally, we will offer an evaluation of its effectiveness.

FIVE TYPES OF INTERVENTIONS

The interventions are presented here in a specific order, organized according to the theoretical rationale underlying their development. The first two interventions—integrated schooling and bilingual education—are based on intergroup contact theory (Allport, 1954). The goal here is to provide contact that is individualized, equal in status, cooperative, and supported by authorities. Through contact, students are expected to acquire communication and cooperation skills, as they engage in respectful interactions and relationships. However, because students for one reason or another do not always make use of opportunities for contact, and because contact is not always feasible in relatively homogeneous settings, other types of interventions are also important.

The third type of intervention, concerned with multicultural and anti-racist education, may be implemented with or without contact. This type of intervention is based on socialization theory, which argues that children adopt the attitudes and behavior of significant others in their culture, through mechanisms such as imitation, paired associate learning, and conformity. Similarly, it is expected that students will acquire new associations, behaviors, and norms for positive race relations, following exposure to appropriate films, stories, and other curriculum materials. However, children are not always receptive to information that runs counter to their biases. Because most children arrive in school with biases already in place, it is often desirable to modify programs to fit the cognitive and emotional constraints and capabilities of students at different ages.

The last two interventions focus on training social-cognitive skills and utilizing emotional involvement through empathy and role-playing. Based on Piaget's cognitive developmental theory (Piaget & Weil, 1951), these interventions try to strengthen cognitive and emotional capabilities that facilitate prejudice reduction, while creating opportunities for peer collaboration that provoke engagement and change.

Racially Integrated Schooling

In many ethnically and racially heterogeneous societies, children experience their first close encounter with peers of another group at school. It may make a difference whether the school has a racially mixed student body because it was forced to desegregate or because it draws from such a population. Initially, the goal of desegregation in the United States was to provide equal educational opportunities, and not explicitly to improve intergroup relations through contact. Researchers have nonetheless examined the effects of intergroup contact, in its varying forms, on attitudes and peer relations. Consequently, this section discusses the effects of intergroup contact, in the absence of any special cooperative learning or multicultural education program.

The organizing framework for this research is Allport's (1954) contact theory. Interventions tend to be categorized in terms of four central variables: (1) individualized contact, (2) equal-status contact, (3) cooperation, and (4) support from authorities. These four are emphasized because they can potentially be modified through school practices. If contact has the above qualities and is long enough in duration, students are expected to develop positive and individualized relationships with outgroup members, a differentiated schema of the outgroup, and skills of cooperation and communication. Such relationships, cognitions, and skills are expected to generalize to new intergroup encounters and to translate into positive attitudes. While most of the experimental support for Allport's theory initially came from research on young adults (e.g., Amir, 1976; Cook, 1985), the theory continues to be the major inspiration for new school programs seeking to approximate the ideals embodied in these four constructs.

Overall, the results demonstrate that simply providing the opportunity for contact does not necessarily lead to cross-race tolerance and respect (e.g., Patchen, 1983; Schofield, 1982). The short-term effects on outgroup attitudes of desegregated compared to segregated schools are mixed at best. Various studies show positive or negative outcomes for Black and/or White students, or no differences (e.g., Schofield, 1995). Stephan (1999) concluded from his extensive review of studies on desegregation in elementary and secondary schools that Black students were more likely to become positive than negative, whereas White students were more likely to become negative. However, he pointed out that most of this research examined outcomes after one or two years of desegregation, when it was still a disturbing change for many students and parents. The questions most frequently addressed now are: What school practices facilitate Allport's conditions for quality contact, such as individualized and equal-status contact, and does this lead to prejudice reduction and positive intergroup relations?

The mediating variable through which integrated schooling has an impact on attitudes is positive peer relationships. Data from a number of studies suggest that having a cross-race close or best friend in childhood prepares people to have cross-race friends in adolescence and adulthood, and to adopt positive attitudes at this later date (Ellison & Powers, 1994; Jackman & Crane, 1986; Patchen, 1983). Cross-race conflict has also been studied extensively, but more detrimental is the avoidance and exclusion of cross-race contacts (e.g., Patchen, 1982). Because students in segregated schools have few cross-race contacts, research on peer relations is conducted in mixed-race schools, examining a variety of student and school variables that might promote friendship. Friendship, more than other types of peer relations, approximates the ideal contact in that friendship is individualized, equal-status, and voluntary.

One large study examined best-friend nominations of Black and White students in grades 4 to 7 in California (Hallinan, 1982; Hallinan & Teixeira, 1987a). Less than 20% of the students had a cross-race best friend, a finding similar to Patchen's (1983), though more recent studies of integrated schools show figures closer to 50% (e.g., Aboud & Mendelson, 1999; DuBois & Hirsch, 1990). In Hallinan's sample, White students had on average 0.82 cross-race friends and 2.48 same-race friends; Black students had 1.53 and 4.11, respectively. Thus, students actually had few cross-race best friends. Black students made more such nominations than Whites, and received fewer from Whites, particularly from White girls. Moreover, the number of cross-race best friends dropped strikingly between fourth and seventh grade.

Concerning the question of what school practices facilitate Allport's individualized contact, the size and composition of classroom and extracurricular groups were important, according to Hallinan's research. The racial composition of classes, varying from 10% to 90% Black, was somewhat influential in that cross-race best-friend nominations increased with availability. However, in racially balanced classes, where half the students were Black, students were least likely to have cross-race friends. Students were more likely to have a cross-race friend if they were in a smaller class, were involved in sports, or were girls in the same reading group. Other studies concur that specially created opportunities for positive, individualized contact in the early grades enhance the chances that contact will translate into friendship (e.g., Miller; 1983; Patchen, 1983; Schofield, 1995; Slavin & Madden, 1979; Weigel, Wiser, & Cook, 1975). Conversely, practices such as tracking students in ability-level groups tend to resegregate students and reduce the number of cross-race friendships.

Teacher training may be required to achieve the criterion of equal status in the contact situation. Cohen and Lotan (1995) argued that, even in small learning groups, children have differential performance expectations for themselves and their classmates, based on status characteristics such as language proficiency and race. Accordingly, teachers and students act in a way that unintentionally fulfills their status expectations. Students who enter the class with higher status attributes are expected to be more competent, and are given more opportunities to talk, to participate, and to take leadership roles, thereby fulfilling the expectation.

To combat this effect, Cohen and her colleagues intervened at the level of the child. They provided lower status students with a unique competence—e.g., how to build a radio—and found that the participation rates of such students increased dramatically in the group. In order to make this idea useful in a classroom setting, Cohen and Lotan trained 13 second-to-sixth-grade teachers to raise the status of lower status children. Teachers were trained for two weeks to be attentive to special abilities in low-status students, and then to provide the student with specific, favorable, and public evaluations so that high-status students would also hear and accept the teacher's evaluation. The intervention was evaluated through observation of the teachers' use of competence-assigning talk on a number of occasions, and the resulting participation rate of low- and high-status students in the classrooms taught by these teachers. Students' status was determined by the number of nominations received from classmates as fitting the two descriptors "best in math and science" and "best friend." Status and participation were highly correlated in some but not all of the classrooms before the intervention, providing partial support for the assumption that academic and social status translates into higher group participation. Observations taken after the intervention revealed that, on average, teachers used the competence-assigning talk once every two 10-minute observations—perhaps an appropriate rate for something that should be seen as special. However, some teachers had scores of zero. The analysis of low-status students demonstrated that teachers' use of the competence-assigning talk predicted the students' level of participation, even after controlling for a number of variables. Importantly, high-status students' participation did not suffer.

While integrated schooling has benefits beyond the reduction of prejudice and discrimination, it has been a disappointment in this regard to some who expected contact to be the "magic bullet." Because of prior biases, status differences, and school practices that recreate a segregated environment inside the school, many students do not have quality contact with cross-race peers. Those who do, seem to benefit in the long-term. Contact through integrated schooling has had a strong theory to guide it and has been subjected to many years of research (see Pettigrew and Tropp's chapter in this volume). Despite the inevitable limitations of research design and measurement, this research approach has persisted as educators and psychologists continued to examine new, more successful school practices that structure the school environment in ways that facilitate intergroup friendship. One of these is cooperative learning groups (reviewed by Johnson & Johnson in this volume). Most authors agree that integrated schooling should be combined with at least one other type of intervention to have greater impact on attitudes and friendship.

Bilingual Education

Bilingual education has much in common with integrated schooling in that contact with the culture and language of a different ethnolinguistic group is expected to develop the skills and attitudes necessary for intergroup harmony. However, bilingual education accomplishes this by offering students an academic program intended to make them proficient in more than one culture and language. At times, the programs have been directed to students from only one group—for example, Spanish-English programs for Hispanics in the United States (Moran & Hakuta, 1995), or French immersion programs for Anglophones in Canada (Genesee, 1987). More recently, programs have been implemented along with integrated schooling in an attempt to reach intergroup goals through adding direct contact with members of the outgroup. What is noteworthy about these programs is that they attempt to change attitudes indirectly by increasing students' familiarity with a second culture and language, and with members of that ethnolinguistic group. The hope is that familiarity and language competence will increase perceptions of similarity and reduce the feelings of threat and discomfort that often color interactions with outgroup members.

The Canadian French Immersion Experiment. The theoretical and empirical rationale underlying bilingual and immersion programs came from diverse sources. Lambert and Klineberg (1967) combined Piaget and Weil's (1951) cognitive-developmental theory with Allport's (1954) learning theory, to suggest that children learn to distrust people who are different because they hear parents emphasize intergroup differences rather than similarities. Motivated by a desire to identify themselves, young children learn what they *are* by discovering what they are not. Lambert, one of the designers of bilingual education in North America, hoped that by learning the language of an outgroup, students would come to feel similar to that group and therefore favorable toward its members. Second-language acquisition research and theory pointed to the desirability of beginning to learn a second language before the age of 12 in order to acquire communicative fluency.

In the early 1960s, a group of English-speaking parents in Montreal, with the help of Lambert, a psychologist at McGill University, set up what has now become a nationwide movement with 300,000 students, known as the early French immersion program. Children are taught entirely in French by monolingual French teachers at least through grade 2; English is gradually introduced, so that by late elementary school the proportion of courses given in French and English is roughly the same. Although the teachers speak in French only, the students are generally monolingual English speakers, as are the administrative personnel of the school. Thus, the teachers are often the only outgroup members with whom the children have regular contact.

While the goal of creating students who are proficient in French (and other school subjects) is largely achieved by the end of elementary school, a second goal is to instill in students an understanding and respect for French Canadians, their language, and their culture. Although there is no explicit instruction in culture or intergroup relations, the math, science, and social studies texts all use examples of French Canadian life and people, and teachers inevitably model pride and respect for members of their group.

Research on this program has been conducted over a 20-year period in Montreal schools, where there is a potential for language proficiency to translate into positive intergroup relations. Change was measured in comparison with a control group of Anglophone students who were in the regular program, learning French in the traditional way—two hours per week. Attempts were made to eliminate differences that might be due to a selection bias. Measures of perceived similarity indicated that immersion students perceived more similarity (a) between French and

English Canadians, and (b) between themselves and French Canadians than did controls (Genesee, 1987). Attitude measures required students to evaluate French Canadians and English Canadians on a number of trait dimensions. In the early grades, the immersion students' attitudes toward French Canadians were more positive than controls', though by the end of elementary school their attitudes became less positive. It was hypothesized at the time that, while immersion students may have based their initial attitude on their contact with the teacher and the language, for older students this was not enough. Contacts with French Canadians, as revealed in the daily diaries of older elementary students, were generally restricted to public settings, and contact with outgroup peers was still low. The children might also have realized that there was little contact between the French- and English-speaking teachers in their school, a pattern that mirrored the larger society.

Consequently, although perceptions of intergroup similarity increased in immersion students, positive intergroup relations did not necessarily follow. In hindsight, the program lacked some of the components necessary for integrated contact (Allport, 1954). Contact was restricted to teachers from the outgroup. Furthermore, while authority figures, such as teachers and principals, were supportive, they did not themselves model integrated contact, preferring to socialize with teachers from their own ethnolinguistic group. As an alternative to this French immersion program, other Anglophone parents have aimed to maximize peer contact and communication by sending their children to French schools, where proficiency in the language and culture can be gained along with intergroup friendships (Lambert, Genesee, Holobow, & Chartrand, 1993). Sociological studies of peer relations in French-language high schools indicate that, while there is some self-segregation, the overall picture is one of intergroup mixing (Laperriere, 1989).

The American Two-Way Amigos Program. In 1985, a bilingual program was initiated in Cambridge, Massachusetts, with the intent to develop Spanish and English language proficiency in Hispanic and Anglophone students. In addition to the academic and language development of these students, a second goal was to promote intergroup friendship, along with knowledge and respect for the diverse cultures of the students. Since the program included mainly-Spanish-speaking Hispanic students along with White and African American English-speaking students, the opportunity for integrated contact was extensive. Efforts were made to equalize the status of students in the classroom. For example, during the half-day when instruction was given in Spanish, the Hispanic students might be perceived as advantaged as a result of their greater proficiency in the language. However, the Hispanic students would be at a disadvantage during the other half-day of English instruction. Despite this attempt to create an equal-status (or balanced status) classroom (Cohen & Lotan, 1995)—a key factor in integrated contact—the program developers recognized that the status of ethnolinguistic groups in the larger society can intrude on classroom activities and set expectations for performance that are difficult to eradicate.

The effectiveness of this program has been evaluated with approximately 50 students from grades 4 to 8, in comparison with students enrolled in all-English schools and in transitional bilingual programs (where Hispanic students are gradually introduced to an all-English program). Measures of academic performance and intergroup relations have been analyzed. Language and math scores indicate that Amigos students excel in these subjects, performing equal to or better than controls (Cazabon, Nicoladis, & Lambert, 1998). English-speaking Amigos were asked about their contact with and attitudes toward Spanish-speaking people. Concerning friendships, 85% had made friends from both ethnolinguistic groups, and all said they liked having students from different groups in their class (Lambert & Cazabon, 1994). This compared favorably with the Spanish Amigos who, however, had more friends from the other group. The English-speaking students' perceptions of similarities and differences between the two ethnolinguistic groups were mixed and comparable to the Spanish Amigos—one-third thought the two groups were very similar, almost one-half saw similarities and differences, and a smaller proportion perceived mostly differences. Slightly over half of the English-speaking Amigos said they would be just as happy to be a Spanish-speaking American had they been born into such a family, while most of the rest were not sure how they would feel. Because this item was the only attitudinal question, it is difficult to determine whether the students' language training and intergroup contact had translated into positive attitudes toward Hispanic Americans. At least half seemed to feel as positive toward Hispanics as to their own group, while the rest were probably ambivalent at best. Interestingly, the distribution of responses by Spanish Amigos was similar (Lambert & Cazabon, 1994).

In conclusion, the results of the French Immersion and the Two-Way Bilingual programs indicate that being instructed in a second language posed no academic problems for the students. They became proficient in both languages and also mastered their academic subjects. Because cultural knowledge was introduced incidentally in the curriculum material, the children learned about another culture and perceived themselves to be similar in many respects to people from that culture. However, it is now apparent that contact with outgroup peers is important for the maintenance of continued intergroup contact and positive attitudes. At the present time, with 30% of Anglophone Montreal students in fully French schools and 182 schools across the United States providing two-way bilingual programs for 50,000 students, the trend toward increased contact through second-language learning is promising (Genesee & Gandara, in press).

Multicultural and Anti-Racist Education

Multicultural or, more specifically, multiethnic education has been inspired by an ideology that seeks to reform the process of schooling for all children, with the goal of promoting cultural diversity and equal opportunity (Banks, 1995; Sleeter & Grant, 1994). In this area, the most common types of school programs aim to provide students with the knowledge and attitudes necessary to understand, respect, and in teract harmoniously as equals with members of different ethnic groups (Bennett, 1990; Sleeter & Grant, 1987). A subset of programs, known as anti-racism education, aims to provide students with a heightened awareness of institutional racism and with the skills to reduce it within their sphere of influence (Dei, 1996; Derman-Sparks & Phillips, 1997). At times, the programs are directed to students from one ethnic group—for example, to White students with the goal of improving their knowledge of and attitudes toward African Americans. The approach may also be used to good effect in integrated settings where, for example, a mixed-race class of students jointly discusses experiences of racism.

Washburn (1996) reported a survey of 713 school districts which each served 10,000 or more students. He found that 46% of the districts had a multicultural education program. Of these, 88% targeted all students (not just minority students), close to 50% used ethnic studies curricula in social studies or language arts courses, almost 30% had an anti-racism program to deter racism, and 11% had a program directly aimed at developing intergroup harmony. We will focus here on two types of programs—general multicultural ones, and more specific anti-racism ones.

Multicultural Education. The theoretical and empirical rationale for multicultural education comes from varied sources, mainly socialization theories (Sleeter & Grant, 1994). The central assumption is that, if prejudiced attitudes and discriminatory behaviors are learned from parents through imitation, paired association, and reinforcement (Allport, 1954), new ones can be learned at a later time through the same mechanisms. Various research findings have raised questions about the assumption that children initially learn prejudice from their parents. For instance, most studies find only a small correlation between the attitudes of a child and those of the parent (e.g., Aboud & Doyle, 1996b; Branch & Newcombe, 1986; Carlson & Iovini, 1985). Despite this fact, children may egocentrically assume that others think as they do, because of distortion or a lack of information to the contrary (Kofkin, Katz, & Downey, 1995). Nonetheless, there is evidence that children show more positive attitudes toward outgroup members who are explicitly approved by the experimenter (Madge, 1976). Furthermore, while children do not necessarily imitate their parents' behavior, they do seem to seek and imitate regularities in their social world (Perry & Bussy, 1979). It seems that one regularity they notice is the lack of cross-race close contact.

In recognition of the need to provide explicit and consistent models for tolerant behavior, some programs provide materials for anti-bias activities that extend through elementary and secondary schooling (e.g., Hawkins, 1995; Heller & Hawkins, 1994). However, many programs simply provide knowledge about the historical and social contribution of certain groups and their culture, assuming that positive attitudes will develop out of a complex understanding of the group. Yet if such learning is to have a persistent effect, it will have to form a schema that replaces or is more accessible than the previous prejudiced attitudes. Another mechanism involved in socialization theory is conformity to norms—i.e., the standards that delineate beliefs, attitudes, and behaviors that a particular group feels are correct and approved. While younger children to not appear to be unduly conformist (cf. Gavin & Furman, 1989), they will tailor their public behavior to fit norms, particularly if counter-normative behavior provokes disapproval. For this reason, schools seek to establish a norm for tolerant and respectful behavior, with the hope that children's attitudes will eventually fall into line with their behavior, as dissonance and consistency theories would predict. As the above comments indicate, some aspects of socialization theory appear to be more suited than others to reducing prejudice, and these differences can be seen in the examples below.

Multicultural education may become commonplace simply because it is an obvious direction for an education system seeking to produce cosmopolitan citizens. Whether intentionally or not, however, teachers and students often draw comparisons between themselves and other cultures, thereby making more salient the intergroup differences. Consequently, it is important to notice how the information about ethnic groups is presented, and whether it serves to stereotype groups or present their heterogeneity.

Several studies in this area have started with the assumption that White children in the early primary grades might develop positive attitudes as a result of listening to stories about African American children. The theoretical rationale for the intervention was that exposure to material portraying African Americans in a positive manner would increase familiarity and help form positive associations to Black people. Using an experimental-versus-control pre-post design, Litcher and Johnson (1969) studied the attitudes of second graders to a 4-month intervention featuring multiethnic readers. The teachers were not to initiate any discussion of race, and the children apparently did not comment on the fact that many of the story characters were non-White. While the experimental and control groups did not differ on the pretest, experimental children were less prejudiced on all four attitude measures at the posttest. However, overall levels of prejudice were still fairly high.

The same authors conducted a *4-week* replication study, but this time found no differences between experimental and control children (Litcher, Johnson, & Ryan, 1973). Similarly, listening to and discussing stories about African-American characters in another 4-week intervention produced no significant change (Yawkey, 1973). Though the intention was for children to unlearn negative associations and relearn positive associations to outgroup members, this paired associative learning was not strong enough to overcome prior biases. Furthermore, children may have grown to like the book characters, but their attitude did not generalize to others—a problem commonly found in cooperative learning groups (Weigel, Wiser, & Cook, 1975). In these studies, the teacher did nothing to convey his/her attitudes or establish a classroom norm in support of positive attitudes toward African Americans (Litcher & Johnson, 1969). Without these supportive factors, programs that simply expose children to stories about other groups are not sufficient to change attitudes.

A similar conclusion was drawn about earlier versions of *Sesame Street* television programs which, despite showing children from many different ethnic and racial groups, did little to reduce the ethnocentrism of their young viewers. Since the mid-1990s, there has been a concerted effort to highlight and explicitly discuss racial differences in both child and adolescent television programs, and more scenes have been specifically aimed at modeling cross-race friendships. In addition, programmers are interested in determining viewers' interpretations of the scenes, recognizing that viewers of different ages and racial backgrounds may attach different meanings to the behaviors shown. Given the power of televised images, it is reassuring to know that this form of multicultural education is being monitored (Graves, in press).

Research has also been conducted on a 16-week multicultural program with students in seventh and eighth grade, which also used reading material and movies, in this case to provide information on the culture and experiences of different American ethnic groups (Fuhr, 1996). Only about half the material was rated highly by the students as promoting tolerance and appreciation of other cultures. While there was no control group, the intervention students endorsed only slightly fewer stereotyped traits at posttest than at the pretest. Almost two-thirds thought it was important to learn about other ethnic backgrounds at school, but this support was lower after the program. This outcome is consistent with the results of another program, which used a control group, where no change was found from pre- to posttest for either the control or the intervention group (Lessing & Clarke, 1976). Comparing the effects of three different approaches to multicultural education, Slavin and Madden (1979) found that White tenth graders' attitudes and cross-race friendships were significantly affected by discussions on race, but not by multiethnic texts or a minority-group history course. Black students were not strongly affected by any of the three interventions.

Anti-Racist and Anti-Bias Programs. Classroom discussions on race could focus on a number of issues. Among relatively young children, the discussions tend to focus on tolerance and anti-bias. Instructional and curriculum materials encourage discussion of racial differences and similarities in a way that will help young children understand and feel comfortable with people from different groups (e.g., Derman-Sparks, 1989; Tatum, 1992; Thomson, 1993). These programs tend to be eclectic in the theories they use to support their methods, but in general they seek to re-socialize children to be unprejudiced through activities, films, readings, and discussions. Because of the demand for such programs, they continue to be created and used without clear evidence of their effectiveness. For one popular series, called *Teaching Tolerance* (see Bullard, 1996; Heller & Hawkins, 1994), only a few outcome evaluations are available (e.g., Klein, 1992; Mileski, 1998).

With high school students, classroom discussions of race generally focus on racism. Anti-racist teaching seeks to make students aware of the institutionalized system of relations that ensures a power differential between racial groups (e.g., Dei, 1996; Derman-Sparks & Phillips, 1997). While many different instructional techniques are available, they differ from multicultural education in their emphasis on student discussion, rather than simply passive exposure to media information. The discussion, often supplemented with media, focuses on the manifestations and deleterious consequences of prejudice, stereotypes, and discrimination, The goals of anti-racist teaching include greater awareness of one's own racial identity and attitudes, learning how racism affects social life, understanding and empathizing with the cultural realities of those from a different background, and developing the skills and confidence to become an agent of social change.

Theoretical and empirical support for anti-racist teaching comes from socialization and self-insight work. The assumption is that racism is acquired by most White members of society as a result of learning and conforming to the norms of society (cf. Dovidio et al., in this volume). An emphasis on self-insight through group discussion, however, places this strategy in a domain quite different from socialization theory. Whether by design or not, it capitalizes on Piaget's view that challenge and conflict from peers produce cognitive conflict, which in turn leads to the construction of a more complex understanding of social relations and one's place in that system. Furthermore, this approach draws support from research with young adults on self-insight. In particular, when people who believe they are tolerant become aware that they have unintentionally reacted in a prejudiced manner, they feel mild guilt. To reduce feelings of guilt, they become vigilant about expressing tolerance and positive attitudes (Devine, Monteith, Zuwerink, & Elliot, 1991; cf. Devine et al., in this volume). However, such change does not usually take place with high-prejudice people who do not feel any guilt.

One of the most explicit descriptions of anti-racist teaching is found in the technique used by Derman-Sparks and Phillips (1997) to train teachers. Topics for their course include experience with interracial encounters, overt and covert racism, activist role models for anti-racism, and development of a personal action project. They describe the personal reactions of White and Black Americans as they confront each other while presenting experiences of being the perpetrators and targets of racism.

Evaluations of anti-racist teaching are rare, but McGregor (1993) found that the effect size of seven intervention studies having control groups was moderately positive. Although the duration of the program and the age of students may have affected the outcomes, there were too few studies to draw firm conclusions. Unfortunately, some programs, especially with adults, have a negative effect on participants, increasing rather than decreasing prejudice levels (see also Kehoe & Mansfield, 1993). Perhaps insight into their prejudiced reactions arouses a feeling of self-righteousness in some people, rather than guilt. This might turn into anger toward instructors and toward the target ethnic group.

In summary, multicultural education has been used extensively in schools, yet has received little careful evaluation of outcomes. It seems clear that simply providing information to reduce ignorance does not reduce prejudice. While learning about different cultures is a useful component of education, it may contribute to a stereotyped knowledge of an ethnic group if presented in a simplified manner for younger students. Material that purposely counters stereotypes is necessary, but not sufficient, because young children often distort the information to fit their preconceived biases. Some discussion of race and racism, along with presentation of multiethnic texts and ethnic studies, appears to be necessary. Obviously, discussions about racism need to be geared to the developmental level of the student. Elementary school children, who lack emotional sophistication, may cope with feelings of guilt in unproductive ways, such as by blaming the victims or denying wrongdoing. Their belief that people get what they deserve—the "just world" belief—may lead them to conclude that minority groups deserve their poor treatment (Glasberg & Aboud, 1981). However, at this point in time, there is too little research available to inform educators about which anti-racist programs successfully reduce prejudice and stereotyping.

Training Social-Cognitive Skills

Interventions to strengthen social-cognitive skills make a concerted effort to have students practice new ways of processing information. Particular skills, known to be related to prejudice reduction, are selected, and practicing them is seen as one way to make the learning long-lasting. This type of intervention, more than the previous ones, attempts to alter the schemas and age-related cognitive structures, such as simple categorization, that often distort the way children process multicultural information.

The rationale for focusing on social cognition derives from Piaget's application of his theory to intergroup relations (Piaget & Weil, 1951) and later research on the development of prejudice (Aboud, 1988; Katz, 1976). Because so many White children arrive in school with already high levels of prejudice (e.g., Bar-Tal, 1996; Katz & Kofkin, 1997), interventions must take into account these pre-existing biases and their cognitive supports. Certain social cognitions appear to develop between ages 4 and 7 and are associated with the rise of prejudice. These include fixation on a single, often racial, classification rather than on classification using multiple defining characteristics, and an exaggeration of the differences between groups and the similarities of members within groups (Katz, Sohn, & Zalk, 1975). In older children, important research had identified cognitive capabilities associated with lower levels of prejudice—in particular the ability to accept and integrate multiple criteria for organizing social information (Bigler & Liben, 1993; Black-Gutman & Hickson, 1996; Doyle & Aboud, 1995; Katz et al., 1975; Levy & Dweck, in press). For example, prejudice is lower in children who understand that people may differ on one dimension yet be similar on another, that people may be different in the future than they are today, and that opposing opinions may both be right. Because children are receptive to information that is consistent with, or slightly ahead of, their current construction of the world, interventions attempt to change their construction of the world, often with the help of peers and a social context that facilitates debate (see Aboud & Doyle, 1996b; Doise, Mugny, & Perret-Clermont, 1975). Within this framework, change is more likely to occur if children are actively involved in reworking both the new information and their existing biases, to create a match.

A common research strategy has been to identify specific social cognitions that vary across age and individuals, and that are associated with lower levels of prejudice. A subsequent phase of studies has demonstrated that short-term interventions to train these cognitions were successful in reducing prejudice and stereotyping. The model for this strategy was set by Katz and her colleagues (Katz, 1973; Katz et al., 1975; Katz & Zalk, 1978), who studied the capability to differentiate individuals within an outgroup. Related research has been continued by others who have worked on other social cognitions, such as multiple classification (Bigler & Liben, 1992, 1993) and lay theories of human change (Levy & Dweck, in press).

In a series of carefully designed pretest-posttest, experimental-control studies, Katz and her colleagues addressed the outgroup homogeneity bias (in which outgroup members are seen as similar to one another). The most comprehensive of these studies, by Katz and Zalk (1978), compared four 15-minute interventions with White second and fifth graders. The most successful intervention was one in which children were trained to learn distinctive names for each pictured outgroup member. The children in this condition expressed less prejudice after the intervention and again two weeks later, compared to controls. In contrast, an intervention designed to promote contact while engaged in a fun activity, and another designed to give positive reinforcement for selecting Black stimuli had no effect. Listening to a story about African American children had some effect on second graders, but not on fifth graders. Such age differences point to the need to tailor interventions to the developmental level of the child. Taken together, these findings suggest that strengthening children's ability to differentiate among members of an outgroup can reduce prejudice (see Katz, Acosta, Bartlett, & Arango, 1992, for an extension of this work).

Elaborating on Katz and Zalk's findings, and moving outside the laboratory into a classroom setting, Aboud and Fenwick (in press) evaluated an 11-week curriculum unit designed to improve students' ability to process information about individual rather than racial attributes. Fifth graders were the participants because Katz et al. (1975) had found that sixth graders but not fourth graders were beginning to base dissimilarity judgments on internal individual differences. Through a series of entertaining exercises, students in the intervention were required to learn a variety of internal attributes about 30 pictured students from a multiracial class. The intervention was conducted in a multiracial school in Montreal with four cohorts in a pretest-posttest experimental-control design. The effectiveness of the unit was assessed two months after the program's completion. Results from the White participants were encouraging: Intervention students showed a significant increase in the proportion of internal attributes they were able to generate when comparing pairs of photographed children. Moreover, children who were identified as high-prejudiced on the basis of their pretest MRA scores reported less prejudice after completing the curriculum unit. Notably, the curriculum unit had no detrimental effects on low-prejudice children or minority children, who at the least benefited by strengthening a social-cognitive skill.

Similar research has evaluated multiple classification as a social-cognitive skill associated with reduced bias (e.g., Hohn, 1973). Bigler and Liben (1992, 1993)

compared the effects of training kindergartners through fifth-graders to classify social and nonsocial stimuli on multiple dimensions. Using a pre-post experimental-
control design, they evaluated the impact of training on gender stereotyping. Each
day for one week, children spent 25 minutes sorting a set of objects by type and
color (nonsocial training) or a set of pictures of men and women by both gender and
occupation (social training). Results indicated that, compared to children in the
control condition and nonsocial classification condition, those trained in multiple
methods of social classification showed more accurate recall of counter-stereotypic
people presented in story form one to two weeks later. They also gave more egalitarian responses to gender stereotyping measures. These findings suggest that
multiple classification training can successfully reduce stereotyping, but that the
training should be specific to social categories.

A form of social cognition that develops in children, persists into adulthood, and
is strongly related to stereotyping concerns the conception that human nature is
static versus dynamic (e.g., Dweck, 1999; Levy, in press; Levy & Dweck, 1998, in
press; Levy, Stroessner, & Dweck, 1998). Those who hold to the dynamic view
(who feel that people can change their personality over the course of life) tend to
exhibit lower levels of stereotyping when processing information about novel group
members. For instance, fifth- and sixth-graders read about several positive, negative, and neutral behaviors performed by different students from one or more unfamiliar schools. Across the studies, Levy and Dweck found that children who viewed
traits as basically malleable and dynamic, compared with children who viewed traits
as fixed, developed less extreme trait impressions, attributed group members' behavior less to their underlying disposition than to situational factors, and minimized
within-group similarities and between-group differences on traits. Furthermore, it
was possible to change students' lay theories with a 10-minute presentation aimed
at providing evidence in support of either the static or dynamic version. Children
who were temporarily led to adopt the dynamic view rather than the static view
made weaker trait ratings, made more dynamic and situational attributions for the
group's behavior, and viewed outgroup members as less similar to one another. In
sum, these results suggest that a dynamic view of attributes, when habitually present or situationally induced, can lessen stereotyping.

To summarize, interventions to reduce prejudice and stereotyping by training
related social cognitions have shown some success. However, while strong on
theoretical and empirical support, most of these interventions have been conducted
in controlled, short-term settings, rather than as part of a school program. So far,
only a few social cognitions have been targeted—those most relevant to prejudice
reduction in elementary school children. Some strengths of this intervention approach are that it operates on information-processing skills and conceptions that
are rarely used by students, but not entirely unknown to them, and that have value
for all young people, regardless of their initial level of prejudice. Another strength
of the research is that many such interventions were focused and brief, and yet
produced a discernible change. Because they focused on social cognitions rather

than racism, they avoided the oppositional reactions often associated with anti-racist interventions. Moreover, promoting social-cognitive skills can have benefits in domains beyond race relations (see Levy & Dweck, 1998). However, the long-term, general effects of these interventions have not been assessed.

Role-Playing and Empathy

The idea that role-playing and empathy can be used to reduce prejudice has much in common with the previously discussed topic of social-cognitive skills. First, the interventions focus on capabilities that are considered to be useful for all forms of interpersonal and intergroup relations. Second, they focus on capabilities that change developmentally, vary across individuals, and can potentially be situation-ally induced (i.e., they can be developmental state-trait mediators of prejudice reduction).

Taking the role of a child from a different ethnic group has been used as a technique to reduce prejudice and discrimination. The role-playing techniques that have been employed vary, but basically follow the same theme. A child is encouraged to walk in the shoes of an outgroup member—to play the role of a child who is the target of discrimination. Through this experience, children learn to adopt a perspective different from their usual one, to understand the painful feelings of others who may be the targets of discrimination, and thereby to empathize with their experiences. It is assumed that, through empathy, which involves both cognitive perspective-taking and emotional sharing, children will perceive themselves to be similar to outgroup members. Furthermore, empathy is expected to motivate children to want to alleviate others distress as if it is their own, by acting in less discriminatory ways in the future. Role- playing, then, may be a useful technique to reduce prejudice and discrimination by encouraging perceptions of similarity and the desire to act in a more respectful manner.

Although role-playing was introduced as a prejudice-reduction technique at least as early as 1957 (Culbertson, 1957), it has not been used extensively. The technique is based on the theoretical rationale that prejudice and antisocial behavior derive from an egocentric orientation. According to Piaget and Weil (1951), young children are cognitively unable to take the perspective of someone different from themselves (this is termed *egocentrism*) or of someone different from their group (*sociocentrism*). Such shifts in perspective taking are particularly difficult when the child's own perspective and preferences are salient and different. Levels of prejudice are reduced when children acquire the ability not only to understand, but also to accept as legitimate, the different perspective of an outgroup member (Doyle & Aboud, 1995). Prosocial behaviors are also facilitated by the experience of empathy (Feshbach & Feshbach, 1998; Gimmestad & DeChiara, 1982). While the ability to experience vicariously others' emotions seems to develop at a younger age than do role-taking skills, both may be necessary when playing the role of an outgroup member.

Probably the most well-known prejudice reduction role-taking technique is the classroom demonstration devised by Jane Elliot (see the film, *The Eye of the Storm*: Peters, 1971). Jane Elliot was a third-grade teacher in a predominately White, rural, elementary school in Iowa in the 1960s. She wanted to teach her students how it felt to be the target of discrimination, so one day, she told her class that students with blue eyes were superior to students with brown eyes. All day, she showed preferential treatment to the blue-eyed children. The next day, she told her class the brown-eyed children were actually superior and proceeded to praise and give special attention to them. In short, for one day, each group of children had a first-hand experience with discrimination on the basis of something as arbitrary as eye or skin color.

Unfortunately, empirical tests of the Blue-Eyes/Brown-Eyes simulation (as it is often called) with children have been rare (see Byrnes & Kiger, 1992, for a simulation with college students). As an exception, Weiner and Wright (1973) tested a variation of the Blue-Eyes/Brown-Eyes simulation with 32 White third graders. In this case, the classroom teacher told children that they were members of Green or Orange groups and asked to them to wear colored armbands. Like Jane Elliot, the teacher encouraged discrimination against each group for one day. Compared to a control classroom, participants in the simulation reported more willingness to attend a picnic with Black children. These results provide an encouraging bit of support for the impact of role-playing the target of prejudice on subsequent intergroup behavior.

In another variation of the Blue-Eyes/Brown-Eyes technique, Breckheimer and Nelson (1976) had a group of mixed-race high school students discuss and role-play student prejudice and discrimination. Five students participated in six group sessions over three weeks. A number of behavioral and sociometric dependent measures were administered before and one week after the completion of the sessions. The role-playing condition was compared with three other group methods of reducing racial prejudice (group discussion, social issues discussion, and game-playing) and with a control condition. The role-taking and racial discussion conditions yielded the strongest, albeit weak, effects. Breckheimer and Nelson found that the role-playing condition influenced sociometric measures and intentions to engage in behaviors with outgroup members. Given the small sample size, these findings are encouraging. Unfortunately, however, a measure of empathy was not included to determine whether an increase in empathy mediated these effects.

So far, we have reviewed how role-taking and empathy may elicit changes in attitudes and prosocial behavior. Another form of helping outgroup members is intervening as a bystander when prejudicial remarks are made about them. A prerequisite for bystander helping may be the ability to take the emotional perspective of the person in distress. Although understanding when, why, and how bystanders intervene is a well-researched area in social psychology with regard to helping generally (for a review, see Latane, 1981), bystander interventions have not been tested extensively in relation to prejudice reduction. A notable exception is an intervention by Slaby (1999), in which sixth graders discussed ways of speaking out against name-calling and other schoolyard expressions of prejudice. Bystander efficacy, measured as confidence that one could successfully intervene, increased after the program.

Anti-racist and anti-bias teaching also explicitly mentions as one of its goals that students and teachers should actively intervene to reduce prejudice and discrimination (e.g., Derman-Sparks, 1989). While educators have tried to specify how teachers might comment on remarks made by their students, there is no similar script for how students might properly respond to peer remarks (see Aboud & Fenwick, in press, for bystander interventions among college students). So far, evidence of the effectiveness of teacher training is only anecdotal. Bystander interventions are potentially useful in a number of ways: they may modify the attitudes and behavior of the person who made the racist remark, reduce some of the pain for targets of the remark, and set a norm of nondiscriminatory behavior among those who overheard the discussion. Moreover, each time bystanders intervene, their own behavior may serve to increase their personal commitment to nonprejudiced and nondiscriminatory views. Furthermore, given that racial slurs and jokes occur even among children (Schofield, 1982) and that elementary school children can be trained to successfully manage peer conflicts (Johnson, Johnson, Dudley, & Acikgoz, 1994; Johnson, Johnson, Dudley, & Magnuson, 1995), exploring the effectiveness of bystander interventions in relation to prejudice reduction is a critical need.

Taken together, results from studies on the impact of role-playing and empathy on prejudice provided encouraging results, regardless of the age, sex, and race of the participants. Unfortunately, the development of these programs has not been systematic. Some of them provide direct experience and others vicarious experience, both of which are usually of short duration. Heightening the emotional involvement of students and taking into account their level of emotional development are two important variables here. The emotions best aroused during empathy training need to be clarified and measured. With young adults, Finlay and Stephan (in press) found that anger toward the discriminator rather than pity for the target was aroused by reading personal accounts of being a target, and that this led to reductions in prejudice. However, care must be taken with young children who lack emotional sophistication, for they may develop feelings of pity, rather than respect, for targets of discrimination. Perceived similarity to the target of discrimination is another hypothesized mediator that has not been evaluated. Young children may cope with the pain of being discriminated against by distancing themselves from minority groups rather than by perceiving themselves to be similar. This type of empathy-inducing intervention seems to have a strong potential if it can become better informed by theoretical and empirical research on the development of children's empathy.

CONCLUSIONS

There are many criteria to use when evaluating interventions to reduce prejudice and discrimination. One of these is the methodological rigor used in determining their effectiveness. We looked for research designs that used both intervention and control groups, and where students and/or classrooms were randomly assigned. We also looked for replications, either cross-sectionally or longitudinally, or with an entirely different population. Measurement of prejudice or discrimination, both pre- and post-intervention as well as several months later, is also important in order to provide convincing results. However, Schofield (1995) has pointed out that unreasonably stringent use of certain measures can potentially mask the benefits of many interventions. For example, attitude measures that allow for only one choice of a person who is "friendly" or "smart" would require students to withdraw such an evaluation from their ingroup and assign it to a member of the outgroup in order to show improvement. Providing a multiple-option format would be preferable in this case. Likewise, peer relations should not be measured solely in terms of friendship because this may not change much over the course of a short-term intervention; instead, weaker associates and chumship groups should also be included. Another important methodological step is to measure mediating variables, such as equal status in the classroom, knowledge about an ethnic group's contribution to society, empathy, or perceptual/cognitive differentiation. We hope that these methodological concerns will be addressed more fully in future evaluations of interventions.

In this review, while we have given greatest weight to the program's effectiveness in meeting its stated goals of prejudice reduction and harmonious interaction, other considerations have also been raised. One concerns the theoretical basis of the program. Because many interventions were initiated at the request of educators or parents, their connections to theories were often weak, and little distinction was made between teaching academic material and teaching race relations. We have therefore often stressed the need for clearer identification of the mechanism by which children and adolescents are expected to change, along with evidence of theoretical and empirical support for such a mechanism. In this regard, there is probably more support for social-cognitive and contact theories than for socialization theory. However, key tasks for future researchers are to rethink the theories we rely on and to elaborate on the mechanisms of change.

A major strength of the integrated and bilingual schooling interventions is that they have a guiding framework in Allport's contact theory. So, while neither has managed to produce all the conditions desired for favorable contact, they have gradually come to approximate them. Both types of programs have had some short- and long-term successes, notably in the domain of positive relations with cross-ethnic peers, but they have also had some disappointments. Students do not make as many cross-ethnic friends as hoped for, and contact has not always reduced prejudice. However, these approaches are a promising route, and an obvious one to take whenever different groups live in proximity. Claims for the success of contact under certain optimizing conditions have been backed by a great deal of outcome evaluation over many years (cf. Pettigrew & Tropp, in this volume).

A major strength of the multicultural and anti-racist approaches is their ease of application even in relatively homogeneous schools where cross-ethnic contact is minimal. Also, many teachers are willing to use these interventions because they are produced as curriculum units or instruction manuals. Unfortunately, the proposed mechanisms for change—imitation, paired-associate learning, and conformity—have not received much empirical support in the context of reducing prejudice and discrimination. These interventions have also not been well evaluated. At this point, the anti-racist or anti-bias approach is more promising because prejudice and discrimination are explicitly discussed in the context of race, and children have the opportunity to discuss actively their conflicting views and to find one that is convincing and long-lasting.

A major strength of the empathy and social-cognitive approaches is their support from previous theoretical and empirical work. However, they have not yet developed broad interventions targeting large numbers of students. Because they target emotional and cognitive capabilities—ones that a child may or may not be ready for—there is a need to tailor the program to the student population. Also, teachers may not always understand the rationale for the specific interventions, and so may need some special training.

The challenge for future researchers is to evaluate rigorously the many interventions currently used in educational settings, while continuing to examine in more controlled settings the mechanisms underlying prejudice reduction. Because there is not a one-to-one correspondence between prejudice and discrimination, we must also be prepared to implement several intervention programs directed differentially at emotional, cognitive, and behavioral change. Such work also requires a stronger partnership between educators, psychologists, and parents, who need each others' input when designing, evaluating, and implementing interventions. In this process, research on interventions targeting adults (as reviewed in other chapters of this book) goes hand in hand with the childhood interventions described here. We may hope that the next decade of research and program development will provide a blueprint for how to sequence specific interventions throughout the school-age years in order to maximize their impact.

REFERENCES

Aboud, F. E. (1988). *Children and prejudice*. New York: Blackwell.

Aboud, F. E., & Doyle, A. B. (1996a). Parental and peer influences on children's racial attitudes. *International Journal of Intercultural Relations, 20,* 371-383.

Aboud, F. E., & Doyle, A. B. (1996b). Does talk of race foster prejudice or tolerance in children? *Canadian Journal of Behavioral Science, 28,* 161-170.

Aboud, F. E. (1999, April). *The emergence of racial prejudice in white children: Social cognitive correlates.* Paper presented at American Educational Research Association meeting, Montreal.

Aboud, F. E., & Fenwick, V. (in press). Evaluating school-based interventions to reduce prejudice in preadolescents. *Journal of Social Issues.*

Aboud, F. E., & Mendelson, M. J. (1999, April). *Do cross-race friendships decline with age in quantity and quality?* Paper presented at Society for Research in Child Development meeting, Albuquerque.

Allport, G. W. (1954). *The nature of prejudice.* Cambridge, MA: Addison-Wesley.

Amir, Y. (1969). Contact hypothesis in ethnic relations. *Psychological Bulletin, 106,* 74-106.

Banks, J. A. (1995). Multicultural education: Its effects on students' racial and gender role attitudes. In J. A. Banks & C. A. M. Banks (Eds.), *Handbook of research on multicultural education* (pp. 617-627). New York: Macmillan.

Bar-Tal, D. (1996). Development of social categories and stereotypes in early childhood: The case of "the Arab" concept formation, stereotype and attitudes by Jewish children in Israel. *International Journal of Intercultural Relations, 20,* 341-370.

Bennett, C. (1990). *Comprehensive multicultural education: Theory and practice.* Needham Heights, MA: Allyn & Bacon.

Bigler, R. S., & Liben, L. S. (1992). Cognitive mechanisms in children's gender stereotyping: Theoretical and educational implications of a cognitive-based intervention. *Child Development, 63,* 1351-1363.

Bigler, R. S., & Liben, L. S. (1993). A cognitive-developmental approach to racial stereotyping and reconstructive memory in Euro-American children. *Child Development, 64,* 1507-1518.

Black-Gutman, D., & Hickson, F. (1996). The relation between racial attitudes and social-cognitive development in children: An Australian study. *Developmental Psychology, 32,* 448-456.

Branch, C. W., & Newcombe, N. (1986). Racial attitude development among Black children as a function of parental attitudes: A longitudinal and cross-sectional study. *Child Development, 57,* 712-721.

Breckheimer, S. E., & Nelson, R. O. (1976). Group methods for reducing racial prejudice and discrimination. *Psychological Reports, 39,* 1259-1268.

Brown, R. (1995). *Prejudice: Its social psychology.* Cambridge, MA: Blackwell.

Bullard, S. (1996). *Teaching tolerance: Raising open-minded empathic children.* New York: Doubleday.

Byrnes, D. A., & Kiger, G. (1992). Social factors and responses to racial discrimination. *Journal of Psychology, 126,* 631-638.

Cairns, R. B., Leung, M. C., Buchanan, L., & Cairns, B. D. (1995). Friendship and social networks in childhood and adolescence: Fluidity, reliability and interrelations. *Child Development, 66,* 1330-1345.

Carlson, J. M., & Iovini, J. (1985). The transmission of racial attitudes from fathers to sons: A study of Blacks and Whites. *Adolescence, 20,* 233-237.

Cazabon, M. T., Nicoladis, E., & Lambert, W. E. (1998). *Becoming bilingual in the Amigos two-way immersion program.* Santa Cruz, CA: Center for Research on Education, Diversity, & Excellence.

Cohen, E. G., & Lotan, R. A. (1995). Producing equal-status interaction in the heterogeneous classroom. *American Educational Research Journal, 32,* 99-120.

Cook, S. W. (1985). Experimenting on social issues: The case of school desegregation. *American Psychologist, 40,* 452-460.

Culbertson, F. M. (1957). Modification of an emotionally held attitude through role-playing. *Journal of Abnormal and Social Psychology, 54,* 230-233.

Dei, G. J. S. (1996). *Anti-racism education: Theory and practice.* Halifax, Canada: Fernwood.

Derman-Sparks, L. (1989). *Anti-bias curriculum tools for empowering young children.* Washington, DC: National Association for the Education of Young Children.

Derman-Sparks, L., & Phillips, C. B. (1997). *Teaching/learning anti-racism: A developmental approach.* New York: Teachers College, Columbia University.

Devine, P. G., Monteith, M. J., Zuwerink, J. R., & Elliot, A. J. (1991). Prejudice with and without compunction. *Journal of Personality and Social Psychology, 60,* 817-830.

Doise, W., Mugny, G., & Perret-Clermont, A. (1975). Social interaction and the development of cognitive operations. *European Journal of Social Psychology, 5,* 367-383.

Doyle, A. B., & Aboud, F. E. (1995). A longitudinal study of White children's racial prejudice as a social-cognitive development. *Merrill-Palmer Quarterly, 41,* 209-228.

DuBois, D. L., & Hirsch, B. J. (1990). School and neighbourhood friendship patterns of Blacks and Whites in early adolescence. *Child Development, 61,* 524-536.

Dweck, C. S. (1999). *Self-theories: Their role in motivation, personality, and development.* Philadelphia: Psychology Press.

Ellison, C. G., & Powers, D. A. (1994). The contact hypothesis and racial attitudes among Black Americans. *Social Science Quarterly, 75,* 385-400.

Feshbach, N. D., & Feshbach, S. (1998). Aggression in the schools: Toward reducing ethnic conflict and enhancing ethnic understanding. In P. K. Trickett & C. J. Schellenbach (Eds.), *Violence against children in the family and the community* (pp. 269-286). Washington, DC: American Psychological Association.

Finlay, K. A., & Stephan, W. G. (in press). Reducing prejudice: The effects of empathy on intergroup attitudes. *Journal of Applied Social Psychology.*

Fuhr, E. (1996). *Promoting tolerance through multicultural education* (ERIC Document Reproduction Service No. ED411188).

Gavin, L. A., & Furman, W. (1989). Age differences in adolescents' perceptions of their peer groups. *Developmental Psychology, 25,* 827-834.

Genesee, F. (1987). *Learning through two languages: Studies of immersion and bilingual education.* Boston: Heinle & Heinle.

Genesee, F., & Gandara, P. (in press). Bilingual education programs: A cross-national perspective. *Journal of Social Issues.*

Gimmestad, B. J., & De Chiara, E. (1982). Dramatic plays: A vehicle for prejudice reduction in the elementary school. *Journal of Educational Research, 76,* 45-49.

Glasberg, R., & Aboud, F. E. (1981). A developmental perspective on the study of depression: Children's evaluative reactions to sadness. *Developmental Psychology, 17,* 195-202.

Graham, J. A., Cohen, R., Zbikowski, S. M., & Secrist, M. E. (1998). A longitudinal investigation of race and sex as factors in childrens' classroom friendship choices. *Child Study Journal, 28,* 245-266.

Graves, S. B. (1996). Diversity on television. In T. MacBeth (Ed.), *Tuning in to young viewers* (pp.61-86). Thousand Oaks, CA: Sage.

Hallinan, M. T. (1982). Classroom racial composition and children's friendships. *Social Forces, 61,* 56-72.

Hallinan, M. T., & Teixeira, R. A. (1987a). Students' interracial friendships: Individual characteristics, structural effects and racial differences. *American Journal of Education, 95,* 563-583.

Hawkins, J. A. (1995). Technology for tolerance. *Teaching Tolerance, 4,* 16-21.

Heller, C., & Hawkins, J. A. (1994). Teaching tolerance: Notes from the front line. *Teachers College Record, 95,* 337-368.

Hohn, R. L. (1973). Perceptual training and its effect on racial preference of kindergarten children. *Psychological Reports, 32,* 435-441.

Jackman, M. R., & Crane, M. (1986). "Some of my best friends are Black...": Interracial friendship and Whites' racial attitudes. *Public Opinion Quarterly, 50,* 459-486.

Johnson, D. W., Johnson, R. T., Dudley, B., & Acikgoz, K. (1994). Effects of conflict resolution training on elementary school children. *Journal of Social Psychology, 134,* 803-817.

Johnson, D. W., Johnson, R. T., Dudley, B., & Magnuson, D. (1995). Training elementary school students to manage conflict. *Journal of Social Psychology, 135,* 673-686.

Katz, P. A. (1973). Stimulus predifferentiation and modification of children's racial attitudes. *Child Development, 44,* 232-237.

Katz, P. A. (1976). The acquisition of racial attitudes in children. In P. A. Katz (Ed.), *Towards the elimination of racism* (pp.125-154). New York: Pergamon.

Katz, P. A., Acosta, D. W., Bartlett, M., & Arango, S. (1999). *Fostering positive intergroup attitudes in young children.* Unpublished manuscript, Institute for Research on Social Problems, Boulder, CO.

Katz, P. A., & Kofkin, J. A. (1997). Race, gender, and young children. In S. S. Luthar, J. A. Burack, D. Cicchetti, & J. Weisz (Eds.), *Developmental psychopathology: Perspectives on adjustment, risk and disorder* (pp. 51-74). New York: Cambridge University Press.

Katz, P. A., Sohn, M., & Zalk, S. R. (1975). Perceptual concomitant of racial attitudes in urban grade-school children. *Developmental Psychology, 11,* 135-144.

Katz, P. A., & Zalk, S. R. (1978). Modification of children's racial attitudes. *Developmental Psychology, 14,* 447-461.

Kehoe, J. W., & Mansfield, E. (1993). The limitations of multicultural education and anti-racist education. In K. A. McLeod (Ed.), *Multicultural education: The state of the art* (pp. 3-8). Toronto: University of Toronto Press.

Klein, T. E. (1992). *Teaching tolerance: Prejudice awareness and reduction in secondary schools* (ERIC Document Reproduction Service No. ED356165).

Kofkin, J. A., Katz, P. A., & Downey, E. P. (1995, April). *Family discourse about race and the development of children's racial attitudes.* Paper presented at Society for Research in Child Development meeting, Indianapolis.

Lambert, W. E., Genesee, F., Holobow, N., & Chartrand, L. (1993). Bilingual education for majority English-speaking children. *European Journal of Psychology of Education, 8,* 3-22.

Lambert, W. E., & Klineberg, O. (1967). *Children's views of foreign peoples: A cross-national study.* New York: Appleton-Century-Crofts.

Lambert, W. E., & Cazabon, M. T. (1994). *Students' views of the Amigos program.* Santa Cruz, CA: Center for Research on Education, Diversity, & Excellence.

Laperrière, A. (1989). *La construction sociale des relations interethniques et interraciales chez les adolescent(e)s.* Unpublished manuscript, Université du Quebec à Montreal.

Latane, B. (1981). The psychology of social impact. *American Psychologist, 36,* 343-356.

Lessing, E. E., & Clarke, C. C. (1976). An attempt to reduce ethnic prejudice and assess its correlates in a junior high school sample. *Educational Research Quarterly, 1,* 3-16.

Levy, S. R. (in press). Reducing prejudice: Lessons from cognitive factors underlying perceiver differences in prejudice. *Journal of Social Issues.*

Levy, S. R., & Dweck, C. S. (1998). Trait- versus process-focused social judgment. *Social Cognition, 16,* 151-172.

Levy, S. R., & Dweck, C. S. (in press). The impact of children's static vs. dynamic conceptions of people on stereotype formation. *Child Development.*

Levy, S. R., Stroessner, S. J., & Dweck, C. S. (1998). Stereotype formation and endorsement: The role of implicit theories. *Journal of Personality and Social Psychology, 74,* 1421-1436.

Litcher, J. H., & Johnson, D. W. (1969). Changes in attitudes toward Negroes of White elementary school students after use of multiethnic readers. *Journal of Educational Psychology, 60,* 148-152.

Litcher, J. H., Johnson, D. W., & Ryan, F. L. (1973). Use of pictures of multiethnic interaction to change attitudes of White elementary school students toward Blacks. *Psychological Reports, 33,* 367-372.

Madge, N. J. (1976).Context and the expressed ethnic preferences of infant school children. *Journal of Child Psychology and Psychiatry, 17,* 337-344.

McGregor, J. (1993). Effectiveness of role playing and anti-racist teaching in reducing student prejudice. *Journal of Educational Research, 86,* 215-226.

Mileski, J. (1998). *The outcome of teaching tolerance: A research report* (ERIC Document Reproduction Service No. ED425101).

Miller, N. (1983). Peer relations in desegregated schools. In J. L. Epstein & N. Karweit (Eds.), *Friends in school* (pp. 201-217). New York: Academic Press.

Moran, C. E., & Hakuta, K. (1995). Bilingual education: Broadening research perspectives. In J. A. Banks & C. A. M. Banks (Eds.), *Handbook of research on multicultural education* (pp. 445-462). New York: Macmillan.

Patchen, M. (1982). *Black-White contact in schools: Its social and academic effects.* West Lafayette, IN: Purdue University Press.

Patchen, M. (1983). Students' own racial attitudes and those of peers of both races, as related to interracial behavior. *Sociology and Social Research, 68,* 59-77.

Pate, G. S. (1995). *Prejudice reduction and the findings of research* (ERIC Document Reproduction Service No. ED383803).

Perry, D. G., & Bussy, K. (1979). The social learning theory of sex differences: Imitation is alive and well. *Journal of Personality and Social Psychology, 37,* 1699-1712.

Piaget, J., & Weil, A. M. (1951). The development in children of the idea of the homeland and of relations to other countries. *International Social Science Journal, 3,* 561-578.

Peters, W. (Producer & Director). (1971). *The eye of the storm.* [Film]. New York: American Broadcasting Company.

Schofield, J. W. (1982). *Black and White in school: Trust, tension, or tolerance?* New York: Praeger.

Schofield, J. W. (1995). Review of research on school desegregation's impact on elementary and secondary school students. In J. A. Banks & C. A. M. Banks (Eds.), *Handbook of research on multicultural education* (pp. 597-616). New York: Macmillan.

Slaby, R. G. (1999). *Above prejudice and beyond tolerance: A bystander approach to reducing prejudice and improving intergroup relations.* Newton, MA: Final report to Carnegie Foundation.

Slavin, R. E., & Madden, N. A. (1979). School practices that improve race relations. *American Educational Research Journal, 16,* 169-180.

Sleeter, C. E., & Grant, C. A. (1987). An analysis of multicultural education in the United States. *Harvard Educational Review, 57,* 421-444

Sleeter, C. E., & Grant, C. A. (1994). *Making choices for multicultural education.* New York: Macmillan.

Stephan, W. G. (1999). *Improving intergroup relations in the schools.* New York: Columbia Teachers College Press.

Tatum, B. D. (1997). *"Why are all the Black kids sitting together in the cafeteria?" and other conversations about race.* New York: Basic Books.

Thomson, B. J. (1993). *Words can hurt you: Beginning a program of anti-bias education.* New York: Addison-Wesley.

Washburn, D. E. (1996). *Multicultural education in the United States.* Philadelphia: Inquiry International.

Weigel, R. H., Wiser, P. L., & Cook, S. W. (1975). The impact of cooperative learning experiences on cross-ethnic relations and attitudes. *Journal of Social Issues, 31*(1), 219-244.

Weiner, M. J., & Wright, F. E. (1973). Effects of undergoing arbitrary discrimination upon subsequent attitudes toward a minority group. *Journal of Applied Psychology, 3,* 94-102.

Williams, J. E., Best, D. L., Boswell, D. A., Mattson, L. A., & Graves, D. J. (1975). Preschool Racial Attitude Measure II. *Educational and Psychological Measurement, 35,* 3-18.

Yawkey, T. D. (1973). Attitudes toward Black Americans held by rural and urban White early childhood subjects based upon multi-ethnic social studies materials. *Journal of Negro Education, 42,* 164-169.

13 Moderators and Mediators of Prejudice Reduction in Multicultural Education

Michele A. Wittig
Ludwin Molina
California State University, Northridge

The contact hypothesis (Allport, 1954/1979) is among the most often researched psychological principles for reducing racial/ethnic prejudice (Brewer & Brown, 1998; Cook, 1985; Pettigrew, 1986; Stephan & Brigham, 1985). It emphasizes the social situation, aims to change individual prejudiced attitudes, and proposes several conditions necessary for intergroup contact to be successful in reducing prejudice and enhancing tolerance. Prominent among these conditions in Allport's original formulation were:

1. normative support by authority figures;
2. equal status of participants within the situation (e.g., via role assignments);
3. cooperative interdependence among participants; and
4. individualized association or personal contact (e.g., having the potential to promote friendships).

In this chapter, our contribution to the literature on contact theory is threefold. First, we consider two paradoxes: (1) Is intergroup contact a problem that precipitates racial/ethnic conflict or a solution to it? and (2) Is social recategorzation a positive or a negative influence on interracial/ethnic prejudice? Both paradoxes are based on the premise that contact between racial/ethnic and other culturally-distinct groups is likely to bring their respective values, traditions, perspectives, or interests into potential competition. Using the moderator-mediator distinction of Baron and Kenny (1986), we conceptualize the first dilemma as asking about the nature and the sign of important moderators of the contact–prejudice relationship, and the second as specifying competing views of the mediators of this relationship. Both paradoxes have implications for the design, implementation, and evaluation of multicultural educational programs.

The second part of the chapter presents results from a theory-based program evaluation that built on the answers proposed for the above dilemmas. Using data from participants in a multicultural educational program, we tested two alternative models of the psychological processes that mediate between Allport's conditions of contact and individual changes in intergroup prejudice. The first model emphasized the mediating role of a common (superordinate) ingroup identity, while the second stressed the mediating role of openness to other groups and racial/ethnic (subgroup) identity.

The third section of the chapter uses the principles and results presented earlier to make practical suggestions for the development and implementation of multicultural education programs designed to reduce intergroup prejudice. Moving beyond contact theory toward diversity theory (Jones, 1997, 1998; Jones, Lynch, Tenglund, & Gaertner, in press), we suggest that promoting or maintaining aspects of one's own group identity need not be a barrier to reducing intergroup prejudice, as long as openness to interactions with members of other racial/ethnic groups is fostered.

TWO PARADOXES CONFRONTING EFFORTS
TO REDUCE INTERGROUP PREJUDICE

Paradox One: Contact as the Problem or the Solution?

Although contact between culturally distinct groups often precipitates conflict, individuals who get to know each other better tend to like each other more. That is, conflict usually involves some contact between groups (suggesting a positive relationship between contact and prejudice); but also, contact, properly managed, can reduce intergroup prejudice, discrimination, and conflict (indicating a negative relation). This seeming contradiction in the direction of the correlation between contact and prejudice has been noted by a number of authors (e.g., Forbes, 1997; Pettigrew, 1998), including Allport himself (Allport, 1954/79).

To deal with this contradiction, contact theory maintains that certain third variables and their combinations explain the difference in direction of correlations between contact and prejudice obtained in different types of situations (Allport, 1954/79). The search for such third variables (i.e., various conditions of contact) can be viewed as a search for moderators of the contact–prejudice relationship, for moderators are conditions that affect the direction and/or strength of the relation between predictors and outcomes (Baron & Kenny, 1986).

Stephan and Stephan (1996) noted that the number of such potential moderating conditions has become so large and the theory has become so complex as to be a liability. In an attempt to resolve the dilemma posed by the possibility of more and more conditions of contact, Forbes (1997), a political scientist, conducted an extensive review of the empirical social science literature on the topic. He found a strong pattern of "different correlations between contact and prejudice at different levels of analysis—a negative correlation at the individual level and a positive one at the aggregate level" (pp. 194-195). His perspective brings coherence to an otherwise chaotic empirical literature by distinguishing between relationships based on (a) individual interaction, (b) groups in proximity within neighborhoods, and (c) ethnic group proportions in a population.

Forbes concluded that those who design multicultural educational programs are justified in focusing on the opportunities presented by intergroup contact at the individual level, where contact has the potential of being managed in ways that will promote positive intergroup attitudes. However, he also called attention to the increased antipathy that such contact can generate in the wider social context, due to the relative slowness of assimilation at the aggregate level (Forbes, 1997, pp. 166-169). We would add that hostilities at the aggregate level could also negatively influence attempts to construct positive intergroup contact among individuals. For both reasons, one should consider distal (e.g., neighborhood), as well as proximal (e.g., classroom and school) sources of influence when designing, implementing, and evaluating multicultural educational programs in school settings.

Pettigrew (1998) also conducted an extensive review of the social psychological literature on intergroup contact. He explained the paradoxical relationship between intergroup contact and conflict in a somewhat different way, According to his view, increased contact at a superficial level (e.g., different racial/ethnic groups migrating into a neighborhood or interacting in a work setting) may increase prejudice, but having racially diverse interpersonal associations decreases prejudice. If one assumes that Forbes' aggregate-level contact is similar to Pettigrew's superficial contact, and that Forbes' individual-level contact has a high potential for promoting Pettigrew's interpersonal associations, their two perspectives seem to be in agreement.

In sum, resolving the first contact–conflict paradox requires us to view intergroup contact as both the problem and the solution (Jones, 1997). As Pettigrew (1998) has shown, superficial contact heightens the opportunity for intergroup prejudice, as compared to no contact between groups. Noninteractive contact between individuals, and aggregate-level contact, tend to be superficial in this sense. However, under certain (moderating) conditions, individual, interactive contact can be harnessed to bring about improvement in individuals' affective intergroup attitudes. Because the conditions and effects of individual-level contact are not independent of tensions at the group level, monitoring the distal, group-level relations (e.g., in the neighborhood) is an important part of any such intervention program.

Paradox Two: Social Recategorization as
A Positive or Negative Mediator?

It has long been realized that to improve the effects of individual-level contact between members of different racial/ethnic groups, we need to understand better the psychological mediators of the intergroup contact–intergroup prejudice relationship—that is, the variables or processes by which contact influences prejudice (cf. Baron & Kenny, 1986).

Social psychologists have proposed a variety of psychological mediators of the intergroup contact–intergroup prejudice relationship. One current widely-held view is that the way the parties in an intergroup situation categorize themselves and others into social groups is critical in determining the outcome of intergroup interactions (e.g., Brewer & Brown, 1998). Accordingly, several lines of research based on social categorization theory attempt to show that getting people from the respective subgroups to (a) decategorize or personalize (Brewer & Miller, 1984), (b) recategorize or form a common ingroup identity (CII, e.g., Gaertner, Dovidio, Anastasio, Bachman, & Rust, 1993), (c) subcategorize or form distinct social identities (Hewstone & Brown, 1986), and/or (d) cross-categorize on two nonparallel dimensions (Doise, 1978) decreases intergroup prejudice and improves intergroup relations.

Beginning with classic studies by Sherif, seeing one's self and one's group as part of a larger, superordinate group has been shown to reduce intergroup prejudice. However, even those studies were not as clear-cut as is often represented (see Cherry, 1995). Furthermore, recent research suggests that recategorizing subgroup members exclusively as one superordinate group may have no effect or may even increase intergroup prejudice and discrimination (Hornsey & Hogg, in press a & b). Hornsey and Hogg (in press b) summarize three potential explanations for the outcome of increasing intergroup prejudice: (a) the recategorization is viewed as a threat to the subgroups' respective identities, (b) the subgroups may be viewed as essentially incompatible, or (c) the superordinate identity is considered to be too inclusive, triggering a countervailing need for distinctiveness (in accord with optimal distinctiveness theory—Brewer, 1991).

In brief, although laboratory studies have traditionally shown that social recategorization into a superordinate group reduces intergroup prejudice, recent evidence has highlighted its potential contradictory influence. Further research is needed to unravel this paradox. Multicultural educational theorists have much to gain from, and much to contribute to, this discussion of psychological mediators of intergroup prejudice. As Hornsey and Hogg (in press, b) suggest, multiculturalism emphasizes that people are motivated to retain their cultural heritage. If pressure to adopt a superordinate group identification can elicit feelings of threat, incompatibility, or a need for distinctiveness in natural settings, educational programs that strongly emphasize assimilation run the risk of inadvertently intensifying subgroup identities and exacerbating intergroup prejudice.

Implications

Our discussion of these two paradoxes confronting efforts to reduce intergroup prejudice suggests that: (a) multicultural education programs focusing on individual-level change are justified, though potential impacts to and from the larger sociocultural context (e.g., neighborhood conditions of contact) should not be neglected, and (b) attempts to get various ethnic group members to adopt a superordinate group identity may have potentially countervailing effects, which need to be considered when designing, implementing, and evaluating multicultural educational programs.

A TEST OF TWO MEDIATIONAL MODELS
OF INTERGROUP PREJUDICE REDUCTION

In this section, we provide a rationale for competitively testing two mediational models of intergroup prejudice reduction, and we report the method and results of such a test, conducted in the context of evaluation of a multicultural educational program.

Rationale

Much of the recent basic research on prejudice reduction that stems from Allport's original theorizing has been concerned with the psychological processes that mediate between contact conditions and reduction in intergroup bias (for reviews see Brewer & Brown, 1998; Brown & Hewstone, 1995; Jones, 1997). For example, several of the chapters in this volume (Dovidio et al.; Stephan & Stephan) present theory and data linking external conditions of contact, on the one hand, with improvements in intergroup relations on the other, and they hypothesize specific psychological processes (e.g., absence of perceived intergroup threat, blurring of intergroup boundaries, feelings of being in a common group, etc.) that mediate between them. With few exceptions (notably Dovidio, Gaertner, and their colleagues), researchers have failed to assess participants' own perceptions of the situational conditions of contact.

Meanwhile, applied research in elementary and secondary schools has tended to focus on which educational policies and practices improve interracial/interethnic relations (see Fishbein, 1996 for a recent review). The term *multicultural education* in this context refers to both an educational philosophy and a collection of policies and practices, which have often been implemented in schools across North America and in Europe. Such policies and practices include desegregation, mainstreaming, cooperative interaction, simulations, and individuation. However, systematic studies of multicultural education have been hampered by the lack of a taxonomy with which to characterize similarities and differences between programs.

Cashmore's (1996) *Dictionary of Race Relations* described multicultural education as education that is concerned with meeting "the particular educational needs of ethnic minority children," as well as "preparing all children for life in a multicultural society" (p. 107). A useful articulation of the concept as it is applied in organizations more generally (not only schools) was provided by Bendick, Egan, and Lofhjelm (1998), based on categories developed by Wrench and Taylor (1993). Bendick et al.'s (1998) taxonomy crosses four training strategies (information provision, attitude change, behavior change, and organizational change) with three types of training content (multicultural, antidiscrimination/antiracist, and broader issues).

In sum, little theoretically based, controlled research has been done on the extent to which students' own perceptions of their classroom, school, or neighborhood interracial climate predicts their interracial/interethnic attitudes and behaviors. In particular, theory-based research on the potential of multicultural education to reduce interracial/interethnic prejudice has been neglected.

In this section we summarize research that bridges this gap between basic and applied research on interracial prejudice reduction. We then present a theory-based study of multicultural education, which uses data from a multicultural educational program (RAP—Racial Awareness Program) to test two alternative models of the psychological processes that mediate between interracial contact and prejudice reduction. These models are: the Common Ingroup Identity (CII) model (Gaertner, Dovidio, Anastasio, Bachman, & Rust, 1993; Gaertner, Rust, Dovidio, Bachman, & Anastasio, 1994), and one based on Outgroup Orientation and Ethnic Identity (OO/EI).

The analyses we report here focus on the psychological processes that mediate between Allport's four conditions of contact and students' intergroup affective bias. We are also interested in the strength of the relationship between students' perceptions of the conditions of contact and their affective intergroup bias.

The Common Ingroup Identity (CII) Mediator
Model of Intergroup Bias Reduction

The CII model of prejudice reduction proposes that "the conditions for successful contact, in part, transform members' cognitive representations of the memberships from separate groups to one, more inclusive group" (Gaertner et al., 1994, p. 226). Gaertner and his colleagues (1994) designed a school-based field study that assessed whether common ingroup identity mediates between student perceptions of the conditions of contact and intergroup affective bias. They analyzed one-time survey data from approximately 1,400 U.S. high school students.

Using a special series of multiple regressions (outlined by Baron & Kenny, 1986; Judd & Kenny, 1981), Gaertner et al. (1994) provided modest support for the mediating role of common ingroup identity. They showed (a) that items tapping perceptions of being in "one group" and "on the same team" as other students accounted for 2% of the variance in Affective Intergroup Bias, after student perceptions of School Interracial Climate were taken into account, and (b) that the perceptions of School Interracial Climate related significantly less strongly to Affective Bias when the Common Ingroup Identity variables were included in the analysis. The R^2 of the full model was 12% ($p < .001$). Unfortunately, this research lacked pre- and post-intervention data, precluding an assessment of change and a direct test of the authors' claim of a mediational role for CII.

The Outgroup Orientation Mediator
Model of Intergroup Bias Reduction

Our framework for explaining how interracial contact conditions influence changes in student affective bias was developed in the context of multicultural education and theories of acculturation. It assumes that one's own ethnic identity and openness to other racial/ethnic groups need not be in opposition. Consistent with this view, Berry, Trimble, and Olmedo (1986) proposed a conceptual framework that emphasized two central issues in the process of acculturation: (a) one's degree of concern with maintenance of one's cultural identity and characteristics, and (b) one's degree of concern for developing and maintaining relationships with other groups. According to this framework, one can vary along each of these two dimensions independently, resulting in four varieties of acculturation. *Assimilation* means being low on (a) and high on (b), while *separation* is indicated by the opposite pattern. *Integration* means being high on both, and *marginalization* is indicated by being low on both (Berry, Trimble, & Olmedo, 1986, p. 307). We use the terms "ethnic identity" and "outgroup orientation," respectively, for these psychological constructs, and we employ them as potential mediators between conditions of intergroup contact and prejudice reduction.

Phinney (1992) conceptualized outgroup orientation as one's attitude toward other racial/ethnic groups and proposed that it interacts with ethnic identity "as a factor in one's social identity in the larger society" (p. 161; see also Tajfel & Turner, 1986). Phinney's Multigroup Ethnic Identity Measure (MEIM), designed for use with racial/ethnic majority group members as well as minorities, includes scales tapping several aspects of ethnic identity and one scale assessing outgroup orientation.

In this chapter, we propose and test a three-part model of intergroup prejudice reduction. The predictors are the target respondents' perceptions of four interracial contact conditions, corresponding to Allport's main dimensions of contact. Situations that are perceived as high on these dimensions are expected to promote greater openness to interactions with people from other racial/ethnic groups. This outgroup orientation is predicted to be at least a partial mediator between the external conditions and reduction in intergroup affective prejudice. The potential mediating influence of ethnic identity is also explored in the present study.

Description of the RAP Multicultural Education Program

The RAP program (a pseudonym) is a school-based intervention designed by educators (Sauceda, Guillean, & McKenna, 1998) to increase students' comfort in talking about racial issues, to decrease their racial and ethnic prejudice, stereotyping, and discrimination, and to promote their appreciation of the equal worth of different ethnic groups. This school-district-approved program trains college students during a one-day, six-hour session. Following training, they are placed in mixed-race pairs to lead a series of eight weekly one-hour sessions for students in middle- and high-school classrooms throughout Los Angeles County, using a common curriculum guide. All discussions take place during regular class time in the presence of the regular classroom teacher. In this study, most target classes consisted of 30 to 40 students and received eight sessions, but some classes received as few as four sessions due to academic schedule conflicts. In brief, the program encompasses information about the history and contributions of various racial/ethnic groups in the U.S., antidiscrimination and antiracist concepts, cultural awareness training, training for equal treatment, and respect for all racial/ethnic groups. Overall, the RAP curriculum aims to initiate discussions among middle- and high-school students and their facilitators, dealing with the concept of race (Sauceda, Gillean, & McKenna, 1998).

INITIAL STUDY

The present research extends the work of Gaertner et al. (1994) in several ways. First we attempt to replicate their finding of a mediating role for CII among students in our sample, separately at Time 1 (prior to their RAP participation) and at Time 2 (at the conclusion of their RAP participation). Then we test a model of prejudice reduction that proposes a mediating role for Outgroup Orientation (OO) and Ethnic Identity (EI). Third, we competitively test Gaertner et al.'s CII model versus the alternative OO/EI model, using combined data from Time 1 and Time 2 (prior to and following student participation in the prejudice reduction program). This last procedure allows for a more powerful mediational test than Time-1 or Time-2 analyses alone. While similar in important respects to Gaertner et al.'s (1994) original field test of the CII, our database is an improvement over theirs in two respects: (1) pre-post assessments, rather than one-time data are used; and (2) a validated assessment of intergroup affective bias is used as the dependent variable.

Participants

Participants were 796 middle- and high-school students (46% male and 54% female) from various schools in Los Angeles County. They were included in the study if they provided at least some responses to both pre- and post-intervention surveys as part of their participation in the Racial Awareness Program (RAP). The participants' mean age was 15 years. Based on self-reports, they were 18% Asian American, 15% African American, 31% Hispanic American, 19% non-Hispanic White, 2% Native American, 7% multiracial, 4% Middle Eastern, 4% missing, and 1% Other.

Procedure

At the conclusion of the training session for college students, the newly trained facilitators were given packets of pre- and post-intervention surveys to deliver to the school teachers. The teachers were asked to administer them to students, seal them in envelopes, and return them to the facilitators, who returned the sealed envelopes to the researchers. Participants completed a self-report questionnaire assessing their racial attitudes and experiences at the beginning of the first of the eight weekly one-hour classes, and an identical questionnaire at the end of the last RAP class. The questionnaire consisted of six sections on three pages. Except for demographic questions, all items used a 7-point Likert format ranging from 1 ("Strongly Disagree") to 7 ("Strongly Agree"). Further procedural information is presented by Wittig and Grant-Thompson (1998).

Measures

Predictor Variables. The predictor variables consisted of 13 items adapted from Green, Adams, and Turner's (1988) School Interracial Climate Scale, making up four subscales of several items each. Wording changes were made to make the items more suitable for use with a more racially and ethnically diverse sample. Each subscale assessed perceptions of the school's interracial climate along one of the four dimensions specified by the contact hypothesis. Items retained for use in the present study were ones that had the highest loadings on their respective factors when administered to a sample of RAP students the semester prior to the present study. Illustrative items from each of the four subscales were:

1. Teachers encourage students to make friends with students of different races. (Norms)
2. Teachers at this school are fair to students of all races. (Equal Status)
3. Students of different races at my school are all working together for the same things. (Interdependence)
4. My friends would think badly of me if I ate lunch with students of a different race. (Individualized Association, reverse scored)

Answers to the 13 items comprising the School Interracial Climate Scale were averaged to form a composite School Interracial Climate (SIC) score at Time 1 and again at Time 2. The Time-1 assessment was used as a predictor in the subsequent model testing.

Mediator Variables. The Common Ingroup Identity (CII) mediating variables comprised four items (identical to those used by Gaertner et al., 1994). The items assessed student perceptions of "one group," "on the same team," "different groups," and "individuals" within their school. These items were:

1. Despite the different groups at this school, there is frequently the sense that we are all just one group.
2. Although there are different groups of students at this school, it feels as though we are all playing on the same team.
3. At this school, it usually feels as though we belong to different groups.
4. At this school, it usually feels as though we are individuals and not members of any particular group.

The Outgroup Orientation and Ethnic Identity mediating variables (Phinney, 1992) consisted of eight items, four tapping each concept. The full scale of 20 items had been administered to a sample of RAP students the semester prior to the present study, and the items retained for use here had the highest loadings on their respective factors. Outgroup Orientation (OO) was assessed by averaging responses to the following items:

1. I like meeting and getting to know people from ethnic groups other than my own.
2. I often spend time with people from ethnic groups other than my own.
3. I am involved in activities with people from other ethnic groups.
4. I enjoy being around people from ethnic groups other than my own.

Ethnic Identity (EI) was measured by averaging responses to the following items, which Phinney (1992) used to tap "affirmation/belonging" to one's own ethnic group:

1. I am happy that I am a member of the group I belong to.
2. I have a strong sense of belonging to my own ethnic group.
3. I have a lot of pride in my own ethnic group and its accomplishments.
4. I feel a strong attachment towards my own ethnic group.

Criterion Variable. The criterion variable was students' intergroup Affective Bias at Time 2. Affective Bias was measured by three items from the Quick Discrimination Index, affective subscale (QDI—Ponterroto, 1995). The seven items comprising the original subscale had been administered to a sample of RAP students the semester prior to the present study, and the three items retained were the ones that showed the highest factor loadings for that sample. They were:

1. I feel I could develop an intimate relationship with someone from a different race (reverse scored).
2. I would feel O.K. about my son or daughter dating someone from a different race (reverse scored).
3. I think it is better if people marry within their own race.

Descriptive Statistics

Means, standard deviations, and Cronbach's alphas for the predictor, mediator, and outcome variables at Time 1 and Time 2 are presented in Table 13.1, together with Time-1 versus Time-2 *t*-tests. The data show that Affective Bias increased, while School Interracial Climate and Ethnic Identity decreased; perceptions of being on the "Same Team" with other students in the school decreased, while perceptions of themselves as "Individuals" increased.

Although our focus here is on theory-based model testing, rather than on the utility of the RAP program, the increase in Affective Bias underscores the need to revise the RAP program. Students in the control classrooms, who received regular instruction from a credentialed teacher during the times that the target students participated in college-student-led discussions, showed no change on any of these variables except for a decrease in perceptions of themselves as "Individuals."

Correlations among the variables measured at Time 1 and Time 2 are presented in Table 13.2.

Initial Tests of the Common Ingroup Identity Mediation Model Within Time Periods

In preliminary analyses within each time period (Molina & Wittig, 1999), we attempted to replicate Gaertner et al.'s (1994) finding that CII functions as a mediator between School Interracial Climate and Affective Bias within each time period. Using techniques summarized by Kenny, Kashy, and Bolger (1998), we found that mediational analyses of the Time-1 data replicated both the relatively

TABLE 13.1
Cronbach's Alphas, Means, Standard Deviations, and
t-test Values for the Main Variables at Time 1 and Time 2

Variable	α	Time 1 M	SD	α	Time 2 M	SD	t
Affective Bias	.73	3.02	1.61	.72	3.24	1.57	4.07***
School Interracial Climate	.81	5.10	0.98	.84	4.96	0.99	-3.49***
Outgroup Orientation	.73	5.15	1.33	.79	5.16	1.38	0.25
Ethnic Identity	.77	5.68	1.25	.83	5.58	1.32	-2.00*
Common Ingroup Identity							
One Group		4.55	1.85		4.49	1.80	-0.75
Same Team		4.87	1.77		4.72	1.72	-1.99*
Different Groups		4.06	1.82		4.17	1.79	1.21
Individuals		3.93	1.81		4.16	1.72	2.74**

Note. Only participants who answered items on a given scale at both Time 1 and Time 2 are included (N = 540-692). *p < .05. **p < .01. ***p < .001.

TABLE 13.2
Intercorrelations of Predictor, Mediator, and
Outcome Variables at Time 1 and Time 2 ($N = 428$)

Variable	1	2	3	4	5	6	7	8	9	10	11	12	13	14	15	16
Time 1																
1. Affective Bias	--															
2. School Interracial Climate	-.35	--														
3. One Group	-.23	.41	--													
4. Same Team	-.26	.53	.44	--												
5. Different Groups	.14	-.26	-.12	-.25	--											
6. Individuals	-.04	.19	.00	.06	-.07	--										
7. Outgroup Orientation	-.53	.48	.25	.30	-.10	.14	--									
8. Ethnic Identity	.07	.18	.08	.06	.04	.02	.13	--								
Time 2																
9. Affective Bias	.68	-.27	-.19	-.21	.06	.02	-.44	.00	--							
10. School Interracial Climate	-.30	.57	.28	.34	-.18	.09	.42	.14	-.40	--						
11. One Group	-.13	.30	.40	.27	-.15	.01	.19	.01	-.18	.45	--					
12. Same Team	-.17	.37	.27	.35	-.19	.04	.21	.07	-.23	.55	.46	--				
13. Different Groups	.10	-.09	-.08	-.13	.33	-.01	-.02	.04	.19	-.20	-.17	-.22	--			
14. Individuals	-.03	.15	.12	.17	-.13	.24	.17	-.02	.01	.14	.19	.16	.01	--		
15. Outgroup Orientation	-.44	.37	.20	.26	-.07	.02	.65	.10	-.53	.54	.23	.26	-.10	.15	--	
16. Ethnic Identity	.03	.19	.06	.13	.00	-.08	.11	.53	-.06	.26	.06	.17	.06	.04	.26	--

Note. $r = .095$ ($p < .05$); $r = .126$ ($p < .01$); $r = .158$ ($p < .001$).

large magnitudes and the direction of relationships between School Interracial Climate and CII. The R^2 for their data was 12% ($p < .001$), while our data produced an R^2 = 14% ($p < .001$) for the pre-intervention CII model. However, the modest support that Gaertner et al. had found for the role of CII in mediating the School Interracial Climate–Affective Bias relationship (R^2 = 2%, $p < .0001$) was not replicated in our pre-intervention data (R^2 = 1.4%, ns).

The same analyses were performed on Time-2 data. Again, we replicated both the magnitude and direction of relationships between School Interracial Climate and CII. Our data produced an R^2 = 20% ($p < .001$) for the post-intervention CII model. Once again, we found no support for the role of CII in mediating the School Interracial Climate–Affective Bias relationship (R^2 = 0.9%, ns). In summary, neither our pre- nor post-intervention series of mediational analyses revealed any support for a significant mediating role of CII.

**Competitive Test of the CII Versus OO/EI
Mediation Models Across Time**

Two series of regressions were performed to compare the CII versus OO/EI mediation models across time. Each series assessed whether the proposed mediators for a given model function both as outcomes of School Interracial Climate (SIC), as well as antecedents of Affective Bias (ABias). The amount of mediation was assessed by, in effect, demonstrating that the influence of SIC on ABias when the proposed mediators were simultaneously considered was significantly less than the influence of SIC on ABias when the proposed mediators were not in the equation (Kenny, Kashy, & Bolger, 1998).

Each series of regressions included three steps corresponding to the following conditions:

(1) SIC predicts ABias (when the proposed mediators are not in the equation);
(2) SIC influences the proposed mediators (CII or OO/EI scales); and
(3) the proposed mediators influence ABias, when SIC and the proposed mediators are considered simultaneously.

Test of Common Ingroup Identity Mediation Model. So as to facilitate direct comparisons of magnitudes of influence, Figure 13.1 shows the standardized coefficients, and their respective signs, along with other aspects of the test of the CII model.

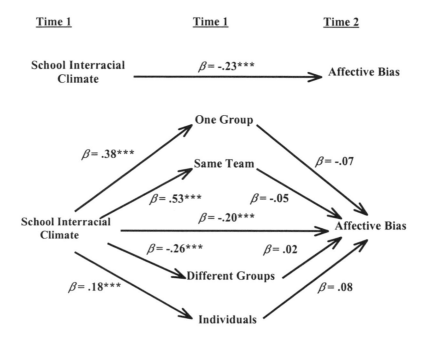

Time 1   Time 1   Time 2

School Interracial $\beta = -.23^{***}$ Affective Bias
Climate

One Group

$\beta = .38^{***}$ Same Team $\beta = -.07$

$\beta = .53^{***}$ $\beta = -.05$

School Interracial $\beta = -.20^{***}$ Affective Bias
Climate

$\beta = -.26^{***}$ $\beta = .02$

Different Groups

$\beta = .18^{***}$ $\beta = .08$

Individuals

FIG. 13.1. Mediation of school interracial climate on affective bias by common in-group identity items (i.e., one group, same team, different groups, and individuals). $N = 558$, $R^2 = .069$, $***p < .001$.

Steps in this series, and their results were as follows ($N = 558$ for all equations):

(1)   Time 1   Time 2
         SIC $\longrightarrow$ Abias $r^2 = 5.5\%$ $p < .001$

(2)   Time 1   Time 1
         SIC $\longrightarrow$ One Group $r^2 = 14.3\%$
         SIC $\longrightarrow$ Same Team $r^2 = 27.9\%$ $p < .001$
         SIC $\longrightarrow$ Different Groups $r^2 = 6.5\%$
         SIC $\longrightarrow$ Individuals $r^2 = 3.4\%$

(3) CII at Time 1 failed to predict Abias at Time 2, when SIC at Time 1 was taken into account simultaneously.

         Time 1   Time 2
         SIC
         One Group   overall
         Same Team   ABias $R^2 = 6.9\%$ $p = .001$
         Different Groups
         Individuals

Although step 2 showed a significant relationship between SIC and the proposed mediators, step 3 showed that none of the proposed mediators significantly predicted Affective Bias. The r^2 for the four CII variables was 1.4% ($p = ns$). Therefore, mediation was ruled out.

Test of Outgroup Orientation / Ethnic Identity Mediation Model. A second series of regressions tested the OO/EI mediation model. As before, Figure 13.2 shows the standardized coefficients and their respective signs, for this test.

Steps in this series, and their results were as follows ($N = 544$ for all equations):

(1)   <u>Time 1</u>   <u>Time 2</u>

      SIC $\longrightarrow$ Abias $r^2 = 6.9\%$ $p < .001$

(Results are somewhat different than for the first step of the previous series, due to the different N of cases. The N of cases is consistent within each series, but different between series, due to different responsiveness to various parts of the survey.)

(2)   <u>Time 1</u>   <u>Time 1</u>

      SIC $\longrightarrow$ Outgroup Orientation $r^2 = 18.8\%$ $p < .001$

      SIC $\longrightarrow$ Ethnic Identity $r^2 = 3.0\%$ $p < .001$

(3)   OO/EI at Time 1 did predict ABias at Time 2 when SIC at Time 1 was taken into account simultaneously.

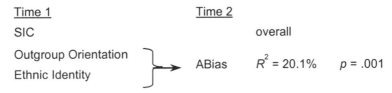

              <u>Time 1</u>   <u>Time 2</u>

              SIC   overall

              Outgroup Orientation   ABias $R^2 = 20.1\%$ $p = .001$

              Ethnic Identity

Because step 2 showed that each of the proposed mediators was influenced by School Interracial Climate, and step 3 showed that at least one of the proposed mediators significantly predicted Affective Bias, mediation was possible. Therefore, a final step was performed. It assessed the significance of the proposed predictor-to-mediator coefficient as well as of the proposed mediator-to-outcome coefficient for each proposed mediator (Kenny, Kashy, & Bolger, 1998). Our results showed that each of these two coefficients for Outgroup Orientation was significantly different from zero ($Z = -7.16$, $p < .001$); and the corresponding two coefficients for Ethnic Identity were also significantly different from zero ($Z = 2.05$, $p < .05$). The r^2 of the Outgroup Orientation / Ethnic Identity variables was 13.2% ($p = .001$).

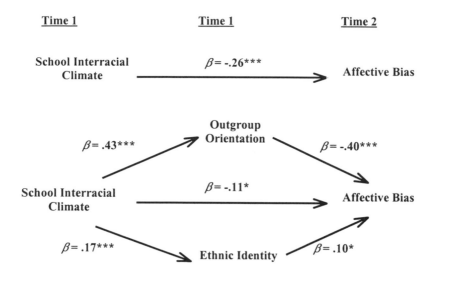

FIG 13.2 Mediation of school interracial climate effect on affective bias by outgroup orientation and ethnic identity. N = 544, R^2 = .201, *p< .05, **p< .01, ***p < .001.

Hierarchical Multiple Regression of Post-Intervention Affective Bias

A hierarchical multiple regression provided an overview of the importance of pre- and post-intervention School Interracial Climate, pre- and post-intervention Out-group Orientation and Ethnic Identity, as well as of pre-intervention Affective Bias as predictors of post-intervention Affective Bias. The order of entry of vari- ables reflected the hypothesized chronological sequence of influence. Results are shown in Table 13.3. Each step added significantly to the prediction of post- intervention Affective Bias. The R^2 of the hierarchical Outgroup Orientation / Ethnic Identity model was 56%.

Discussion of Competitive Model Testing

Using data from middle- and high-school students who participated in a racial awareness program in a multiethnic school setting, we showed that common in- group identity did not mediate between their perceptions of the school interracial climate at the inception of the program and their affective intergroup bias at its conclusion. Instead, support was obtained for the alternative model, which em phasized participants' outgroup orientation and, to a lesser extent, their ethnic identity, as mediators of this relationship. Because the mediational analyses re- ported here used variables assessed at Time 1 to predict affective intergroup

TABLE 13.3
Hierarchical Multiple Regression of
Post-Intervention Affective Bias on Major Predictors (N = 457)

Step and Variable	R^2	ΔR^2	ΔF
1. School Interracial Climate (Time 1)	.08	.08	36.89***
2. Outgroup Orientation & Ethnic Identity (Time 1)	.20	.12	34.99***
3. Affective Bias (Time 1)	.49	.29	253.68***
4. School Interracial Climate (Time 2)	.53	.04	38.72***
5. Outgroup Orientation & Ethnic Identity (Time 2)	.56	.03	14.80***

***p < .001.

bias at Time 2, we can be confident that the pre-intervention outgroup orientation and ethnic identity constructs influenced post-intervention affective bias, rather than the reverse.

Two psychological constructs mediated affective bias in the present study. The more important aspect was one's openness to other ethnic groups, as evidenced by the reported extent of day-to-day interactions with other racial/ethnic groups and the attitudes held toward these interactions. In predicting affective intergroup prejudice, the beta weights showed that this orientation to outgroups was about four times as important as the other mediating variables, affirmation of and feelings of belonging to one's own ethnic group.

There are several possible reasons for the absence of support for Gaertner et al.'s (1994) common ingroup identity model in the present data. First, we employed a pre- and post-intervention design that allowed an assessment of *change* in prejudice, whereas Gaertner et al.'s one-time-only assessment could only assess differences between respondents, rather than changes in prejudice. Second, our measure of affective bias was different from the one developed and used by Gaertner et al. (1994). We used a subset of items from a scale of intergroup affective discrimination, validated in 1995, which was not available to Gaertner et al. (1994). Third, their sample was two-thirds non-Hispanic Whites, as compared to our sample, which was only 19% non-Hispanic Whites. Fourth, samples drawn several years apart and from different parts of the U.S. may have been different in other respects as well. We note, however, that all the relations Gaertner et al. found—except a significant mediational role for perception of group cohesiveness—were reconfirmed in our data. In addition, the amount of variance in affective bias accounted for by the group cohesiveness measure was about the same in both studies: 2% (p < .0001) in the Gaertner et al. (1994)

study and 1.4% (p = ns) in the present research. In our opinion, differences in statistical significance between the two studies were mainly due to differences in sample size (about 1165 vs. 550 respondents, respectively).

The hierarchical multiple regression across time demonstrated the importance of Allport's moderating conditions and our mediating psychological process variables in predicting intergroup affective bias. The outgroup orientation/ethnic identity mediational analysis and its accompanying hierarchical regression showed a significant negative relationship between student perceptions of school-based interracial conditions and intergroup prejudice—a finding that supports Allport's conception of contact theory in this context. As expected, students' openness to other groups was negatively related to their intergroup affective bias. Ethnic identity played less of a mediating role, but acted in the direction of increasing such bias.

A FOLLOW-UP STUDY

Rationale

Although the original RAP evaluation provided important information from a theory-testing perspective, the program showed mixed results with respect to changing student intergroup attitudes. The target students' mean affective bias significantly increased from week 1 to week 8, while for the approximately 100 control students, there was no change. There was no improvement in openness to cross-racial friendships in either group. However, the target group showed significantly greater improvement in reported comfort in talking about racial issues from Time 1 to Time 2, F (1, 773) = 77.5, p < .001. The mean level of comfort for participating RAP students at the end of the intervention was 5.2, as compared to the non-RAP controls' mean of 4.7, after adjusting for initial differences in comfort level.

Intriguing findings came from an examination of attitude change among the 42 college-student facilitators (33% male and 67% female), who completed relevant items on brief pre- and post-facilitation surveys about ten weeks apart. The sample included 10% Asian Americans, 5% African Americans, 19% Hispanic Americans, 45% Euro Americans, and 19% multiracial respondents (2% declined to respond). Their mean age was 21 years. In contrast to the target students, the facilitators showed large improvements on the three outcomes designed to assess intergroup bias. A comparison of their end-of-training to end-of-intervention agreement with the following statements indicated:

1. "White people's racism constitutes a major problem in America."
   Mean at Time 1 = 2.6; mean at Time 2 = 5.9 (t = 9.30, df = 42, p < .001).
2. "I feel comfortable talking about racial/ethnic issues."
   Mean at Time 1 = 2.2; mean at Time 2 = 6.4 (t = 15.59, df = 41, p < .001).

3. "My friendship network is very racially mixed."
   Mean at Time 1 = 2.1; mean at Time 2 = 6.6 (t = 12.57, df = 41, p < .001).

These results led us to develop and test a modified intervention, while retaining the original curriculum (Wittig & Molina, 1999). The modification was designed to engage the target students as peer discussion leaders, in an effort to achieve a similar degree of success as had been obtained with the college-student discussion leaders in the original study.

Participants

Participants consisted of 202 students (46% male, 40% female, 14% no response) in one of five classes taught by one teacher in a Los Angeles County high school. They were included in the study if they provided at least some responses to both pre- and post-intervention surveys as part of their participation in RAP during Spring, 1999. Their mean age was 15 years. Based on self-reports, they were 20% Asian American, 4% African American, 18% Hispanic American, 25% non-Hispanic White, 1% Native American, 13% multiracial, 5% Middle Eastern, and 14% no response.

Purposes and Measures

The purposes of the follow-up study were four-fold. First, we hoped to replicate our initial results (reported above) showing outgroup orientation to be a mediator of prejudice reduction, and to test whether the smaller role played by ethnic identity would again be found, as well as to reconfirm the lack of a mediating role for common ingroup identity. Second, because the RAP program is a classroom-based intervention, special emphasis was placed on adequately measuring the classroom climate. Eleven items were adapted from the Green, Adams, and Turner (1988) School Interracial Climate scale for this purpose. They tapped very similar constructs as had been assessed at the school level in the original study, primarily by changing the word "school" to "class" or "classroom" in each item. Third, in an effort to assess more distal interracial climate conditions, we wrote and incorporated four items to tap Allport's four dimensions of intergroup contact in the students' home neighborhood. Fourth, we wished to demonstrate which method of RAP implementation (standard vs. modified) is better suited to reducing intergroup prejudice among middle- and high-school students.

Design

The design was implemented in five cultural awareness/career preparation classes taught by one social studies teacher, who uses cooperative learning strategies every day throughout each ten-week term. His classroom is furnished with 10 tables, at each of which sit three- to four-person discussion groups, mixed by race and gender, during each of the five 50-minute sessions they attend weekly. Students at each table rotate responsibility for leading class discussions during most class sessions of the academic term. This teacher's classes had received only four weeks of RAP during the previous year, due to scheduling conflicts.

Eight college-student facilitators, whose academic schedules were compatible with those of the target students, were trained as usual, and used the original RAP curriculum. Two classes received the "standard RAP," in which the college-student facilitators led the target students (seated at their usual tables in groups of three or four) in "whole group" discussion during the one hour per week they visited. Two classes received "modified RAP," in which the college-student facilitators encouraged each of the ten groups to engage in small-group discussion during part of each RAP class session, in addition to being led as a class through the session by the college-student facilitators part of the time. A fifth (control) class received a regular curriculum, without RAP, throughout the eight weeks. All classes completed pre- and post-surveys.

Results

Descriptive Statistics. Means, standard deviations, Cronbach's alphas, and Time-1 versus Time-2 t-tests for the main variables for all groups combined in this follow-up study are presented in Table 13.4. The only significant change was that the RAP students' perceptions of themselves as "One Group" with their classmates increased. In the control class, the only change on any of these variables was that students' scores on the Neighborhood Interracial Climate Scale increased over time.

Mediation Between Classroom Interracial Climate and Affective Bias. Results showed that pre-intervention Common Ingroup Identity did not significantly mediate between the pre-intervention *Classroom* Interracial Climate and post-intervention Affective Bias (Z = .68 for One Group; Z = 1.09 for Same Team; Z = - .13 for Different Groups; and Z = -.77 for Individuals; all ps = ns). However, Outgroup Orientation was a significant mediator of the relationship between Classroom Interracial Climate and Affective Bias (Z = -3.66, $p < .001$), while the contribution of Ethnic Identity as a mediator was not significant (Z = 1.41, p = ns). OO/EI accounted for 13.3% of the variance in post-intervention Affective Bias ($p < .001$). The R^2 of the overall pre-post-intervention Outgroup Orientation / Ethnic Identity mediation model was 25.7% ($p < .001$).

Mediation Between Neighborhood Interracial Climate and Affective Bias. Mediational analyses for the *Neighborhood* Interracial Climate showed the same pattern as that just reported for the Classroom Interracial Climate, despite the

TABLE 13.4

Cronbach's Alphas, Means, Standard Deviations, and *t*-Test

Values of the Main Variables at Time 1 and Time 2 in the Follow-Up Study

Variable	Time 1			Time 2			
	α	M	SD	α	M	SD	t
Affective Bias	.72	2.76	1.44	.78	2.59	1.45	-1.63
Classroom Interracial Climate	.72	5.27	0.72	.74	5.42	0.71	1.84
Neighborhood Interracial Climate	.61	4.91	1.20	.79	4.84	1.37	-0.63
Outgroup Orientation	.84	5.58	1.26	.86	5.76	1.24	1.38
Ethnic Identity	.87	5.51	1.27	.87	5.66	1.36	1.29
Common Ingroup Identity							
One Group		4.06	1.86		4.46	1.61	2.10*
Same Team		4.25	1.91		4.64	1.70	1.90
Different Groups		4.48	1.76		4.62	1.67	0.71
Individuals		4.25	1.57		4.25	1.75	0.00

Note. Only participants who answered items on a given scale at both Time 1 and Time 2 are included (N = 112-120). *p < .05.

fact that the classroom scale consisted of 11 items adapted from Green, Adams, and Turner (1988) while the neighborhood scale consisted of 4 items composed for this study. CII did not mediate the Neighborhood Interracial Climate–Affective Bias relationship (Z = .23 for One Group; Z = .76 for Same Team; Z = -.13 for Different Groups; and Z = -1.19 for Individuals; all ps = ns). Outgroup Orientation was a significant mediator of the relationship between Neighborhood Interracial Climate and Affective Bias (Z = -3.07, p < .001), while Ethnic Identity was not (Z = 1.10, p = ns). OO/EI accounted for 12.4% of the variance in post-intervention Affective Bias (p < .001). The R^2 of the overall pre- post-intervention Outgroup Orientation / Ethnic Identity mediation model was 22.9% (p < .001).

Comparison of Effectiveness of Program Implementations on Prejudice Reduction

Because the correlations between Affective Bias scores at Time 1 and Time 2 were greater than .50, we used the Time-1 Affective Bias response as a covariate and the Time-2 Affective Bias response as the outcome variable in a treatment-wise ANCOVA. This procedure adjusted for individual differences on the Time-1 measure. After adjustment by the covariate, Affective Bias varied significantly with the intervention condition, F (2, 137) = 3.44, p < .05. Pairwise comparisons showed that the Affective Bias scores of students in the modified RAP (M = 2.50) and standard RAP (M = 2.65) conditions were significantly lower than those of the control group (M = 3.19). The modified RAP and standard RAP conditions did not differ from each other.

CONCLUSION AND IMPLICATIONS FOR MULTICULTURAL EDUCATION

Given the greater prejudice reduction in the modified and standard implementation conditions, we plan to refine the RAP intervention. The mediating role shown for outgroup orientation in the classroom, school, and neighborhood domains supports the approach of encouraging students' dispositions to participate in cross-ethnic interactions, so as to increase their liking and enjoyment of such activities—not only in the classroom, but in the school setting more generally, as well as in their home neighborhoods.

The two studies reported here of middle- and high-school students in a multicultural educational setting reconfirm the importance of meeting Allport's conditions of contact for reducing intergroup prejudice. Prior research (Gaertner et al., 1994) had shown the utility of focusing on the school interracial climate as a measure of Allport's situational criteria. It is apparent from our results that assessments of the classroom and neighborhood interracial climates can also play a predictive role in the evaluation of classroom-based prejudice-reduction programs.

The results of the above mediation tests call into question the reliability of the small, though statistically significant, role of common ingroup identity in mediating the interracial climate–interracial bias relationship, which had been found by Gaertner et al. (1994). Instead, our results provide evidence of a mediating (not merely predictive) role for outgroup orientation.

The fact that items tapping ethnic identity showed little or no mediating influence on prejudice suggests that reducing intergroup prejudice may not require eschewing one's ethnic identity. What role does this leave for ethnic identity? In the context of educational programs, having a strong racial/ethnic identity may or may not constitute a barrier to overcoming intergroup bias, depending on other factors, such as the type of educational program (e.g., cultural awareness, antiracist, multiculturalist), its goals (e.g., tolerance, assimilation, integration), and the specific curriculum (e.g., promoting ethnic identity alone or in combination with a superordinate identity). The pattern of results we obtained provides empirical support for attempts to overcome intergroup prejudice through programs that promote participants' retention of their respective ethnic identities, as long as the programs also encourage their greater openness to other ethnic groups. This is consistent with diversity theory and related concepts based on cultural pluralism (e.g., Jones, 1997, 1998; Jones, Lynch, Tenglund, & Gaertner, in press).

The mediating role that we found for outgroup orientation provides a bridge between the theorizing of cultural psychologists, who are mainly concerned with its role in acculturation, and the empirical work of social psychologists who study mediators of intergroup prejudice.

REFERENCES

Allport, G. W. (1954/1979). *The nature of prejudice*. Reading, MA: Addison-Wesley.

Baron, R., & Kenny, D. A. (1986). The moderator-mediator variable distinction in social psychological research: Conceptual, strategic, and statistical considerations. *Journal of Personality and Social Psychology, 51*, 1173-1182.

Bendick, M., Jr., Egan, M. L., & Lofhjelm, S. (1998). *The documentation and evaluation of anti-discrimination training in the United States*. Geneva: International Labour Office.

Berry, J. W., Trimble, J. E., & Olmedo, E. L. (1986). Assessment of acculturation. In W. J. Lonner & J. W. Berry (Eds.), *Field methods in cross-cultural research* (pp. 291-324). Thousand Oaks, CA: Sage.

Brewer, M. (1991). The social self: On being the same and different at the same time. *Personality and Social Psychology Bulletin, 17*, 475-482.

Brewer, M. B., & Brown, R. (1998). Intergroup relations. In D. T. Gilbert, S. K. Fiske, & G. Lindzey (Eds.), *Handbook of social psychology* (4th ed., Vol. 2, pp. 554-594). Boston: McGraw-Hill.

Brewer, M. B., & Miller, N. (1984). Beyond the contact hypothesis: Theoretical perspectives on desegregation. In N. Miller & M. B. Brewer (Eds.), *Groups in contact: The psychology of desegregation* (pp. 281-302). Orlando, FL: Academic Press.

Brown, R., & Hewstone, M. (1995). Contact hypothesis. In A. S. R. Manstead & M. Hewstone (Eds.), *Blackwell encyclopedia of social psychology* (pp. 123-125). London, England: Basil Blackwell.

Cashmore, E. (1996). *Dictionary of race relations*. London, England: Routledge.

Cherry, F. (1995). *The "stubborn particulars" of social psychology: Essays on the research process*. New York: Routledge.

Cook, S. W. (1985). Experimenting on social issues: The case of school desegregation. *American Psychologist, 40*, 452-460.

Doise, W. (1978). *Groups and individuals: Explanations in social psychology*. Cambridge, England: Cambridge University Press.

Fishbein, H. D. (1996). *Peer prejudice and discrimination: Evolutionary, cultural, and developmental dynamics*. Boulder, CO: Westview.

Forbes, H. D. (1997). *Ethnic conflict: Commerce, culture, and the contact hypothesis*. New Haven, CT: Yale University Press.

Gaertner, S., Dovidio, J., Anastasio, P. A., Bachman, B. A., & Rust, M. C. (1993). The common ingroup identity model: Recategorization and the reduction of intergroup bias. In W. Stroebe & M. Hewstone (Eds.), *European review of social psychology* (Vol. 4 pp. 1-26). London, England: Wiley.

Gaertner, S. L., Rust, M. C., Dovidio, J., Bachman, B. A., & Anastasio, P. A. (1994). The contact hypothesis: The role of a common ingroup identity on reducing intergroup bias. *Small Group Research, 25*, 224-249.

Green, C. W, Adams, A. M., & Turner, C. W. (1988). Development and validation of the school interracial climate scale. *American Journal of Community Psychology, 16*, 241-259.

Hewstone, M., & Brown, R. (Eds.). (1986). *Contact and conflict in intergroup encounters*. Oxford, England: Blackwell.

Hornsey, M. J., & Hogg, M. A. (in press a). Intergroup similarity and subgroup relations: Some implications for assimilation *Personality and Social Psychology Bulletin.*

Hornsey, M. J., & Hogg, M. A. (in press b). Subgroup relations: A comparison of the mutual intergroup differentiation and common ingroup identity models of prejudice reduction. *Personality and Social Psychology Bulletin.*

Jones, J. M. (1997). *Prejudice and racism* (2nd ed.). New York: McGraw-Hill.

Jones, J. M. (1998). Psychological knowledge and the new American dilemma of race. *Journal of Social Issues, 54*(4), 641-662.

Jones, J. M., Lynch, P. D., Tenglund, A. A., & Gaertner, S. L. (in press). Toward a diversity hypothesis: Multidimensional effects of intergroup contact. *Journal of Applied and Personality Psychology.*

Judd, C., & Kenny, D. A. (1981). Process analysis: Estimating mediation in treatment evaluations. *Evaluation Review, 5,* 602-619.

Kenny, D. A., Kashy, D. A., & Bolger, N. (1998). Data analysis in social psychology. In D. T. Gilbert, S. T. Fiske, & G. Lindzey (Eds.), *Handbook of social psychology* (4th ed., Vol. 1, pp. 233-265). Boston: McGraw-Hill.

Molina, L., & Wittig, M. A. (1999, April 30). *Does common ingroup identity mediate the interracial climate–interracial bias relationship?* Paper presented at Western Psychological Association meeting, Irvine, CA.

Pettigrew, T. F. (1986). The intergroup contact hypothesis reconsidered. In M. Hewstone & R. Brown (Eds.), *Contact and conflict in intergroup encounters* (pp. 169-195). Oxford, England: Blackwell.

Pettigrew, T. F. (1995, April). *Generalized intergroup contact effects on prejudice.* Unpublished manuscript, University of California, Santa Cruz.

Pettigrew, T. F. (1998). Intergroup contact theory. *Annual Review of Psychology, 49,* 65-85.

Phinney, J. A. (1992). The multigroup ethnic identity measure: A new scale for use with diverse groups. *Journal of Adolescent Research, 7,* 156-176.

Ponterotto, J. G. (1995). Quick discrimination index. In J. G. Ponterotto, J. M. Casas, L. A. Suzuki, & C. M. Alexander (Eds.), *Handbook of multicultural counseling.* Thousand Oaks, CA: Sage.

Sauceda, J., Guillean, A., & McKenna, J. H. (1998). *[Racial awareness program]: Curriculum guide.* Los Angeles: People for the American Way.

Stephan, W. G., & Brigham, J. C. (Eds.). (1985). Intergroup contact [Special issue]. *Journal of Social Issues, 41*(3), 1-179.

Stephan, W. G., & Stephan, C. W. (1996). *Intergroup relations.* Chicago: Brown & Benchmark.

Tajfel, H., & Turner, J. C. (1986). The social identity theory of intergroup behavior. In S. Worchel & W. G. Austin (Eds.). *The psychology of intergroup behavior* (pp. 7-24). Chicago: Nelson Hall.

Wittig, M. A., & Grant-Thompson, S. K. (1998). The utility of Allport's conditions of intergroup contact for predicting perceptions of improved racial attitudes and beliefs. *Journal of Social Issues, 54*(4), 795-812.

Wittig, M. A., & Molina, L. E. (1999, October). *When students talk about race: Psychological processes underlying the relationship between conditions of intergroup contact and prejudice in school settings.* Paper presented at the British Psychological Society meeting, Social Section, Lancaster, England.

Wrench, J., & Taylor, P. (1993). *A research manual on the evaluation of anti-discrimination training activities.* Geneva: International Labour Office.

14 Promising Practices in Reducing Prejudice: A Report from the President's Initiative on Race

Stuart Oskamp
Claremont Graduate University

James M. Jones
University of Delaware

> When people of goodwill join hearts and hands, we can free our-
> selves from the destructive grip of prejudice and discrimination.
> —President Bill Clinton, 1999

In June, 1997, President Clinton announced a program, which became termed the President's Initiative on Race, as a featured step toward his goal of building "One America in the 21st Century." He named an Advisory Board of seven eminent Americans from diverse backgrounds, chaired by the historian John Hope Franklin, to oversee the One America program. The Board planned a series of programs and eventually produced a report which occupies 1414 kilobytes on the World Wide Web (www.whitehouse.gov/Initiatives/One America). In 1999, their work was extended in a New President's Initiative, to further the many steps that they had already begun.

The part of this work which we will focus on here, the President's Initiative on Race, was a creative idea for addressing racial conflicts, and it is well worth publicizing to the professional community. Its staff conducted a number of activities directed at understanding and improving race relations in the U.S. The Initiative on Race was conceived with several broad objectives in mind:

- Dialogue—to promote a constructive national dialogue on race
- Education—to increase the nation's understanding of race relations and diversity
- Community Building—to bridge racial divides through community leadership
- Problem Solving—to identify race-related problems and their possible solutions

These objectives were first approached through a series of Advisory Board meetings and planning activities. It is important to note that social science's contributions to understanding race and race relations in America were an important aspect of the education objective of the Initiative. The second Advisory Board meeting focused on the topics of racial demographics and research on racial attitudes. It was addressed by a panel of social scientists including sociologists Lawrence Bobo and Reynolds Farley, social psychologists John Dovidio and James Jones, and clinical psychologist Derald Wing Sue. A later Advisory Board meeting was addressed by social psychologists Phyllis Katz, Susan Fiske, and Claude Steele, political psychologist Shanto Iyengar, and sociologist Joe Feagin. The Board's attempts to understand the attitudes and cognitive processes that underlie racial antagonism and discrimination necessarily called upon the cumulative knowledge that social science has developed during the 20th century.

THE *PROMISING PRACTICES* REPORT

As of 1999, the most visible product of the Initiative on Race was a report on *Promising Practices for Racial Reconciliation* (President's Initiative, 1999). This nearly 200-page report collected and briefly described outstanding examples of both local community-based groups and national organizations that have been working toward improved racial and ethnic relationships. Interestingly, these accounts are very similar to the concept of local community activism that President Bush in 1992 termed "a thousand points of light." In the President's Initiative (1999) report, their efforts are described as follows:

> Across America groups of concerned and committed people are working effectively to facilitate constructive dialogues and to establish opportunities to bridge racial and ethnic divides....These organizations and groups provide all Americans with examples of how we can successfully and fruitfully work together to overcome the historical obstacles of intergroup separation and distrust (Albert Camarillo, p. iii).

Many of these organizations are local and largely anonymous, and it was a difficult task for the staff to locate them and collect descriptive data about them. The report on *Promising Practices* explained that the staff concentrated primarily on "non-profit, community-based efforts" (p. 186), though they also included some programs from the business sector and quite a few that had expanded to a regional or national scope. They collected a large amount of written material about each program and also conducted phone interviews with the program director and with "other people familiar with the program's operations and outcomes" (p. 186).

The *Promising Practices* report clearly is not a scientific evaluation nor a definitive research report. Nevertheless, it contains descriptions of a wide variety of creative and exemplary community programs that are aimed at racial reconciliation. Our analysis of it showed that many of the programs (about half) are directly aimed at combating prejudice and discrimination, and so they are relevant to the topic of this book. As functioning, often award-winning community programs, they should have much to teach us about the practical aspects of setting up and maintaining such programs. And in turn, psychological analysis can bring greater clarity to understanding their operation and suggest reasons why they may or may not be as effective as desired.

Thus, this chapter summarizes facts about the programs described in the *Promising Practices* report, classifies them in various ways, and discusses their goals, the methods by which they aim to reach those goals, the psychological (and other) mechanisms apparently implied by their methods, and the degree to which their efforts have been professionally evaluated. Next, it focuses on the programs specifically aimed at improving intergroup relations, reviews their characteristics, and discusses their practices in the light of established social psychological theories and guiding principles for prejudice reduction. Finally, it briefly describes current efforts to gain more in-depth knowledge of "what works" in community organizations that are attempting to improve race relations in the United States.

Overview of Programs in Report

The *Promising Practices* report gives only brief 1-2 page summaries of 124 programs that were judged by the staff to be outstanding on one or more criteria of relevance. The World Wide Web report gives similar brief reports on a broader collection of 351 programs, of which these 124 are a subset that was judged most relevant and excellent. The fuller information that was submitted by the organizations is not publicly available from the Initiative. Since the published descriptions of the programs are so brief, the account of each organization drastically compresses the information about its founding, background, goals and purposes, methods of operation, and outcomes. Thus, our summary of their characteristics should be understood as a lower-bound estimate of whatever characteristic is being considered—an estimate that might have been increased if the accounts had fully described the work of the organizations. Nevertheless, the points that were highlighted give a capsule summary of the features that the organizations felt were most important or outstanding about their activities.

The *Promising Practices* report made it clear that the 124 included programs were by no means all of the valuable community efforts directed toward improving race relations. Rather, it said, they were highlighted because of their "proven effectiveness" (p. vii), though, as we shall see, that did not mean that many had been professionally evaluated. The Initiative staff defined a "promising practice" as follows:

> an effort or program intended to increase awareness of racial issues, improve the lives of individuals who are affected by past and/or present discrimination, or eliminate racial prejudice and discrimination from societal institutions such as work-

places, schools, or retail establishments. These programs range from mentoring and tutoring support for people of color to innovative ways communities are banding together across racial lines. They may vary in scope, duration, and intensity, but all are making important contributions to racial reconciliation. (President's Initiative, 1999, p. vii)

Further, the staff judged the programs that were nominated for consideration on eight key characteristics or criteria that they thought were most central to racial reconciliation. These were:

1. promotes racially inclusive collaboration
2. educates on racial issues
3. raises racial consciousness
4. encourages participants' introspection
5. expands opportunity and access for individuals
6. fosters civic engagement
7. affects systemic change
8. assesses the program's impact on the community

The staff's decision process specified that a program only had to possess one of these key characteristics in order to be considered for inclusion in *Promising Practices*, though clearly many of the featured programs met several of the criteria. For purposes of this chapter on reducing prejudice and description, we felt that characteristics 1, 2, 3, 4, and 7 were most relevant. By contrast, programs that met criteria 5, 6, and 8, though possibly of great social value, were not directly relevant to reducing prejudice unless they also met some of the other criteria. However, the staff's ratings on these eight characteristics were not presented in the report nor available to us, so we made our judgments based on the descriptive material that was included in the published report.

The report classified the 124 programs into nine domains based on the substantive area on which they focused. Each program was classified under the domain that "seemed to best capture the program's activities" (p. 187), though many of them were relevant to several domains. As one example, a program classified under Youth might also have elements relevant to Education, Health, and/or Community Building. Table 14.1 lists the nine domains, together with the number of programs classified in each, the number of these that were considered national in scope, and the median year when the programs were started.

Table 14.1 shows that the report concentrated more heavily on programs that were classified as Community Building or Youth, and much less heavily on programs classified as Business or Health and Human Services. About 30% of the programs included were national in scope (actually meaning broader than a single large metropolitan area). The table also shows that a majority of the programs were begun in the 1990s (the median year was 1992), and that, on aver-

TABLE 14.1
Domains of Promising Practices Programs

Domain	N in Report	National in Scope		Year Started	
		N	%	Median	Range
1. Arts, multi-media, and sports	14	3	21	1994	(1968-1998)
2. Business	7	4	57	1994	(1984-1996)
3. Community and economic development	12	2	17	1981	(1947-1996)
4. Community building	26	10	38	1991	(1927-1997)
5. Education	16	5	31	1993	(1959-1996)
6. Government	10	4	40	1993	(1981-1997)
7. Health and human services	6	0	0	1983	(1969-1995)
8. Religious	13	4	31	1991	(1903-1997)
9. Youth	20	5	25	1989	(1963-1996)
Total	124	37	30	1992	(1903-1998)

age, the Community and Economic Development and the Health and Human Services programs were considerably older than the other categories. Starting with the oldest programs, the earliest program begun in each of the categories was as follows:

- Religious—Catholic Charities, Archdiocese of Boston (1903)—local, Boston
- Community building—National Conference for Community and Justice (1927)—national, New York
- Community and economic development—Phoenix Indian Center (1947)—local, Phoenix
- Education—Center for Applied Linguistics (1959)—national, Washington, DC
- Youth—A Better Chance (1963)—national, Boston
- Arts, multi-media, and sports—Community Change (1968)—local, Boston
- Health and human services—Delhi Center (1969)—local, Santa Ana, CA
- Government—Cultural Sensitivity: Orientation for the New Juvenile Justice Professional (1981)—local, Harrisburg, PA
- Business—American Institute of Managing Diversity (1984)—national, Atlanta

In Box 14.1, we present an example of the full information that was available about a program that was relevant to our topic of prejudice reduction:

Center for Prejudice Reduction
Great Neck, New York

Contact(s): Amy Levine, Executive Director
516-446-4650

Purpose: To encourage dialogue and education to reduce violence and discrimination brought about by hate and bigotry.

Background

The Center for Prejudice Reduction (CPR) was founded in 1991 by the American Jewish Congress as a communitywide project serving Long Island. It is a clearinghouse for information on combating bigotry and discrimination. CPR provides schools, government agencies, religious and community groups, and businesses with resources on how to reduce the incidence of prejudice. To best serve the community on this issue, CPR created its Community Advisory Council, consisting of more than 100 organizations that work on eliminating prejudice and racism in the community. The Council serves as an important hub for sharing solutions on race and religious issues.

Program Operations

Each year, CPR hosts a conference on prejudice reduction for educators in the New York counties of Nassau and Suffolk. Organized by a racially diverse planning committee, the event aids school districts in the replication of anti-bias curriculums that address cultural, religious, and racial tensions on campuses. As a followup to the conference, CPR operates as a clearinghouse of speakers and programs for local community members.

Additionally, CPR has created the CPR Library, a multi-media collection that features books, films, videotapes and audiotapes, curriculum materials, and other items, all of which are available for use by schools, government agencies, religious and community groups, businesses and others. Moreover, CPR has developed the Crisis Response Service, which refers victims of all forms of prejudice to appropriate police and government officials, county human rights commissions, fair housing organizations, and religious and psychological resources. Moreover, American Jewish Congress staff members conduct vigorous followup on all cases.

Through the services that CPR offers, educators are provided with the resources necessary to use innovative strategies for teaching tolerance; employers are provided with the resources necessary for fostering diversity and tolerance in the workplace; synagogues, churches, and civic organizations are taught how to handle community relations issues; and police, district attorneys, and officers of the court are provided with materials needed for programs on educating bias crime offenders.

Another CPR accomplishment is its StopBias Program, created in 1994. CPR and the Suffolk County district attorney work with adults and youth who have been charged with racial-bias offenses. Through StopBias, these offenders receive counseling on their negative behavior toward various cultural and religious groups.

Outcomes

The annual conference for educators on prejudice reduction typically attracts hundreds of educators, law enforcement personnel, and community leaders. These community members represent 128 school districts from Suffolk and Nassau Counties. During the past 7 years, CPR has reached more than 1,200 educators through these conferences. Through StopBias, more than 100 bias offenders have been counseled, and the program has achieved a zero-percent recidivism rate.

> "The CPR educators' conference was an invaluable resource to our staff and provided a unique opportunity to view an entire spectrum of prejudice reduction techniques in one place and at one time." Raymond J. McDonough, Dean of Students, Hicksville High School

Source: President's Initiative on Race (1999, pp. 51-52).

METHODOLOGY OF OUR REPORT

Based on the published material, we classified each program on 38 characteristics. These included its domain in the report, the year the program started, whether it was national or local, whether the goal of reducing prejudice/discrimination was indicated in the program's brief stated purpose or anywhere in its description, whether the program was described as having received public awards, recognition, or wide publicity, whether its expansion to other major cities was mentioned, and whether evaluation of the program was mentioned or demonstrated anywhere in the description (beyond the simple number of participants that it had enrolled or assisted).

In addition to these eight characteristics, we rated each program as to whether or not its description mentioned its use of 30 different methods or mechanisms, many of which were psychological in nature. These mechanisms are listed in Table 14.2, classified within one of five basic categories: (a) education and publicity (knowledge-based), (b) training (skill-based), (c) contact or interactions (either intergroup or interpersonal), (d) resource allocation of materials, opportunities, or services (to individuals or groups), or (e) community-building (involving organizations, neighborhoods, or whole communities). Our rating of

TABLE 14.2
List of Psychological Mechanisms Rated for
Each Program, Classified Within Five Major Categories

Category and Mechanism

Education and Publicity
  Education—to whom?
  Research
  Public conference, exhibition, tournament
  Summary report of findings or activities
  Media publicity
  Providing educational materials

Training
  Job skills training
  Diversity training
  Leadership training
  Conflict resolution training

Contact or Interaction
  Dialogue—what groups?
  Contact—what groups?
  Contact with favorable situational features
    (e.g., equal status)

Other methods or mechanisms

Resource Allocation of Materials, Services, etc.
  Mentoring or counseling
  Providing educational opportunities
    (including financial aid for students)
  Providing recreational opportunities
  Providing job opportunities
  Providing home ownership opportunities
  Providing consultants
  Support in career
  Support of minority organizations and/or
    businesses
  Services to immigrants, families, etc.

Community Building
  Financial support for community projects
  Certification of businesses
  Ownership and renovation of land and/or
    buildings
  Preservation of neighborhood diversity
  Providing model diversity programs
  Building community coalitions
  Activism in general on community issues

---

the programs' methods is the feature of our report that is most clearly a lower-bound estimate, because each program normally only mentioned a few of the mechanisms that we had identified (range = 1-8), and it is certainly possible that a program may have used others that were not featured as central in its write-up.

It is interesting to consider these mechanisms used by racial reconciliation programs in terms of their disciplinary status. The ones that are most strongly related to psychological theory are contact and interaction, which are based on the contact hypothesis (Allport, 1954). Other mechanisms are clearly psychological in nature, though not relying on intergroup contact—particularly the training group, and mentoring/counseling within the resource allocation group. Most of the mechanisms within the education/publicity group also involve psychological processes and expertise, though several require media or public relations skills as well. The resource allocation group and the community building group of mechanisms rely mainly on economic methods (e.g., providing job opportunities; financial support for community projects) or on social work kinds of skills and training (e.g., activism; building community coalitions).

The list of program mechanisms in Table 14.2 makes it clear that many methods and many sorts of skills may be both useful and necessary in attacking the evil of racism in our society. Further, the programs in the *Promising Practices* report seem to fall into two major groups—ones aimed mainly at improving racial intergroup relations and others focused primarily on raising the quality of life for ethnic minority groups, though quite a few of the programs try to work toward both of these major goals.

FINDINGS AND DISCUSSION

In Table 14.3 we list, by domain, the percentage of programs that indicated a goal of prejudice reduction (in the stated purpose, or anywhere in the description), that revealed evaluation of their outcomes, that mentioned having received awards, recognition, or wide publicity, and that described expansion beyond their original metropolitan area. The next several sections briefly discuss each of these topics.

Prejudice Reduction

We defined prejudice reduction broadly, to include any mention of reducing stereotypes, prejudice, discrimination, racism, or racial bias, or promoting racial tolerance, reconciliation, friendship, or race relations. As Table 14.3 shows, only about one-fourth of the programs mentioned this goal in their brief, one-sentence statement of purpose (we will refer to this mention as a central goal), but about half did so somewhere in their program description. This goal was listed as central most often in the religious programs (62%) and next most often in the community-building programs (31%), business programs (29%), and youth programs (25%). It was never listed as a central goal in the health and human services programs. As at least a subsidiary goal, prejudice reduction was listed most often in community-building programs (77%), religious programs (62%), arts, multimedia, and sports programs (50%), and youth programs (45%). The community/economic development programs were very unlikely to state prejudice reduction as a goal, and both the business and health/human services programs were also relatively low in focusing on it.

The goals of the programs that didn't emphasize prejudice reduction can be deduced from the other mechanisms that were mentioned most often (shown later in Table 14.4). For example, some of these were multicultural education, leadership training, presenting public conferences or exhibitions, providing a wide variety of community services, job skills training, and mentoring young people. All of these, of course, are valid goals of programs that aim to improve the living conditions of racial minorities, whether or not they directly attack racial prejudice. Other frequently mentioned mechanisms, which were often (but definitely not always) featured in programs having the specific goal of prejudice reduction, included intergroup dialogue, contact between diverse individuals, and conflict resolution training.

Evaluation of Outcomes

Overall, 41% of the programs gave some information (beyond merely the number of people that they served) that indicated an attempt to evaluate their success on some dimension. However, only six programs (5%) emphasized the fact of having been evaluated, or presented relatively extensive evaluative findings (within their space limitations). These six were all in the domains of youth programs or arts, multi-media, and sports. Some indication of evaluation was most common in the community/economic development programs (67%), youth programs (60%), government programs (60%), and education programs (50%). It was never mentioned by the health and human services programs, and it was rarely mentioned by the religious programs. Taken together, these findings suggest that probably less than 10% of these highly regarded programs have been rigorously examined by outside professional evaluators, while only about 30% more have even performed any internal investigation of the outcomes attained by their clients. If that is the case, it demonstrates a major need for careful professional evaluation to help these programs learn what they are doing well and where they need to improve in their impact.

Examples of the strongest evaluation information given were programs that mentioned regular use of an outside evaluation agency or that gave specific data about outcome research. More typical were simple statements that outcomes were measured or that listed a particular outcome, such as fewer discipline referrals in schools.

TABLE 14.3

Percentages of Programs, by Domain, that Indicated Prejudice Reduction Goals,
Evaluation of Outcomes, Receipt of Awards or Publicity, and Expansion to Other Cities

Program Domain	Prejudice Reduction Goals		Evaluation of Outcomes	Receipt of Awards or Publicity	Expansion to Other Cities
	In Purpose	Anywhere			
1. Arts, multi-media, and sports	14%	50%	29%	21%	14%
2. Business	29	29	43	71	14
3. Community and economic development	8	8	67	17	17
4. Community building	31	77	31	31	31
5. Education	7	38	50	19	13
6. Government	20	40	60	30	10
7. Health and human services	0	33	0	33	0
8. Religious	62	62	15	31	15
9. Youth	25	45	60	35	35
Total	23	48	41	30	20

Awards or Wide Media Publicity

Overall, 30% of the programs made specific mention of having received awards
or wide media publicity. However, it seems certain that many programs that did
not devote space to emphasizing their favorable publicity must also have received widespread and positive public attention in the media. This seems particularly likely for the 25 programs that reported having expanded from a single
city or area to a number of additional ones, yet only 8 of these specifically mentioned having received awards or media publicity. Thus, these mentions of
awards or wide media publicity have the nature of testimonials to the program's
effectiveness. This kind of emphasis was most common among the business
programs (71%), and least common in the community/economic development
programs (17%), education programs (19%), and arts, multi-media, and sports
programs (21%). Though these awards and publicity suggest that the programs
are being successful in their goals, they clearly do not represent careful scientific
evaluations of the programs' impacts. Typical examples include: "has been featured in the Washington Post and on ABC News' "Nightline..."(p. 2) and "has received the Amoco Leader Award and is being used as a model by the National
Conference for Community and Justice" (p. 165).

Expansion to Other Cities

This outcome was not relevant and not rated for the national programs, which constituted 30% of the sample. Among all the programs, 20% mentioned having expanded beyond their original metropolitan area. This occurred most often among the youth programs (35%) and the community-building programs (31%), and not at all among the health and human services programs. Again, such expansion suggests that the programs are being effective, but it does not scientifically demonstrate the value of their outcomes.

Methods or Mechanisms Described

The 30 different mechanisms that were mentioned in the program descriptions (listed above in Table 14.2) were coded separately. Thus a program could be scored for each of several related mechanisms, such as education in general, dialogue, mentoring or counseling, and holding a large public conference, exhibition, or other production. It might also be scored for each of: job skills training, diversity training, leadership training, conflict resolution training, career support, or any of the other mechanisms that were specifically alluded to. However, the average number of mechanisms mentioned in the program descriptions was only 3.9 (range = 1-8).

Table 14.4 shows the mechanisms that were mentioned most often in describing the programs, and the program domains in which each mechanism was most frequently mentioned. As it indicates, general education was by far the most often mentioned technique (54% of programs), followed by intergroup dialogue (34%), and leadership training (31%). Intergroup contact came next at 24%, and a very large majority of those programs mentioned one or more of Allport's (1954) favorable conditions for contact, such as support by authorities, equal status, or cooperative activities, or personalized relationships (20% of all programs). As shown in Table 14.4, three other mechanisms were mentioned by more than 20% of the programs, six more by 10% or more, while each of the remaining 16 mechanisms was mentioned by less than 10% of the programs.

Table 14.4 also shows interesting differences in the mechanisms that were most common in programs of different types. For instance, programs in the domain of health/human services were particularly high in using education alone and in providing a community service. Community building programs were highest in the use of intergroup dialogue, leadership training, and intergroup contact. Government programs were highest in the provision of educational materials, while arts programs were highest in putting on public exhibitions. Community/economic development programs were highest in job skills training, while business programs were highest in providing job opportunities. Youth programs were highest in mentoring and/or counseling, whereas religious programs were highest in community activism. Many of these emphases follow naturally from the

TABLE 14.4
Mechanisms Most Frequently Mentioned in Program Descriptions

Mechanism	% of Programs	Domains Where Most Commonly Mentioned and %
Education	54	Health 83, Arts 71, Business 71, Education 62, Youth 60
Dialogue	34	Community building 69, Business 43, Religious 38, Arts 36
Leadership training	31	Community building 50, Youth 50
Contact	24	Community building 38, Religious 31, Youth 30, Arts 29
Providing educational materials	24	Government 40, Community building 38, Education 38, Health 33, Business 29
Public conferences, exhibitions, etc.	23	Arts 36, Community building 31, Religious 31, Government 30
Providing community services	23	Health 67, Youth 35, Religious 31, Community/ economic development 25
Diversity training	19	Health 50, Religious 31, Business 29, Community building 27, Education 25
Job skills training	17	Community/economic development 75, Health 33, Arts 29
Mentoring or counseling	13	Youth 55
Conflict resolution training	12	Health 33, Youth 20, Community building 19
Activism in general	12	Religious 38, Youth 20, Community/economic development 17
Providing job opportunities	11	Business 29, Arts 21, Youth 20, Health 17

nature and goals of the particular type of program, and they demonstrate that there are many paths toward improving the lot of ethnic minorities in our society. It should be interesting to psychologists to realize that many of the mechanisms used were not specifically psychological in nature—for instance, putting on public exhibitions, providing community services (e.g., health care, or literacy education), or providing job opportunities.

PROGRAMS AIMED AT REDUCING PREJUDICE AND DISCRIMINATION

We turn our attention now from these broader goals to the subset of 59 programs that stated reduction of prejudice, discrimination, or racism, or improvement of race relations as one of their goals. What were these programs like, how did they operate, and how successful did they appear to be? First, and perhaps surprisingly, only half of them (49%) stated prejudice reduction as a *central* goal in their statement of purpose. The others were apt to mention education as a main goal, and many also mentioned intergroup dialogue as a goal.

Second, only 31% of the prejudice reduction programs described any *evaluation* of their outcomes—substantially below the 51% figure for the other 65 programs. This may indicate that the goal of reducing prejudice is more nebulous and harder to measure than some other program goals, or alternatively it may suggest that these programs haven't thought much about the need for evaluation of their efforts.

Third, the prejudice reduction programs were slightly higher than the other programs in the percentage that mentioned having received awards or wide publicity. However, they were similar in their age (their median starting date was 1992), the percentage of national programs, and the percentage of local programs that reported having expanded to other cities.

Fourth, as noted above, prejudice reduction was most likely to be mentioned as a goal by programs in the domains of community building (20 programs— 77%) or religion (8 programs—62%). It was quite unlikely to be mentioned as a goal by programs in the domains of community/economic development (1 program), business (2 programs), or health/human services (2 programs).

Methods or Mechanisms Described

Table 14.5 is parallel to Table 14.4 and shows, for the 59 programs aimed at prejudice reduction, what mechanisms they mentioned using in their program descriptions. These programs were surprisingly similar to the total group of programs in many ways. Like the total group, they typically mentioned using about four mechanisms (mean = 4.1, range = 1-8). Moreover, the particular methods they listed were almost identical. The order of the top five mechanisms listed in Tables 14.4 and 14.5 is the same with only one exception. The prejudice reduction programs most often used general education (47%) and intergroup dialogue (47%), followed in order by leadership training, providing educational materials, and public conferences or exhibits.

Comparing the percentages in the two tables, the prejudice reduction programs were higher in the percentage using all of the mechanisms on their list except education and providing community services. They were substantially higher in providing educational materials and in the use of dialogue, diversity training, leadership training, and conferences and exhibits.

Intergroup Contact. Probably most surprising is the fact that the prejudice reduction program's emphasis on intergroup contact was only a little higher than the whole group of programs and was seventh highest on their list (at 29%), compared to fourth highest on the list for all programs. As with the total group of programs, almost all of the programs that listed contact also mentioned one or

TABLE 14.5
Mechanisms Most Frequently Mentioned in
Descriptions of Programs Aimed at Prejudice Reduction

Mechanism	% of programs
Education	47%
Dialogue	47
Leadership training	41
Providing educational materials	39
Public conferences, exhibitions, etc.	34
Diversity training	31
Contact	29
Conflict resolution training	19
Providing community services	17
Activism in general	17
Providing consultants	10

more of the conditions that Allport (1954) listed as conducive to its favorable effects (but that number constituted only 25% of the prejudice reduction programs). Here are a few examples of descriptions of such favorable conditions for contact:

- "multi-racial student teams that lead school-based efforts to prevent and reduce racial conflicts and violence" (p. 175—common goals)
- "Through teaching one another about their religions, students begin to develop awareness and understanding about each other as individuals." (p. 148—personalized acquaintance)
- "an effort to bring together political, business, and community leaders in [city] to foster racial healing" (p. 67—authority support)
- "to focus on a common cause, foster team building across racial lines ....The best [city] players are required to serve as coaches and referees for designated hours during the week." (p.7—equal status, common goals)

Other Mechanisms. Since less than 30% of the prejudice reduction programs emphasized intergroup contact, what other mechanisms did they use in their efforts? Of those programs that did not mention contact, the largest group emphasized education (48%), generally in combination with one or more of the following techniques, each of which was mentioned by 35% or more of them: dialogue, conferences, providing educational materials, leadership training, and diversity training. Fortunately, hardly any of these programs listed the knowledge-oriented techniques of education, conferences, or providing educational materials *without combining them* with other more-interactive methods, such as dialogue, or various types of training activities. Thus, it seems that most of them have profited from the social psychological findings that education or information alone is seldom sufficient to change attitudes or behavior (e.g., McGuire, 1986). In addition, these interactive techniques usually involve a fair amount of intergroup contact, so that variable may be playing an implicit part in their effects.

The program described in Box 14.1 presents a good illustration of prejudice reduction efforts that are not primarily focused on intergroup contact. Its main activities appear to be an annual conference and providing educational materials to many users through its library. In addition it provides services to prejudice victims and counseling to bias-crime offenders. Though dialogue is involved in many of these activities, it is not stressed, and intergroup contact is not mentioned as a focus of the program's activities.

FURTHER IN-DEPTH STUDY OF PROGRAMS

Though this chapter has been confined to analysis of the summary report of the President's Initiative (1999), that is not the end of the story. It should be possible to conduct more in-depth studies of apparently successful prejudice reduction programs, to learn more about their methods and to evaluate their results more carefully. In fact, such efforts are actually going on, and we close this chapter with a brief description of one such study.

This effort is headquartered at Claremont Graduate University in the Institute for Democratic Renewal, under the direction of John D. Maguire. Its basic approach is to conduct multi-person, multi-day site visits to a limited number of exemplary organizations that are working toward racial reconciliation, and in each community to hold in-depth interviews with a wide variety of informants about the methods, successes, and failures of the organization. This program started with the list of 300-plus "promising practices" programs gathered by the President's Initiative staff, and added to them similar lists of outstanding programs gleaned from the Ford Foundation, the Rockefeller Foundation, and the National Conference for Community and Justice (1999). The total list of nearly 500 organizations was then screened based on the available information, and a subset of 37 was selected for telephone interviews with the director to check on their coverage, methods, and apparent success. From that group a final number of 13 was chosen for the multi-day site visits. The main criterion for selecting these finalists was *variety*, in four different features of their work—in the aspect of racial issues that they addressed, in their methods, in geographic diversity around the U.S., and in service to different racial and ethnic groups. Not all of them were found to be outstanding successes, but all of them exemplified important principles of organizational operation that contributed to their successes and failures.

When a multi-racial team of interviewers visited each of these organizations, they talked not only to leaders of these organizations, but also to community leaders, elected and appointed officials, newspaper editors, and other informed citizens, to get a broad-gauged view of the program's operation from all viewpoints. The notes from these interviews were transcribed and collated into a summary report on each visited program (Institute for Democratic Renewal,

2000). The lessons learned from these program assessments have been collected in a handbook that is designed to be useful to other organizations that are trying to emulate their successes and avoid their failures in working on ethnic and racial issues (Maguire & Leiderman, 2000). As that volume states, the goal of this research is to help any group of concerned citizens "toward building healthy, effective, interracial/multicultural communities" (p. 2).

CONCLUSIONS AND IMPLICATIONS

The goal of reducing prejudice and improving intergroup relations is one that demands the efforts of both academic researchers and community-based organizations. Many social science researchers and many community-based organizations other than the ones described in the *Promising Practices* report are working toward similar goals of racial reconciliation. This chapter has been aimed at making the community-level efforts better known to psychologists and other researchers, and at enlisting more social scientists in these efforts—at every level, from research studies through community activism to broad public policy programs.

The President's Initiative (1999) collection of *Promising Practices* is essentially a "bully pulpit"—a useful starting place that summarizes many organizations and approaches dedicated to promoting better race relations and improving the quality of life for ethnic minorities. These organizations can be aided with knowledge from social science theories and research and, reciprocally, social scientists can benefit from a deeper understanding of the complex issues and problems that these organizations encounter in their practical work. Additionally, our analysis of the *Promising Practices* report indicates the need for thorough empirical evaluations of the activities of such organizations, in order to help disseminate knowledge of "what works" (or doesn't work) more broadly and effectively.

REFERENCES

Allport, G. W. (1954). *The nature of prejudice*. Reading, MA: Addison-Wesley.

Institute for Democratic Renewal. (2000). *Reports on site visits to thirteen project partners*. Claremont, CA: Author.

Maguire, J. D., & Leiderman, S. (2000). *How to build healthy, effective interracial/multicultural communities: A handbook on how democracy is renewed*. Claremont, CA: Claremont Graduate University, Institute for Democratic Renewal.

McGuire, W. J. (1986). The myth of massive media impact: Savagings and salvagings. In G. Comstock (Ed.), *Public communication and behavior* (Vol. 1, pp. 173-257). Orlando, FL: Academic Press.

National Conference for Community and Justice. (1999). *Intergroup relations in the United States: Programs and organizations*. New York: Author.

President's Initiative on Race. (1999, January). *Pathways to one America in the 21st century: Promising practices for racial reconciliation*. Washington, DC: Author.

About the Authors

Frances E. Aboud is Professor of Psychology at McGill University in Montreal, Canada, where she also earned her Ph.D. She has been conducting research on the development of prejudice and ethnic identity in children for the past 25 years. In addition to her publications in child development journals, she authored *Children and Prejudice* (1988). Another area of her interest areas is international health psychology, which has motivated her to work in community problem solving. After several years of teaching and research in Ethiopia, she published a textbook entitled *Health Psychology in Global Perspective* (1998).

Marilynn B. Brewer received her Ph.D in social psychology at Northwestern University in 1968 and is currently Professor of Psychology and Eminent Scholar in Social Psychology at the Ohio State University. Her primary area of research is the study of social identity and intergroup relations, and she is the author of numerous research articles and co-author of several books in this area, including *Groups in Contact: The Psychology of Desegregation* (1984) and *Intergroup Relations* (1996). Dr. Brewer received the 1995 Kurt Lewin Memorial Award from the Society for the Psychological Study of Social Issues (SPSSI), and she has served as President of SPSSI, the Society for Personality and Social Psychology, and the American Psychological Society.

Brenda N. Buswell is a doctoral candidate in psychology at the University of Wisconsin–Madison. Her current research focuses primarily on prejudice and prejudice reduction as influenced by differences in the source of motivation to respond without prejudice. Her other research interests include work on emotion, in particular self-conscious emotions such as embarrassment, guilt, and shame.

Patricia G. Devine earned her Ph.D. at the Ohio State University, and is Professor of Psychology at the University of Wisconsin–Madison. Her research primarily focuses on prejudice and intergroup relations. Her research on prejudice was honored by her receipt of SPSSI's 1990 Gordon Allport Intergroup Relations Prize and the 1994 APA Award for a Distinguished Early Career Contribution to social and personality psychology. She is currently the editor of the Journal of Personality and Social Psychology: Attitudes and Social Cognition.

John F. Dovidio earned his M.A. and Ph.D. from the University of Delaware, and is Charles A. Dana Professor of Psychology at Colgate University. His research interests are in stereotyping, prejudice, and discrimination; nonverbal communication; and altruism and helping. He has served as editor of the *Personality and Social Psychology Bulletin,* is currently associate editor of *Group Processes and Intergroup Relations*, and has been elected president of the Society for the Psychological Study of Social Issues (SPSSI).

Susan T. Fiske, Distinguished University Professor of Psychology at the University of Massachusetts at Amherst, will move to Princeton University in 2000. A Harvard Ph.D., she has published over 100 articles and chapters, co-edited *The Handbook of Social Psychology* and the *Annual Review of Psychology,* and co-authored *Social Cognition*. The U.S. Supreme Court and the President's Initiative on Race have used her expert testimony. She won the American Psychological Association's Early Career Award for Distinguished Contribution to Psychology in the Public Interest, and with Peter Glick, she recently was awarded the Gordon Allport Intergroup Relations Prize from the Society for the Psychological Study of Social Issues.

Samuel L. Gaertner received his Ph.D. from the City University of New York Graduate Center in 1970, and is Professor of Psychology at the University of Delaware. His primary research interests involve strategies for reducing intergroup bias and stereotyping. Currently his work focuses on the Common Ingroup Identity Model (developed with J. Dovidio) and its relation to other category-based strategies for reducing bias. An article describing this work was awarded the 1998 Gordon Allport Intergroup Relations Prize by SPSSI.

David W. Johnson received his doctoral degree from Columbia University, and is Professor of Educational Psychology at the University of Minnesota, and Co-Director of the Cooperative Learning Center. He held the Emma M. Birkmaier Professorship in Educational Leadership at the University of Minnesota from 1994 to 1997. He has authored over 350 research articles and book chapters and is the author of over 40 books. He is a past editor of the *American Educational Research Journal.* With his brother, he has received numerous awards for outstanding research—from the American Psychological Association, the American Personnel and Guidance Association, the American Society for Engineering Education, the National Council for Social Studies, the American Association for Counseling and Development, and the American Educational Research Association.

Roger T. Johnson holds a doctoral degree from the University of California at Berkeley, and is Professor of Curriculum and Instruction at the University of Minnesota and Co-Director of its Cooperative Learning Center. He is the author of numerous research articles, book chapters, and books. With his brother, he has received numerous awards for outstanding research—from the American Psychological Association, the American Personnel and Guidance Association, the American Society for Engineering Education, the National Council for Social Studies, the American

Association for Counseling and Development, and the American Educational Research Association.

James M. Jones earned his B.A. from Oberlin College, his M.A. from Temple University and his Ph.D. from Yale. He has taught at Harvard University, Howard University, and is currently Professor of Psychology at the University of Delaware. He is a past president of the Society of Experimental Social Psychology, has served on the editorial boards of numerous scientific journals, and is well known for his book, *Prejudice and Racism* (2nd ed., 1996). For many years he has been Director of the Minority Fellowship Program for the American Psychological Association, and he has also served as head of the Public Interest Directorate and Affirmative Action Officer for APA.

Kerry Kawakami received her Ph.D. in social psychology from the University of Toronto and is currently Assistant Professor of Psychology at the University of Nijmegen in the Netherlands. Her primary area of research is stereotyping and prejudice. The main focus of her research is examining the automaticity of stereotyping and factors that influence this process, with the goal of learning how to reduce the activation and application of stereotypes.

Sheri R. Levy is an assistant professor of Psychology at SUNY Stony Brook. She earned her B.A. in psychology from the University of Michigan and her Ph.D in psychology from Columbia University in 1998. Her dissertation on children's static versus dynamic conceptions of people won the 1999 SPSSI dissertation award. Her research interests include lay theories of psychology, determinants of prejudice during childhood and adulthood, prejudice reduction, hate group membership, intragroup and intergroup relations, group identification and its functions, and the role of children's social concerns on their report of stereotype-based beliefs.

Brenda Major earned her Ph.D. at Purdue University, and is Professor of Psychology at the University of California at Santa Barbara. From 1978-1985 she taught at the State University of New York at Buffalo. She has been an Associate Editor of the *Personality and Social Psychology Bulletin*, and is on the editorial boards of numerous professional journals. She received SPSSI's Gordon Allport Prize for research in Intergroup Relations in 1986, and again in 1988. Her research centers around psychological resilience—how people cope with, adapt to, and overcome adversity. Her current research interests include the psychology of stigma, the psychology of legitimacy, self-esteem, and predictors of coping with abortion.

Shannon K. McCoy earned her B.A. from St. Mary's College and is now a doctoral candidate in social psychology at the University of California, Santa Barbara. Her research interests include the antecedents and consequences of perceiving discrimination, just-world beliefs and legitimizing ideologies, and self-esteem.

Ludwin Molina received a B.A. in psychology from UCLA, and is currently a Sally Casanova predoctoral scholar in psychology at California State University, North-ridge. His research interests include intergroup relations, superordinate/subgroup identity, optimal distinctiveness theory, and social identity theory. His research on psychological mediators of prejudice reduction is being supported by an applied social issues internship from the Society for the Psychological Study of Social Issues.

Stuart Oskamp earned his Ph.D. at Stanford and is Professor of Psychology at Claremont Graduate University. His main research interests are in the areas of attitudes and attitude change, environmentally responsible behavior such as recycling and energy conservation, intergroup relations, and social issues and public policy. His books include *Attitudes and Opinions* (1991), *Applied Social Psychology* (1998), and *Social Psychology: An Applied Perspective* (2000). He has served as president of the American Psychological Association Division of Population and Environmental Psychology and the Society for the Psychological Study of Social Issues (SPSSI) and as editor of the *Journal of Social Issues* and the *Applied Social Psychology Annual.*

Thomas Pettigrew is Research Professor of Social Psychology at the University of California, Santa Cruz. He received his Ph.D. from Harvard University in 1956, and has also taught at the Universities of North Carolina, Harvard, and Amsterdam. His books include *A Profile of the Negro American* (1964), *Racially Separate or Together* (1971), *Racial Discrimination in the U.S.* (1975), *The Sociology of Race Relations* (1980), and *How To Think Like a Social Scientist* (1996).

E. Ashby Plant is a doctoral candidate in psychology at the University of Wisconsin–Madison. Her research focuses on the source of people's motivation to respond without prejudice and its consequences for people's attitudes, affect, and behavior in prejudice-relevant situations. Her most recent work has explored the implications of the source of people's motivation to respond without prejudice for their implicit and explicit expressions of prejudice and their responses to anti-prejudice social pressure.

Wendy J. Quinton earned an M.A. from the University of California, Santa Barbara, where she is currently a doctoral candidate in social psychology. Her interests include the social and dispositional antecedents of perceiving discrimination, the affective consequences of perceiving discrimination, group identification, political ideologies, and collective action.

Toni Schmader earned her Ph.D. in social psychology at the University of California at Santa Barbara, and is an assistant professor of psychology at the University of Arizona. Her research examines the consequences of social stigma and ideology for people's self-definition, self-esteem, performance, and social identity.

Jim Sidanius received his Ph.D. in political psychology in 1977 at the University of Stockholm, Sweden, where he also taught for ten years. Since returning to the United States in 1983, he has taught at Carnegie-Mellon University, the University of Texas at Austin, New York University, and Princeton University, and he is currently Professor of Psychology at UCLA. His work focuses on the interface between political ideology and cognitive functioning, the political psychology of gender, group conflict and institutional discrimination, and evolutionary psychology. Professor Sidanius served as vice-president of the International Society of Political Psychology in 1998-1999, and he has authored more than 80 research articles. His recent books include *Social Dominance: An Intergroup Theory of Social Hierarchy and Oppression* (1999) and *Racialized Politics: Values, Ideology, and Prejudice in American Public Opinion* (2000).

Cookie White Stephan is Professor of Sociology at New Mexico State University. She received her Ph.D. in psychology from the University of Minnesota in 1971. Her major research focus is intergroup relations. She is the co-author of *Two Social Psychologies* (1985), *Intergroup Relations* (1996) and "What are the functions of ethnic identity?" in P. Spickard & W. J. Burroughs (Eds.), *We Are a People* (1999).

Walter G. Stephan received his Ph.D. in psychology from the University of Minnesota in 1971. He has taught at the University of Texas at Austin and at New Mexico State University, where he holds the rank of Professor. He has published extensively on attribution processes, cognition and affect, intergroup relations, and intercultural relations. He co-authored *Two Social Psychologies* (1985) and *Intergroup Relations* (1996), and his most recent book is *Reducing Prejudice and Stereotyping in Schools* (1999). In 1996 he won SPSSI's Otto Klineberg award for research on intercultural relations.

Marylee C. Taylor is Associate Professor of Sociology at The Pennsylvania State University, where she has taught since receiving her Ph.D. from Harvard's Department of Psychology and Social Relations. Her research on racial attitudes includes a study of the impact of workplace affirmative action on the views of White employees. Using census data and crime statistics linked to General Social Survey responses, she is now examining questions about the influence of the local context on the psychological well-being of Black Americans and on the racial and ethnic attitudes of Whites.

Linda R. Tropp is an advanced doctoral student in the social psychology graduate program at the University of California, Santa Cruz. She received her B.A. from Wellesley College and her M.Sc. in social psychology from the University of California, Santa Cruz. Her main areas of research deal with outcomes of intergroup contact for members of minority and majority groups, group identification and responses to prejudice among members of socially devalued groups, and conceptualization and measurement of constructs pertaining to identity and the self-concept.

Rosemary C. Veniegas received her Ph.D. in social psychology from UCLA in 1999, and is currently a post-doctoral fellow in the psychology at the University of California at Berkeley. Her work focuses primarily on the social psychology of gender and the dynamics of intergroup relations. She has written research articles and book chapters on these topics, and a book entitled *Gender, Culture, and Ethnicity: Current Research About Women and Men.*

Michele A. Wittig earned her Ph.D. at the University of Illinois, Urbana-Champaign, and is Professor of Psychology at California State University, Northridge. She has co-edited *Sex-Related Differences in Cognitive Functioning* (1979), *Approaching Pay Equity Through Comparable Worth* (1989), and *Social Psychological Perspectives on Grassroots Organizing* (1996). Her recent publications focus on social identity and political activism and on psychological mediators of prejudice reduction. She is a past president of APA's Division of the Psychology of Women and of the Society for the Psychological Study of Social Issues.

Author Index

Subject Index